# Month-By-Month™

## WHAT TO DO EACH MONTH TO HAVE A BEAUTIFUL GARDEN ALL YEAR

# GARDENING
# IN ALABAMA &
# MISSISSIPPI

Published by Cool Springs Press, 101 Forrest Crossing Boulevard, Franklin, Tennessee 37064
Visit the Cool Springs Press website at **www.coolspringspress.net**

Polomski, Robert, 1960–    .
    Month-by-month gardening in Alabama & Mississippi : what to do each month to have a
beautiful garden all year / Bob Polomski.
        p. cm.
    Includes bibliographical references and index.
    ISBN-10: 1-59186-254-X (pbk.)
    ISBN-13: 978-1-59186-254-3
    1. Gardening—Alabama.  2. Gardening—Mississippi.  I. Title.
SB453.2.A2P663  2007
635'.09761—dc22

                                    2006037245

Printed in the United States
10 9 8 7 6 5 4 3

Managing Editor: Billie Brownell
Designer: James Duncan, James Duncan Creative
Production Design: S. E. Anderson

## PHOTOGRAPHY AND ILLUSTRATION CREDITS (Copyright © all photographs & illustrations)

**Lee Anne White, Lee Anne White Photography:** (cover): Cherokee Rose

**Jupiter Images Stock:** page 7 (bottom of page): Camellia

**Bill Kersey, Kersey Design:** all illustrations

**Thomas Eltzroth:** pages 14 (cosmos, top of page); 27; 28; 39; 30 (summer snowflake, top of page); 45;
56; 62; 67 (tomatoes, top of page); 70; 80; 82; 94 (landscaped lawn, bottom of page; zoysia, top of page);
123 (hibiscus, top of page); 151 ('Peace' hybrid tea, top of page); 159; 171; 177 (sasanqua camellia, top
of page); 188; 199; 205 (live oak landscape, bottom of page); 211; 219; 226; 231 (pachysandra walkway,
bottom of page; morning glory, top of page); 238; 242; 245; 257 (lotus, top of page); 264

**Neil Soderstrom:** pages 18; 50; 55; 58; 60; 71; 74; 79; 89; 119; 125 (both photos); 127; 130; 131; 134;
142; 149; 154; 162; 169; 173; 190; 192; 195; 202; 224; 247

**Jerry Pavia:** pages 14 (pansy, bottom of page); 32; 36; 146; 151 (rose arbor, bottom of page); 181; 239;
254; 257 (water feature, bottom of page); 266; 271; 273; 274; 276

**Liz Ball and Rick Ray:** pages 48; 64; 67 (harvest bench, bottom of page); 177 (azalea landscape, bottom
of page); 205 (ginkgo, top of page); 251; 252; 261; 268

**William Adams:** pages 47; 107; 111; 117

**Lorenzo Gunn:** frontmatter and backmatter photo at top of page (Southern magnolia)

**Pam Harper:** page 221

**Charles Mann:** page 40 (dahlias and crocosmia, bottom of page)

**J. Paul Moore:** page 72

**Clint Waltz:** page 121

**David Winger:** page 123 (perennial landscape, bottom of page)

# Month-By-Month™

### WHAT TO DO EACH MONTH TO HAVE A BEAUTIFUL GARDEN ALL YEAR

# GARDENING IN ALABAMA & MISSISSIPPI

## BOB POLOMSKI

### COOL SPRINGS PRESS

*Growing Successful Gardeners*™

www.coolspringspress.net

FRANKLIN, TENNESSEE

# DEDICATION

To my mother and father who ignited my passion for reading, writing, and gardening.

# ACKNOWLEDGMENTS

I am grateful to Cool Springs Press for the opportunity to write this book and for their support during the entire process.

Many thanks to the following gardeners and organizations who shared their time and expertise with me—reviewing portions of the manuscript and offering helpful suggestions and advice:

Alison Arnold • American Rose Society • Bonnie Lee Appleton, Ph.D. • Richard E. Bir • Linda Cobb • Jenks Farmer • Bill Head • Robert M. Lippert, Ph.D. • Joe Maple • Linda T. McHam • Don and Cherrie McKinney • L. B. McCarty, Ph.D. • Bob Head • The Netherlands Flower Bulb Information Center • Rekha Morris, Ph.D. • Peter J. Reynolds • Barbara Smith • Howard "The Rambling Rosarian" Walters • Sheree "The Rose" Wright • William B. Miller, Ph.D. • P. Diane Relf, Ph.D. • Roger B. Swain, Ph.D. • F. Clint Waltz, Ph.D. • Jim Wilson

I am indebted to Lois Trigg Chaplin for skillfully editing this book. Thank you, Lois, for sowing handfuls of keen horticultural information and advice in each chapter and for pruning out wayward portions of the text.

Finally, this book would never have been written without the love and support of my spouse and soulmate Susan. Thank you for making me complete.

—Bob Polomski

# FOREWORD

When invited to edit this book for Alabama and Mississippi, I was glad, for I saw a chance to help provide gardeners in this region a guide for proper timing of garden activities. Wondering when to plant? When to fertilize your lawn? When not to fertilize? How to start seeds and when? How to share an old rose with friends? This and more are spelled out in this guide. There is much to learn by reading this book cover to cover. Helpful Hints point out things such as choosing peonies that will have half a chance in our hot weather or knowing how many ground cover plants to buy. So take this book with you on a trip, to the doctor's office, or anytime that you have a few minutes to yourself. It's easy to read in snippets, and a little bit of our advice may save you a lot of money and time while adding to the good looks of your home. Happy gardening!

—Lois Trigg Chaplin

# CONTENTS

# INTRODUCTION

## GARDENING IN ALABAMA & MISSISSIPPI

If you are new to gardening or new to gardening in Alabama or Mississippi, we hope that this book will help you discover the joy of gardening in our long growing season. Knowing what to do is obviously important, but knowing *when* to do it is often just as critical. Creating a flower bed that draws admiring looks; complementing the look and style of your home with well-placed trees, shrubs, and ground covers; and brightening your indoor living area with the colorful blooms and enchanting fragrances of indoor plants do not happen by chance. You can be assured that all of these are achieved with careful planning, know-how, and proper care.

*Month-by-Month Gardening in Alabama & Mississippi* helps you achieve such goals, guiding you throughout the year. If you follow our calendar format during the year, you will be reminded when it's time for certain garden and landscape tasks.

Every season presents a gardening opportunity. Start vegetables in the summer for a fall garden. Divide and replant fall-flowering perennials in the spring when their new growth emerges. Start or renovate a lawn in late spring and early summer. Just knowing how and when to perform certain tasks makes gardening easier and greatly improves your chances of success.

Ten plant categories are described in this book. Each chapter takes you month-by-month through the year with

reminders, "how to" items, and "helpful hints" that sharpen your gardening skills.

With the help of a number of seasoned gardeners, I have attempted to place each activity into the appropriate month for both states. However, some fine-tuning will be necessary in your own garden and landscape. The seasons do not always arrive when expected, and most landscapes have microclimates within them—nooks and pockets that have environmental conditions that are different from the other areas.

### BENEFITS OF A GARDENING PLAN

Folks smitten by the beauty and excitement of gardening quickly discover that they need two additional gardening tools: pen and paper. Although you can write in the margins of this book, I strongly encourage you to start a gardening diary in a separate notebook. I use 100-page wide-ruled composition notebooks. I record observations on weather, especially first and last freezes;

the names of vegetables, flowers, and shrubs that I've grown; and the bloom dates of choice flowering plants. I also make notes about fertilizer applications and pest problems. When I talk with and learn from other gardeners, I jot down interesting techniques or plants that I need to grow. All these handwritten comments have become my "gardening mem-

ory." My journal is a tool, just like my shovel and hoe. Besides, a notebook also gives me the freedom to stuff old seed packets between the pages.

Throughout the book, I refer to "your regional Extension agent." Part of Auburn University, or Mississippi State University, these agents are based in most counties and are able to access the latest information from research and findings at the land grant colleges. You can find a list of agents for your county at http://ACES.edu/counties (Alabama) or http://msucares.com/counties/index.html (Mississippi).

# GENERAL GARDENING PRACTICES

## BUILDING HEALTHY SOIL

Gardeners often get caught up in the beauty of their plants without remembering that the foundation for any healthy garden, landscape, or lawn is the soil. Good soil allows air, water, and nutrients to be absorbed by plant roots and lets those roots roam freely.

How do you build healthy soil? Begin with a soil test through your local Cooperative Extension Service. The test will tell you the pH level of the soil and the levels of nutrients available for plant growth. Stated in numbers, pH is a measurement of the acidity or alkalinity of the soil. On a scale of 0 to 14, a pH of 7 is neutral. Numbers below 7 indicate acid conditions and readings above 7 are basic or alkaline. Soil pH affects not only plant health, but also the availability of nutrients. If the soil is too acidic or too alkaline, minerals such as nitrogen, phosphorus, potassium, calcium, and magnesium can be "tied-up" and unavailable to your plants. Adding more fertilizer will not help. The soil pH will have to be corrected by either mixing in the recommended amount of limestone to raise the pH or "sweeten" the soil, or adding sulfur if you need to lower the soil pH.

Maintaining the right soil pH is very important. It affects the uptake of nutrients by plants and creates an environment that supports helpful soil-dwelling organisms, including earthworms.

The results of your soil test will indicate the amount of limestone or sulfur required to bring the soil pH into an ideal range, between 5.8 and 6.5 for most vegetable and flower gardens, shrubs, trees, and lawns. Mix pulverized or pelletized limestone into the top 6 inches of soil to raise the pH; mix in sulfur to lower it.

The soil test also measures the levels of phosphorus, potassium, calcium, and magnesium. Since calcium and phosphorous move slowly in the soil, these minerals should be incorporated into the top 6 inches of soil.

Knowing which nutrients are already present will save you money. If your test shows your soil already has high levels of phosphorus and potassium, there's no need to add a fertilizer containing these two nutrients.

Good gardeners also add organic matter. It improves soil tilth—its physical condition or structure. When added to clay soil, organic matter holds the clay particles apart, improving air and water movement in the soil. This translates to deeper and more extensive root development from our plants.

The kind of organic matter you mix into your soil is your choice. My grandfather liked to use rabbit and chicken manure for his vegetable and flower beds. My mother liked using fish in her rose garden. As a child, I buried fish heads, tails, and other inedible parts around her roses. If you are squeamish about using these organic materials, then add compost or shredded leaves. Cover crops or "green manure" such as crimson clover or annual rye are relatively inexpensive sources of organic matter. Sow these crops in the fall and then turn them under in the spring to enrich the soil.

# GENERAL GARDENING PRACTICES

Organic fertilizers derived from naturally occurring sources are a good alternative to synthetic plant foods. They include composted animal manure, cottonseed meal, and bloodmeal, among many others. Although they contain relatively low concentrations of actual nutrients compared to synthetic fertilizers, they increase the organic matter content in the soil and improve soil structure.

To avoid damaging soil structure, never dig or cultivate when the soil is too wet or too dry. Follow this simple test: If the soil sticks to your shovel—the soil is too wet. Postpone digging until the soil dries out.

Coarse-textured sandy soils have excellent drainage but hold little water. Add organic matter to them to increase fertility and water retention.

Sand has often been touted as the perfect fix for improving drainage in clay soils. Unless you add it at the rate of at least 6 inches of sand per 8 inches of soil, your soil will be better suited for making bricks than growing plants.

## PLANTING

Plant properly. The health and long-term survival of plants that you set into their new home—indoors or out—is affected by how they're planted. Follow the step-by-step planting instructions in the introduction to each chapter to learn about proper planting. Your plant's survival depends on it.

## WATERING

Anyone can water; however, watering efficiently to meet the demands of the plant while conserving water requires some attention to detail. The chapters provide information on when and how often to water. The aim is to avoid the common mistakes of overwatering or underwatering—two practices that can injure or kill plants.

Water needs depend on the plant and the situation. Moisture-loving plants require more-frequent watering than plants adapted to dry conditions. Newly-set-out plants need to be watered after planting and during their establishment period. Once they become established, however, they may not require supplemental watering even during the hot, dry summer months. Some shrubs and trees are quite drought-tolerant and can withstand long periods without rain or irrigation.

Soil also affects watering. Plants growing in clay soils need to be watered less often than plants growing in sandy soils because sandy soils drain so rapidly.

Whether you water with a garden hose or an automatic belowground irrigation system, water wisely. Refer to the Watering sections in the chapters for information on watering efficiently.

## FERTILIZING

Fertilizing could be the gardening practice that causes the greatest confusion. Besides knowing when, how often, and how much to fertilize, the choices seem endless. Should you choose a fast- or slow-release nitrogen fertilizer? Would your plants prefer a diet of organic or inorganic nutrients? What do those numbers on the bag mean? Should you choose the 10-10-10 or the 16-4-8? Dry or liquid fertilizer? Before making an application, realize that fertilizing should be guided by soil-test results, the appearance of the plants, and the purpose of fertilizing.

Fertilizers are minerals added when the soil does not supply enough of those nutrients. The three most important—nitrogen, phosphorus, and potassium—are represented by three numbers on a fertilizer bag. For example, a ratio of 16-4-8 gives the percentage by weight of nitrogen (N), phosphate ($P_2O_5$), and potash ($K_2O$). In this case, nitrogen makes up 16 percent of the total weight, phosphate—which supplies phosphorus—accounts

for 4 percent, and potash, a source of potassium, makes up 8 percent. The remaining weight (the total must add up to 100 percent) is comprised of a nutrient carrier.

A fertilizer containing all three nutrients, such as a 16-4-8, is referred to as a "complete" fertilizer. If soil tests indicate high levels of phosphorus and potassium, then apply an "incomplete" fertilizer, one that supplies only nitrogen, such as 21-0-0.

In addition to the primary elements (N-P-K), the fertilizer may contain secondary plant nutrients including calcium, magnesium, and sulfur, or minor nutrients such as manganese, zinc, copper, iron, and molybdenum. Apply these nutrients if dictated by soil-test results.

You can choose dry or liquid fertilizers. Dry fertilizers are applied to the ground around your plants. They are available in fast- or slow-release-nitrogen forms.

Fast- or quick-release-nitrogen fertilizers dissolve readily in water and are almost immediately available to plants. They can also be quickly leached out of the root zone in fast-draining, sandy soils.

Liquid fertilizers can be absorbed through the leaves as well as the roots of plants. These have to be applied more frequently than granular types, usually every two to four weeks.

Slow-release fertilizers make nutrients available to the plant for an extended period of up to several months. These are also called timed-release or controlled release. The nutrients are coated so they release gradually. While more expensive than conventional fertilizers, they reduce the need for supplemental applications and the likelihood of fertilizer burn. Select a slow-release fertilizer that has at least one-half the total amount of nitrogen listed as "water insoluble nitrogen."

An alternative to synthetic slow-release fertilizers are organic fertilizers derived from naturally occurring sources such as composted animal manure, cottonseed meal, and blood-meal, among many others. Although they contain relatively low concentrations of actual nutrients compared to synthetic fertilizers, they increase the organic matter content in the soil and improve soil structure.

A slow-release fertilizer is a good choice, especially for sandy soils, which tend to leach, or for heavy clay soils where runoff can be a problem. If the soil is properly prepared at the start, supplemental fertilization may not be necessary for several years after planting. When fertilizing your perennials, let their growth rate and leaf color guide you. Rely on soil-test results to help you make the right decision. If the bed is already highly fertile, the soil test will save you from the other, equally undesirable results of overfertilizing, such as encouraging a lot of leafy growth at the expense of flowers.

## PRUNING

Pruning improves the health and appearance of plants. It can be as simple as nipping the spent flowers from your zinnias (deadheading) or removing a large limb from your maple tree. In the following chapters, read the step-by-step instructions for pruning roses, shrubs, and trees.

You'll find that pruning will require you to have a purpose in mind. It can be to encourage more flowers on perennials, to reduce the height of plants, or to create a strong structure of trunk and limbs to support future growth in young trees.

## PROBLEMS

You are bound to confront the three most common pests in your garden: insects, diseases, and weeds. (Deer, voles, and rabbits can also be considered pests and are addressed in the chapters.)

Deal with them sensibly. In the Problems sections of this book, I use the term "Integrated Pest Management" or "IPM." IPM is a commonsense approach to managing pests that brings Mother Nature into the battle on the gardener's side.

It combines smart plant selection with good planting and maintenance practices, and an understanding of pests and their habits. It starts with planning and proper planting to produce strong, healthy plants that, by themselves, can prosper with minimum help from you. As in nature, an acceptable level of pests can be accommodated. Control is the goal, rather than elimination. Several techniques can be used in a home garden/landscape IPM approach.

## IPM CULTURAL PRACTICES

**Proper soil management:** Maintain the appropriate soil pH for your plants by testing your soil at least every three years. Add generous amounts of organic matter to build up soil fertility.

**Plant selection:** Match plants suited to the soil and climate of your area, and select species and cultivars resistant to pests. These plants are resistant—not immune—to damage. Expect them to exhibit less insect or disease injury than susceptible varieties growing in the same environment.

**Watering:** Water late at night or early in the morning when dew has formed. Avoid watering in early evening when leaves may remain wet for an extended period of time. This favors fungal infections.

**Mulching:** Apply a shallow layer of organic mulch such as compost, shredded leaves, or bark to conserve moisture, suppress weeds, and supply nutrients as they decompose.

**Sanitation:** Remove dead, damaged, diseased, or insect-infested leaves, shoots, or branches.

## IPM MECHANICAL CONTROLS

**Handpicking:** Remove any insects by hand, or knock them off with a strong spray of water from the hose.

**Exclusion:** Physically block insects from attacking your plants. Aluminum foil collars can be placed around seedlings to prevent cutworms attacking plant stems. Plants can be covered with muslin or spun-bonded polyester to keep out insects.

## IPM BIOLOGICAL CONTROLS

**Predators and parasites:** Some bugs are on our side. Known as beneficial insects, they are the natural enemies of damaging insects. They fall into two main categories: predators and parasites. Predators hunt and feed on other insects. They include spiders, praying mantids, lady beetles, and green lacewings. Parasites, such as braconid wasps and Trichogramma wasps, hatch from eggs inside or on another insect and they eat their host insect as they grow.

Releasing beneficial insects into your landscape or garden may offer some benefit, but it is better to conserve the beneficial insects already there. Learn to distinguish between pests and beneficial insects in your garden and landscape. Avoid applying broad-spectrum insecticides that will harm beneficial insects if it looks as if the harmful insects are already being kept to tolerable levels.

**Botanical pesticides and insecticidal soaps:** Botanical pesticides or "botanicals" are naturally occurring pesticides derived from plants. Two common botanicals include pyrethrins, insecticidal chemicals extracted from the pyrethrum flower (*Tanacetum cinerariifolium*), and Neem, a botanical insecticide and fungicide extracted from the tropical Neem tree (*Azadirachta indica*) which contains the active ingredient azadirachtin. Insecticidal soaps have been formulated specifically to control insects. Soaps are effective only against those insects that come into direct contact with sprays before they dry.

These "natural" pesticides break down rapidly when exposed to sunlight, air, and moisture and are less likely to kill beneficial insects than insecticides that have a longer residual activity.

**Microbial insecticides:** These insecticides combat damaging insects with microscopic living

organisms such as viruses, bacteria, fungi, protozoa, or nematodes. Although they may seem like out-of-the-ordinary insecticides, they can be applied in ordinary ways—as sprays, dusts, or granules. The bacterium *Bacillus thuringiensis* (Bt) is the most popular pathogen. Formulations from *Bacillus thuringiensis* var. *kurstaki* (BTK) are the most widely used to control caterpillars—the larvae of butterflies and moths.

**Horticultural oils:** When applied to plants, these highly refined oils smother insects, mites, and their eggs. Typically, horticultural oils such as Sunspray®, Scalecide®, and Volck® are derived from highly refined petroleum products that are specifically manufactured to control pests on plants. Studies have shown that horticultural oils derived from vegetable oils, such as cottonseed and soybean oil, also exhibit insecticidal properties.

Dormant applications generally control aphid eggs and the egg stages of mites, scale insects, and caterpillars like leafrollers and tent caterpillars. Summer applications control adelgids, aphids, mealybugs, scale insects, spider mites, and whiteflies.

Oils have limited effects on beneficial insects, especially when applied during the dormant season. Additionally, insects and mites have not been reported to develop resistance to petroleum or vegetable oils.

**Traditional, synthetic pesticides:** Synthetic pesticides, developed by people, should be your last resort when confronted by damaging pest levels. Use them sparingly to control the targeted pest. Specific names of synthetic pesticides are avoided in this book because products and their labels change rapidly along with the pesticide registration and use process. When buying any pesticide, read the label and follow all directions and precautions before mixing and applying it, and before storing or disposing of it.

## FURTHER HELP

The Alabama Extension Service and Mississippi Extension Service have Extension offices in most counties. Many are staffed by Master Gardeners trained in horticulture. These volunteers are also available to answer your questions at many arboreta, botanical, and other public gardens.

Help is available from botanical gardens and an array of societies devoted to specific plants, and from seminars and informative newsletters as well.

# GENERAL OVERVIEW

The garden plants in this book are divided into ten groups and arranged alphabetically to help you find the information you need for each month of the year.

Annuals and biennials are relied upon to deliver brilliant color and a long-lasting display of flowers all season long. In this chapter you will learn when to start them from seed indoors, when to transplant them outside, and how to care for them during the year so they look their best.

Bulbs, corms, rhizomes, and tubers are below-ground storage structures that encompass an exciting array of beautiful and durable plants. I refer to them collectively as bulbs for simplicity's sake. The chapter offers guidance on when to plant them and how and when to divide them.

Fresh herbs and vegetables can be grown and harvested year-round in most of Alabama and Mississippi. Knowing when to start seeds indoors and when to set transplants in the garden will help you keep your garden productive throughout the year. Refer to this chapter for monthly reminders. The Problems sections highlight common pests and what to do about them.

The chapter on lawns deals with the cultural requirements of turfgrass, and includes some basic turf establishment and maintenance practices to keep your lawn healthy and attractive.

Perennials, technically "herbaceous" perennials, are so called to separate them from woody trees and shrubs. Over the years their popularity has grown, and with good reason. This group includes flowering plants, ferns, and ornamental grasses that can deliver unique colors and textures with flowers, seedheads, and leaves. Perennials have specific needs regarding pruning, dead-heading, dividing, and transplanting. Treat them properly to get the most from this truly extraordinary collection of plants.

The rose—the emblem of our nation—has been around since ancient times and continues to infat-

uate gardeners with its grace and beauty. This chapter focuses on "easy-care" roses that are suitable for gardeners who love them but aren't interested in intensive management. You'll learn in this chapter that selecting the right rose to fit your easy-going management style is only part of growing roses successfully.

Shrubs come in a dizzying array of shapes, sizes, forms, and colors. Some have soft, naturally billowy forms, others sport showy, fragrant flowers or brightly colored berries, and still others deliver stunning fall color. Planting, pruning, fertilizing, and watching for pests should be done at specific times of the year.

Trees are permanent landscape investments that grow in value with each passing year. Select them carefully, place them wisely, and plant them properly. They will need smart pruning and timely feeding to grow and look their best. Insects and diseases are a constant threat, but pest-resistant trees help. Refer to this chapter for advice and "how-to" help in caring for your trees.

Vines and ground covers are the workhorses of the landscape, combining functionality and beauty. Vines have traditionally been used to hide chain-link fences and unsightly views, and to provide some shade and privacy on the front porch. Ground covers are called upon to control soil erosion on steep slopes, to hide red clay in places where nothing else will thrive, and to replace lawn grass in shady or wet areas where it just won't grow, even after several exasperating attempts. This chapter suggests how to use them to solve unyielding problems.

Water gardening offers a different set of challenges and experiences than does "terrestrial" gardening. Water and bog plants include a wide range of unique plants that like "wet feet." Select the right kinds of plants for your water garden and give them the proper care each month.

Now let's look at these plants in more detail.

# ANNUALS & BIENNIALS

Annuals are the workhorses of the garden. They deliver brilliant color in leaves and flowers for up to three seasons. Some of the best known include impatiens, marigolds, and coleus. You can plant them in large sweeps for a massive show of color, or just use them as "fillers" to dress up open spaces that haven't yet been filled in by permanent plantings of perennials or shrubs. The tallest ones even work as seasonal screens. In containers, they'll give you months of nonstop color and texture—literally anywhere you choose.

Some annuals attract hummingbirds and butterflies; some have exquisite fragrance; some make long-lasting and inexpensive cut flowers. Many adapt readily to containers and hanging baskets to provide a spot of color. All of this from a group of plants whose entire life lasts less than a year!

Biennials, which are often grouped with annuals, are a little different because they complete their life cycle in two years. Common biennials are hollyhock and foxglove. The first year they produce stems, leaves, and roots. In their second year, biennials flower, set seed, and die. Mild winters can trick some biennials into blooming in less than a year. Sowing the seeds of biennials in midsummer allows the plants to develop during the fall. After exposure to winter cold, biennials will bloom the following season. In general, care for biennials like you would annuals. Plant most biennials in the fall to bloom the following spring.

Annuals differ in their ability to tolerate cold so they're categorized as hardy, half-hardy, or tender. The categories help you know when to plant. The two important dates that determine planting time are the last expected freeze in spring and the first expected freeze in fall.

Hardy annuals are the most cold tolerant; they withstand frosts or light freezes. The best known is the pansy. Transplants are set out in fall. Start seeds a few weeks before the last freeze in spring or in fall after freezing temperatures have arrived but while the soil can still be worked. Other hardy annuals include calendula, larkspur, poppy, and stock. Most hardy annuals are not heat tolerant and usually decline and die with the onset of summer.

Half-hardy annuals can tolerate cool, wet weather but are damaged, slowed down, or killed by freezes. Sow seeds of most half-hardy annuals after the last anticipated freeze in spring. Although most do not require warm soil to germinate, some do. Refer to the seed packet for specific information about optimum temperature ranges for good germination. Many half-hardy annuals decline in the midsummer heat but may bloom again in late summer or fall.

Most tender annuals are native to tropical regions and cannot tolerate cold soils and air temperatures. Popular ones are impatiens, coleus, and zinnia. They need warm soil and long warm summers to produce the best flower display. Typically, seeds or transplants are planted two to three weeks after the last spring freeze. But as we will discuss later, if you grow your own transplants, you can get a head start by starting the seeds indoors so that they are ready to set out when the time comes.

## PLANNING THE ANNUAL FLOWER GARDEN

Annuals can change the look and feel of your landscape in a short time. Pay attention to their color, form, texture, and habit. Create a plan with these guidelines in mind:

- **Season:** Annuals have a peak season. Warm-season annuals (the tender tropicals), such as impatiens, are showy from spring (after frost) until frost kills them in fall. Cool-season annuals (hardy and half-hardy), such as pansies, look best in late fall, winter, and early spring. With the right selection, you can have a beautiful display during each of the four seasons.

- **Cultural needs:** Annuals vary considerably with respect to their environmental and cultural requirements. Some perform best in full sun while others do best in shade. Drought tolerance varies; plants that tolerate drier conditions should be grouped together and those that need more moisture should be planted near each other, making watering easier. Ideal planting times differ also.

- **Spacing requirements:** Know the expected height and spread of the annuals to determine the number of plants needed. Plant annuals the right distance apart so they will grow into their allotted space as they mature. Avoid overcrowding at all costs. Leave enough space between plants to encourage air movement. Their leaves will dry off quickly to thwart the spread of fungal diseases that require moisture to grow and spread.

- **Color, form, and texture:** Serious gardeners spend time studying flower and leaf color, the form, or habit, of each plant (upright or spreading), and textures (from the fine needlelike leaves of cosmos to coarse sunflower leaves). Gardeners blend and contrast these features to create different impacts. There are some excellent reference books that offer a variety of designs and instructions on creating incredible displays. When working with color, you may want to work with a color wheel to help you visualize complementary or contrasting shades. You can create solid beds of one color or mix them. Beds can be simple in all white, cool with blues, or hot with reds. There are design rules, but the bottom

line is this: your garden is an expression of your taste. Consider leaves when selecting plants. Some, like coleus and dusty miller, are cultivated just for their foliage. Group the plants in threes, fives, or sevens to create a natural, flowing look.

Commercial catalogs and the Internet provide detailed information on many varieties, colors, and sizes.

## STARTING ANNUALS AND BIENNIALS FROM SEED

Garden centers offer many annuals and biennials, but you can widen your selection beyond those normally available, by starting plants from seed. To grow your own transplants from seed, you must provide them with adequate light. Low light levels result in weak, spindly seedlings that "stretch," becoming long and lanky and eventually flopping over. To avoid relying on sunlight, buy or build an artificial light stand and grow your seedlings under lights. A portable light stand can be taken apart and stored in a closet when the seed-starting season is over. This clever design is inexpensive and is easily constructed out of $1/2$-inch PVC pipes. I've built light stands out of $1/2$- and $3/4$-inch PVC pipe and found that $3/4$-inch pipe produces a sturdier stand.

See January Planting p. 18 for information on starting seeds indoors. To direct-sow seeds outdoors, see February Planting p. 20.

## PREPARING THE GROUND

Annuals need a soil that is porous and drains well yet holds enough moisture and nutrients. Prepare your soil several weeks before planting by following these steps:

1. Dig the planting bed to a depth of 8 to 12 inches.

2. To improve drainage and fertility in clay soils, incorporate at least 2 inches of compost or bagged soil conditioner into the top 8 inches of soil.

Using inorganic materials can improve drainage in clay soils, especially when organic materials are also used. The inorganics include chicken grit, small (pea) gravel ($3/8$ inch or less), or stalite (marketed as Perma-till®, which has the appearance of pea gravel but weighs much less since each particle is filled with air). Apply a 2-inch layer to the surface of the bed and mix it in to a depth of 6 to 8 inches.

To improve the water-holding capacity of sandy soils, amend the soil with compost, composted pine bark, or peat moss. As with clay soils, at least 2 inches of material (but no more than half the digging depth) should be amended.

3. Have your soil tested through your local Cooperative Extension Service. A pH of 5.5 to 6.5 is fine for most annuals.

If a soil test hasn't been done for at least three or more years, apply 5 pounds of dolomitic limestone and 2 pounds of a fertilizer high in phosphorus and potassium with a 1-2-2 ratio, such as 2 pounds of 5-10-10 per 100 square feet. This is a fast-release fertilizer.

Instead of using a fast-release fertilizer such as 5-10-10, a slow-release fertilizer may be a good choice, especially in sandy soils prone to leaching. Apply the fertilizer using the label instructions.

4. Mix pulverized lime or sulfur and fertilizer as recommended by soil-test results into the top 6 inches of soil, paying special attention to phosphorus or calcium, both of which move very slowly in the soil.

5. Rake the bed smooth.

## TRANSPLANTING ANNUALS

Plant annuals at the appropriate time.

1. Moisten the potting medium before taking the plant out of the container. Moisten plants in peat pots before planting, pot and all.

2. Dig a hole a little wider than the rootball and the same depth.

3. Hold your hand over the top of the pot with the plant stems between your fingers. Tip over the pot and tap the plant into your hand. Annuals growing in cell-packs can be pushed out from the bottom.

4. Plant the rootball level with the soil surface.

5. Firm the soil around the plants and water them in. Apply a layer of mulch.

## CARE

You may have spent a lot of time raising, or a fair amount of money purchasing, healthy transplants, and you may have selected and prepared appropriate sites, but you can still meet with disappointment if you do not continue to give your flowering annuals the care they need.

## WATERING

Adequate water is necessary for annuals to grow vigorously and bloom continuously, especially during hot, dry summers. Some annuals require a continuous supply of water, while other, more drought-tolerant types can prosper with minimal regular watering.

Frequent watering, perhaps twice daily, is necessary when sowing seeds outdoors until the seeds sprout. Seedlings or newly planted annuals should be watered once a day. Once established, you can gradually water them less frequently. Water deeply to encourage deep rooting. Established plants may need to be watered once a week in clay soils that hold more water than sandy soils. Sandy soils may need to be watered twice a week. Instead of following the calendar, water when the top 2 or 3 inches of soil feels dry.

There are several ways to water annual beds. Refer to Shrubs May Planning p. 190, for several efficient approaches.

## FERTILIZING

Annuals need adequate nutrients to sustain them during the growing season. Before making any supplemental fertilizer applications, let their growth rate, leaf color, and a soil test be your guides. If the bed is already highly fertile, the soil test will save you from the undesirable results of overfertilizing. The rule of thumb for fertilizing is to apply a dry, granular, complete, fast-acting type of fertilizer such as 10-10-10, at a rate of one pound per 100 square feet monthly. That works out to 2 cups per 100 square feet, or 4 tablespoons per 10 square feet. Keep this up throughout the growing season; stretch the intervals between feedings up to six weeks, based on your observations.

Water-soluble fertilizers usually call for shorter intervals between applications. They are not only quickly available, but also quickly used up. Most should be mixed with water and applied every two weeks, following label directions. These fertilizers can be absorbed by both leaves and roots.

Slow-release or controlled-release fertilizers deliver small amounts of nutrients gradually over an extended period. Depending on soil moisture and temperature, release of the coated nutrients may extend over several weeks or months. Typically, the first application is mixed into the bed just before planting. Some products will have to be applied a second time midway through the growing season. How much you apply and how often should be based on the manufacturer's instructions.

## CONTROLLING PESTS

To control pests, practice IPM (Integrated Pest Management). This is a practical approach focusing on establishing and maintaining healthy plants and understanding pests. See p. 10 for more information.

# JANUARY
## ANNUALS & BIENNIALS

 PLANNING

Organize your seed packets to create a sowing schedule. Check the instructions on the seed packets to find the number of weeks of growth required before each seedling can be transplanted outdoors. Count the number of weeks back from the last expected freeze to know when to sow your seeds.

Make a growing chart, either on a spreadsheet on your computer or in a gardening journal. Record the name of the plant and the day the seed should be sown. Write down the expected time of germination and when the plant will be ready for outdoor planting.

 PLANTING

Growing your own transplants from seed offers you a wider choice of varieties. It can also be a challenge. Be sure to pay attention to timing. Avoid sowing seeds too early because they may be ready for transplanting before outdoor conditions permit. See Planning, above.

There are two ways of growing transplants from seed. In the one-step method sow seeds directly into individual containers. Transplant them directly

It takes some organization and planning, but you can grow your own transplants from seed.

outdoors when they can be easily handled.

In the two-step method sow seeds in trays or flats until the "true leaves" emerge, then transplant them to pots for further growth before moving them to their permanent homes outdoors. Use aluminum foil pans if nursery flats are not available. Punch holes in the bottom of the pans for drainage.

Here's how to sow seeds for either method:

1. Moisten a soilless seed-starting mixture and fill the pots or trays to within 1/4 inch of the top.

2. Mix very fine seeds with vermiculite or sand and pour into the center of a folded sheet of paper. Tap it gently over the medium to sow the seeds.

If planting in individual pots, make a hole in the mix with a pencil point, chopstick, or other "dibble." Plant the seeds no deeper than recommended on the package label. A general rule is to cover seeds to a depth equal to twice their diameter. Drop one or two seeds in each hole.

When sowing medium to large seeds in the two-step method, use the end of a pencil to create furrows about 1 to 2 inches apart and about 1/8 to 1/4 inch deep across the surface of the growing medium. Sow the seeds in rows for easier labeling and transplanting.

3. Press extremely fine seeds, such as **begonia**, lightly into the medium, or water them in with a fine mist spray. Cover the seed if light is not required for germina-

tion. A thin layer of vermiculite will do. Otherwise, leave the seed uncovered, exposed to light.

4. Label the pot or flat with the name of the crop and the date it was planted. Read the packet and make note of the date the seed is expected to germinate so you will know when to expect sprouts to appear.

5. Spray-mist the seeds to water them in. If watering from the top may dislodge the seeds, place the entire container into a tub, sink, or bucket containing a few inches of water. After the potting mix is saturated, set it aside to drain.

6. Cover the pots or trays with plastic wrap, or put them in a plastic bag secured at the top to retain moisture. They won't have to be watered until the plastic wrap is removed.

7. Unless the seeds require cool temperatures, move them to a location between 65 and 75 degrees F. in bright but indirect sunlight. Germination can be hastened by providing warmth. Follow instructions on the seed packet; if there are no instructions, provide bottom heat of 75 to 85 degrees F. Use a bot-

tom-heat mat or a waterproof insulated heating cable, or set the tray on top of the refrigerator.

When the seeds have sprouted, expose them to bright light to keep them short and stocky. Remove the plastic covering and put them under fluorescent lights. Two 40-watt cool white fluorescent lights are a cost-effective choice and provide the right quality of light. Set the trays on your light stand and lower the lights so they're almost touching the topmost leaves. Keep the lights on for sixteen hours each day. An automatic timer will help. As the seedlings grow, raise the lights. Temperature can be 60 to 70 degrees F., 10 degrees lower at night. Tape aluminum foil to the back and sides of the light stand to concentrate light on plants.

When the soil can be worked, direct-sow **bachelor's button**; **sweet alyssum**; **sweet pea**; **larkspur**; and **California**, **Iceland**, and **Shirley poppies** later this month. Although they're better suited to fall sowing, you can still sow them now. Sprinkle seeds on a roughly raked surface and water in.

## WATERING

Determine the need for watering by squeezing the top $1/2$ inch of medium between your thumb and forefinger. If water squeezes out easily, there's enough moisture. If the medium feels slightly moist but water is difficult to squeeze out, add water.

## FERTILIZING

Seedlings growing in soilless mixes need to be fertilized when the first true leaves appear. Feed at every other watering with a water-soluble fertilizer to promote faster growth until the plants are ready to plant outdoors.

## PROBLEMS

Damping-off can be a problem with seedlings. This common fungal disease attacks the seedlings at ground level, rotting the stems and causing plants to topple over. Their stems look as if they have been pinched. See February Problems p. 21.

# FEBRUARY

## ANNUALS & BIENNIALS

### PLANNING

When planning your garden, think in splashes—not drops—of color. High-impact, car-stopping beds are achieved when annuals are planted en masse. Before you buy any plants or seeds, draw your garden plan on a sheet of graph paper. Draw it to scale and decide on the kinds of colors you want. As you look through catalogs, examine plant descriptions carefully. Take note of these features:

• Are they cool- or warm-season annuals?

• What is their expected height and spread at maturity? Will they require staking?

• Are they "self-cleaning?" The spent flowers of some modern varieties are shed by the plant and quickly disappear. Others need spent flowers removed (called deadheading) to get rid of the old, faded blooms. This task is necessary for **cosmos**, **marigold**, **pansy**, and **pinks**. Deadheading prevents the formation of seeds and stimulates continued flowering.

Keep this information in a gardening journal to help you plan your season and evaluate the performance of annuals in your landscape. Record your observations this year so that next year you can review your list and make the best choices.

### PLANTING

**Indoors:** When seedlings produce their first set of true leaves, it's time to transplant them from the tray to individual containers.

1. You can fill the containers with the same soilless mix used for germinating the seeds. You'll get better results, however, if you mix one part perlite with two parts of the soilless mix. Perlite improves drainage and aeration.

2. Firm the moistened mix to within $1/2$ inch of the top of the container.

3. Loosen the medium around a seedling with a pencil and lift it out. Hold on to a cotyledon, or "seed leaf," the pair of first leaves that the seedling produces; they are oval or round in shape. Avoid squeezing the stem.

4. Use your pencil to poke a hole in the medium that is large enough to accommodate the fragile roots and plant the seedling.

5. Firm the soil lightly around the plants, and water them in so the soil and roots are in good contact.

Don't leave the seedlings in the flat too long, or you'll be left with a tangled mess. Then you may have to sacrifice some seedlings. To thin them simply pinch off their stems close to the surface of the medium.

Warm-weather annuals that require six to eight weeks from sowing to transplanting outdoors can be sown this month: **African daisy**, **ageratum**, **annual phlox**, **China aster**, **flowering tobacco**, and **Mexican sunflower**.

The point of a pencil makes a good dibble to use when transplanting seedlings.

Warm-season annuals that require four to six weeks can also be sown indoors now. These annuals include **coleus, marigold, salvia, snow-on-the-mountain, strawflower**, and **zinnia**.

If your overwintered **coleus** has become leggy and gangly looking, take cuttings by clipping off the ends and root them to produce short, stocky plants for planting this spring. Refer to August Care p. 33 to learn how to propagate **coleus** from cuttings.

**Outdoors:** When the soil can be worked, continue sowing seeds of **bachelor's button, sweet alyssum, sweet pea, nasturtium, larkspur** and **California, Iceland,** and **Shirley poppies**. Follow the recommended seeding date, depth, and spacing on the packet. Prepare the bed and pay close attention during germination and when they begin to grow. Most outdoor-grown seedlings should be thinned to the recommended spacing to allow remaining plants to have adequate light, water, nutrients, and space to develop fully above and below ground. Water them in after sowing.

Sow seeds of **sweet alyssum** four to six weeks before the last frost.

Plant transplants of annual **dianthus (pinks), calendula, pansy, viola, snapdragon**, and sweet **William** as they become available.

## CARE

**Indoors:** Seedlings receiving inadequate light become spindly and floppy. Keep them in a south-facing window or place them under artificial lights for sixteen hours a day.

If you overwintered **geraniums** indoors, take stem cuttings and root them now or next month. See March Care p. 22 for the step-by-step details.

**Outdoors:** Pinch off **pansy** flowers when transplanting to encourage branching and focus the plant's efforts on rooting and getting established.

## WATERING

See January p. 19.

## FERTILIZING

Feed indoor-grown transplants with a water-soluble fertilizer such as 20-20-20 at half strength every other week.

Fertilize **pansies** when new growth resumes. A liquid fertilizer may have to be applied every two weeks.

## PROBLEMS

Control any winter annual weeds such as bittercress, common chickweed, and henbit by handpulling. Suppress them with a shallow layer of mulch.

Damping-off is a serious disease that attacks and kills seedlings. It especially attacks weak seedlings when growing conditions are unfavorable. Overwatering, lack of drainage, poor ventilation, and crowding can foster an attack. With seedlings, the stem rots at or close to the soil surface. This is mainly caused by the fungi present in the seed-starting medium.

Damping-off is easier to prevent than cure. Use clean containers. If necessary, disinfect them with a 10 percent bleach solution (1 part bleach to 9 parts water). Use a sterile, well-drained medium. Provide good conditions for rapid seed germination and development. Avoid waterlogging the medium when watering. Damping-off can be reduced by cutting back the frequency of watering and increasing the amount of light. Several fungicides are available that may help. They are applied as a drench or heavy spray as soon as evidence of damping-off appears.

# MARCH
## ANNUALS & BIENNIALS

 PLANNING

Before visiting the garden center, make a list of the kinds and quantities of annuals you need. Planning beforehand will help you avoid overindulging so you purchase only what you need.

1. Measure the length and width of the flowerbed and calculate the area in square feet (area = length x width). If the bed is irregularly shaped—oval, round, or long and winding—make a rough estimate.

2. Jot down the kind of sun- or shade-loving annuals you would like to plant in the bed. Include their spacing requirements. Refer to the seed packet or catalog for the correct spacing.

3. Determine the number of plants you need by following April's Helpful Hints p. 25.

 PLANTING

It's still too early to plant warm-season annuals, but almost too late to plant some cool-season annuals. Plant **pansies** and **violas** (**Johnny jump-ups**) in pots or beds that just need a short show. By May, they'll be fading.

You can plant **snapdragon** and **petunia**, which tolerate frost and have also been bred to be more heat tolerant.

You can sow seed of **calliopsis**, **coreopsis**, and **red mustard**.

Follow these steps to plant properly:

1. Moisten the potting medium before taking the plant out of the container. This will keep the soil intact when you slide it out.

2. Dig a hole as little wider than the rootball and the same depth. Plants growing in peat pots can be planted pot and all. Moisten the plants in the peat pot before planting.

3. Hold your hand over the top of the pot with the plant stems between your fingers. Tip over the pot and gently tap the plant into your hand. Annuals growing in cell-packs can be pushed out from the bottom with your thumb. If they are reluctant, slice the walls of the container and peel it away. If there is a mat of tangled roots on the base, tease the bottom third of the rootball to loosen it up.

4. Plant the rootball level with the soil surface. Remove any exposed portion of peat pots (the exposed peat can act like a wick, drawing moisture away from the roots and soil, causing the plant to dry out quickly).

5. Pinch off any open flowers to direct the plant's energy into building roots for speedy establishment.

6. Firm the soil around each plant with your fingers and water. Allow the plants the cor-rect spacing. Refer to the seed packet for suggested spacing.

Once you have finished planting, cover the bed with a 2- to 3-inch layer of mulch, tapering to a $1/2$-inch layer near the crown but not covering it. During the next few weeks, keep the plants well watered to help them become established.

 CARE

Any **geraniums** stored upside-down in the basement or crawl space over the winter should be brought out and rejuvenated at the beginning of this month.

1. Prune back dead shoots.

2. Repot the **geranium** using fresh soil.

3. Water and set in a warm place.

As growth begins, move the plants into a sunny window and begin regular watering and fertilizing.

 WATERING

Indoors, continue watering seed-lings planted last month.

# FERTILIZING

When the weather warms and growth resumes, fertilize your **pansies**, **violas**, and other winter annuals with a slow-release fertilizer, or give them a quick pick-me-up with a liquid such as 20-20-20, mixed according to label directions.

# GROOMING

Pinch out the growing tips of plants that have become rangy. They will branch from below the pinch and regain their bushy form.

Cut off dead blooms to encourage continued flowering of **pansies**.

# PROBLEMS

Spider mites can be a problem on indoor seedlings. See p. 284 for a description and controls.

Damping-off can be triggered by waterlogged conditions in the growing medium. See February Problems p. 21 for more information.

Preemergent herbicides are available for use around many common bedding plants. These herbicides kill germinating weed seedlings before they appear. When selecting a preemergent herbicide, keep these points in mind:

• Identify the weed that you want to control.

• Select a herbicide that will control this weed but can be applied to the flowering annuals you're growing.

• Read the label carefully and apply only as recommended. For example, some pre-emergent herbicides are safe to use only on established bedding plants. If applied shortly after transplanting, injury may result.

# HELPFUL HINTS

If you're toying with the idea of raising your own transplants, concentrate on annuals that require only a little attention. **Cosmos**, **marigold**, and **zinnia** need only a month or two of daily care. Let nurseries grow **geranium**, **petunia**, and **dwarf snapdragon**, which require three to four months to reach market size. Here's a table showing the time needed in weeks from seed to planting size for common bedding plants.

| | |
|---|---|
| Ageratum | 8–10 |
| Celosia | 7–9 |
| China Aster | 8–10 |
| Cleome | 8–10 |
| Cosmos | 4–6 |
| Flowering Tobacco | 9–11 |
| Geranium | 13–18 |
| Impatiens | 9–10 |
| Marigold, Dwarf | 8–10 |
| Marigold, Tall | 5–6 |
| Pansy | 12–14 |
| Petunia | 11–15 |
| Portulaca | 10–12 |
| Salvia, Dwarf | 10–12 |
| Salvia, Tall | 8–10 |
| Snapdragon, Dwarf | 12–14 |
| Snapdragon, Tall | 8–10 |
| Verbena | 8–10 |
| Zinnia, Dwarf | 6–8 |
| Zinnia, Tall | 4–6 |

# APRIL
## ANNUALS & BIENNIALS

 PLANNING

In addition to using annuals to show off their flowers and leaves outdoors, make plans to cultivate a cutting garden to enjoy the flowers indoors. With careful planning you can have flowers blooming from spring until fall. A cutting garden requires regular watering, the prompt removal of dead or dying leaves, and the continuous removal of spent flowers to encourage the production of more flowers. Try these flowers in the cutting garden: **celosia**, **China aster**, **gaillardia**, **globe amaranth**, **heliotrope**, **lisianthus**, **marigold**, **phlox**, **snapdragon**, **strawflower**, **poppy**, and **zinnia**.

 PLANTING

Start hanging baskets early in April. **Impatiens** and **begonias** do well in shade. For sunny locations, try **dwarf marigold**, **petunia**, **scaevola**, **verbena**, and **annual vinca**. **Portulaca** is wonderful in baskets, as it tolerates hot sun and drought. For a bushier basket planting, keep the plant tips pinched. Start pots for your patio or porch.

Two weeks before the last frost, plant **cleome** seeds and **gloriosa daisy**.

Two to three weeks after the last freeze when the soil temperatures have warmed, **cosmos**, **gomphrena**, **marigold**, **portulaca**, **sunflower**, **zinnia**, and other warm-season annuals can be sown directly in the beds where they are to grow. Keep the seeded area moist until the seeds emerge. Thin out as soon as they are large enough to transplant. Any extras can be transplanted to other areas.

 CARE

Tender annuals started indoors should gradually be "hardened off" before planting them in the garden. Hardening is a procedure that prepares indoor-grown plants for the rigors of the outdoors. Reduce watering and set them outdoors during the day. Bring them inside at night. Continue this for three to four days. If the temperature drops below 50 degrees F., take the plants inside. After four days, allow the plants to be outside all day and night. After about a week or two, the plants should be hardened off and ready to be transplanted with a minimum of shock. Alternatively, place plants in a cold frame for a week or two, monitoring the temperature and adjusting the cold-frame cover accordingly. See November Care p. 38.

Some annuals will produce hundreds of seedlings from last year's flowers. Look for "volunteers" of **cosmos**, **cleome**, **melampodium**, **impatiens**, **silk flower**, **vinca**, and others. Thin out the seedlings or transplant them to other parts of your garden.

As you remove cool-loving **larkspurs**, shake the plant over the soil to scatter seeds. Alternatively, shake the seeds over a sheet of newspaper, collect them, and sow them next fall.

Other cool-season annuals can be removed to make room for warm-season annuals.

 WATERING

Keep transplants well watered and mulched to help them get settled in before summer's heat and humidity arrives.

 FERTILIZING

If you fertilized at planting with a slow-release fertilizer, you may not have to fertilize until midsummer or later, depending on the fertilizer brand and formulation. Follow the label directions to learn the desired amount and frequency of application. Fast-release granular fertilizers can be applied every four to six weeks during the growing season. Plants can absorb liquid

# HELPFUL HINTS

If you want to plant your annuals on a square spacing, where each plant is spaced an equal distance from one another, refer to the square spacing chart in Vines and Ground Covers March Helpful Hints p. 239. For more uniform beds, use a triangular spacing instead of a straight row or a rectangular grid. Triangular spacing requires more plants per square foot, but the resulting effect will be more attractive than plants placed in rows. To determine the number of plants needed for a given area, use the following formula: Area of Bed in Square Feet x Spacing Multiplier = Number of Plants Needed.

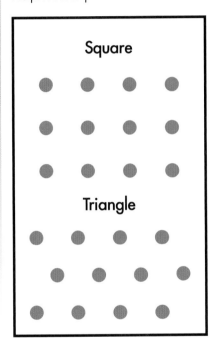

Square

Triangle

| In-row Spacing (inches) | Triangular Spacing Spacing Multiplier (# of plants needed per 1 sq. ft.) |
|---|---|
| 14 | 10.4 |
| 16 | 14.6 |
| 18 | 12.6 |
| 10 | 11.7 |
| 12 | 11.2 |
| 14 | 10.8 |
| 16 | 10.7 |
| 18 | 10.5 |
| 24 | 10.3 |

fertilizers through their leaves and roots and they will have to be applied more frequently (typically every two weeks).

## GROOMING

Prune or shear **alyssum** and **lobelia** after blooming—this will make them look neater and encourage them to produce more flowers. Remove spent flowers from **snapdragon** for another crop of flowers. The blooms will not be as large, but they will provide garden color.

## PROBLEMS

Watch out for aphids and whiteflies on **China aster, impatiens,** and others. See pp. 283 to 287 for descriptions and controls.

See p. 31 for weed controls.

Damping-off can still be a problem on indoor seedlings. Use sterile seed-starting medium and avoid overwatering.

Gray mold is a fungus that commonly attacks **geraniums,** covering the flowers with a fuzzy grayish mold. It often infects dead or dying tissues first, and then spreads into living tissue such as leaves, stems, and flowers. Cool, damp weather favors the development and spread of this disease. Remove spent flowers, dying leaves, and other dead tissues. Use fungicides according to label directions.

# MAY

## ANNUALS & BIENNIALS

### PLANNING

Too busy to enjoy your garden during the daylight hours? Then plan to create an "evening garden" with annuals that look their best at twilight. These flowers open in the evening or release fragrances at night to attract night-flying pollinators such as moths. One of the more familiar night-blooming annuals is **flowering tobacco** (*Nicotiana alata*). **Petunias** open by day and release their scent at night. Try the varieties 'Celebrity White', 'Ultra White', or 'Apollo'.

Other night-blooming annuals to consider are the **moonflower vine** (*Ipomoea alba*), **angel's trumpet** (*Datura inoxia*), **night phlox** (*Zaluzianskya capensis*), and **night-scented stock** (*Matthiola longipetala*). For a more comprehensive list, read *The Evening Garden: Flowers and Fragrance from Dusk till Dawn* by Asheville, North Carolina, garden writer Peter Loewer.

### PLANTING

Plant warm-season annuals for summer color. Set out those you started indoors. Continue to plant **zinnia** seed at intervals to have cut flowers until frost.

Overplant bulb beds with annuals using seeds or transplants. Take care to avoid injuring the bulbs when planting.

Although cool-season annuals such as **pansy** and **viola** may still be flowering, the heat will make them stretch and get leggy. Pull them out and replace them with heat-loving summer annuals such as **African daisy**, **ageratum**, **celosia**, **cockscomb**, **marigold**, **pentas**, **vinca** or **Madagascar periwinkle**, **petunia**, **portulaca**, **salvia**, and **zinnia** for sunny areas. **Geranium** and **New Guinea impatiens** are excellent if you have afternoon shade. For shady areas, use **begonia**, **coleus**, and **impatiens**.

Grow your own dried flowers. Start seeds of **statice**, **globe amaranth**, **strawflower,** and other everlastings for this year's arrangements.

### CARE

Thin out direct-seeded annuals to the correct spacing.

To make room for warm-season annuals, remove cool-season annuals when they begin to decline.

Although plant breeders have developed compact, sturdy varieties that require no support, other tall-growing types need support for protection from buffeting

winds and rain. See Perennials May Care p. 136 for techniques.

### WATERING

Newly set transplants should not be allowed to dry out. But keep the leaves dry—extended periods of wetness on the leaves promotes the growth and spread of diseases.

### FERTILIZING

Continue to apply fast-release fertilizer every four to six weeks if necessary. Follow the label instructions. Water the fertilizer in to make it available to the plants.

### GROOMING

To promote bushy growth, pinch back annuals when they are 4 to 6 inches tall:

• Pinch out the shoot tips of **marigold**, **petunia**, **salvia**, and **zinnia**.

• Pinch the shoot tips of **cosmos** to encourage branching. If left unpinched, the stems may require staking to keep them upright.

• Shear **alyssum** and **lobelia** after flowering.

• Remove the spent flowers of **sweet William**.

• Remove the yellow flowers of **dusty miller** to keep the leaves looking good throughout the growing season. If the plant gets leggy, cut it back to about half its height to encourage branching and denser growth.

When reworking flower beds, use a slow-release fertilizer, especially in sandy soils. The nutrients are released over an extended period, perhaps three or four months, depending on the product. Use as recommended on the label.

## PROBLEMS

Aphids, spider mites, whiteflies, snails, and slugs can be a problem. See pp. 286 and 287 for descriptions and controls of snails and slugs.

Watch out for cutworms, which feed on plant stems near the soil surface. In their wake they leave the fallen stems gnawed off at the base. They feed at night, so use your flashlight to inspect the seedlings in the dark. Handpick them when you see them. To control cutworms, till up the soil thoroughly

before planting. Protect the transplants with a stiff paper collar made out of a paper cup with the bottom cut out and pushed 1 to 2 inches deep into the ground and about 1 to 2 inches high. Or create a collar with strips of cardboard 2 inches wide by 8 inches long and stapled into a band which is placed around the plants. Press the collar about an inch into the soil. Bt (*Bacillus thuringiensis*), Neem extract, and other insecticides will also control cutworms.

Avoid leaf spot diseases by watering your annuals from below, keeping the leaves dry. Proper spacing with plenty of air movement will also reduce fungal infections.

Nicotiana is a fragrant, night-blooming annual.

# JUNE
## ANNUALS & BIENNIALS

### PLANNING

This is a good month to visit public gardens to view the tremendous variety of annuals on display. Of special note are the All-America Selections (AAS) display gardens that exhibit the most recent All-America Selections Winners. See pp. 288 to 291 for a list of AAS display gardens in Alabama and Mississippi.

### PLANTING

It's not too late to plant annuals. If your needs are great or your budget small, consider sowing seeds directly into prepared garden beds. **Cosmos**, **cleome**, **marigold**, **Mexican sunflower**, **portulaca**, **sunflower**, and **zinnia** are good choices for direct-sowing. Just remember to keep the seedbed moist during the first few weeks after establishment.

Stagger the plantings of **sunflower** and **zinnia** a couple of weeks apart so you can enjoy fresh blooms longer.

### CARE

Pull up and discard **pansies** as the heat causes them to look ratty. Replace them with trans-plants or seeds of warm-season annuals.

Look for a crop of self-sown seedlings or "volunteers" from last year's **impatiens**, **cleome**, **annual vinca**, **melampodium**, and other annuals. Look around for them and transplant them as you like.

With the approach of midsummer, **geraniums** may go into a slump and start to decline: flowers are sparse and the plants begin to look ragged. This condition is most likely due to high nighttime temperatures. This is a common problem with plants that prefer cooler summers.

High nighttime temperatures cause the plants to consume more carbohydrates through respiration than can be produced by photosynthesis during the day. If you are determined to keep your **geraniums**, here are some tips for late summer:

• Prune them back one-half to three-quarters the length of the stems. Make your cuts above a node on the stem.

• Fertilize each plant to encourage root and stem growth. This should encourage **geraniums** to bloom until they are killed by freezing weather.

• Try growing the humidity- and heat-tolerant cultivars 'Bingo Rose' and 'Freckles'.

### WATERING

A crusty surface on the walls of clay pots or over the potting medium indicates a salt problem. Leach containers occasionally to remove any mineral salt deposits that accumulate from

The yellow daisy-like flowers of melampodium are a good hot weather annual choice.

fertilizer and hard water. To leach the container, allow the water to run until it drains freely from the bottom holes. Wait a few minutes, then repeat.

When watering, apply sufficient moisture to soak the soil deeply to the root zone.

## FERTILIZING

Annual beds can use a boost, especially where the soil is sandy or the season has been rainy. Apply slow-release fertilizer for maximum benefit with minimum effort. For a quick but brief response, water plants with a liquid fertilizer such as 20-20-20.

Do not overfertilize **cosmos** or **nasturtium** or you will run the risk of having a lot of leaves and few, if any, flowers.

## GROOMING

Some annuals need to be jump-started either now or next month. Trim back **petunias** toward the end of the month to keep them bushy and encourage the formation of new flowers. After watering and fertilizing, they'll soon be full and attractive again. Remove spent blossoms on annual flowering plants as often as possible. This encourages further flowering rather than seed production. Seed collectors and those who want the dried seed-pods for arrangements might ignore this rule. In most cases, however, seed collectors should delay until the end of the blooming season. Then the last few blooms may be kept for seed. Seeds of hybrids will not reproduce true from the parent plant.

**Cosmos** reseeds readily. Shear the spent blooms, leaving some to germinate and grow during the warm summer weather.

## PROBLEMS

Be on the lookout for aphids, spider mites, snails, and slugs.

Allow beneficial insects such as lady beetles to reduce aphid numbers. Aphids can sometimes be washed from plants with a strong stream of water. Many safe insecticides are available, including insecticidal soaps, horticultural oils, or Neem. Apply according to label directions.

Avoid overhead watering, and remove spent flowers and dead or dying leaves. Keeping plants clean will reduce the chance of infection.

Look for signs of powdery mildew on your garden **zinnias**. Infected leaves have a whitish-gray powder on both sides. Heavy infestations can cause the leaves to become curled and eventually yellow and die. Remove any infected plants and discard them. Thin out the bed to improve air movement. Fungicides can be applied when the symptoms appear; continue applications as long as symptoms are present. In the future, select varieties that are resistant to powdery mildew.

Handpull or hoe out any weeds to prevent them from stealing water and nutrients from your annuals. Suppress their emergence with a layer of mulch.

Rabbits and deer can be a problem. Commercially available mammal repellents can be applied on or near your flowers. To make your own repellent, see Shrubs, October Problems p. 201.

## HELPFUL HINTS

• Self-cleaning flowers save time and work in the garden by dropping dead blooms, thus requiring no trimming or dead-heading. Among them are **cleome**, **impatiens**, **New Guinea impatiens**, **pentas**, **wax begonia**, and **narrowleaf zinnia**.

• Weed seedlings and annual seedlings look similar when they're emerging. Make weeding easier by sowing annual seeds in patterns such as rows or circles. You will be able to readily identify and remove any weed seedlings that are out of formation early enough that they won't compete with the flowering annuals.

# JULY
## ANNUALS & BIENNIALS

 PLANNING

If you're going on vacation, plan to have someone take care of your plants. To make things easier for the caregiver, group plants in containers near a water source and out of the afternoon sun. There may be some pots that need more attention than others; use colorful flags to mark those pots, or tie a bright ribbon around a few of the plants to remind your caregiver that these pots or beds need to be inspected more often. Before you leave, water everything thoroughly, weed, and deadhead any spent flowers.

 PLANTING

Look for empty spaces in the landscape and fill them with warm-season annuals. If you're planting among bulbs or perennials that have gone dormant such as **bleeding heart**, inspect the area carefully to avoid damaging the perennial's crown.

**Cleome**, **cosmos**, **marigold**, **sunflower**, and **zinnia** can still be planted or sown for bloom until frost. When the seedlings are about 2 inches tall, thin them where they're too crowded, or transplant them to other parts of the garden. Some quick-growing and -flowering annuals that can be planted now from seed include **cosmos**, **gomphrena**, **Klondyke marigold**, **Mexican sunflower**, **dwarf sunflower**, and **zinnia**. For the price of a few seeds, they will make a spectacular late-summer show in five to six weeks.

 CARE

See August p. 32.

 WATERING

To learn how to water efficiently, refer to the Roses July Helpful Hints p. 167.

 FERTILIZING

If you use a slow-release fertilizer, now is the time to make your second application (your first application should have been incorporated into the bed at planting time). Fast-release fertilizers should be applied every month or six weeks throughout the growing season. Water afterwards to make the nutrients available to your plants.

 GROOMING

Continue to deadhead spent flowers and cut back leggy annuals such as **salvia** and **zinnia**. This encourages bushiness and produces more flowers.

Good grooming—deadheading spent flowers—encourages bushiness and stimulates repeat flowering.

Low-growing **marigolds** tend to get leggy and produce fewer blooms in midsummer. Shear them down to within 6 inches.

Some types of **petunias** "stretch" during the summer with the onset of higher temperatures. Their long, slender stems produce few flowers. Pinching them back—removing an inch or two from the ends of the stems—repeatedly during the growing season will encourage branching below the "pinch," keeping them stocky and well endowed with blooms. If you took a hands-off approach for the first half of summer, then you need to prune them back now to encourage branching and flowering. Cut back the shoots to half their length. This will force the plant to produce shoots or branches from below the cut. These branches will produce flower buds. Practice "staggered pruning." Stagger your pruning by cutting back one-third of a bed or container (every third plant) each week. By the third week, the first group of pruned plants will be blooming again, assuring some color during the entire pruning period.

**Impatiens** tend to grow leggy in the South in response to high nighttime temperatures. They may grow a third taller than their labeled height. Cut them back by one-third, or grow **impatiens** tolerant of high temperatures such as the Impulse and the Super Elfin series.

Pinch the tips of **coleus** every few weeks to keep them dense and compact. Pinch off any flower stalks as they appear.

## HELPFUL HINTS

Cutting flowers for bouquets is best done with sharp shears or a knife to avoid injury to the growing plant. You can buy a special pair of cutting scissors that holds the cut-off stem, allowing the removal to be a one-handed operation. A slanted cut exposes a larger absorbing surface to water. It also prevents the base of the stem from resting on the bottom of the vase, interfering with its water intake. Instead of the familiar cutting basket, carry a bucket of water to the garden for collecting blooms.

**Cleome** often grows vertically with few flowering stalks. Snip off a few inches from the tip before it blooms. Two flowering stalks will replace one. If pinched two or three times, the plant will be covered with flowers.

Hanging baskets of **portulaca** should be cut back every month to keep them full in the center of the basket. Snip away old blooms to keep the plants flowering until the first frost.

Shear annual **coreopsis** to encourage another round of blooming in the fall. Leave some flowers to produce seed for next year.

## PROBLEMS

Aphids, spider mites, and whiteflies continue to be on the prowl this month. They can be washed from plants with a strong stream of water. Insecticidal soap, insecticides, and miticides will keep their numbers in check.

Watch out for Japanese beetles. The adults eat flowers and foliage. See p. 283 for controls.

Watch out for powdery mildew on **zinnia**. Pull out and discard infected plants. Reseed the vacant areas. In the future, select **zinnias** that are resistant to powdery mildew.

Pull weeds out by hand or lightly hoe them.

# AUGUST

## ANNUALS & BIENNIALS

PLANNING

The heat and humidity of August can be a time to reflect on the past season and update your garden journal. Over a glass of iced tea, jot down the names of annuals that didn't perform as well as you would like. List any that performed better than you expected. Make a note of any insect or disease problems.

As you collect your thoughts, begin making plans for next year. Avoid varieties that didn't do well. Focus on varieties that performed well in your garden or that you've noticed in display gardens.

PLANTING

Seeds of hardy annuals that will bloom in the fall and winter can be started this month. They include **alyssum**, **calendula**, and **ornamental cabbage** and **kale**. Biennials that can be planted for transplanting later include **foxglove**, **money plant**, and **sweet William**.

If you have any leftover seed, make a final planting of **marigold**, **zinnia**, and other fast-growing annuals.

Sow seeds of cool-season annuals that will be transplanted to the garden this fall. Plant **calendula**, **snapdragon**, and **stock** from seed by sowing in sterile soilless mix in individual pots, and transplant seedlings to individual containers before they become too crowded. Water as needed, give them plenty of sun, and fertilize weekly with a liquid fertilizer.

The seeds of **cabbage** and **kale** should be sown about eight weeks before the first freeze. Keep them cool after they sprout and move them outside when night temperatures begin to cool down in early fall.

Coleus root easily, allowing you to overwinter them for next year.

Take cuttings of favorite annuals or sow seeds in pots for winter flowering indoors. The following bedding plants root easily, allowing you to preserve your favorite varieties for next year: **geranium**, **impatiens**, **coleus**, and **wax begonia**. Here's how to root **coleus**:

1. Select a terminal shoot that's at least 3 inches long and has two or three nodes or buds that will open into new leaves.

2. Place the cutting in a small pot filled with a soilless mix, such as three parts perlite to one part peat moss.

3. Place the potted cutting in a plastic bag twist-tied at the top, and move it to a warm location between 70 and 75 degrees F. The warmer the temperature, the faster the cuttings will root. Roots will sprout within ten days and the plants should be ready to transplant within two or three weeks.

Keep the cuttings in a cool location, ideally between 40 and 50 degrees F., and under cool white fluorescent lights for up to twelve hours a day.

CARE

Do not disturb the soil in your flower beds during hot, dry August days. Loosening the soil can damage surface roots and increase water loss from the soil.

Inspect the mulch in flower beds. If wind, rain, and natural decay have reduced its thickness to an inch or less, apply more mulch to raise the level to 2 to 3 inches, but only about $1/2$ inch around the bases of the plants. Use compost, pine straw, pine bark, or hardwood mulch.

If the cutting garden looks bedraggled, clear out the annuals that have finished blooming or are overgrown.

## WATERING

Check the soil in flower beds to determine if you need to water. Water deeply to wet the entire root zone of the plants.

Container-grown flowers can dry out quickly, especially when located in full sun. Feel the soil in containers at least once a day to check for moisture. When water is necessary, apply it long enough so that it runs out of the drainage holes. Keep in mind that clay pots will need to be watered more often than plastic pots. Also, small pots will dry out faster than large planters.

Check hanging baskets daily in the summer. Wind and sun dry them much more quickly than plants in other kinds of containers.

## HELPFUL HINTS

When selecting flowers for dried arrangements, be mindful that bright-yellow, orange, pink, and blue flowers preserve their colors best. Red and purple petals become darker and less attractive, while white flowers usually fade to a buff or tan color.

## FERTILIZING

If they haven't been fertilized in over six weeks, leggy plants that were cut back will benefit from a light feeding with a fast-release fertilizer. Apply a water-soluble fertilizer, such as 20-20-20, to container-grown annuals, according to label directions. Water the soil first, then apply the fertilizer.

## GROOMING

Early this month, pinch flowers from **coleus** to produce bushier plants. Deadhead any faded flowers or seedpods from **snapdragons** that survived the summer; this will encourage another round of flowers this fall.

## PROBLEMS

Be on the lookout for aphids and spider mites. Plants infested by spider mites have faded, stippled leaves. Remove these pests with a strong spray of water. Resort to a pesticide if their numbers are high and damage is great. If these plants are going to be removed and replaced by cool-season annuals, spraying with a pesticide may be unnecessary.

Nematodes may threaten your plants as well. See Roses, July Problems p. 166.

Fungal leaf spots, powdery mildew, and other diseases could be afflicting your warm-season annuals. Evaluate the extent of damage to determine if a fungicide application is necessary. Heavily infested plants should be removed and discarded. Avoid wetting the leaves when watering.

Control weeds by handpulling and maintaining a layer of mulch. Keeping the beds weed-free will also remove over-wintering sites for spider mites.

# SEPTEMBER

## ANNUALS & BIENNIALS

 PLANNING

 PLANTING

 CARE

### PLANNING

Plan to obtain seeds or transplants early this month for fall planting. Let your journal be your guide. It should document the annuals that performed well in your garden, or those that you've admired during your travels. Try your hand at annuals mentioned in conversation with friends and acquaintances.

Be adventurous: Experiment with something new. Mix delicious winter greens to provide pretty foliage and foil for cool-season annuals in beds and containers. For example, try a palette of winter annuals with the following colorful greens: **purple mustard** (*Brassica juncea* var. *rugosa* 'Red Giant'), **mizuna** (*Brassica rapa* var. *nipposinica*), **Japanese mustard-spinach** (*Brassica rapa* var. *peviridis*), **tatsoi** or flat **pak choi** (*Brassica rapa* var. *rosularis*), and **arugula** or **roquette** (*Eruca vesicaria* ssp. *sativa*). These minimum-care greens can be terrific fall and winter bedding plants that make a great foil for **pansies** and **calendulas**.

### PLANTING

Plant seeds of **California, Iceland**, and **Shirley poppies**:

1. Place seeds in a small jar with two or three small nail holes in the lid.

2. Shake seeds out where you want them.

3. Create a shallow V-shaped trench and sow seeds in the trench.

4. Cover the seed very lightly with soil.

Start setting out **marigolds** and **petunias** for fall color. In the warmer areas of Zone 8, **petunias** planted earlier, especially the **species petunia** (*P. integrifolia*) and those in the Wave series, can generally be left in place. They usually bounce back unperturbed after cold snaps and continue flowering.

Sowing seeds of hardy annuals (such as **calendula, calliopsis, sweet alyssum, larkspur**, and **pinks**) now will give the seedlings time to get established and develop good root systems before the coldest part of winter. This gives them a head start on growth and flowering next spring. You will need to shade them and keep them moist early in the month.

### CARE

Start taking cuttings of your annual plants to bring indoors to carry through the winter. **Coleus, geranium, impatiens, wax begonia**, and others do best when stem cuttings are rooted and kept in pots indoors during cold weather. Be sure to place pots where they receive plenty of light and cool temperatures. Root some cuttings of bedding **geraniums** by following these steps:

1. Use a sharp knife or razor blade to take 3- to 4-inch cuttings of terminal growth. Make an angled cut just below a node (the point where the leaf joins the stem). Remove the lowest leaf or two.

2. Dip the cut end into rooting hormone suited for herbaceous plants (0.1 percent indolebutyric acid or IBA).

3. Fill a small pot with equal parts peat moss and perlite.

4. Use a pencil to poke a hole in the potting medium before inserting the cutting. This will prevent the rooting powder from being scraped off.

5. When you have stuck in all the cuttings, water them well and place the pots in plastic bags that are closed at the top with twist-ties.

Set the pots in a bright location, but not direct sunlight. Rooting should occur in two to three weeks. When the cuttings have rooted, remove the pots from the bag and move them into direct sunlight in a cool room between 55 and 65 degrees F. You will end up with bushier, more floriferous **geraniums** if you pinch each of these young plants back at least once.

## WATERING

Fall is the driest season in Alabama and Mississippi. Keep newly set-out transplants well watered to help them establish quickly.

## FERTILIZING

Apply a slow-release fertilizer when planting cool-season annuals.

## GROOMING

Trim back leggy annuals and continue removing faded flowers to encourage more blooms.

---

## HELPFUL HINTS

This is the ideal time for taking soil samples to be tested by your Cooperative Extension Service. Pick up soil boxes and forms at your local Extension office, garden centers, or "feed 'n seed" stores. Follow directions carefully. Identify each sample by what is to be grown in that area so the testing lab can offer you specific recommendations for the particular grass, flower, or shrub. Results should be available in time for you to take any corrective measures this fall and early winter.

Fall is a perfect time to take a soil sample to test.

## PROBLEMS

Discouraged by powdery mildew on your **zinnias**? This late in the season, fungicides may not be warranted. **Zinnias** will soon be removed to make way for cool-season annuals. Make a note in your gardening journal to select mildew-resistant **zinnias** next year.

Check for evidence of snails and slugs. Set out baits or traps for them as the weather turns cooler and wetter.

Do not turn your back on the weeds in your flower beds. Summer annual weeds like crabgrass and goosegrass have matured and are going to seed. Winter annual weeds like annual bluegrass and chickweed are germinating. Hoe them out or handpull them now.

# OCTOBER
## ANNUALS & BIENNIALS

### PLANNING

With the onset of cooler temperatures, begin planning new beds or converting the beds to new plantings of perennials or shrubs. Refer to your journal to guide your decisions to expand your beds, reduce them, or add different kinds of plants. Start making lists of the plants you will need. You will be ready when catalogs arrive in the next couple of months.

To help you design new beds, use a garden hose to outline the shape. Enrich the soil with organic matter as explained on p. 38. Take a soil sample and send it in for testing.

### PLANTING

Sow seeds of **calliopsis**, **foxglove**, **larkspur**, **money plant**, **Johnny-jump-ups**, **stock**, and **Shirley**, **Iceland**, and **California poppies** directly into well-prepared garden soil before the first expected freeze. These plants need cool temperatures to germinate. Fall sowing tends to produce stronger plants than seeds sown in early spring. Leave the soil surface bare or use a very light mulch.

Plant **ornamental cabbage** and **ornamental kale**, **pansy**, and **viola** to help them get established quickly before cold weather sets in. Allow at least six weeks before the first expected freeze. Now is also a good time to set out **calendula**, **dianthus**, **sweet William**, **snapdragon**, **stock**, and **sweet alyssum** before the night temperatures drop consistently below 40 degrees F.

### CARE

**Pentas**, or **Egyptian star cluster**, long grown as a houseplant in Zone 10, has become popular as a heat- and drought-tolerant outdoor annual. **Pentas** grows 2 to 3 feet high and produces 4-inch flat-topped clusters of small, star-shaped flowers in white, pink, lilac, or red all summer long. Because plants will be killed by freezing temperatures, make cuttings in the fall by taking 3- to 4-inch stem cuttings of nonflowering shoots just below a leaf. Follow the same rooting procedure that was described for **geraniums** in September Planting p. 34. When rooting occurs, usually after one month, uncover the new plant and grow it indoors as a houseplant. Next year, plant it outside after the last freeze in spring.

Pot up and bring **geraniums** indoors for the winter before the first frost. In February you will be able to take cuttings to produce a bevy of new plants for next year's garden. If you decide to do this, cut back the plant now so it will have produced a number of new shoots for cutting by January.

You can also shake the soil off the **geraniums'** roots and hang them upside-down with twine or place them in a paper bag in a cool, dry location such as a crawl space or basement. This old-fashioned method of storing **geraniums** is possible because their thick, fleshy stems allow them to survive periods of

Sow Johnny-jump-up seeds now for a delightful show next spring.

drought. The location must remain above freezing yet be cool and moist enough to avoid excessive dehydration of the bare roots. Periodic moistening of the roots may be necessary. Light is neither necessary nor desirable, provided the temperature is cool enough.

Despite this drastic treatment, the **geraniums** can be repotted in the spring, their tops cut back by half or two-thirds, and returned to bright light and regular watering. New roots will emerge from the green stems below the soil surface, new shoots above.

Pull up frost-tender plants like **marigold, impatiens,** and **zinnia** toward the end of the month before the first expected freeze. Although it may be disconcerting to lift up completely healthy plants, you need the space to plant cool-season annuals, like **pansies** in their place. The cool-season annuals will need time to root before temperatures cool down.

## WATERING

Keep an eye on the watering needs of your annuals, especially emerging seedlings and newly set-out transplants. Check the soil for moisture; don't wait until the plants begin to wilt.

### HELPFUL HINTS

Collect seeds of annuals such as **cleome, cosmos, flowering tobacco, sunflower,** and **zinnia** for next year. Keep the seeds in an envelope and put them in a jar or film canister in the refrigerator (not the freezer) during winter. Hybrid varieties probably won't come back true-to-type. Other open-pollinated types, however, will reproduce faithfully. The offspring of hybrids may come in different heights and colors from the original parents.

Rake up fallen pine needles and use them for mulch.

## FERTILIZING

Use a slow-release fertilizer at planting time to lightly fertilize hardy annuals such as **calendula, pansy,** and **sweet alyssum.** This will encourage establishment and flowering.

## GROOMING

Deadhead spent flowers from **pansies** planted last month.

## PROBLEMS

Inspect the annuals you brought inside for the winter. Whiteflies and spider mites could have hitchhiked their way inside. Keep the plants quarantined, and control pests before you introduce them to your other indoor plants. Insecticidal soap applied to the upper and lower leaf surfaces will control these pests. If the plant is not listed on the label, you may have to test a small area on your plant for injury. It may take seven to ten days to see if any damage occurs. If your plant shows sensitivity, rinse the soap off once the whiteflies and spider mites are killed.

Leaf spots may be a problem on **zinnias** and other warm-season annuals. Since they're going to be removed, or killed by impending cold temperatures, a fungicide may not be necessary. Any heavily infected plants can be pulled out immediately.

See September p. 35 for weed controls.

# NOVEMBER
## ANNUALS & BIENNIALS

### PLANNING

Garden tools can add up to a large investment. Make plans this month to clean them off and repair or replace any broken ones. As soon as seed flats and pots are emptied of fall transplants, wash and sterilize them with a 10-percent bleach solution (1 part bleach to 9 parts water) before storing them so they'll be ready in the spring.

This is also a good month to think about building a cold frame, which is like a halfway house for seedlings as they make their way from the windowsill or light table to the outdoors. The cold frame is basically a bottomless box made of wood, stone, or brick, with a transparent or translucent cover—like a miniature unheated greenhouse outdoors.

Cold frames are typically rectangular in shape, 3 by 6 feet or so. The back of the cold frame should face north and should be 18 to 30 inches high. The front should be slightly lower, between 12 and 24 inches to allow enough headroom for the plants inside. Tilt the cover to the south by sloping the sides about 1 inch per foot. More adventurous gardeners can even add an automatic opener to the cover. These devices lift the cover automatically as the temperature rises during the day, and gradually close it with the falling evening temperatures.

### PLANTING

Set out **forget-me-nots**, **snapdragon**, **pansy**, **sweet William**, **pinks**, **viola**, and other hardy plants for flowers and leaves in winter and early spring.

If you didn't sow them last month, go ahead and sow the seeds of **calliopsis**, **foxglove**, **Johnny-jump-ups**, **money plant**, **larkspur**, **stock**, and **Shirley**, **Iceland**, and **California poppies**.

### CARE

Clean up the garden. Remove spent plants, chop them up, and compost them. Add organic matter to beds. Either shred leaves and use them as mulch or compost them to improve soil. Cover the garden with mulch to prevent soil loss.

Move containers of live plants to a protected spot if possible. Protect the roots by covering the soil and the container with a thick layer of straw or leaves. Check the moisture level of the pots every few weeks, and water if needed. Annuals overwintered indoors should be kept in a cool location in bright light.

### WATERING

If the month is dry, water newly planted transplants.

### FERTILIZING

If you didn't incorporate a slow-release fertilizer last month at planting, lightly fertilize with a liquid fertilizer such as 20-20-20 now.

### PROBLEMS

See September p. 35 for weed controls.

---

## HELPFUL HINTS

Put packets of unused seed inside screw-top glass jars. Add a small tissue packet of powdered milk to the jar to serve as a desiccant, soaking up moisture from the air inside the jar that would otherwise get into the seeds and reduce their longevity. Store them in the refrigerator. If there isn't any room, keep them in a cool, dry location.

# DECEMBER

## ANNUALS & BIENNIALS

 PLANNING

There's not much to be done with annuals this month except enjoy them. Fall-planted **pansies**, **violas**, **greens**, or **ornamental cabbages** and **kales** should be sitting pretty. If you've kept up with the autumn chores outdoors and your green thumb still itches, swing your focus to your houseplants.

Review your journal to draw some conclusions. Could you have grouped your annuals better? Remember the rule of threes: three plants, each set at the point of a triangle, grow together to multiply their impact. Could you have streamlined the care process? Plants with similar growing needs (sun, water, feeding, etc.) thrive better and are easier to care for if grouped together. Incorporate these principles in your design for next year's beds. Have a plan ready before the seed catalog bombardment starts. Steel yourself to resist the tugging and pulling of the seed merchants that takes you out of your plan. And if you find a way to do this, please tell me!

 PLANTING

Hardy cool-season annual transplants may still be set out in areas near the coast.

Ornamental cabbage and kale are perfect for this time of year.

 CARE

**Pansies** and other winter annuals can be pushed out of the ground in the winter in areas where the ground freezes. This "frost-heaving" (when the freezing and thaw- ing of the soil lifts plants out of the ground and damages roots) can be minimized by mulching. Cut up your Christmas tree and lay some of the branches over flower beds to insulate the soil.

 WATERING

Water cool-season annuals after fertilizing. Newly planted transplants should be watered more often to speed up establishment. If there is a warm spell, check to be sure nothing in the garden is getting too dry; water as necessary.

 FERTILIZING

Lightly fertilize winter annuals such as **pansy** and **ornamental cabbage** and **kale** between bouts of cold weather. If you didn't fertilize last month and the weather is mild, use a liquid fertilizer that contains a nitrate source of nitrogen because it is most readily available in cold soil.

## HELPFUL HINTS

A small envelope of seeds collected from your garden makes a thoughtful gift to enclose in your holiday cards. Label the envelope with the collection date and the name of the flower.

# BULBS, CORMS, RHIZOMES, & TUBERS

This group deserves a place in your garden. When you think of easy-care, no-fuss-no-muss plantings, think of bulbs. Their wide range of sizes and colors allows them to fit in any corner of the garden.

Technically, they're geophytes—literally "earth plants." Geophytes contain in their subterranean storage structures everything needed to sprout and flower. Their leaves produce food that recharges the bulb for the next cycle.

They can be divided into six types: true bulbs, corms, rhizomes, tubers, tuberous roots, and enlarged hypocotyls. Collectively, they're called bulbs. Knowing something about the different types helps with planting and propagating them.

Bulbs are also traditionally classed by blooming period: Spring/early-summer-flowering bulbs, the so-called Dutch bulbs, are planted in the fall. Most are completely hardy in the northern parts of Alabama and Mississippi. But they need refrigeration in southern parts of the states. Summer/fall-flowering bulbs include both hardy and tender bulbs that are planted in the spring, summer, or fall.

Some bulbs bloom through late fall and winter. Depending on your location, you can select bulbs to provide a colorful outdoor display the year round. But if winter temperatures won't let you, consider "forcing" bulbs into bloom indoors.

## PLANNING AND PREPARING THE BULB GARDEN

Location is the key to successful bulb culture. Plan with the following two factors in mind.

# CHAPTER TWO

**Soil:** Good drainage is a must. Test the drainage before planting. Fill a foot-deep hole with water. The next day, fill it again. If that refill drains away in less than ten hours, most bulbs will thrive there. If drainage is a problem, consider creating a raised bed—or add organic matter such as composted yard trimmings or composted pine bark to improve drainage. In sandy soils that lose water too fast, add organic matter. Mix in no less than 2 inches of organic matter, to a depth of 8 to 12 inches. If you want, you can add organic matter until it makes up half the soil volume. Some bulbs thrive in waterlogged soil (sometimes known as "hog wallows"), but choices are limited. Try moisture-loving bulbs such as canna, summer snowflake (*Leucojum aestivum*), Dutch iris (*Iris x hollandica*), rain lily (*Zephyranthes*), crinum, and spider lily (*Hymenocallis*).

**Light:** Most spring-flowering bulbs prefer light shade to full sunshine. Pick a location that offers at least six hours of direct sunlight a day. It doesn't have to be full sun year-round. A spot near deciduous trees that gets sunlight before the trees leaf out is perfect for spring bulbs. A few bulbs that tolerate partial shade are crocus, daffodils, squill, and wood hyacinths. Summer-flowering bulbs are not so fastidious about light. Be mindful that inadequate light usually results in poor flowering. Too much light during the summer months, however, can bleach the flowers and leaves of some bulbs.

## PLANTING

Plant spring- and early-summer-flowering bulbs in the fall to satisfy their cold requirement and to develop a good root system by bloom time. That cold requirement ranges from six to sixteen weeks, depending on the species or cultivar. Delay planting until the soil temperature at planting depth is below 60 degrees F. This usually occurs around the time of the first expected freeze, or when trees begin to lose their leaves. October and November are good months for planting in the northern parts of Alabama and Mississippi. South of Montgomery, AL, and Jackson, MS, wait until after Thanksgiving—but before early January—to plant, after proper chilling periods.

Summer-flowering and fall-flowering bulbs except for autumn crocus (also called meadow saffron) (*Colchicum autumnale*) and fall-blooming crocuses (*Crocus niveus, C. speciosus,* and others) should be planted in the spring after the last expected freeze.

Here's how to plant the bulbs: Arrange the bulbs on the surface of the bed before you plant them individually. Set them at the right depth. In general, plant small bulbs (1 inch in height) in holes 3 inches deep, and larger bulbs in holes 6 inches deep. Space small bulbs 1 to 2 inches apart, medium-sized bulbs about 3 inches apart, and large bulbs 4 to 6 inches. When in doubt, follow this simple rule of thumb: Plant at a depth two times the bulb height, measured from the base to the "nose" or top of the bulb.

For large beds, an easy method is to excavate the bed to the right depth and set the bulbs at the right spacing. Then just fill in with soil. For smaller areas among other plants or with fewer bulbs, cultivate as large an area as possible, then dig each hole with a trowel or bulb planter. To finish up, press the soil firmly around the bulbs. Water thoroughly to settle the soil and cover with 2 or 3 inches of mulch.

## CARE

Nearly all bulbs eventually become overcrowded. Clumps must be divided and bulbs replanted. Some large producers of bulblets require division every two or three years. Others can remain in place for years. At the end of their growth cycle when their leaves turn brown and wither, gently lift the bulbs without damaging them and pull them apart. Corms can also be divided this way.

Cut rhizomes and tubers into sections, either at the end of their growing season or just as it

begins. Make sure each division contains at least one eye. Replanted, each will produce a new plant. Tuberous roots such as dahlia can be split apart. Each division should have a small piece of crown tissue attached. After dividing, either replant them right away or store them for planting later in the season.

## WATERING

Spring-flowering bulbs usually receive enough moisture from natural rainfall, so watering is usually unnecessary. Summer-flowering bulbs, however, may have to be watered weekly during dry spells while they're actively growing. Water deeply to soak the ground thoroughly.

Covering with a 2- to 3-inch layer of mulch will conserve moisture. Compost, bark, pine needles, and many other materials are suitable.

## FERTILIZING

If the plants look robust and are growing in a well-prepared, fertile site, fertilizing may not be needed.

You can, however, encourage spring-flowering bulbs to bloom resplendently in subsequent years with a shot of a bulb-booster type fertilizer in the fall. Use a slow-release nitrogen fertilizer to reduce the likelihood of fertilizer burn. Follow the manufacturer's recommendations. Fast-release plant food works, too, but you'll need to apply again in the spring when 1 or 2 inches of the shoots show.

Do not fertilize spring-flowering bulbs when they're blooming or immediately after they flower. At these times the nitrogen in the fertilizer can encourage the development of the fungal disease Fusarium. You can recognize it by the sour smell it gives to rotting bulbs.

Feed summer-flowering bulbs with a slow-release fertilizer when the shoots appear in the spring. Depending on the formulation, a second application may be needed in mid- to late summer. Follow the manufacturer's directions.

Water-in the fertilizer so that it becomes available to the plant.

## PROBLEMS

Good gardening practices will thwart many diseases. Prepare a well-drained, fertile bed, and plant healthy bulbs, discarding any diseased or damaged ones. Bulb rot, gray mold or botrytis, and powdery mildew are a few of the common diseases that may afflict bulbs. Remove any heavily infected leaves or dig out the bulbs.

Aphids, thrips, and spider mites are the most common bulb pests. Watch for them and learn to identify them. As you visit your garden, take a moment to examine the leaves and flowers. Try to accept less-than-perfect-looking plants.

When trouble strikes, turn to nonchemical controls first. Insects such as aphids can be hosed off with a strong spray of water. Sometimes it is necessary to resort to more potent measures such as insecticidal soap and Neem (a botanical insecticide extracted from the tropical Neem tree) to control soft-bodied insects such as aphids and spider mites.

You may have to occasionally resort to the more toxic pesticides, especially when you feel the damage is more than you or your bulbs can tolerate. Consider spot-treating heavily infested plants instead of making a blanket application that can destroy beneficial insects such as ladybugs, predatory mites, and green lacewings. Use recommended pesticides and apply according to label directions.

Voles, rabbits, and deer relish many kinds of flower bulbs such as crocus and tulip. To protect bulbs from voles, cover the bulbs with heavy wire mesh screening that allows the shoots to grow through. Dig down about 10 to 12 inches and spread the 1/2-inch mesh across the bottom, up the sides, and over the top. A simpler technique that offers less protection is to spread a handful of sharp crushed pea-sized gravel around the bulbs at planting.

# HELPFUL HINTS

**True bulbs** include ornamental onions, tulips, daffodils, Dutch iris, hyacinths, and others. On the bottom of the egg-shaped bulb is a basal plate which gives rise to roots. The bulb itself is comprised of scales—fleshy modified leaves which store food and enclose the flower bud. Some bulbs, like tulips, have tightly packed scales protected by a dry papery "skin" or tunic. Others, such as crown imperial (*Fritillaria*) and lily (*Lilium*), lack a protective covering. They're easily damaged and can quickly dry out when they're out of the ground. Plant true bulbs with the broader, root-forming end facing down. Lift them, when necessary, after their leaves turn brown and die back. While they are out of the ground, look for the new bulblets attached to the basal plate. Some types, such as lilies, produce bulblets underground and small above-ground bulbils in the joints of their leaves. Replant them immediately in the garden, or pot them for nurturing in a cold frame.

**Corms** are like bulbs, but they're more flattened and have "eyes" from which the topgrowth emerges. Each year a new corm forms atop the old one. Tiny corms known as cormels form around the base of the parent corm, as with crocus, freesia, or gladiolus, or in long chains as with crocosmia. Plant corms with the wide side facing down and the "eyes," or buds, looking up.

**Tubers**. The best-known tuber is the potato. In flower beds, caladiums are a good example of tubers. Growth buds, or "eyes," scattered over the surface give rise to both roots and shoots. Plant them with the eyes up.

**Tuberous roots**. Dahlias and sweet potatoes grow from tuberous roots, as do anemone and ranunculus. Buds form only on the crowns and roots grow from the opposite end. Lay them horizontally when planting. Rhizomes grow horizontally, usually below the soil surface but sometimes on top of the soil as with many iris. Roots grow from the underside and shoots develop from buds on the top and sides, usually near the tip. Calla lily, canna, certain species of iris, and lily-of-the-valley are examples.

**Hypocotyls**. Cyclamen and tuberous begonias store food in thickened stems that grow larger every year. It is a bit difficult to discern which end is up. On tuberous begonias, look for crater-like markings where the stem once sprouted—that's the top. The bottom should show traces of spiny roots. Cyclamen has a concave side that should be planted facing up.

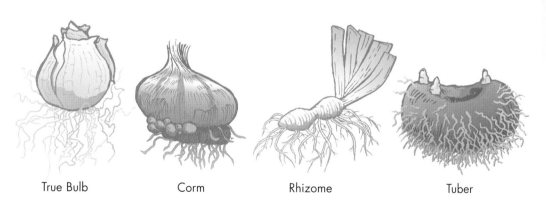

True Bulb      Corm      Rhizome      Tuber

# JANUARY
## BULBS, CORMS, RHIZOMES, & TUBERS

 PLANNING

As garden catalogs arrive each day, enjoy the spectacular pictures and mouth-watering descriptions of summer- and fall-flowering bulbs. While reading the descriptions of the bulbs, pay attention to bloom time, color, height, and hardiness. Keep your gardening journal handy so you can take notes. The journal can be as simple as a spiral-bound notebook, or as high-tech as a spreadsheet program on your computer. Whatever you use, make records of your activities so you can improve your techniques and learn from experience. Some of the information worth recording in your journal are:

- Name of variety
- Where the bulbs were cooled (for example, in a cold frame outdoors, crawl space, or garage)
- Length of chilling period (weeks or months)
- Observations about rooting and flowering (write down the cultivars that performed best and those that didn't do very well).
- Records of techniques that have to be fine-tuned next fall when you force another crop of bulbs to flower outside their normal season.

 PLANTING

Coastal gardeners in Zone 8b can plant **tulips** and **daffodils** that have been precooled or refrigerated for at least six to eight weeks. Refer to October Planting p. 62 for details. If you're going to be preparing a new border for bulbs, now is a good time to mix compost, lime, or other amendments into the bed. If the soil is wet and sticks to your shovel, wait a few days or you could do more harm than good. When the soil crumbles easily in your hand, it's a good time to dig.

 CARE

If a few mild days of winter have encouraged shoots to emerge, don't fret about the health of your bulbs. The leaves are quite cold hardy and will not require any special protection. If they are damaged, expect new leaves to emerge.

Maintain a blanket of mulch at the feet of your bulbs, especially where freezing and thawing can lift the bulbs out of the ground, leaving them to dry out or be harmed by cold. An insulating layer of mulch will break the cycle of freezing and thawing.

If you planted bulbs in pots to force indoors, bring out one or two pots of bulbs each week so you will have a steady stream of flowers in your home. Start them out in the coolest spot in your house, which will allow the flowers to last longer in bright, but indirect, light. When the leaves turn green and begin to grow, place in a sunny window and flowers should open up soon.

As blossoms fade, either compost the bulbs or put the pots in a sunny place where the leaves can recharge the bulbs so they can be planted outdoors.

 WATERING

Check the potting mix in pots that will be forced indoors. The mixture should be evenly moist but not soggy. The easiest way to determine moisture is to lift the pots. A dry pot will be lighter than a wet one.

 PROBLEMS

Check the condition of stored bulbs such as **caladium**, **dahlia**, and **tuberous begonia**. Discard any that show signs of rot, which attacks improperly stored tubers in warm, humid conditions. Discard all diseased tubers. Avoid damaging tubers when digging them up, and store them in a cool, dry, dark place.

# HELPFUL HINTS

There are more than 4,000 **tulip** cultivars that represent virtually all colors, but many are not notably persistent in the South and usually decline after the first year. This decline is typically the result of the high night temperatures, which sap the storage reserves in the bulbs, and the warm summer soils that encourage attacks from insects and diseases. There are some things you can do to encourage **tulips** to perennialize:

Provide good drainage as described in the introduction to this chapter on p. 41. **Tulips** grow best in a partially shaded or full-sun location with a soil pH between 6 and 7. (Have the soil tested by your local Cooperative Extension Service to determine its pH and fertility levels.)

1. **Tulip** bulbs require a cool moist winter and warm summer, but the bulbs should not be exposed to temperatures above 70 degrees F. Plant the bulbs a full 8 inches deep measured from the bottom of the bulb to the soil surface. I also recommend planting annuals or perennials over the bulbs so the shade of their leaves will keep the soil and the bulbs cool. Fertilize in the fall with a slow-release fertilizer such as 9-9-6.

2. After the bulbs have bloomed and the flowers begin to fade, clip off the flower stalks. This prevents seed development and encourages the plants to focus their energy on the bulbs. Allow the **tulip** leaves to "ripen" and turn brown naturally to replenish the bulbs. You can hide or draw attention away from the dying **tulip** leaves by interplanting or bordering the bed with summer-flowering annuals or perennials.

3. Choose varieties that will perennialize. You can expect encore performances most often from perennializing **tulips** that come from cultivars of **triumph tulips** ('Don Quichotte', 'Kees Nelis', and 'Oscar'), Darwin hybrids ('Golden Parade,' 'Parade', and 'Oxford'), single late **tulips** ('Demeter', 'Ile de France', and 'Make Up'), and **species tulips** such as *T. fosteriana, T. greigii, T. bakeri*, **lady** or **candy tulip** (*T. clusiana*), **waterlily tulip** (*T. kaufmanniana*), and others.

This lady tulip is a good choice for our climate, and it perennializes too!

# FEBRUARY
## BULBS, CORMS, RHIZOMES, & TUBERS

 PLANNING

Make plans now to order summer-flowering bulbs for new beds or as complements to existing plantings. Give some thought to trying new varieties of tried-and-true standbys, such as **lilies**, which offer newer colors and long-lasting color in midsummer. Experiment with some of the "little" bulbs with long flowering periods between summer and fall, such as the **summer scillas** (*Scilla autumnalis* and *S. scilloides*), **alliums** (*Allium globosum* and *A. senescens*), **hardy cyclamens** (*Cyclamen graecum* and *C. hederifolium*), and **zephyr lily** (*Zephyranthes candida*). Though small in stature, they're ideal for adding sparkle to containers and small cozy spots in the garden.

 PLANTING

Gardeners in northern Alabama and Mississippi who want to try **tuberous begonias** for spring and maybe summer flowering in pots, beds, or hanging baskets outside should start the tubers indoors late this month or early next month. To sprout the tubers:

Use a mix of equal parts perlite, sphagnum peat moss, and vermiculite. This should be kept damp (not soggy) in a shady

window with a temperature in the lower 60s F.

Place the tubers, hollow side up, fairly close together in shallow, well-drained pans.

Transplant the tubers to pots when growth starts, normally within three weeks.

Place them outside only after all threat of freezing temperatures has passed.

 CARE

It's not unusual for some spring-flowering bulbs to send up a few leaves in late fall or early winter. The bulbs will remain safe and still produce flowers next spring. It's not too late to send soil samples to your local County Extension office for testing. Since some additives, like limestone, take time before increasing the soil pH (ideally between 6 and 7), the sooner you submit a sample, the better. Continue to take out potted bulbs for forcing indoors.

 WATERING

As the bulbs are being forced, keep the potting mix moist. Do not, however, keep the medium waterlogged.

 FERTILIZING

The best fertilizer for bulbs is a soil that's rich in organic matter. Adding nutrients periodically to replace nutrients absorbed by the growing plants, however, will help them bloom in top form. Spring bulbs whose shoots have emerged should be fertilized with a complete fertilizer such as 10-10-10. Apply 1 rounded teaspoon per square foot. Brush off any fertilizer from the leaves. If you fertilized with a slow-release fertilizer last fall, it is not necessary to fertilize now.

 PROBLEMS

Watch out for aphids on forced bulbs. These soft-bodied insects suck plant sap with their piercing-sucking mouth parts, causing the leaves to curl and become malformed. Aphids can be controlled with insecticidal soap and other insecticides.

A number of fungal diseases attack both growing plants and stored bulbs. Fungi invade planted bulbs through wounds, causing them to rot in the ground. The plants may look stunted, their leaves become yellow, and the plant dies. Bulbs attacked by these rots include **daffodil**, **dahlia**, **gladiolus**, and

# HELPFUL HINTS

• Not all bulbs need a cold period in order to bloom reliably. Some magnificent tropical flowering bulbs require no cold. **Amaryllis** (*Hippeastrum* cultivars) and **canna** are the most famous. Others you should seek out include **gloriosa lily** (*Gloriosa superba*), **Aztec lily** (*Sprekelia formosissima*), **spider lily** (*Hymenocallis caroliniana*), **Peruvian daffodil** (*Hymenocallis narcissiflora*), **pineapple lily** (*Eucomis* species), **hurricane lily** (*Lycoris aurea*), **society garlic** (*Tulbaghia violacea*), and **zephyr lily** (*Zephyranthes* species). In areas where the ground freezes, these bulbs may be safely overwintered outdoors with a hefty mulch layer or lifted and stored.

• **Daffodils** make nice tabletop bouquets; they differ from other cut flowers, however, when it comes to conditioning. To get the longest vase life (a week or more) here's what you should do:

Harvest the **daffodils** very early in the morning. To avoid any skin irritation from the sap, use a gloved hand to remove the flower stem or scape at its base. Gently pull it to one side and twist it off. Pick single-flowered **daffodils** when the neck is bent roughly at a 90-degree angle to the stem; this is called the "gooseneck" stage. The flower bud should just barely be open to reveal its color. Multiflowered stems with several flowers should be picked when at least one from the bunch is fully open.

To prevent any stem-clogging air bubbles from interfering with water uptake, cut the white, pith-filled bottom end of the scape at an angle underwater with a clean sharp knife or razor blade. Put the stems in warm water that has a little household bleach added ($1/2$ teaspoon per quart). Keep the flowers in a cool, dark area for twelve hours or, ideally, overnight.

Since **daffodil** sap can harm other cut flowers, notably **carnations**, **freesias**, **irises**, **roses**, and **tulips**, condition them separately. **Daffodils** should be placed in water for twenty-four hours, then rinsed before combining them with other flowers.

Gloriosa lily is a magnificent tropical flowering bulb that does not require a chilling period.

**tulip**. Stored bulbs may become infected through wounds or nicks in the tissue. Bulbs feel spongy and are discolored.

Fungicides can be used to treat healthy bulbs dug from infected beds prior to replanting in another part of the garden. The infected area can be treated with an appropriate fungicide at least six months before replanting. Depending on the disease and the course of action, the diseased bed may have to be avoided for several years. In the future, purchase and plant healthy bulbs.

Since cultivars vary in their resistance to diseases, cultivate the more resistant types. Use care when digging up bulbs to avoid damaging them.

# MARCH

## BULBS, CORMS, RHIZOMES, & TUBERS

 PLANNING

As your spring-flowering garden begins to go into glory this spring, take photographs so you can refer to them later in the year. The photos will come in handy when you're making plans to spruce up your garden or extend your beds with spring-flowering plants this fall. In addition to taking photographs, sketch a planting map in your gardening journal to show where the bulbs are located. With an accurate plot plan, you will know where to plant spring-flowering bulbs this fall. You'll also be able to plan for continuous flowering by sowing or transplanting annual or perennial flowers among the bulbs after their display has ended.

 PLANTING

If you've forced **paper-white narcissus** (*Narcissus tazetta*) indoors (see December Helpful Hint p. 66), plant them directly in the garden after the last spring freeze. **Paper-whites** will thrive outdoors in Zones 7 to 9. They should flower next spring if you forced them in a medium that has available nutrients, such as a soil-based mixture or a soilless peat-based mix with added nutrients. If you forced them in water,

you may have to wait a couple of seasons before they bloom. Choose a well-drained location in full sun or filtered shade, and plant them at a depth that's twice the height of the bulb. Encourage your **paper-whites** to perennialize by applying a complete slow-release fertilizer once a year in the fall. Potassium is most important for **daffodils**, so apply a 5-10-12 or 5-10-20 fertilizer according to label directions.

If you received an **amaryllis** (*Hippeastrum* hybrids) over the holidays, you can move it to a permanent location outdoors in the garden if you live in the central or southern parts of Alabama or Mississippi, and if you keep it mulched during the winter months. After the last spring frost, plant your **amaryllis** in a well-drained fertile site in full sun to partial shade. The neck of the bulb where the leaves

emerge should be 2 to 4 inches below the soil surface. Mulch with a 2- to 3-inch layer of compost to conserve moisture and suppress weed growth. Make a single application of a slow-release complete fertilizer after planting and then in subsequent springs when the shoots appear. Expect your **amaryllis** to bloom every year in early summer.

 CARE

After flowering, the leaves of your spring-flowering bulbs will turn an unsightly yellow. Temper your urge to remove the leaves, or braid them into attractive ponytails. The bulbs need the leaves to harvest energy that's channeled to the bulb for next year's flowers. Bulbs that were forced indoors can be fertilized while in bloom, then planted in

Amaryllis aren't just for holidays; in our climate, they bloom in summer.

your garden to allow the leaves to mature and replenish the bulb. Expect the bulbs to flower again next year.

 ## WATERING

Outdoor-growing bulbs seldom need watering this time of year. When plants are a few inches tall, begin watering to keep them evenly moist throughout the period of growth and bloom. Bulb roots grow deeply, so water thoroughly—don't just sprinkle the surface. How much water you add depends on the weather and the rate of growth. Bulbs need a lot of water when they are actively growing. Continue to water them after the blooms fade and until the leaves start to turn yellow.

 ## FERTILIZING

When the leaves of spring-flowering bulbs emerge, apply a complete fertilizer to ensure quality blooms next year. Do not fertilize them after they've bloomed; these bulbs are going dormant.

 ## GROOMING

Snip off the spent blooms of spring-flowering bulbs to prevent

## HELPFUL HINTS

Occasionally the flower buds of **daffodils** fail to open, and when you cut them open, they are brown and dry inside. This disorder is called "bud blast" and commonly affects late-blooming **daffodils** and double-flowering cultivars. It's been speculated that drastic temperature changes, inadequate moisture, and wet autumns are responsible. Studies involving irrigation, mulching, and shading treatments, however, have not prevented bud blast from occurring. Late-blooming cultivars that may perform better in your landscape include 'Baby Moon', 'Grace Note', 'Geranium', and most of the *Narcissus poeticus* hybrids.

seedpods from forming. If you expect them to repeat their show next spring, allow leaves to mature and die down naturally before removing. Unless the leaves have an opportunity to store a good supply of carbohydrates and nutrients in the underground bulb, the plants won't flower next year.

 ## PROBLEMS

Gray mold, or botrytis blight, is a springtime disease that is most active during cool and wet weather. It attacks dead or dying leaves and flowers and can quickly spread to healthy tissues. Bulbs and corms may also be infected, leading to rot. A wide range of plants are infected, including **amaryllis**, **bulbous iris**, **dahlia**, **hyacinth**, and **tulip**. Warm, humid, rainy conditions foster this fungal disease which

produces yellow, orange, brown, or reddish-brown spots on the leaves and flowers. The spots on the leaves and flowers grow together, causing them to collapse and become slimy. Eventually they're covered with a telltale gray fuzzy mold.

To control botrytis, collect and discard faded flowers. Fungicides can be applied at the first sign of disease. Provide good air movement by not overcrowding the plants. Space plants far apart to allow leaves and flowers to dry off quickly. Avoid overhead watering; this fungus spreads through splashing water and wind. Most important, keep the plants healthy. Examine your stored bulbs and discard any that show signs of rot.

If weeds occur in bulb beds, do not remove them by cultivation. Pull them by hand so the bulbs and roots will not be disturbed.

# APRIL
## BULBS, CORMS, RHIZOMES, & TUBERS

## PLANNING

Evaluate your spring-flowering bulbs. Note in your gardening journal which bulbs and cultivars met or exceeded your expectations. If any looked disappointing, make plans to replace them or give them another year or two to settle in.

Also include remarks about the growing environment and culture. Were winter and spring unseasonably warm or mild? Were there unexpected freezing temperatures? Did you fertilize the bulbs last fall with a slow- or fast-release fertilizer? When was the last time you tested the soil for pH and fertility levels? It is ideal to have soil tested by your Cooperative Extension Service every three years.

## PLANTING

Summer-flowering bulbs such as **crocosmia**, **dahlia**, and **lily** can be planted after freezing temperatures have passed.

In the warmer parts of Alabama and Mississippi, dig, divide, and replant **cannas** and **dahlias**. The best time to do this is after the eyes have sprouted but before they have grown more than an inch. Each tuber should have a short piece of old

This is a good time to dig, divide, and replant cannas.

stem attached. Discard those that show signs of growth. Dust the newly cut surfaces with a fungicide before putting them in the ground.

Stake **dahlia** tubers as you are planting so you can insert the stake without skewering the tuber.

Plant **gladiolus** corms every two weeks until July to create a continuous succession of flowers. Plant the corms at least 4 inches deep to stabilize them as they produce their long flower stalks. You can also mound soil around the base to avoid having to stake them.

Avoid planting **caladium** tubers too early in the spring because

they can rot. The soil temperature must be above 70 degrees F. Plant the tuber shallowly, only an inch or two deep. Since roots and shoots emerge from the top, place it knobby side up.

Bulbs forced indoors that have finished flowering can be moved outdoors. Cut off the faded flowers and transplant bulbs into the garden.

Wait until the last freeze before transplanting **Easter lilies** (*Lilium longiflorum* var. *eximium*) outdoors (they are hardy to Zone 6) in a well-drained location. Space the plants 12 to 18 inches apart. Since **lilies** like their "feet in the shade and their heads in the sun," mulch with a 2-inch layer of compost, pine straw, or shredded leaves. As the leaves and stems of the original shoots die back, prune them off. New growth will soon emerge, sometimes producing a second round of flowers. **Easter lilies**, which are forced to flower under controlled greenhouse conditions in March or April, will flower naturally in May or June. In addition, you will get a taller plant, one that grows to a height of 3 feet or more.

When the bulbs go dormant as signaled by the yellowing, dying leaves, dig up and transplant **red spider lily** (*Lycoris radiata*) and **magic lily** or **naked lily** (*Lycoris squamigera*) immediately. Plant them shallowly, with their "necks"—the point where the leaves emerge and the tunic ends—just sticking out of the ground. Planting too shallow is better than planting too deep since the bulbs possess contractile roots that will pull the bulb down into the soil until it is the right depth. When planted too deep, *Lycoris* species will spend a few nonflowering years producing a completely new bulb.

## WATERING

Spring is usually a wet time of year, so supplemental water may not be necessary. If you have to water, keep leaves and flowers dry.

## FERTILIZING

Fertilize summer bulbs when new leaves emerge, using a single application of a slow-release nitrogen fertilizer. Instead of a slow-release fertilizer, you may use a balanced fast-release nitrogen fertilizer such as 8-8-8 or 10-10-10. An application every month or two during the growing season may be necessary to satisfy the needs of **dahlias**, **gladiolus**, and **lilies**. Avoid overfertilization, which can encourage the production of leaves at the expense of flowers. Let the appearance of the plant guide you. If plants look robust and are growing in a well-prepared, fertile bed, fertilizing may not be necessary.

## GROOMING

When the flowers fade on your spring-flowering bulbs, cut them off to prevent seeds from developing. Don't cut or remove the leaves, which should be allowed to die naturally. Overcome the urge to braid the leaves or tie them into neat bundles.

## PROBLEMS

Inspect the leaves of your bulbs for aphids and spider mites. Dislodge them with a strong spray of water in early morning, giving leaves plenty of time to dry before evening.

When **iris** leaves appear thin and limp, check for iris borers. These grublike insects can ruin an entire planting if not detected and eradicated early. Eggs overwinter in old, dried **iris** leaves and other debris. They hatch in mid- to late spring when the tiny larvae crawl up the young **iris** leaves and feed, producing telltale notches. Then they enter the leaves, producing pinpoint holes. As they slowly mine their way down toward the rhizomes, the borers leave a ragged, water-soaked tunnel in their wake. When you spot such a tunnel, squash the borer inside by pressing the leaf between your thumb and forefinger. Alternatively, spray your plants with an insecticide when the leaves are 5 to 6 inches tall.

See March p. 49 for details on diseases.

Handpull winter annuals such as common chickweed, henbit, and Carolina geranium to prevent them from reseeding. A shallow layer of mulch will suppress them.

# MAY

## BULBS, CORMS, RHIZOMES, & TUBERS

### PLANNING

As spring-flowering bulbs begin to fade, make plans to fill their voids with flowering annuals that are either direct-sown as seed, or planted from transplants. Avoid injuring bulbs when planting over them.

Summer- and fall-flowering bulbs also make good fillers for a continuous floral display. When selecting bulbs for the summer and fall landscape, use your list of recommended types and cultivars. Pay particular attention to height and spread, bloom time, flower color, and fragrance. Finally, determine how many bulbs you'll need so you won't come home shorthanded.

### PLANTING

After the last freeze, plant tender summer bulbs such as **canna**, **dahlia**, **ginger lily**, and **tuberose** that have been stored over the winter or purchased from mail-order com- panies or garden centers. Plant **caladium** bulbs when soil temperature goes above 70 degrees F. **Caladiums** prefer shade to partial shade; recently introduced cultivars called the Florida series (which includes 'Florida Pride', 'Florida Queen', and 'Florida Sweetheart'), however, tolerate sun and have a dense growth habit.

### CARE

After blooming, cut off spent flowers and stalks from **bearded iris**. Stake **lilies** and **dahlias** early in their growth to avoid skewering them.

Lilies benefit from staking early in the season.

### WATERING

Water newly planted bulbs to settle them in. Apply a shallow 2- to 3-inch layer of mulch to conserve moisture, suppress weeds, and keep the soil cool.

### FERTILIZING

Lightly fertilize summer bulbs when their shoots emerge, using a slow-release fertilizer. Follow the manufacturer's instructions regarding the amount and frequency. Water-in thoroughly afterwards.

There is no benefit to fertilizing spring-flowering bulbs during or after bloom. In fact, as the soil warms up after flowering, nitrogen in the fertilizer can encourage the development of the fungal disease Fusarium. Rotting bulbs infected with Fusarium have a sour smell.

### GROOMING

Cut flower stalks back to the ground on **daffodils** and other spring-flowering bulbs as flowers fade. Do not cut the leaves until they die naturally. (Leaves are necessary for producing strong bulbs capable of reflowering.) If you have to hide the dying leaves, consider these tips:

• Interplant with perennials that will grow above and hide the bulb leaves.

• Plant taller flower bulbs behind lower-growing shrubs.

• Intersperse clump-forming plants such as **liriope**, **ornamental grasses**, and **daylilies**.

• Underplant with low-growing, sprawling ground covers like **junipers** and some **cotoneasters**, which allow you to tuck the leaves beneath the branches.

 PROBLEMS

There are several insect pests that afflict bulbs. Watch out for aphids and spider mites. See April Problems p. 51 for controls.

Japanese beetles skeletonize the leaves of **canna**, **dahlia**, and others. They can be hand-picked and discarded in a jar of soapy water.

Flower thrips are tiny (1/16-inch-long) yellowish-brown to amber-colored insects that damage the flowers of **dahlia**, **gladiolus**, **lily**, and others by rasping the tissues and then sucking up oozing sap. Their feeding causes buds to become streaked with brown. Often the buds fail to open or the flowers look distorted. To check for thrips, open up a suspected flower over a sheet of white paper and search for what look like tiny scurrying slivers of wood. Thrips are difficult to control. Fortunately, they're preyed upon by minute

pirate bugs, ladybugs, lacewings, and big-eyed bugs. Remove and discard any infested flowers. Apply recommended insecticides.

Narcissus bulb flies are specific pests of **daffodils**. The life cycle of the narcissus bulb fly begins with the adult, which looks like a small bumblebee. The adult fly lays eggs on leaves near the soil's surface, or on the crowns. When eggs hatch, the plump, grayish-white-to-yellow larvae tunnel into the bulbs, where they feed on the soft tissue. The larvae overwinter in the bulbs, then move into the surrounding soil to pupate and begin their life cycle all over again. A bulb that has been attacked is soft and spongy. It usually has a telltale entry hole through the basal plate and is difficult to save. Most often, just dispose of an infested bulb promptly. You can attempt to kill the maggot by stabbing it with a

needle inserted through the hole in the basal plate. There is always a chance of not hitting the maggot and simply adding damage to the plant tissue. The best strategy is to keep your **daffodils** healthy by maintaining a shallow mulch layer and fertilizing your bulbs in the fall. When you divide your **daffodils**, discard any bulbs that show signs of infestation.

Several leaf spots will affect the leaves of summer bulbs. Depending on the level of infection, fungicides may not be necessary. Remove any heavily infested leaves and discard them.

Handpull or hoe weeds in beds. Pre-emergent herbicides will control weeds before they emerge; make sure that the bulbs are listed on the herbicide label.

# JUNE
## BULBS, CORMS, RHIZOMES, & TUBERS

 PLANNING

Visit public gardens to witness the splendor of summer-flowering bulbs. Refer to Public Gardens (pp. 288 to 291) for a list of gardens and their addresses. Bring your camera and gardening journal to take pictures and notes of some favorite high-performing bulbs. Don't forget to update your gardening journal by recording the performance of spring-flowering bulbs in your own garden. Were there any outstanding **daffodil** cultivars? Are there areas of your garden that need to be replanted or beds that need to be renovated this fall? The information will help you order the bulbs you need.

 PLANTING

**Bearded iris** can be planted now while in bloom. Wait until late summer or early fall to divide or transplant existing clumps. **Bearded irises** form the beginnings of next year's flowers in the six or eight weeks after blooming. Disturbing the plants at that time risks next year's flowers.

Plant **autumn crocus** (*Colchicum autumnale*) now, as soon as you purchase them. These unusual bulbs flower on bare stems in fall and produce leaves the follow-

ing spring. Use golf tees to mark their position so you can plant something that will fill the void left when their leaves die down next summer.

**Dahlia** tubers may still be planted for fall bloom. Place them 6 to 8 inches deep and 3 to 4 feet apart.

Since the leaves of most spring bulbs have finished maturing by now or have died back, they can be cut back to ground level. Dig up any crowded bulbs that have declined and produced few, if any, flowers. Replant larger bulbs and discard smaller ones, unless you are willing to wait for them to reach blooming size, which may take two years or more. The spaces vacated by spring-flowering bulbs can be seeded or planted with annual transplants to provide summer and fall color.

Divide overcrowded **daffodil** bulbs after the foliage has ripened and died down. Use a flat-tined garden fork to unearth the bulbs. Carefully pry out a clump of bulbs. Handle them gently to avoid bruising them. Brush off the excess soil with your fingers, and separate the bulbs as you remove the soil.

Carefully break apart the bulbs that are loosely connected to one another, but leave the offsets or small bulbs that are firmly attached to the mother bulb. Any

damaged, soft, or rotten bulbs should be discarded.

Plant the bulbs immediately or store them for planting in the fall. If you choose to store them, let the bulbs cure by putting them on an old window screen in a well-ventilated shady spot. After a few days of curing, put the bulbs into paper bags and store them in a cool, dark, well-ventilated place.

Replant the bulbs, saving the largest ones for planting where you want the showiest display. The smaller offsets will not flower for the first few years, so you can use them in a naturalized area where a few bulbs that haven't flowered won't be obvious. Select a well-drained location that receives full sun or part shade. Loosen the soil 8 to 12 inches deep and mix in several inches of compost. After watering, cover the bulbs with an inch or two of mulch such as shredded leaves or compost to conserve moisture and suppress weeds.

 CARE

Loosely tie **gladioli** to stakes, or mound soil around the base of the plants to prevent them from toppling over.

## WATERING

Be prepared to water summer bulbs if little rain occurs this month. Keep water off the leaves.

## FERTILIZING

If summer-flowering bulbs were not fertilized when their shoots emerged, it may be necessary to fertilize them now. Follow the manufacturer's instructions regarding the rate and frequency of application. Avoid overfertilization, which can encourage the production of leaves at the expense of flowers. Let the appearance of the plant guide you. If the **dahlias**, **gladioli**, and **lilies** look robust and are growing in a well-prepared, fertile bed, fertilization may be unnecessary.

## GROOMING

If you are lucky enough to still have **tuberous begonias**, remove the spent blooms. They may be infected by the fungus disease gray mold. Clip off **amaryllis** and **iris** blooms after they've faded.

## PROBLEMS

Pests to watch for include aphids, spider mites, thrips, and Japanese beetles. Handpick Japanese beetles and discard them into a jar of soapy water. Neem can be applied to the leaves to reduce feeding by the adults. Use other insecticides for heavy infestations. If the rhizomes of your **bearded irises** are riddled with holes, they could be infested with iris borers. See April Problems p. 51 for a description and controls.

Watch out for fungal leaf spot diseases during wet spring and summer seasons. To control leaf spot diseases, remove blighted leaves during the season. Remove and discard any infected foliage in the fall. Fungicides can be applied to control certain leaf spot diseases.

Powdery mildew may be a problem on **dahlias**. This fungal disease commonly occurs during the spring and fall seasons, when the days are warm and humid and the nights are cool. This fungus is more severe on plants that are shaded or crowded. To reduce the chance of infection, improve air movement by siting them in an open location and by selectively pruning out interior growth to eliminate congestion. Pick off and destroy infected leaves.

Handpull weeds when they are young and easier to remove. Suppress them with a shallow layer of compost. Another way of handling weeds is to plant companion plants among your bulbs whose leaves will shade the soil and deprive the young weeds of sunlight.

Leaves infected with powdery mildew should be picked off and composted.

# JULY
## BULBS, CORMS, RHIZOMES, & TUBERS

PLANNING

Your summer bulbs can be enjoyed outdoors or indoors as cut flowers. Create a cutting garden where you won't have to worry about color combinations and other design features. A cutting garden produces lots of flowers for tables, picnics, or sharing with friends. The U. S. Netherlands Flower Bulb Information Center (**www.bulb.com**) recommends the following list of cut flowers. They have sturdy stems, interesting flowers with color that doesn't fade, and lots of fragrant blossoms.

**African corn lily** (*Ixia*): lush petals in red, cream, orange, pink, or yellow, atop wiry stalks

**Calla lily** (*Zantedeschia*): sheath-shaped flower of flawless beauty in white and pastel shades

**Crinum lily**: majestic white blossoms with rosy-red markings

**Fragrant gladiolus** (*Acidanthera*): delicate cousin of the **gladiolus** with creamy white flowers and a delicate scent

**Gladiolus**: a flower made for cutting, tall stately stalks covered with huge florets, in every color imaginable

**Pineapple plant** (*Eucomis*): creamy-white flowers on a pineapple-like flower head

**Liatris**: tall, spiky wand of magenta florets, long-lasting

**Asiatic lily**: generally early summer bloomers

**Oriental lily**: the most flamboyantly flowered of the **lilies**, blooming in mid- to late summer

**Summer hyacinth** (*Galtonia*): bell-shaped flowers atop 2- to 3-foot stems; bloom when **gladioli** do, so use them together in arrangements

**Tuberose** (*Polianthes*): tall, exceedingly sweet, waxy white blossoms

PLANTING

Plant **reblooming irises**. Those that have performed well in the South Carolina Botanical Garden, which has conditions similar to northern Alabama and Mississippi, include 'Autumn Tryst', 'Clarence', 'Harvest of Memories', 'Raven's Return', and 'Violet Music'. They require a little more attention to fertilizing and watering, but their two seasons of flowering in late spring and early fall are well worth the effort.

CARE

Support any leaning **dahlias**, **glads**, and **lilies** to prevent them from toppling over.

There is a gladiolus bloom in every color imaginable.

WATERING

Water regularly and adequately. Water early in the day to keep leaves dry. Spring-flowering bulbs do not require water while they're dormant. **Caladiums** are especially sensitive to drying. Once they wilt badly, the plants will go dormant, so keep them watered.

## FERTILIZING

Evaluate the growth rate and appearance of your summer-flowering bulbs prior to fertilizing them with a fast-release fertilizer. If they look robust, fertilizer won't be necessary. To enrich the soil, topdress the beds lightly with composted manure.

## GROOMING

As flowers fade from your summer bulbs, clip them off. This will prevent them from producing seeds, allowing the bulbs to replenish themselves for next season. Removing old flowers from **tuberous begonias** will control gray mold, tidy them up, and encourage continuous flowering.

## PROBLEMS

Japanese beetles skeletonize leaves and feed on buds and flowers. Aphids occur in clusters near the tips of shoots and their feeding cause leaves to become wrinkled, sticky, and sometimes coasted with black sooty mold. Spider mites cause yellow or bronze stippling on the leaf surface. Thrips damage flower buds, creating streaks or spots on the open blooms and brown

## HELPFUL HINTS

To cut flowers for indoor arrangements, use sharp shears or a knife to avoid injury to the growing plant. A special pair of cutting scissors can hold the cut-off stem, allowing the removal to be a one-handed operation. A slanting cut will expose a larger surface to absorb water and will prevent the base of the stem from sealing off by resting on the bottom of the vase. It is best to carry a bucket of water to the garden for collecting blooms, instead of the familiar cutting basket.

edges on flower buds that fail to bloom.

Watch out for the lesser canna leaf roller. It attacks young growth, causing **canna** leaves to become frayed, tattered, and shot full of holes. Some will appear sealed together with webbing. The adult brown moths with 1-inch wing spans emerge in March and April, and the females lay yellowish-white eggs in small patches on the emerging foliage. When the tiny caterpillars hatch, they tunnel into the **canna** leaves, as many as six invading a single rolled leaf. The larvae, which eventually grow to nearly an inch in length, have cream to greenish bodies and yellow heads.

The caterpillars typically feed only on the upper surface of the leaf, but will sometimes bore through the furled leaf, creating a series of holes when the leaf unfurls. To shelter themselves, the caterpillars often fasten the edges of leaves with silk to pre-

vent them from unrolling, and older larvae can reroll opened leaves and hold them closed with silk. When fully grown, the caterpillars pupate inside a filmy cocoon. There are usually two generations per year. The easiest way to control the lesser canna leaf roller is with early applications of *Bacillus thuringiensis* (Bt). Direct the spray into the center of furled leaves, where the caterpillars are feeding. Cleaning up and discarding aboveground portions of **cannas** after the first freeze will also remove overwintering caterpillars.

Nematodes are microscopic, soil-inhabiting, eel-like worms that damage the roots of **dahlias** and other bulbs. No chemicals are available for homeowners to combat these troublesome pests. If nematodes are a threat, the best defense is a healthy plant. See p. 166 for more information. In the future, plant in sites free of nematodes.

# AUGUST
## BULBS, CORMS, RHIZOMES, & TUBERS

 PLANNING

As your summer bulbs approach the end of their season and the fall-flowering bulbs start theirs, lift and divide the overcrowded, poorly flowering clumps of summer bulbs and corms. Periodic dividing will improve their performance as well as give you a lot of extra plants. The best time to divide most summer-flowering bulbs is at the beginning of their dormant period when the leaves start to turn brown and die.

Bulbs such as **ornamental onion** (*Allium*), **magic lily** (*Lycoris*), and **spider lily** (*Hymenocallis*) produce daughter bulbs or offsets, which are attached to the basal plate where the roots emerge. After lifting the bulbs or corms, detach the offsets carefully. Replant hardy bulbs and store tender ones.

Tiny corms called cormels can be planted right after you lift your **gladioli** or **crocosmias**. Tender corms can be stored indoors along with their offspring.

When you lift and divide **lily** clumps, be careful not to bruise or break the fragile scales. Plant them immediately. Bulbils—tiny bulbs in the leaf axils (the nook where the leaf joins the stem)—can also be planted or potted up and overwintered in a cold frame outdoors.

 PLANTING

Plant or move summer-flowering bulbs that have already bloomed, such as **amaryllis**, **crocosmia**, **iris**, and **lily**.

Divide **bearded irises** so the plants will have plenty of time to become established before cooler weather arrives. Gardeners in the warmer parts of Alabama and Mississippi can wait until September, which will allow the divisions to settle in after the heat of summer has passed.

1. Loosen the soil around the rhizomes (horizontally creeping stems) with a spading fork. Watering the bed the day before will make digging easier.

2. Dig up the clumps and separate the rhizomes. Divide each rhizome into sections with a sharp knife, making sure that each section has at least one bud or fan of leaves. The young rhizomes will be growing from the sides of the older, spongy rhizomes.

3. Cut the young rhizomes away from the older sections with a sharp knife. Discard the older pieces and any sections that are undersized or diseased. (Don't think twice about throwing away the old rhizomes. They bloom only once and then become a flowerless food reservoir). The rhizomes may be infested with borers. Discard heavily infested rhizomes. Salvage others by digging out the pinkish larvae with a pocketknife and trimming away any damaged tissue. Because the larvae's feeding creates opportunities for bacterial soft rot, soak the damaged rhizomes for half

Bearded iris can be trimmed and divided this month.

an hour in a 10 percent solution of household bleach and water. Then dust them with powdered sulfur and allow the cut surfaces to air-dry in a shady place for several hours before replanting. Before you replant the **irises** in their original location, comb the soil carefully for signs of brown pupal cases. Collect and destroy them to prevent the dusky brown adult moths from emerging in the fall and laying eggs on or near your plants.

4. Trim leaves to about one-third to one-half their height to reduce moisture loss. Make sure that each division consists of a firm rhizome with a fan of healthy leaves.

5. To help prevent infection, dust the cut ends with powdered sulfur. Lay the trimmed plants in a shady spot for a few hours to allow the cut ends to dry and heal.

6. Replant the **bearded irises** in a sunny, well-drained location. Dig the hole 8 to 12 inches deep, then form a cone of soil in the center, making it high enough so the rhizome will be planted just above ground level in heavy clay soils. For lighter sandy soils, the top of the rhizome may be 1/2 inch or less below ground level. Spread the roots around the top of the cone, pressing them firmly into the soil. Space the divisions about 12 to

18 inches apart. Plant them in groups of three to form a natural-looking clump.

7. Cover the freshly planted rhizomes lightly with soil. Use about 1/2 inch of soil—less for very small rhizomes.

8. Water the young plants to settle soil around the roots. Mulch to prevent freezing and thawing of the soil, which can heave the plants out of the ground. Remove the mulch in early spring, or too much moisture may remain around the rhizomes.

## CARE

The leaves of your summer-flowering bulbs may look tattered and unattractive, but don't remove them until the foliage and shoots turn yellow. Cut them off a few inches above the ground.

## WATERING

Water regularly and thoroughly. During hot, dry, August days, avoid deep cultivation in your flower beds. Loosening the soil under these conditions reduces water uptake by increasing loss of soil water and damaging surface roots.

## FERTILIZING

Fertilize **bearded, Louisiana,** and **Siberian irises** lightly early this month with a low-nitrogen fertilizer such as 5-10-10. Water the fertilizer in afterwards.

## GROOMING

Remove spent flowers as they fade. If the weather is hot and the flowers are in afternoon sun, blooms will not last very long. Cut the flowers and use them in arrangements.

## PROBLEMS

Spider mites are especially troublesome during the hot, dry weather of this month. See April Problems p. 51 for controls.

Watch out for powdery mildew. Warm, humid days and cool night temperatures favor the growth of this grayish-white foliar disease.

Handpull any weeds and suppress their growth with a layer of mulch. Watch out for particularly aggressive weeds such as ground ivy and Indian mock strawberry.

# September
## BULBS, CORMS, RHIZOMES, & TUBERS

### PLANNING

As you make plans to visit a garden center to purchase spring-flowering bulbs, begin with a shopping list. Rely on your gardening journal and local newspaper and magazine sources. Be wary of catalogs unless you are shopping for specific cultivars that you know to be well adapted to Alabama or Mississippi. This becomes most critical in the southern and central parts of the states as they get

If you want to add or expand beds, you can use a garden hose and lime to "outline" the shape before starting to dig.

few chilling hours. Look at color, bloom period, and height.

Check the merchandise carefully. Remember that "bigger is better" when it comes to bulbs. Bigger bulbs produce bigger blossoms. However, do not dismiss bargain bulbs that are smaller in size and less expensive than the larger ones. They may not give you the big impact you are looking for next year, but they will bring some color to large areas of the landscape (by the backyard fence, along the driveway, etc.) for the right price. In a few seasons they will bulk-up sufficiently so no one will know they were bargain bulbs. Stay away from soft, mushy, moldy, or heavily bruised bulbs. It doesn't matter if the tunic (the dry, papery, onion-skinlike covering) is loose or torn, but it should not harbor any insects or diseases.

Finally, plan to try something new. It may be a bulb that has screaming pink flowers, or one that has a botanical name that's difficult to pronounce, but produces extraordinary blooms. Record your purchases in your journal so you can document their performance next year.

### PLANTING

Plant fall-blooming bulbs, such as **autumn crocus** (*Colchicum*),

**autumn daffodil** (*Sternbergia lutea*), **fall-blooming crocus** (*Crocus speciosus*), and **nerine lily** (*Nerine*), as soon as you receive them.

Plant the summer-flowering **madonna lily** (*Lilium candidum*) now or in early spring with no more than 1 inch of soil covering the "nose" of the bulb.

Plant **lily** bulbs soon after you receive them because they do not have a truly dormant period.

Prepare beds for spring-flowering bulbs as soon as possible. Cultivate the soil and add generous amounts of organic matter to improve drainage. Bulbs will rot without proper drainage. Although you can buy Dutch bulbs now, it's too early to plant the spring-flowering bulbs such as **daffodils**.

### CARE

Store Dutch bulbs in a cool (60 to 65 degrees F.) location to prevent them from drying out before planting. Temperatures higher than 70 degrees F. can damage the flowers inside spring-flowering bulbs. The bulbs can be stored in ventilated bags but not in paper or plastic bags unless specified. Since rhizomes, tubers, and tuberous roots dry out faster than bulbs and corms, store them in peat, perlite, or vermiculite.

Bulbs can be stored for several weeks in a cool place (35 to 55 degrees F.) such as a refrigerator. Vegetable crisper drawers can be used, but avoid storing bulbs in the same drawer as ripening fruit or vegetables, which give off ethylene, a gas that can cause problems with flowering. Since some bulbs are poisonous, this storage method is **not** recommended for households with young children.

Dig and store **caladium** bulbs before frost. Here's how:

Lift the tubers from the ground before frost. Shake the soil from the tubers and leave them in a sunny location to dry for seven to ten days. If rain or frost is forecast, move the tubers indoors temporarily.

After this drying period, pluck off the withered leaves from the tuber and brush off any remaining soil.

Store the tubers over the winter in a box or basket filled with dried vermiculite or perlite. Place the container where the temperature will not drop below 60 degrees F. Next spring, plant the tubers in the garden when the soil temperature rises to 70 degrees.

## WATERING

September and October tend to be dry months. Continue watering regularly.

## HELPFUL HINTS

For naturalizing large areas with **daffodils**, consider purchasing smaller, less expensive bulbs so that you can buy more. **Daffodils** multiply and grow larger each year, so if you can be patient and wait a year or two, these bulbs will enlarge and produce bigger flowers.

## FERTILIZING

It's not necessary to fertilize newly planted spring-flowering bulbs that you are going to treat like annuals for one season of bloom. The bulbs can grow and bloom without any additional nutrients.

For bulbs that you expect to naturalize or perennialize, fertilize with a slow-release bulb-booster type fertilizer at planting. Or instead of making one annual application of a controlled-release fertilizer, apply a fast-release fertilizer at planting and a second application the following spring when the new shoots emerge. Water after fertilizing to make nutrients available to the roots.

Winter-blooming bulbs such as **cyclamen** and **crocus** do not have to be fertilized in most well-prepared garden soils. A light topdressing, however, with a balanced fertilizer such as 10-10-10 will encourage abundant blooms and keep corms healthy.

## PROBLEMS

Aphids and spider mites are still active. Mites get worse in dry weather. Evaluate the extent of injury and decide if pest control measures are warranted. Use a water wand on a weekly basis, preferably early in the morning, to wash mites from plants.

Clean up dead, fallen leaves. They can harbor disease and insect pests over the winter if allowed to remain on the ground.

Handpull any young winter annual weeds, or cover them with a shallow layer of compost. Weeding is never fun, but the cooler temperatures can make it more bearable.

Voles, rabbits, and deer relish many kinds of flower bulbs, such as **crocuses** and **tulips**. To learn how to protect bulbs from voles, refer to the Problems section in the introduction on p. 42.

# OCTOBER

## BULBS, CORMS, RHIZOMES, & TUBERS

### PLANNING

Though not as famous as "major" bulbs like **daffodil**, **hyacinth**, and **tulip**, "minor" spring-flowering bulbs such as **crocus**, **cyclamen**, **Dutch iris**, **snowdrop**, and **winter aconite** are quite easy to grow and can be used in a variety of landscape situations:

So called "minor" bulbs can still have a major impact, like this Dutch iris.

• Plant them beneath the rising stems of **tulips** and **daffodils** to highlight the color and forms of their taller brethren.

• Interplant early spring-flowering **crocuses** with ground covers such as **vinca**.

• Plant **anemone**, **grape hyacinth**, or **crocus** en masse in borders.

• Plant them as a focal point for a perennial border or mixed planting with shrubs. Eye-catchers include **giant onion** (*Allium giganteum*), with its towering purple globe-shaped flower heads, and **crown imperial** (*Fritillaria imperialis*), with pendulous flowers topped by a pineapple-shaped crown.

### PLANTING

Spring-flowering bulbs require an extended cold period to bloom reliably. When bulbs do not receive sufficient weeks of cold treatment (usually in the central and southern parts of Alabama and Mississippi), they produce flowers close to the ground on shortened stalks, often hidden by the leaves. Sometimes you can find pre-cooled **tulips** and other spring-flowering bulbs. Alternatively, chill them yourself by storing them in an old refrigerator for a minimum of ten weeks (and up to sixteen weeks) prior to planting in December or January. After chilling, plant the cooled bulbs immediately.

Making bulbs flower outside their normal season is a wonderful way of ushering spring into your home. Bulbs that can be easily forced include **daffodil**, **hyacinth**, and **tulip**. Minor bulbs good for forcing include **crocus**, **glory-of-the- snow** (*Chionodoxa* spp.), **grape hyacinth** (*Muscari* spp.), **netted iris** (*Iris reticulata*), **Siberian squill** (*Scilla siberica*), **spring snowflake** (*Leucojum vernum*), **snowdrop** (*Galanthus nivalis*), **winter aconite** (*Eranthis hyemalis*), and **wood hyacinth** (*Hyacinthoides nonscripta*). Follow these steps to force bulbs:

Buy bulb cultivars that are recommended for forcing. Pot up the bulbs anytime from mid-September to December in a well-drained potting medium. Use commercial potting soil or make your own mix composed of equal parts potting soil, sphagnum peat moss, and perlite. Since the bulbs already contain enough food for the developing flowers and roots, fertilizing is unnecessary. Select a shallow pot or bulb pan that is at least twice the height of the bulbs. Fill it three-quarters full of mix and set the bulbs in place. Have at least 1 to 2 inches of soil beneath large bulbs. **Tulips** and **daffodils** can be left with their tips showing; completely cover smaller bulbs such as **crocus**, **snowdrop**, and **grape hyacinth**.

When planting **tulips**, position the flat side of the bulb toward the outside of the pot; when the first and lowest leaf emerges, it will gracefully arch over the rim to give a balanced look.

Fill the pot with soil to within $1/4$ to $1/2$ inch of the rim. Add water until it seeps through the drainage hole in the bottom of the pot. Label each pot, marking the name of the cultivar, the planting date, and the date to be brought into the house.

Cool the bulbs by exposing them to temperatures between 35 and 50 degrees F. for twelve to sixteen weeks. Store them in an old refrigerator, unheated basement, cold frame, or in the ground buried up to their rims. Protect the potted bulbs from freezing outdoors by covering them with sawdust, straw, leaves, or peat moss. After twelve weeks of chilling, check the pots. When you wiggle the bulb in the pot and it stays in place and roots can be seen through the drainage holes, bring the pot indoors for forcing.

Gradually expose the pots to light and warm temperatures. Start with a cool, 60- to 65-degree F room in indirect sunlight. When the shoots turn green, expose the pots to warmer temperatures and more light to stimulate flowering.

Rotate the pots regularly so that all the leaves receive an equal amount of light. After a week, move the pot to warmer temperatures and more light to encourage flowering. Keep the soil moist. The flowers will last longer if you move the pots to a cool room at night.

If you wait until after the last freeze, most forced bulbs can be planted in the garden. During their time indoors, keep them in bright sunlight and fertilize them with a water-soluble houseplant fertilizer. Plant hardy bulbs that have been forced into bloom in the garden once spring arrives, or allow them to go dormant in their pots and then plant them in the fall. **Daffodil**, **crocus**, **squill**, and other hardy bulbs can be transplanted into the garden in the spring, and will flower normally the following year. Other bulbs, such as **tulip** and **hyacinth**, are best discarded after forcing.

## CARE

In the fall, cut back **lily** stalks to soil level after they have turned yellow. Lift **dahlia** and **gladiolus** after their foliage is killed by frost. Because they may not survive the winter outdoors in northern reaches of Alabama or Mississippi, they need to be

cleansed of soil and stored indoors in a cool but frost-free location. Also, dig and store **caladium** bulbs before frost. See September Care p. 60.

## WATERING

If the fall is dry, provide sufficient water to newly planted spring-flowering bulbs. Check bulbs being forced in beds or cold frames and water them to keep the potting medium moist (but not sopping wet).

## FERTILIZING

See September on p. 61.

## PROBLEMS

Watch out for storage diseases, including Fusarium bulb rot and botrytis. Avoid damaging bulbs and tubers when lifting them out of the ground to be stored.

Weeds, especially weedy grasses, may be in beds. Hand-pull or hoe out the clumps.

# NOVEMBER
## BULBS, CORMS, RHIZOMES, & TUBERS

### PLANNING

While bulbs are commonly planted in formal beds, borders, and even containers, many lend themselves to naturalized plantings where they bloom and spread in ever-widening drifts. Plan to create some naturalized areas in your landscape in the following ways:

1. Randomly scatter **crocus**, **daffodil**, **grape hyacinth**, **snowdrop**, and **snowflake**, and plant them where they fall. They look better when planted in clumps or drifts, so you may have to move them around. These bulbs will root and establish themselves by spring.

2. Plant spring-flowering bulbs along the edges of woodland areas or beneath the canopies of deciduous trees. They should receive plenty of sunlight there and finish blooming by the time the trees leaf out.

3. Insert bulbs such as **crocus** in your warm-season lawn. The **crocus** will brighten up the lawn before it awakens from its winter dormancy in the spring. By the time the **crocuses** finish replenishing themselves, it will be time to mow the grass and remove the spent **crocus** leaves.

Keep in mind that naturalized bulbs need to be fertilized on an annual basis to encourage perennialization. Failure to fertilize them often results in a gradual reduction in their numbers.

### PLANTING

**Freesias** can be grown indoors in the winter; keep in mind that they have exacting requirements. The delicate spikes of tubular, often fragrant, flowers in a range of colors from white to lavender, purple, blue, yellow, orange, pink, and red are well worth the effort.

1. Plant dormant corms in well-drained sterile potting soil with a neutral pH, such as Pro-Mix BX. If you are blending your own mix, it should contain no more than one-third perlite because **freesias** are sensitive to the fluoride in the perlite. Leaf scorch is a symptom of fluoride toxicity.

2. Fill the pots to within 2 inches of the rim and place the corms, pointed ends up, 2 to 3 inches apart in each pot.

3. Cover the corms with an inch of potting mix and water thoroughly.

4. For the most compact growth, precool these pots for forty-five days in a location where the temperature is 55 degrees F. Until the leaves appear, light is unnecessary; an unheated garage or basement will work fine. After this precooling period, green leaf tips should be visible.

5. Move the pots to a well-lit location that averages 65 degrees—higher temperatures delay flowering and increase bud drop. A combination of coolness and brightness will yield the best plants. Keep soil moist and fertilize every two weeks with a complete fertilizer such as 20-20-20.

6. Stake the straplike leaves to prevent them from falling over. You can use ready-made ring stakes or connect bamboo stakes with lengths of twine. Depending on conditions and the cultivars you choose, blossoms should appear two to four months after planting and continue for a month.

It's not too late to plant crocus for early-spring color.

Now is a good time to plant spring-blooming beauties such as **anemone, crocus, daffodil, scilla**, and **snowdrop**. Use a time-release bulb fertilizer at planting time. When in doubt, follow this general rule: Plant bulbs at a depth equal to three times the height of the bulb.

Summer bulbs which could be killed by winter freezes should be lifted, dried, and stored (if you did not already do so last month). Divide and replant crowded **dahlias** after a freeze kills their top growth. Where they won't survive the winter outdoors (in northern parts of Alabama and Mississippi), they will have to be lifted and overwintered indoors in a cool (35 to 50 degrees F.), dry place. Here's how:

Cut the tops back to 6 inches, lift out the clumps with a spading fork, brush off the soil, and turn them upside-down to dry. Inspect each clump and pare away any damaged parts. Remove infested or dead tubers at the neck. Dust the tubers with sulfur to prevent rot in storage, making sure all the surfaces are coated. Store them in a ventilated crate or basket filled with peat moss. Place each tuber upside-down, stacking them no more than two deep. Inspect them monthly and discard any rotting tubers.

## CARE

Mulch plantings with compost, pine straw, or salt hay to protect tender and semihardy bulbs from the winter cold.

Clean up and remove old, dried **iris** leaves, stems, and other debris in the fall to help eliminate overwintering eggs or iris borers.

## WATERING

Check potted bulbs that will be forced during the winter months.

Bulbs stored outdoors in cold frames or in the ground may need to be watered. Water newly planted bulbs to encourage rooting before cooler temperatures arrive.

## FERTILIZING

Fertilize new and established beds with a slow-release nitrogen fertilizer. Don't wait until spring, because the bulbs are producing roots and foraging for nutrients now.

## PROBLEMS

Examine stored bulbs for signs of rot and discard any diseased ones. In the future, avoid damaging tubers when digging them up, and store them in a cool, dry, dark place.

## HELPFUL HINTS

Some bulbs resist attacks by squirrels, chipmunks, voles, and their kin. In addition to the popular choices of **daffodil** and **colchicum** (also known as **autumn crocus**), you have several other choices. **Common hyacinth** (*Hyacinthus orientalis*), **glory-of-the-snow** (*Chionodoxa*), **tommies** (*Crocus tommasinianus*), **crown imperial** (*Fritillaria imperialis*), **dogtoothed violet** (*Erythronium*), **grape hyacinth** (*Muscari*), **Grecian windflower** (*Anemone blanda*), **spring star flower** (*Ipheion*), **snow iris** (*Iris reticulata*), **ixiolirion**, **ornamental onion** (*Allium*), **star-of-Bethlehem** (*Ornithogalum nutans*), **puschkinia**, **scilla**, **snowdrop** (*Galanthus*), **snowflake** (*Leucojum*), **Spanish bluebell** (*Hyacinthoides hispanica*), and **winter aconite** (*Eranthis hyemalis*) all resist attack. Be mindful, however, that extremely hungry animals will eat almost anything.

# DECEMBER
## BULBS, CORMS, RHIZOMES, & TUBERS

 PLANNING

Despite the holiday rush this month, make plans to spend some quiet time updating your gardening journal. What bulbs stopped you in your tracks when you first noticed them in bloom? Were any bulbs troubled by insects or diseases? Did any "minor" bulbs stand out among the rest?

During the year you may have saved newspaper and magazine clippings of articles from garden writers who touted certain bulbs. Perhaps you wrote down the names of bulbs or growing techniques suggested by friends, staff at public gardens, or speakers at gardening symposia. Now's the time to compile these notes so you can act upon them next year.

 PLANTING

Buy commercially prepared **lily-of-the-valley** pips from your florist or garden center. Plant as many as possible in pots to secure an abundance of fragrant blooms. One bonus of these bulbs is that they tolerate more heat than other commonly forced bulbs. Late-blooming spring bulbs can still be planted, though bulbs that bloom in February (**crocus, snow-**

**drop**, etc.) may not flower if planted now. Try to get them in the ground before midmonth.

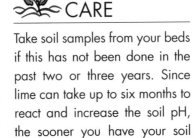 CARE

Take soil samples from your beds if this has not been done in the past two or three years. Since lime can take up to six months to react and increase the soil pH, the sooner you have your soil tested, the sooner you can apply lime to your beds if necessary.

 WATERING

See November p. 65.

 FERTILIZING

See September p. 61.

 PROBLEMS

Discard any bulbs that show signs of rot, which attacks improperly stored tubers in warm, humid conditions.

Handpull any young winter annual weeds, or cover them with a shallow layer of compost. Weeding is never fun, but cooler temperatures can make it more bearable.

Mice may get into outdoor bulb beds or cold frames. Use hardware cloth to keep them out. Voles, also called meadow or field mice, can feed on a wide variety of plants, including your bulbs. See p. 285 for controls.

---

## HELPFUL HINTS FOR FORCING PAPER-WHITES

There are some bulbs that can be forced without cooling. **Paper-white daffodils** (*Narcissus tazetta*) are winter-blooming tender bulbs that can be forced without having to expose them to cool temperatures. Here's how to force them in a soilless mixture: 1) Set them in an undrained decorative bowl or dish that is at least 2 to 3 inches deep, with enough pebbles, pea gravel, or coarse sand to reach about 1 inch below the top. 2) Add water until it's barely below the surface of the gravel. 3) Set the bulbs on top and hold them in place with enough gravel to cover the bottom quarter of each bulb. Carefully maintain the water level. 4) Move them to a cool 50- to 60-degree-F location in low light until they are well-rooted and the shoots appear—usually in about two to three weeks. Bring them gradually into direct sunlight and warmer temperatures.

# HERBS & VEGETABLES

We are lucky in the Deep South because fresh herbs and vegetables can be grown and harvested year-round. Compact varieties can be tucked in almost anywhere in the landscape. With the right conditions, the vacant spots among your shrubs and flowers can accommodate herbs and vegetables that look as good as they taste. Of course, you can take the traditional approach and allot some space in the landscape to these edibles.

Before you plant, make a plan.

## PLANNING THE HERB AND VEGETABLE GARDEN

Before you get swept up with thoughts of harvesting vine-ripened tomatoes or sprigs of homegrown oregano, spend some time planning your garden. Follow these steps to find the right location and make the right selections of herbs and vegetables:

1. Locate a fertile, well-drained spot that gets six to eight hours of sun. That is the amount of light that fruit-producing vegetables, such as peppers and tomatoes, need. Leafy vegetables such as beets, cabbage, lettuce, and the like do all right in partial shade. So do herbs like angelica, parsley, and sweet cicely.

2. List your favorite vegetables—think about taste, cost, nutrition, and appearance—and note their planting dates.

**Cost.** Many people grow the expensive, unique, and flavorful vegetables and buy the others. High-value vegetables for home growing include orange

sweet peppers, gourmet lettuces, tomatoes, and some squash.

**Nutrition.** Some vegetables pack more vitamins and minerals than others. Nutrient-dense vegetables include sweet potatoes, carrots, spinach, collard greens, red pepper, and kale.

**Beauty.** The flowers, leaves and fruits of some herbs and vegetables add beauty to the landscape.

3. Decide on the quantities you will need. Then it's a simple step to allocate the garden space you'll need to devote to each crop.

4. Start planning your garden on paper. Graph paper where 1/4 inch represents a foot works well. A 12-by-16-foot space is enough to grow a good selection of greens, some herbs, and a supply of tomatoes, peppers, beans, and cucumbers.

**Orient the rows east to west.** Allow room to walk between rows to take care of the garden. Put the tallest and trellised plants on the north so they won't shade the shorter ones. Place perennials like asparagus and horseradish to the side where they will not be disturbed. For a four-season garden, use a different sheet of paper for each season.

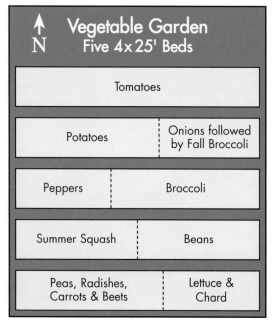

## SOIL PREPARATION

With your plan in hand, stake out your garden and prepare the soil.

1. Check the pH and nutrient levels of your soil. Have the soil tested through your local Cooperative Extension Service at least every third year. A pH of 5.5 to 7.0 is fine for most vegetables.

2. Add organic matter. Compost, old manure, or decaying leaves and weeds release nutrients and improve soil structure. Water and nutrients move less quickly out of the root zone in sandy soils amended with organic matter. In heavy soils, organic matter improves drainage.

3. Cultivate the soil. Dig to at least 8 inches, mixing in nutrients and any lime or sulfur recommended by a soil test.

## PLANTING THE HERB AND VEGETABLE GARDEN

The best time to plant vegetables outdoors depends on the cold hardiness of the species or variety. Vegetables can be divided into two classes based on temperature requirements: cool-season and warm-season crops.

Cool-season vegetables originated in temperate climates and grow best in cool weather. They often continue to produce well past the early fall freezes, but they should be started in time to mature before hard freezes begin.

Warm-season crops came primarily from subtropical and tropical regions. Thus they need warm weather for seed germination and growth. Freezes injure or kill them and they need to be protected from spring frosts. They are planted in the summer to mature in the fall; get them in early enough so they can be harvested before fall's killing freezes arrive.

Before doing anything else, plan your vegetable garden on paper.

# CHAPTER THREE

## STARTING HERBS AND VEGETABLES FROM SEED

Growing vegetables and herbs from seed gives you access to a wider range of varieties than are offered in stores. It also produces transplants fairly inexpensively. Follow the step-by-step instructions for starting seeds indoors in the introduction to the Annuals chapter on p. 16.

Select varieties that are well adapted in your area, with resistance to local insects and diseases. Contact your County Cooperative Extension Service for recommended varieties.

## FERTILIZING

Your soil-test report has told you what nutrients you need. Apply the fertilizer by broadcasting it over the garden, or by individually feeding each plant. Use a cyclone or drop spreader to broadcast, applying half the total in one direction and the other half at a right angle to the first (refer to Lawns, p. 103, to learn how to calibrate your spreader to apply the correct amount of fertilizer). Till it at least 3 inches into the soil.

Better yet, incorporate half the plant food deeply into the soil with a spade or rototiller. Then sprinkle the other half on top and rake it in lightly. This distributes fertilizer throughout the root zone.

A more efficient way of using fertilizer is to apply some in a band about 2 to 3 inches from the side and at least 3 inches below the seeds. Placing fertilizer closer to the seeds may injure or kill emerging plants.

Apply plant food sparingly to leafy, fast-growing herbs. Heavy applications of fertilizer, especially those high in nitrogen, can reduce the concentration of desirable essential oils that make herbs flavorful.

## WATERING

Since vegetables are made up of 80 to 90 percent water, yield, fruit size, and quality can be affected by a lack of water. Water prevents disor-ders such as toughness, off-flavor, poor filling of pods or tips, cracking, blossom end rot, and misshapen fruit. There is no ironclad schedule of how much and how often to water. Correct watering requires common sense and observation. Follow these "ground rules" for proper watering:

• Water often enough to keep the soil from drying out around newly planted vegetables. Gradually reduce the frequency but continue to water deeply to encourage development of a deep, extensive root system.

• Water vegetables in porous sandy soils more frequently than vegetables in dense clay soils.

• Water more often when temperatures are high.

• Water deeply, wetting as much of the root zone area as possible.

• Keep the leaves dry by applying water only to the soil surface. Fungal leaf diseases rely on moisture to infect and spread.

• To reduce evaporation and suppress water-stealing weeds, mulch your herbs and vegetables with a 2- or 3-inch layer of compost.

## PEST CONTROL

When growing vegetables and herbs you are bound to confront insects, diseases, and weeds. Do not be discouraged. Learn about pests and try to outsmart them.

It may mean planting squash early to avoid squash vine borers. Or you might hold off spraying the Mexican bean beetles on your snap beans because the assassin bugs are keeping the pests at levels that can be tolerated by your plants. To thwart any emerging weeds, plant your vegetables close together so they will shade the soil.

All these strategies are summed up in an approach called Integrated Pest Management: using a mix of mechanical, biological, cultural, and chemical techniques to control rather than eradicate pests. Some keys to IPM:

• Practice good soil management to grow healthy plants that can resist pests and diseases.

# HELPFUL HINTS FOR USING WOOD ASHES

Wood ashes are a good source of potassium for plants and they increase soil pH. Before applying wood ashes to a garden, have your soil tested through your County Extension center. If the soil is already in the 5.8 to 6.5 range and no lime is recommended, do not apply ashes—they are likely to make the soil too alkaline, tying up micronutrients such as zinc and manganese that are needed for good plant growth. If lime is recommended, you can spread an equivalent amount of wood ashes over the soil surface and work it into the soil. Wood ashes are low in calcium compared to limestone, and some supplemental gypsum (a source of calcium) will be needed if the calcium level, as indicated on the soil-test report, is medium or low.

Store the wood ashes in a closed container to prevent rainwater from leaching the nutrients away. Because fresh ashes can be caustic, do not spread them directly over the roots of plants or on young seedlings.

• Select plant varieties that are suited to your area and resistant to local pests.

• Rotate crops. Do not grow related vegetables in the same place year after year. Rotate species within the garden or relocate the entire garden (see the March Helpful Hints p. 77).

• Time your planting. Select planting dates that are favorable for the crop and unfavorable for the pest.

• Interplant. Plant different kinds of vegetables together in your garden since many insect pests attack plants of a certain family and avoid unrelated ones. Plants not preferred by pests can act as a buffer to slow the spread of harmful insects to pest-preferred plants.

• Thin out young plants to avoid overcrowding and weak growth that invites problems.

• Keep the leaves dry when watering to thwart the spread of fungal diseases that require moisture to grow and spread.

• Stake or cage plants to keep fruits off the ground and reduce sunscald. Slip boards under melons to prevent rot.

• Avoid injuring plants. Cuts, bruises, cracks, and insect damage invite infection. Cut, rather than pull off, fruit that is difficult to pick, such as cucumbers and watermelons. Avoid cutting into the plant roots when you cultivate.

• Mulch to suppress weeds and reduce water stress and soil splashing.

• Pull weeds as they appear. They often harbor pests and compete for nutrients and water.

• Keep your garden clean. Remove infected leaves or plants as you see them. Clean up

Staking or caging plants in a way to keep the fruit off the ground (tomatoes, in this example). Mulching is also important.

There is a wide variety of amendments and conditioners; make sure you know which ones you may need by performing a soil test first.

debris after harvest to destroy overwintering eggs and pests.

• Handpick egg clusters, bean beetles, caterpillars, and other insects as often as possible. Drop them into soapy water.

• Use biological controls. Rely on natural predators and parasites to control harmful insects. Learn to recognize the eggs and larvae of lacewings, ladybugs, and praying mantids.

A microbial insecticide is a living, insect pathogen that is safe to use on beneficial insects. The bacterium *Bacillus thuringiensis* (Bt) is the most popular pathogen. Formulations from *Bacillus thuringiensis* var. *kurstaki* are the most widely used. BTK (sold as Dipel®, Thuricide®, and others) controls most caterpillars, which are the larvae of butterflies and moths, such as cabbage looper, imported cabbageworm, and tomato fruit worm. When caterpillars ingest the bacteria, they stop feeding and die shortly thereafter. BTK works best when caterpillars are very small, and it remains effective for only a day or two after application because it is broken down by sunlight. Expect to get the best results when you spray BTK as soon as you see the first tiny caterpillars, and repeat applications as additional eggs are laid.

• Use botanical pesticides and insecticidal soaps. Refer to IPM Biological Controls in the Introduction to this book on pp. 11 for more information about these "natural" pesticides.

• As a last resort, turn to synthetic pesticides. Apply them sparingly, according to need and not season, and in strict accordance with manufacturer's instructions. They may kill a broad spectrum of insects and require a waiting time between application and harvest.

Before using any pesticide, read and follow label directions.

# JANUARY
## HERBS & VEGETABLES

### PLANNING

Intensive gardening can be accomplished in a number of ways to increase production from a limited space. You can shift the garden layout from rows to raised beds, which uses most of the ground formerly used for pathways. Make these permanent rectangular beds as long as you like and 3 to 4 feet wide so they can be worked from either side. Plant intensively in these beds. Consider "square-foot gardening," (*All New Square Foot Gardening*, Cool Springs Press, 2006) where the bed is divided into square blocks. Each plant or seed is planted in the center of each square.

Another intensive gardening approach is vertical gardening, which exploits the air space above the bed. Vining and sprawling plants such as **cucumbers**, **melons**, **pole beans**, and **indeterminate tomatoes** can be supported by trellises, nets, strings, or poles. Since they occupy little garden space, the remaining space can be planted with low-growing vegetables.

### PLANTING

Some gardeners grow their seedlings indoors in the bright direct light of a south-facing window, greenhouse, or sun porch. Others prefer the outdoors, using a cold frame (see November Planning p. 92). In the milder areas of Alabama and Mississippi, gardeners can sometimes move seedlings outdoors during warm days to expose them to full sunlight. Be aware that you will have to contend with some cloudy, overcast days. Instead of relying on sunlight, you can buy or build an artificial light stand and grow your seedlings under lights.

See Annuals January p. 18 to find out how to organize your seed packets to create a sowing schedule for your seeds, and for step-by-step information on producing transplants from seed indoors to get a jump on the growing season.

Gardeners in the southern parts of Mississippi and Alabama can sow **basil**, **chives**, **parsley**, **sage**, **summer savory**, and **sweet marjoram** indoors. To encourage **parsley** seeds to sprout more rapidly, soften the seeds by soaking them overnight in warm water. Also sow seeds of **broccoli**, **cabbage**, and **Chinese cabbage** indoors for transplanting within six to eight weeks in southern and central parts of the states. **Head** and **leaf lettuce** can be set out four to six weeks after sowing. Farther north, gardeners can wait until next month before starting these vegetables.

Outdoors, gardeners in the warmer coastal areas can sow **beets**, **carrots**, **garden peas** (**English peas** and **edible pea**

Intensive gardening methods include using raised beds and trellises for vining plants. This photo is an example of a square foot garden.

pods), **lettuce**, **mustard**, **radishes**, **spinach**, and **turnips**. Wait until later this month and early next month in the more inland areas of south Alabama and Mississippi. You can plant **asparagus** crowns throughout the state (see February Planting p. 75 for the step-by-step procedure) if the ground allows.

## CARE

Continue harvesting **carrots**, **radishes**, and **turnips** that were

planted in the fall. **Lettuce** and **spinach** growing in a cold frame or under the protection of a fabric row cover (spun-bonded polypropylene) or plastic tunnel can also be picked.

## WATERING

See Annuals January p. 19.

## FERTILIZING

Fertilize seedlings in soilless mixes when the first true leaves appear.

## PROBLEMS

Damping off is a serious disease that attacks and kills seeds and seedlings. See Annuals February p. 21 for a description and controls.

---

# HELPFUL HINTS FOR STARTING SEEDLINGS

Sowing seeds into pots and then waiting for the seedlings to emerge can be an act of faith. To avoid those feelings of helplessness and anxiety when sowing vegetable seeds, try my father-in-law's sealed-lid seed-starting technique. I have used it for germinating large-seeded vegetables like **tomato**, **pepper**, **cucumber**, **squash**, and **melon**. The materials for the sealed-lid method include a small plastic container that has a clear or translucent plastic lid such as a leftover margarine or whipped-cream container, and a piece of paper towel about 6 inches square.

1. Cut the paper towel into postage stamp-sized squares and place them on the inside of the lid.

2. Wet each square towel with a few drops of water. Then place one seed in the center of each square.

3. For small seeds, picking them up may be a challenge. Break a toothpick, wet the jagged end, and touch the seed with it. The seed readily sticks to the end and can be easily deposited on the paper.

4. Once you have placed the seeds on the lid, close the container, using the lid as the floor and the container as a makeshift greenhouse. Put the container in a warm, out-of-the-way place.

5. Depending on the seed, germination may take place in a few days or it may take a week or more. Inspect the seeds every now and then by looking through the underside of the lid for signs of the "seedling root" or radicle peeking through.

6. Once you see the radicle (seedling root), a welcome sign that germination has occurred, remove the container from the lid. Gently pluck the germinated seeds off the lid with tweezers and plant them in small pots filled with potting mix. Use the eraser end of a pencil to dibble a shallow planting hole. After placing the seed in the pot, run the pointed end of the pencil alongside the hole to cover the seed.

I have found the sealed-lid method to be highly efficient and economical. For example, instead of sowing a whole packet of **tomato** seeds, germinate only the number you want to eventually transplant in the garden.

# FEBRUARY

## HERBS & VEGETABLES

### PLANNING

To keep your garden in continuous production, use any of three intensive approaches:

1. Interplanting or intercropping involves growing different kinds of vegetables together at the same time. Combine a slow-growing or early-maturing crop with a fast-growing or late-maturing crop. The quick-growing vegetable will mature and be harvested before the slow-growing crop needs the space; thus two crops can grow in the same area without crowding each other.

2. Succession planting is another intensive approach in which a crop is grown, harvested, removed, and another planted in its place. Just avoid planting vegetables in the same family in the same place right after one another. For example, try following **peas** with **okra**, or plant **cucumbers** after **spinach**. Planting a spring, summer, and fall garden is another form of succession planting. Cool-season crops (**broccoli**, **lettuce**, **peas**) are followed by warm-season crops (**bean**, **pepper**, **tomato**), and these may be followed by more cool-season plants or even a winter cover crop.

3. Relaying consists of staggering the planting times of one type of crop to extend the harvest season over a long period of time instead of having one big harvest all at once. One approach is to plant one variety several times, at about two-week intervals (allow more time between early plantings in colder soil, but only ten days between the last plantings). For instance, **sweet corn** may be planted at two-week intervals for a continuous harvest. Another relaying approach is to make one planting of two or more varieties that differ in maturity time; for example, try fifty-day with sixty-day **beans** or early, mid-, and late-season varieties of **sweet corn**.

Never work wet soil; if a handful sticks together when you squeeze it, it's too wet.

### PLANTING

In the southern parts of Alabama and Mississippi, sow warm-season vegetables indoors in flats or trays—try plants like **eggplant**, **pepper**, and **tomato**. Cucumber, **cantaloupe**, **summer squash**, and **watermelon** should be sown in individual pots or peat pellets because their growth may be hindered if their roots are disturbed. Wait until next month if you live farther north.

You can also sow **basil**, **chives**, **parsley**, **sage**, **summer savory**, and **sweet marjoram** indoors. To encourage **parsley** seeds to sprout more rapidly, soften the seeds by soaking them overnight in warm water.

Set out (outdoors) hardened-off vegetable transplants of **broccoli**,

cabbage, and **lettuce**. Set out small tubers or "seed pieces"—a piece of a large tuber containing at least one "eye" or bud—of **white** or **Irish potatoes**. The soil temperature should be above 50 degrees F. Wait until next month in northern Alabama and Mississippi.

In southern and central parts of the states, gardeners can sow **mustard**, **garden peas**, **radishes**, **spinach**, and **turnips**. Wait until next month farther north. Plant "short-day" **onion** transplants for **bulbing onions** in southern and central parts of Alabama and Mississippi.

Plant dormant **asparagus** crowns without any green shoots showing into a bed enriched with organic matter such as compost, manure, or shredded leaves. Here's how:

1. Place the crown into the bottom of an 8-inch-deep furrow and cover with about 2 inches of soil (in heavier clay soils set them 6 inches deep). Set the crowns 12 inches apart in the trench.

2. As the new shoots emerge and grow, add another 2-inch layer of soil—do this every two to three weeks until the trench is filled.

3. Mulch with a 2-inch layer of compost to conserve water and control weeds. Weed control is very important. Don't let weeds get started in your **asparagus** bed because they will be very hard to eliminate later as the **asparagus** grows.

4. Begin harvesting **asparagus** spears in the third year. (If you must, harvest lightly in the second year, for no more than two weeks. Harvesting too much and too early results in weak plants).

## CARE

When the soil can be worked, turn under the cover crops planted last fall. Till the soil to a depth of 8 to 12 inches. Never work the soil when it is wet—working wet soils, especially silty or clay types, destroys the structure and makes the soil hard, compacted, and unproductive. There are two indicators of wet soil: (1) soil sticks to the shovel and (2) a handful of soil sticks together in a ball and does not crumble when squeezed.

## WATERING

Do not overwater seedlings or transplants. Water them when the surface of the medium feels dry.

## FERTILIZING

Fertilize indoor-grown transplants with a water-soluble fertilizer such as 20-20-20 at half-strength every other week after they've sprouted and grown the first true leaves. Outdoors, fertilize the newly emerging growth of established asparagus beds with a nitrogen-containing fertilizer. Sidedress **beets**, **carrots**, and **English peas**. See March Fertilizing p. 76.

## PROBLEMS

Damping-off can be a problem on seedlings. Refer to Annuals & Biennials February Problems p. 21 for control recommendations.

Control any winter annual weeds such as bittercress, common chickweed, and henbit by handpulling. Suppress them with a shallow layer of mulch.

# MARCH

## HERBS & VEGETABLES

### PLANNING

If you are serious about growing herbs and vegetables, plan to start a journal this month. It will document your observations, thoughts, and plans for the future. List the herbs and vegetables you planted in the garden. Include the names of seed companies, plant name, variety, planting date, and harvest date.

### PLANTING

Throughout Alabama and Mississippi, sow **basil**, **chives**, **parsley**, **summer savory**, and **sweet marjoram**. To encourage **parsley** seeds to sprout more rapidly, soften the seeds by soaking them overnight in warm water.

In central and northern regions, sow warm-season vegetables in flats or trays—try **eggplant**, **New Zealand spinach** (a heat-tolerant substitute for **spinach**), **pepper**, and **tomato**. Vegetables that resent any root disturbance, such as **cucumber**, **cantaloupe**, **summer squash**, and **watermelon**, should be sown in individual pots or peat pellets. Avoid sowing seeds too early or they may be ready for transplanting before outdoor conditions permit.

**Sweet potatoes** are started from "slips"—shoots that sprouted from last year's crop. Purchase them as transplants to start later, or start your own transplants now by placing a **sweet potato** in a glass half-filled with water. Place it in bright light. Detach the plants from the mother root when they are 6 to 8 inches long, pot them up, and then plant them in the garden about three weeks after the last freeze.

Plant perennial herbs such as **chives**, **oregano**, and **thyme** when they become available in garden centers. You can sow **parsley**, **dill**, **beets**, and **Swiss chard**. Since each **beet** or **Swiss chard** "seed" is actually a dried fruit containing up to six seeds, expect a cluster of seedlings to emerge. When their first "true leaves" appear, thin out the bunches by pinching off the extra seedlings near ground level.

In south Alabama and Mississippi, after the last freeze, set out **eggplant**, **onion**, **pepper**, and **tomato**. Sow seeds of **butter bean (lima bean)**, **pole bean**, **snap bean**, **sweet corn**, **summer squash**, and **watermelon**.

In central and northern regions, buy **seed potatoes** and cut them into egg-sized pieces containing one or two eyes. Allow the cuts to dry and callous for a day or two before planting. Plant them

when the soil temperature remains above 50 degrees F.

In central and northern Alabama and Mississippi, plant **asparagus** crowns before new growth emerges from the buds. Set out transplants of **broccoli**, **cabbage**, and **kale** as well, up to four weeks before the last spring freeze. Sow seeds of **carrot**, **lettuce (leaf** and **head)**, **garden peas**, **mustard**, **radish**, **rutabaga**, **turnip**, and **spinach**.

Divide **chives**, **thyme**, **mint**, and **tarragon** when new growth emerges. A simple way of propagating **rosemary** and **thyme** is by layering. See Shrubs March Planting p. 186 for details.

### CARE

Before moving home-grown or store-bought transplants into the garden, harden them off (see Annuals April Care p. 24).

### WATERING

Continue watering trays or pots of seedlings indoors.

### FERTILIZING

Some vegetables have heavier demands for nitrogen than

others and need extra nitrogen during the growing season. These heavy-feeders benefit from a primarily nitrogen-containing fertilizer applied along one side of the row about 4 to 6 inches from the plants. The application of fertilizer to growing plants is called *sidedressing*. Use a nitrogen fertilizer such as calcium nitrate, bloodmeal, or cottonseed meal.

Sidedress **beets** and **carrots** four to six weeks after planting. **Broccoli, cabbage,** and **cauliflower** benefit from an application two to three weeks after planting and again four to six weeks later. Sidedress **lettuce** soon after the seedlings emerge and grow; a second application is optional and should be based on the appearance and growth rate of the **lettuce** crop. Fertilize **English peas** when they are 4 to 6 inches tall.

## HELPFUL HINTS FOR CROP ROTATION

Rotate your vegetables by not planting the same vegetable or related vegetable in the same location year after year. Rotate at least once every three years. If you have to, and if space permits, rotate the entire garden to another part of the yard the following year and allow the original garden to remain fallow. By rotating vegetables from different families you can prevent the buildup of insect and disease problems. Refer to the following list of vegetable families when rotating your garden.

- Carrot family: **carrot, chervil, celery, coriander, dill, Florence fennel, parsley,** and **parsnip**
- Goosefoot family: **beet, spinach,** and **Swiss chard**
- Gourd family: **cucumber, gourd, cantaloupe, watermelon, pumpkin,** and **squash**
- Grass family: **popcorn** and **sweet corn**
- Lily family: **asparagus**
- Mallow family: **okra**
- Mustard family: **bok choi, broccoli,** Brussels sprouts, **cabbage, Chinese cabbage, cauliflower, collards, cress, kale, horseradish, kohlrabi, mustard greens, radish, rutabaga,** and **turnip**
- Nightshade family: **eggplant, peppers,** Irish **potato,** and **tomato**
- Onion family: **chive, garlic, leek, onion,** and **shallot**
- Pea family: **bean** and **peas**
- Sunflower family: **endive, chicory, globe artichoke, Jerusalem artichoke, lettuce, salsify,** and **sunflower**

## PROBLEMS

Look for imported cabbage worm caterpillars on **cabbage, cauliflower,** and, to a lesser extent, other members of the family including **broccoli, kale,** and **mustard**. Prevent the cabbage worm butterflies from laying eggs in the spring by covering the young plants with a layer of spun-bonded row cover. Hand-

picking the larvae is another way to control them, but their camouflage makes them difficult to locate. Use a biological control, *Bacillus thuringiensis* var. *kurstaki* (BTK), sold as Dipel®, Thuricide®, and others. Spray BTK as soon as you see the first tiny larvae, and repeat applications as additional eggs are laid. Other less specific (and highly toxic) insecticides are available.

They may kill a broad spectrum of insects and require a waiting time between application and harvest.

See February p. 75 for advice on disease control and for details about weed controls.

# APRIL
## HERBS & VEGETABLES

### PLANNING

Summer is around the corner—plan to water your herbs and vegetables efficiently when hot weather arrives. Take a look at the irrigation methods described in Shrubs May Planning p. 190, and select an appropriate one for your garden.

### PLANTING

After the last expected freeze, set out the transplants of herbs you started indoors.

After the last freeze, sow **beans**, **corn**, **cucumbers**, and **southern peas**. Avoid planting **okra** seeds too early. The soil temperature should be above 75 degrees F.; soak **okra** seed overnight before planting in the garden.

Set out transplants of **eggplant**, **cantaloupe**, **watermelon**, **peppers**, **summer squash**, **New Zealand spinach**, and **zucchini** about two weeks after the last freeze when the nights are continuously above 50 degrees F.

Plant **determinate bush-type tomatoes** for canning or preserving so the fruit will ripen all at once, all within a week or two of one other. For vine-ripened **tomatoes**, plant **indeterminate tomatoes** that have an extended

### HELPFUL HINTS

Avoid purchasing **tomato** or **pepper** transplants that are already in bloom. Once the plant starts flowering, it is forced into the dual responsibility of maintaining flowers and trying to produce roots. If a plant is blooming when transplanted, it will concentrate on fruiting rather than growing. The end result will be a small plant that bears little fruit. You are always better off planting one that's not in bloom.

If you can't find any without blooms, then pinch the blooms off when you plant; feed with 20-20-20 liquid fertilizer diluted according to label directions.

fruiting period; they vine, flower, and fruit all the way up to the first frost.

Without providing protection, you can plant **tomatoes** one to two weeks after the last freeze. Plant transplants either on their side in a shallow trench with only the topmost leaves showing, or dig a deep hole with a shovel or posthole digger to set the transplants straight down.

### CARE

To keep the **cauliflower** curds pure white, loosely tie the long outside leaf onto the flat, open head when it is 1 to 2 inches across. Hold the leaves together with a rubber band until the head is ready for harvesting.

Continue to harvest **asparagus** until the spears become thinner than a pencil.

Root crops must be thinned, no matter how ruthless this practice seems. Thin **beets**, **carrots**, **onions**, **Swiss chard**, and **turnips** until you can fit three fingers between individual plants.

You should be enjoying the harvests of your late winter/early spring labor: home-grown **beets**, **carrots**, **lettuce**, **onions**, **peas**, and **turnips**.

### WATERING

The first few weeks after planting and transplanting and during the development of fruit or storage organs are times when plants may be stunted by shortages of water. Be sure they are watered well.

Be sure you water young transplants regularly for the first few weeks after planting.

 FERTILIZING

Fertilize **asparagus** to encourage the production of large ferny growth. Research has shown that the bigger the topgrowth, the better the yield. Sidedress young **garlic** plants when the new growth is 6 inches high. Sidedress **Irish potatoes** when the sprouts begin to break ground.

 GROOMING

Both **lavender** (*Lavandula augustifolia*) and **sage** (*Salvia officinalis*) can be cut back in the spring as new growth begins. In both cases, do not cut below the point of new buds. With **lavender** this is usually 6 or 8 inches above the ground. **Sage** can be cut back lower still, provided you leave at least one pair of healthy green leaves on each stem from whose bases the new shoots will appear. Shearing **lavender** after the blossoms fade will also help keep the plants compact.

 PROBLEMS

Mexican bean beetles—both adults and larvae—feed on **bush**, **pole**, and **lima beans** by skeletonizing the leaves from below. Handpick and destroy beetles and larvae on the leaves, or deposit them in a jar of soapy water. Parasitic wasps help control the beetles. Insecticides are available.

Look for flea beetles on **eggplant**. They are about 1¹/₂ inches long, shiny black in color, and chew tiny holes in leaves.

Control with the appropriate insecticides.

Cutworms damage seedlings and transplants by cutting stems a few inches below or just above ground level. They feed mainly at night. See Annuals May Problems p. 26 for a description and controls.

Leaffooted bugs feed mostly on **tomatoes**, **potatoes**, **beans**, **cowpeas**, and **okra**. Both nymphs and adults suck sap from pods, buds, blossoms, fruit, and seeds, causing distorted leaves and distorted or deformed fruit. Their life cycle lasts about forty days, with many generations per year. Plant early to avoid the first generation. Handpicking and destroying the eggs are time-consuming but effective measures. Insecticides are available.

Control weed seedlings when they are young since they grow rapidly and can be more difficult to remove later. A sharpened hoe is a good friend in the garden.

# MAY

## HERBS & VEGETABLES

### PLANNING

If you lack the ground space for herbs and vegetables, consider growing them in containers. Remember these points:

1. Choose white or light-colored containers which absorb less heat than dark-colored ones in full sun.

2. The container should be large enough to provide root-growing space. A 1-gallon container is suitable for **beets**, **carrots**, **lettuces**, **onions**, and **radishes**. A 2-gallon pot is fine for **bush beans**, **mustard**, and **turnips**. A minimum of 5 gallons would be necessary for **bush squash**, **cabbages** and other cole crops, **cucumbers**, **melons**, and **tomatoes**.

3. Use a premium-quality soil-less potting mix for small containers. Since the expense of prepackaged or soilless mixes can be high for large-container gardens, prepare your own soil by mixing equal parts of peat moss, potting soil, and clean coarse builder's sand or perlite.

4. Container-grown vegetables and herbs have the same requirements for light, moisture, and nutrients as garden-grown plants. Being confined to containers, however, means they require more-frequent watering, which leaches out nutrients, so they also require more-frequent fertilizing. Use a slow-release fertilizer to make fewer applications.

### PLANTING

Sow warm-weather vegetables such as **beans**, **cucumber**, **okra**, and **southern peas**. Extend your **sweet corn** harvest by planting successive crops when the previous crop has three to four leaves, or plant early, mid-, and late-maturing varieties all at the same time. Set out herb transplants. Continue setting out transplants of warm-weather vegetables such as **eggplant**, **cantaloupe**, **New Zealand spinach**, **peppers**, **summer squash**, **sweet potato** slips, **tomatoes**, and **watermelon**. **French tarragon** doesn't like the heat and wet weather in the warmer areas of Alabama and Mississippi. A heat-tolerant substitute is **Mexican mint marigold** (*Tagetes lucida*).

### CARE

Harvest **broccoli** when the florets are still tight and green. After harvesting the main head, **broccoli** will put out smaller-size heads from the side shoots. Pick **cauliflower** before the curds begin to separate, and **cabbage** when their heads are firm. Pick **green**, **sugar snap**, and **snow** **peas** every couple of days to keep more coming. Stop harvesting **asparagus** spears when they get close to pencil size. Fasten **indeterminate tomatoes** to a stake or other tall support. This will keep their fruit off the ground to avoid disease problems. **Determinate tomatoes**, which branch more and ripen their fruit all at once, are best enclosed in a reinforced wire tomato cage. Wind their branches around the inside of the cage as they grow.

### WATERING

Water deeply, keeping the leaves of your vegetables dry. Invest in soaker hoses or drip irrigation.

"Seep-irrigate" with plastic milk jugs. Punch holes in the sides of a jug with a large nail, spacing them about 2 inches. Bury the jug, leaving the neck above the soil. Fill the jug with water (solutions of liquid fertilizer may be used to fertilize at the same time) and screw the cap on firmly.

### FERTILIZING

Sidedress **sweet corn** when it is 8 to 12 inches high and again when the tassel is just beginning to show. Use a nitrogen fertilizer such as 10-10-10 at the rate recommended on the label, bloodmeal, or cottonseed meal.

## GROOMING

With your fingers, you may pinch out the "suckers" of **indeterminate tomatoes** to harvest larger **tomatoes**. Suckers are shoots that develop in the "U" between the main stem and a branch. If left in place, they will eventually become larger branches. Your plant will produce smaller **tomatoes**, but lots of them. The option is yours.

## PROBLEMS

Look for curled or puckered leaves on your vegetables caused by aphids. Slugs and snails produce large, ragged holes on leafy crops, especially **lettuce** and **cabbage**. See p. 286 for descriptions and controls. Watch out for leaffooted bugs. See April Problems p. 79 for controls. Greenstriped cucumber beetles attack the leaves, stems, and fruit of **beans**, **corn**, **cucumber**, **melon**, **pumpkin**, and **squash**. They transmit bacterial

---

### HELPFUL HINTS

When planting **squash** or **cucumbers** in a circle or hill, place a stick upright in the middle of the circle and leave it there. Later, when the main roots are hidden by vines, use the stick to show you where to water them.

wilt disease. Expect two or more generations per year. Hand-picking is time-consuming but effective. Fabric row covers such as spun-bonded polyester provide an effective barrier between the insect and young plants. Remove the covers during flowering to ensure pollination. Insecticides are available.

Early blight is a disease of **tomatoes**. Look for small, sunken, dark-brown spots with yellow haloes on the lower leaves and stem. Eventually the spots enlarge to form a "bulls-eye." Mulch to keep the soilborne fungal spores from splashing onto the leaves, and avoid wetting the leaves when watering. If necessary, apply a fungicide. Squash fruit rot is a fungal disease that attacks **summer squash** blossoms and fruit. Avoid wetting fruit when watering and avoid overcrowding plants. Powdery

mildew infects **beans**, **cantaloupe**, **cucumbers**, **okra**, **peas**, and **squash**. Leaves are covered with patches of whitish to grayish powdery growth. They eventually turn yellow, then brown, then dry up. Plant resistant varieties and avoid crowding. If necessary, use fungicides. Fusarium wilt is a warm-season disease that only attacks **tomatoes**. The best defense against both of these is genetic resistance. Select varieties that have "VF" after their name, signifying that they are resistant to both of these diseases. 'Big Beef', 'Celebrity', 'OG 50', 'Pilgrim', and 'Quick Pick' are a few possibilities.

Prevent weed seed germination, destroy weeds that sprout before they bear seed, and do not use mulches or compost contaminated with weed seeds.

# JUNE
## HERBS & VEGETABLES

### PLANNING

If you've planted more than you can use, share your bounty with friends and neighbors. What about your community? Make plans to share your vegetables and herbs with your community soup kitchen or food bank. Herbs are especially welcome because they provide nutrients as well as flavor. Get the address

Okra 'Burgundy' remains tender even if the pods are long—an exception to most varieties of okra. It's also very attractive as an ornamental.

of the nearest food pantry or soup kitchen that needs fresh produce from a church organization that helps the needy or from the Social Services department at your town hall.

### PLANTING

Sow another batch of **sweet basil** seeds for late summer. You can sow another round of seeds of summer crops such as **beans**, **cucumbers**, **okra**, **pumpkins**, **southern peas**, and **squash**, and a last planting of **sweet corn**. Also, set out transplants of **pepper**, **tomatoes**, and **sweet potato** slips for a good fall harvest. Remove the flowers and fruits from late-season **tomato** transplants before setting them out.

### CARE

The best time to harvest most herbs is just before flowering when the leaves contain the maximum essential oils.

Harvest **beans**, **cucumbers**, **okra**, and **squash** daily to keep the plants producing. Pick **cucumbers** when the fruits are small and before they turn yellow.

Harvest **okra** pods when they are 2 to 4 inches long. Wait much longer and the pods become tough and fibrous and the plant stops producing—an

exception is 'Burgundy', whose pods can stay tender even when 6 to 8 inches long. Pick **yellow squash** when the fruit is 4 to 6 inches long, **zucchini** when it is 6 to 8 inches long, and **patty pan** when it is 3 to 5 inches wide.

Pick **eggplant** after the fruit reaches 3 to 5 inches in length. The skin should be glossy and fully colored. Dull skin indicates overripeness.

Dig **onions** when about half the tops begin to turn yellow and fall over. Brush the soil off and cure them in a dark, warm (80 to 85 degrees F.), well-ventilated space for two to three weeks. Store them in a mesh bag in a dry, dark, cool place.

Harvest **Irish potatoes** when the vines have died back about halfway. Save some of the small **potatoes**, refrigerate them, and plant them whole in the fall.

Watch out for blossom end rot, a disorder that causes **tomatoes** to turn black on the blossom-end. It occurs when there are extremes in soil moisture, which result in a calcium deficiency in the fruit. When rain or irrigation follows a dry spell, the roots cannot take up calcium fast enough to keep up with the rapid fruit growth. Blossom end rot also occurs if the delicate feeder roots are damaged during transplanting or by deep cultivation near the plants. Here's how to fight it:

• Keep moisture levels uniform by regular watering and by maintaining a mulch layer around the base of the plants.

• Maintain a pH between 6 and 6.5 and an adequate calcium level by liming or applying gypsum.

• Finally, avoid overfertilizing, which inhibits calcium uptake.

## WATERING

**Corn** needs water at two crucial times: when the tassels at the top are beginning to show, and when the silk is beginning to show on the ear. If rainfall is scarce at these times, water.

## FERTILIZING

Fertilize the **asparagus** bed to encourage the "ferns" to grow during the summer to store food in the roots for next year's crop. Keep the bed weed-free. After they have set their first fruit, sidedress **eggplants**, **peppers**, and **tomatoes** with a nitrogen fertilizer such as bloodmeal, 10-10-10, or cottonseed meal; sidedress **sweet potatoes** six weeks after planting.

## PROBLEMS

Corn earworm caterpillars chew on **corn** ears, gaining entry through the corn silks. Avoid this pest by planting **corn** earlier in the season, or apply a few drops of mineral oil at the base of the corn silks five days after they emerge from the husk. Insecticides are also available.

Watch out for leaffooted bugs. See April Problems p. 79.

Mites feed on nearly all vegetable crops, but are commonly a problem on **beans**, **tomato**, and **eggplant**. Whiteflies are tiny insects that attack **tomato, pepper, bean, cucumber, squash, melon,** and **okra**. See pp. 285 to 286 for descriptions and controls.

Pickleworms mostly attack **cantaloupe, cucumber,** and **squash.** The young larvae usually feed on leaves and flowers. The older larvae bore into the sides of the fruit and continue to feed. Grow resistant varieties and plant early to harvest before the insects arrive.

Squash vine borers are the larvae of a wasplike clearwing moth which lays oval, flat brown eggs on the stems and leaf stalks of **squash** and **gourds**. Upon hatching they bore into the stem, causing the vine to wilt and die. Squash vine borers are difficult to control with

pesticides. Once inside the stem, they cannot be reached. The best control is prevention:

• Cover seedlings or transplants with a layer of spunbonded row cover to keep the adult moths at bay. This will have to be removed when flowers appear to allow for pollination.

• Stems attacked by borers wilt suddenly; look for the borers' entry hole near the base of the stem and some fine, brown sawdust-like frass (insect feces). Carefully split the stem lengthwise with a penknife and remove the borers or kill them with a long pin or needle. Cover the "surgery" with soil and keep watered to encourage the stem to root; perhaps you can salvage the damaged plant.

Pinch or prune out any diseased leaves or stems on herbs. Watch out for bacterial wilt on **tomatoes**. See July Problems p. 85 for information about this disease.

In most gardens, annual weeds can be controlled by mulching and handweeding. Using a herbicide in a herb and vegetable garden is difficult because there are few herbicides that can be safely applied to the wide range of plant species grown in the garden.

# JULY
## HERBS & VEGETABLES

### PLANNING

Start planning your fall garden. Choose early-maturing vegetables when you can. They will replace those early vegetables you harvested this month and will be ready to pick before freezing weather comes. Sketch out a plan, list the crops, and mark their locations. Note the dates to remind you when to plant them—allow adequate time to mature before the first expected freeze. Check the freeze dates.

### PLANTING

This is your last chance to sow **beans, cucumber, short-season corn, basil, squash,** and **southern peas.** Also plant transplants of **eggplant, pepper,** and **tomato** for a fall crop. Consider varieties that offer disease resistance and earlier yields for fall success.

Sow **pumpkins** early this month for Halloween.

In northern parts of the states, start seeds of **Brussels sprouts, cabbage,** and **cauliflower** for the fall garden. Sow seed indoors or in a partly shaded area outdoors.

Extra attention to watering will be needed during hot, dry

weather to get these up and growing.

### CARE

Continue to cut and dry herbs for winter use. Keep picking **beans, cucumbers, okra, peppers,** and **squash** so they will remain productive. If going away for a few days, invite neighbors to help themselves.

You can tell **cantaloupe** is ripening when the green skin begins to lighten. Pick them when they slip easily from the stem and are fragrant.

A **watermelon** is ready when the underside turns from whitish to creamy yellow and the stem starts to wither. Dig **Irish potatoes** when half their tops have died down. Pick **sweet corn** just before cooking. It's ready when the silks turn brown and the pierced kernel releases a light milky juice (not creamy looking). Most varieties maintain peak sweetness for one or two days. Super-sweet types stay sweet four or five days after picking.

### WATERING

A vegetable garden thrives on an inch of water or more each week of summer. When rain is sparse, water deeply once a

week if you have clay soils and every three days if you have sandy soils to encourage deep rooting. You can measure a 1-inch application by collecting the water in small bowls in the garden. Stop watering when the water is an inch deep.

### FERTILIZING

Restore soil fertility before planting your fall crops by working in fertilizer or manure. Do not fertilize drought-stressed plants. Wait until after watering or rainfall and the plants' leaves have dried.

### GROOMING

Cut back **basil, mint,** and **oregano** to keep them compact and to keep these herbs from going to seed.

### PROBLEMS

Squash bugs feed on **pumpkin** and **squash** plants. Capture them with a shingle. Bugs will gather under it during the heat of the day and can be destroyed.

If your vegetables looked stunted, poorly colored, and wilted, check the roots for signs of a nematode infestation. These microscopic roundworms are commonly found in coarse-textured sandy soils and feed on plant roots. The root knot nematode produces knots or galls in the roots. Have the soil analyzed through your County Extension center. If the findings reveal damaging levels of nematodes, the course of action includes rotating vegetables away from this site, and planting nematode-resistant vegetables such as 'Carolina Wonder' and 'Charleston Belle' **bell peppers**, 'Colossus' **southern pea**, 'Better Boy', 'Celebrity' or 'OG 50' **tomatoes**, and 'Jewel' **sweet potato**. Soil solarization, described in the Helpful Hints, will also reduce their numbers.

See April and June Problems pp. 79 and 83 for help in controlling leaffooted bugs, pickleworms, and spider mites.

Bacterial wilt attacks **tomatoes**, **Irish potatoes**, **eggplants**, and **peppers**. It causes an entire fruiting plant suddenly to wither and die. To control this disease: Remove and dispose of infected plants, roots and all. Rotate susceptible vegetables to different locations in your garden every year. Currently, no chemicals or totally resistant **tomato** plants are available. Two cultivars show promise, and you may want to try 'Tropic Boy' or 'Neptune' **tomatoes**.

## HELPFUL HINTS

• To make a produce cleaning station, replace the bottom of a wooden box with half-inch hardware cloth or chicken wire. Place fresh-picked vegetables in the box and rinse them off in the garden so the soil remains there. Only the final cleaning will be necessary indoors. Or you can use an oversized colander.

• To suppress soil pest problems such as nematodes, bacteria, fungi, weeds, and insects, solarize the soil. Solarizing uses clear plastic or polyethylene to intensify sunlight, which raises soil temperatures and kills soilborne pests. Solarize the soil during the hottest part of summer. Follow these steps:

1. Cultivate the soil to a depth of 6 to 8 inches. Level the soil. Remove weeds, plants, and crop debris, and break up large clods of soil so the plastic will come in close contact with the soil.

2. Moisten the soil to conduct heat more deeply into it.

3. Dig a shallow trench around the plot to hold the edges of the plastic.

4. Stretch a clear plastic sheet that is 1 to 4 mils thick over the bed. A plastic that contains ultraviolet inhibitors will prevent it from deteriorating too quickly. Tuck it into the trench and bury the edges with soil to secure it in place.

5. Leave the plastic in place for four to six weeks in full summer sun.

Soil Solarization

# AUGUST
## HERBS & VEGETABLES

 PLANNING

As you update your garden journal, note the vegetables and herbs that didn't live up to expectations, and those that exceeded them. Make a note of insect and disease problems. In your plans for next year's garden, focus on varieties that performed well for you or that you have noticed did well in other gardens.

Consider heirloom vegetables. They are prized for flavor and tenderness and are saved year after year for generations. Select heirloom vegetables adapted to your area's soil, climate, and pests.

**Beans** and **tomatoes** are popular heirloom vegetables partly because they are easily maintained true-to-type—their seed produces fairly similar plants from one generation to the next. Heirlooms often have unique names like 'Mortgage Lifter' **tomato** and 'Turkey Gizzard' **bean**.

 PLANTING

Set out cloves of **garlic** for a harvest early next summer. For an early start to the fall garden, in cooler parts of Alabama and Mississippi, sow seeds of cool-weather vegetables such as **beet**, **carrot**, **lettuce**, **peas**, **radish**, **spinach**, **rutabaga**, and **Swiss chard**. Plant seeds of greens such as **kale**, **mustard**, and **turnip**, in intervals now and next month to lengthen the harvest season. For the hardiest crops like **cabbage**, **collards**, and **kale**, count back from your average first frost date the number of days the particular variety requires to mature; plant at the appropriate time. For half-hardy crops like **beet**, **carrot**, and **Swiss chard**, allow an additional week. Set out transplants of **kale**, **lettuce**, **broccoli**, **cabbage**, and **collards**. See the Helpful Hints for help starting seeds in midsummer.

 CARE

Dry herbs. Gather bundles of each type of herb and spread on cheesecloth or hang upside-down in a warm, dark, dry place. Harvest **garlic** when the leaves turn yellow. Lift the entire plant and dry it in a well-ventilated, covered space. Save some for replanting and eat the rest. To protect **pumpkins** from rot, slip a shingle under ripening fruits to lift them off the soil. **Winter squash** is ready to harvest when the rind is hard and cannot be punctured with your thumbnail. Pull out plants that have stopped producing, including **bush beans**, early **cucumbers**, and **summer squash**. High

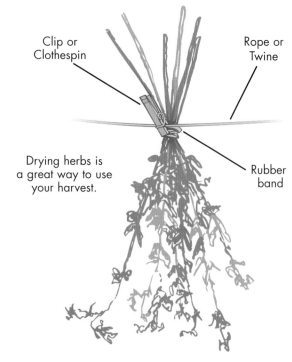

Clip or Clothespin

Rope or Twine

Drying herbs is a great way to use your harvest.

Rubber band

temperatures slow **tomato** production. There is nothing to do but wait for the weather to cool. Then they will start producing again. The same goes for **bell peppers**. Too much fertilizer can cause **pepper** blossoms to fall off. **Peppers** are moderate feeders, needing only a little fertilizer at planting and a light sidedressing after the first fruits have set.

 WATERING

Watering properly is critical in the heat of summer. Slow, deep soakings are best done with trickle irrigation or soaker hoses.

 FERTILIZING

Feed **basil** with a liquid fertilizer to keep it productive into fall. Trim off seedheads so the plants will spend their energy on flavorful foliage.

## HELPFUL HINTS

• Here's an old-time trick for starting seeds in midsummer: Plant and water them well, then set a board over the row. When the sprouts just reach the soil surface, remove the board.

• Before storing root crops like **carrots** and **beets**, cut off the green tops. They pull moisture from the roots, reducing quality.

• Leave 3 inches of stem when you harvest **winter squash** and **pumpkins**; they'll keep longer.

• Herbs make attractive, fragrant wreaths, especially when combined with **boxwood** or **ornamental grasses**. Green herbs are easier to work with, but wreaths must be hung to dry when completed.

• **Sunflower** seeds gain flavor if flower heads are left on until their backs turn brown. Then you can rub two heads together to knock off the seeds. Dry seeds for a few days, pack in airtight jars, and refrigerate to retain flavor. Eat them raw or toast for 15 minutes at 300 degrees F. They are high in minerals, vitamins, and protein.

 PROBLEMS

Pests reach record numbers in the fall months. Remove old plants that have stopped producing to eliminate shelters for insects and disease organisms. Nematodes can be a problem with vegetables. Remove and discard infected plants. Watch for signs of leaffooted bugs and spider mites. See April Problems p. 79.

Gummy stem blight is a fungal disease that mostly infects **cantaloupes, cucumbers**, and **watermelons**. Look for brown lesions on leaves and stems. If the stem is infected, the vine beyond the lesion will wither and die. Pull out and destroy infected vines. Remove and discard crop debris at the end of the growing season. Rotate with other vegetables other than vine crops or melons for two years. Avoid wetting the leaves when watering. Fungicides are available.

# SEPTEMBER

## HERBS & VEGETABLES

### PLANNING

Whether you garden year-round or hang up your hoe at summer's end, start tidying up the garden and take steps to build up the soil for next spring. Certain insects and diseases overwinter in plant debris. Time spent now removing plant stalks, debris, and mulch will eliminate winter havens for pests.

Consider the steps you will take to build the soil for next season. Planting a cover crop or "green manure" this fall that you will turn under in the spring is a great way to improve soil fertility and structure, hold valuable topsoil in place, improve water and nutrient retention in sandy soils, facilitate water and air movement in clay soils, attract earthworms and other beneficial critters, and suppress winter weeds. The most useful cover crop for home gardeners is one of these legumes: **crimson clover**; **Austrian winter pea**; **rough pea**; or **common**, **smooth**, or **hairy vetch**. They can be planted at least a month before the first killing frost, adding nitrogen as well as organic matter to the soil, and they are relatively inexpensive. Non-legume cover crops provide less nitrogen but more organic matter. Mainly grasses like **oats**, **buckwheat**, **rye**, and

barley, they are planted in late summer. In the spring, turn under your cover crop three weeks before planting your garden.

### PLANTING

Pot up **chives**, **parsley**, and other herbs and bring them into the house to extend the growing season.

Take cuttings or buy small plants of **rosemary**, **oregano**, **sage**, and other herbs. Grow them in 6-inch containers in a sunny window. Keep well watered; if possible, set them in a shallow tray containing pebbles and water to increase humidity. Opening the window on mild days can help.

In mild winter areas, plant **cilantro**, a winter annual whose seeds are called **coriander**.

Plant **beets**, **carrots**, **kale**, **lettuce**, **spinach**, **turnips**, and **radish**. Soak seed furrows well before sowing seed, and mulch lightly. Water daily to promote germination and growth.

All sorts of fall vegetables can go in right away, including transplants of **leaf lettuce**, **Swiss chard**, **broccoli**, **Brussels sprouts**, and **cabbage**. Plant **onion** sets anytime this month. Choose small, firm sets that are less than 3/4 inch in diameter for **bulb onions**. Larger sets can be used for **green onions**, since they tend

to "bolt" and produce a seed-stalk instead of a bulb.

Contact your regional Extension office for recommended varieties.

Plant **parsley** and perennial herbs such as **sage**, **thyme**, and **rosemary**, and annual herbs like **dill** and **coriander**.

### CARE

Harvest herbs to dry for winter use. Freeze **chives**. Take cuttings for a windowsill garden.

Start drying herbs such as **basil**, **oregano**, **sage**, **summer savory**, and **tarragon**.

Dig **sweet potatoes** before frost, being careful to avoid bruises and scrapes. Cure them for two or three weeks in the warmest room in the house to toughen the skin. Then store them where it is cool and dark. Every two weeks, cull out any showing signs of decay.

Harvest **luffa gourds** when they begin to turn brown, feel light and dry, and rattle when shaken. Let any that remain after the first killing freeze dry on the vine. To make useful, biodegradable scrubbers for you and your pots and pans:

- Soak in warm water until the sponge can be slipped out.
- Whiten sponges by dipping them into a 10 percent solution of household bleach.
- After thorough drying, store them in mesh bags.
- Discard worn-out sponges in your compost pile.

Harvest **winter squash** and **pumpkins** when fully mature but before they are damaged by frost. Cut the fruits from the vine, leaving a short piece of stem attached. They will keep for several months in a cool, dry basement.

Harvest **garlic** when the tops die. Cure the bulbs for six weeks in a warm, dry, shady, airy place, then move them to a cool, dry, airy spot.

After mid-month, pinch new blossoms off **tomatoes, peppers,** and **eggplants** to help smaller fruits mature before cold weather.

## WATERING

Keep watering. Many crops such as **corn, pepper, squash,** and **tomato** won't mature nicely if stressed due to lack of water.

## FERTILIZING

Apply fertilizer to vegetables as needed.

## HELPFUL HINTS FOR TOMATOES AND HERBS

- **Tomatoes** won't ripen when average daily temperatures fall below 65 degrees F. Then is the time to nip off all blossoms so plant nutrients flow to **tomatoes** already set. Not all green **tomatoes** ripen off the vine to an acceptable taste. Rescue from frost for later ripening only those showing a white or yellow star or a pink tinge at the blossom end. Delay ripening by storing at 50 to 60 degrees. Light is not needed, so put them where you can keep an eye on them.
- Use your microwave oven to dry herbs. Heat them between paper towels for one minute or until leaves are crisp. They'll keep their color and flavor stored in the dark in jars.

## PROBLEMS

Cucumber beetles, squash bugs, Colorado potato beetles, and European corn borers pass the winter in garden debris. Compost dead plants. This will limit your pest population next year to insects that migrate into the garden.

A compost bin is a good way to dispose of all sorts of garden debris.

# OCTOBER

## HERBS & VEGETABLES

### PLANNING

Envision an indoor winter herb garden. Most herbs do very well on a south-facing windowsill where they get plenty of bright, direct sunlight. **Sweet basil**, **lemon verbena**, **summer savory**, and **tarragon** are the exceptions. They either go dormant or shed their leaves excessively.

**Oregano**, **thyme**, **parsley**, and **sage** can all be grown in small pots and trimmed as needed for the kitchen. Pots of **rosemary** and **sweet bay** (*Laurus nobilis*) are equally valuable, though they need more space.

In the **onion** family, windowsill candidates include **chives**, **onion** sets, and **garlic**. The **onions** and **garlic** can be started in pots.

If you have only an east- or west-facing windowsill, try **mints** such as **peppermint**, **spearmint**, or **lemon balm**. Provided they are sheared regularly, these too make excellent houseplants.

If you find you have insect pests, use insecticidal soap spray or discard infested plants rather than use stronger pesticides indoors.

Indoor herbs grow best in a mixture of two parts potting soil to one part coarse sand or perlite. Setting the pots in trays lined with gravel will keep them from getting wet feet should you over-

With just a little effort, you can extend the season by covering your vegetaable bed.

water. Cool temperatures (60 degrees F.), especially at night, will keep herbs at their best.

### PLANTING

**Chives**, **coriander** (cilantro), **dill**, and **parsley** can be direct-sown in the fall in the milder areas of Alabama and Mississippi so they will grow during the fall and winter months. Also divide **chives**, **thyme**, **mint**, and **tarragon** when new growth emerges.

Throughout both states, plant **garlic** now for harvest in late summer next year. It likes a sunny, well-drained spot. Set bulb tips 2 inches beneath the surface.

Most herbs have lost their best flavor by now; discontinue drying for winter use. **Chives** and **parsley**, however, taste better

than ever in cool weather; use them lavishly (French cooks mince fresh **chives** and **parsley** together and let diners spoon desired amounts onto fresh vegetables or baked **potatoes**. The flavors complement each other and **parsley** cuts the oniony aftertaste of **chives**.)

Extend the gardening season well into the winter. **Lettuce**, **radish**, and **spinach** can all be grown through fall and even all winter in the protection of a cold frame. For more about cold frames, see November Planning p. 92. Buy transplants for quicker results. In cooler weather, insulate the outsides of the frame with banked soil or sawdust. Cover the top with sacks stuffed with straw or other insulation during cold nights.

## HELPFUL HINTS FOR SQUASH HARVEST

You can store **Hubbard squash** up to six months, **butternut** about three, and **acorn** up to two. Here's how:

• Pick when they've developed a deep color, an indication of maturity. Leave about one inch of stem.

• Handle the fruit gently. Damaged rinds shorten storage life.

• Cure the rind in full sun for 10 days. If frost is expected, cover the **squash**.

• Pack in single layers in a crate, with crumpled newspapers between the layers.

• Store them between 50 to 60 degrees F. **Squash** are injured by temperatures below this range.

---

You can still plant **onion** sets and **garlic** cloves now to mid-November in warmer parts of Alabama and Mississippi.

### CARE

Listen for frost warnings and be prepared to cover **tomatoes**, **eggplants**, **peppers**, and other tender vegetables from early cold. The weather often warms up again after the first frost, so this protection can prolong the harvest for weeks.

When there is a threat of frost, harvest your **cucumbers**, **eggplant, okra, pepper**, and **summer squash** before the fruits are frost-damaged if you can't protect them.

Bring in **tomatoes** for ripening when daytime temperatures are consistently below 65 degrees F. Pick only those fruits that have begun to change color.

Harvest **sweet potatoes** before frost as well as **gourds, pumpkins**, and **winter squash**. To store

**pumpkins**: Pick only solid, mature **pumpkins** of a deep orange color. Try not to injure the rind; decay-causing fungi attack through wounds. Dip them in a chlorine solution of 4 teaspoons bleach per gallon of water. Allow the fruit to dry, but do not rinse until ready to use. Cure them at room temperature for a week to harden the rind, then store in a cool place. They will keep about two months.

When you can no longer protect your plants, pull them and add them to the compost heap. Till or spade the soil in cleared areas to expose insects that are planning to overwinter. Then plant a hardy cover crop or mulch with shredded leaves, fresh manure, or spoiled hay to minimize winter erosion and provide nutrients for next year.

For bigger and better **Brussels sprouts**, pinch out the top of the plant when sprouts at the bottom are fully grown. The smaller, upper sprouts will grow larger than they would otherwise.

Thin **turnip** and **radish** plantings to give each root enough room to develop.

### WATERING

Cool-season vegetables perk up in the milder areas and grow vigorously. Water during dry spells and feed as necessary.

### PROBLEMS

Clean up the garden. Remove any diseased or insect-infested plant debris. That's where pests spend the winter. Cabbage loopers and cabbageworms are the bane of the fall garden. If your **cabbage** leaves look like lace, spray with BTK (sold as Dipel® or Thuricide®). This microbial insecticide will not harm humans but will put a stop to hungry caterpillars. Control aphids with insecticidal soap.

# NOVEMBER
## HERBS & VEGETABLES

### PLANNING

Map out a plan of action to cut back or close down gardening operations for the winter. Do not forget to:

• Bring in your rain gauge to avoid freeze damage.

• Drain and store water hoses to extend their lives.

• Protect your investment in garden tools. Clean them up. Repair or replace broken ones.

Plan for the spring. As soon as seed flats and pots are emptied of fall transplants, wash and sterilize them. Use a 10 percent solution of household bleach and dry them thoroughly before storing them.

This is also a time to consider building a cold frame. Think of it as a sort of halfway house for seedlings as they make their way from the windowsill or light table to the outdoors. Make the cold frame, which is basically a bottomless box, of wood, stone, or brick with a transparent or translucent cover. It's like a miniature unheated greenhouse.

Typically cold frames are rectangular in shape, 3 by 6 feet or so. The back of the cold frame should face north and should be 18 to 30 inches high. The front should be slightly lower, between 12 and 24 inches to allow enough headroom

### HELPFUL HINTS FOR SOIL

Cultivating the soil this month can leave it exposed throughout fall and winter and can result in problems with soil erosion. Since it's too late to plant a cover crop to hold the soil, apply a blanket of mulch such as shredded leaves or compost to keep the soil in place. To learn more about making compost, refer to Trees September Planning p. 224. You will find information about recycling leaves and other yard trimmings.

for the plants inside. Tilt the cover to the south by sloping the sides about 1 inch per foot. More adventurous gardeners can even add an auto-matic opener to the cover. These devices lift the cover automatically as the temperature rises during the day and gradually close it as the evening temperatures fall.

### PLANTING

Grow leafy vegetables such as **lettuce, endive, arugula, Chinese cabbage**, and **spinach** in a cold frame or beneath a row cover for harvesting all winter long.

Continue enjoying fresh-picked cool-weather crops as they mature.

Harvest **kale** by picking just a few leaves from each plant; this will encourage continued production of new leaves.

### CARE

A light mulch of shredded leaves or straw on **carrots**, **turnips**, and other root vegetables will help protect against freezing. Pick **tomatoes** when frost is predicted and store in a single layer in a cool location. Harvest **broccoli** while the heads are still compact.

### GROOMING

Remove **asparagus** foliage after frost kills it.

A cold frame can also be a very simple frame with a plastic window.

92

# DECEMBER

## HERBS & VEGETABLES

 PLANNING

Take inventory of your seed collection. Decide what to save, trade, or toss out. To decide what stays and what goes, ask yourself:

• How old is the seed? Seeds have a limited shelf life and remain viable (capable of germinating) for a certain period of time. Here are the ballpark ages of several vegetable seeds that when stored under cool, dry conditions should be expected to produce a good stand of healthy seedlings.

1 year or less: **onion, parsley, parsnip,** and **salsify**

2 years: **corn, pepper,** and **okra**

3 years: **bean, southern peas (cowpeas),** and **peas**

4 years: **beet, fennel, mustard, pumpkin, watermelon, rutabaga, squash, Swiss chard, tomato,** and **turnip**

5 years: **Brussels sprouts, cabbage, cauliflower, collards, eggplant, radish, cantaloupe,** and **spinach**

• Is the seed viable? Perform a simple germination test. Take two or three layers of moistened paper towel and lay ten to twenty seeds on the surface. Gently roll up the towels enclosing the seeds and put the roll inside a plastic bag. Label with the variety and date of sowing and place the bag in a location where the temperature is between 70 and 80 degrees F. After two or three days, unroll the paper towels and examine the seeds, and do so daily thereafter. At the end of three weeks, total up the number of seeds that have germinated. If ten of the twenty have sprouted, expect a 50 percent germination rate when you sow the remainder.

• If you collected seed, is the seed the actual variety you wanted to save? If the vegetables are self-pollinated like **beans, peas,** and nonhybrid **tomatoes,** expect to grow true-to-type varieties. Expect surprises, however, when planting the seeds from insect- or wind-pollinated varieties. Cross-pollination will occur between different varieties of insect-pollinated vegetables such as **cucumber, melon, squash,** or **pumpkin.** The same goes for wind-pollinated **beets, sweet corn, spinach,** and **Swiss chard.** You may want to discard these seeds.

• Was the seed collected from a hybrid? Hybrid or $F_1$ hybrid seed is the offspring of a cross made between two parent varieties. If you want the original hybrid, discard these seeds. The offspring from an $F_1$ hybrid will be a mixture of traits, most of which will be inferior to the original parent.

• Do you have any seeds or varieties that a fellow gardener would be willing to swap for? In the eyes of some gardeners, a "Mickey Mantle" or "Joe DiMaggio" could take the form of a 'Sweet Baby Blue' **corn** or a 'Super Italian Paste' **tomato.** Perhaps you can save these seeds and trade them for something else.

 PLANTING

Sow **lettuce, endive, kale,** and other greens in cold frames for winter use.

 CARE

Continue to harvest **chives, cilantro,** and **parsley.** Protect winter greens from hard freezes with a fabric row cover or with plastic tunnels—plastic stretched over metal hoops. **Brussels sprouts, broccoli, mustard, cabbage, turnips,** and most **lettuces** will be damaged by a hard freeze (more than six hours below 26 degrees F.).

# LAWNS

You can achieve a lawn that looks good and is functional and still have your weekends free if you understand the lawn's needs. Remember, each maintenance practice influences another. Fertilizer affects how often you mow. Your mowing height affects watering and the number of weeds.

In Alabama and Mississippi, we can grow a few cool-season, cool-climate grasses well and all the warm-season, warm-climate grasses. Cool-season grasses (Kentucky bluegrass, perennial ryegrass, tall fescue, and creeping red fescue) grow well during the cool months (60 to 75 degrees F.). They will grow best in northern parts of Alabama and Mississippi.

Warm-season grasses (bahiagrass, Bermudagrass, centipedegrass, carpetgrass, St. Augustine or "Charleston grass", and zoysiagrass) thrive when temperatures are 80 to 95 degrees F. They go dormant and turn brown when the weather cools. Most can be grown throughout the states and are the only sane choice in the southern halves of Alabama and Mississippi.

## COOL-SEASON GRASSES

Kentucky bluegrass (*Poa pratensis*) is often the standard by which other grasses are judged. It has shiny leaves with a distinct boat-shaped tip and spreads by underground stems called rhi-

zomes to form a thick lawn. It's often used on athletic fields farther north because it withstands foot traffic and recovers rapidly from injury. Kentucky bluegrass tolerates full or half-day sun, and does best farther north and at the higher elevations in the Smoky Mountains. The price for its beauty is lots of water, fertilizer, and time. It is *not* adapted to Alabama or Mississippi.

Tall fescue (*Festuca arundinacea*) forms clumps and can be grown in the northern halves of the states. It's the best cool-season grass for us. Kentucky 31 is a pasture-type tall fescue that's been replaced by more attractive cultivars referred to as "turf-type" tall fescues. Turf-types have a fine leaf blade. They're darker green, thicker, and tolerate shade better than Kentucky 31. Tall fescue lawns thin out, yellow, and become "clumpy" after summer dry spells and may need reseeding in the fall. If you want a cool-season lawn, that's just something you'll have to live with.

Often, these two turfgrasses are mixed together in packaged lawn seed. Kentucky bluegrass contributes wear tolerance while tall fescue contributes drought tolerance in areas where it grows well. Fine fescues are often combined with Kentucky bluegrass or in a three-way mixture that also includes tall fescue (because of its exceptional shade tolerance). You'll find all of these mixed together in packages at your local mass merchandiser, but for the best luck with cool-season grass in Alabama or Mississippi, avoid these national seed mixes and go with a tall fescue or a blend of tall fescue types.

Perennial ryegrass (*Lolium perenne*) and annual ryegrass (*Lolium multiflorum*) are used to overseed dormant warm-season lawns, to provide green cover when the warm-season grasses are brown. Perennial ryegrass is unreliable as a permanent lawn because of its susceptibility to diseases in hot weather.

## WARM-SEASON GRASSES

Common Bermudagrass (*Cynodon dactylon*) grows rapidly from seed to form a lawn in less than a year. It's extremely drought tolerant, rejoices in hot weather, handles wear-and-tear, and tolerates salt spray. However, it does poorly in shade and is very aggressive. Bermudagrass spreads by both above- and belowground runners, making weeding flower and shrub beds an endless battle (hence its other common names of wiregrass and devilgrass). Except for wide-open spaces where sodding is too expensive, avoid using common Bermudagrass.

Hybrid Bermudagrasses are more refined. Whereas common Bermudagrass produces an open turf with unsightly seedheads, the improved selections— Tifway (Tifton 419) and Tifway II— have finer leaves and darker green color, and are thicker. They also require more frequent fertilizing and mowing. Midiron and Vamont are coarse-leaved, cold-tolerant cultivars. Tifgreen (Tifton 328), Tifgreen II, and Tifdwarf are used on golf courses, football fields, and other recreational areas. It is salt tolerant and can be used along the coast.

Centipedegrass (*Eremochloa ophiuroides*) makes a dense lawn requiring little mowing and fertilizing in central and southern regions. It has a light green color, grows slowly, and can be used in full sun to part shade anywhere except the northern parts of Alabama or Mississippi. Centipedegrass produces aboveground runners called stolons and can be controlled near flower beds and walkways. It is easiest started from sod, but can be plugged or even started from seed, which you'll find expensive compared to common Bermudagrass. Although centipede requires little effort, it has no tolerance for too much fertilizer, succumbing to a disorder called "centipede decline." The grass may fail to green-up in the spring or die in late spring or summer. See the May Helpful Hints p. 109.

# CHAPTER FOUR

Zoysiagrass (*Zoysia* spp.) forms a dense lawn in full sun or very light shade. In winter it turns a beautiful beige. Zoysiagrass grows very slowly, which is why it is almost exclusively started from sod. It's also very drought tolerant. Although it browns quickly in dry weather, it greens up after rain. Also, it recovers slowly from injury. However, the slow growth is an advantage in that the lawn is easy to contain and won't work you to death. Zoysiagrass can be bad about forming thatch (a spongy accumulation of dead, decaying plant matter on the soil surface), but you can manage this by mowing properly and avoiding too much fertilizer. For more information on thatch, see January Helpful Hints p. 101. Mowing the tough, wiry leaves requires a sharp blade. The prettiest "finish" comes from mowing with a reel-type mower, but a good rotary mower is most common and perfectly acceptable.

Two popular zoysiagrass cultivars are 'Meyer', often advertised as "super" grass. It has good cold tolerance and spreads more rapidly than most zoysias, but has a coarse texture. 'Emerald' zoysia is fine textured, darker green, and more shade tolerant than 'Meyer', though less winter hardy.

St. Augustinegrass (*Stenotaphrum secundatum*) or Charleston grass will grow in partial shade and tolerates salt spray. It is recommended for the southern parts of Alabama and Mississippi and is the best choice along the beach. This fast-growing grass has large flat stems, broad coarse leaves, attractive blue-green color, and forms a fairly dense turf. It spreads along the ground with aboveground stolons. Although it's an aggressive grower, it can be easily confined with strong edging.

When fertilized or watered frequently, St. Augustinegrass can become thatchy. Some cultivars are cold-sensitive and often suffer in the few areas where people have used it in the central and north central parts of Alabama and Mississippi. A major insect pest of St. Augustinegrass is chinch bugs, whose feeding causes the leaves to wilt and turn brown; resistant cultivars are available. For more information on chinch bugs, see May Problems p. 109.

Carpetgrass (*Axonopus affinis*) is ideally suited for wet, poorly drained, acid (pH 4.5 to 5.5) soils where ease of establishment and care are more important than quality. It is only occasionally used in acidic, piney flatwoods with spots of poor drainage along the coast; mow at 1 to 2 inches height.

## STARTING A LAWN

Cool-season grasses can be established using seed or sod. Often, they are mixes of more than one type to take advantage of the strengths of each. Warm-season grasses can be started using seed, sod, or grass pieces called sprigs or stolons. But most are started from sod because it creates an instant lawn that is much easier to manage. Also, warm-season grasses are rarely mixes because their habits, textures, and characteristics are so different that they don't mix well. Whatever method you choose, follow these steps prior to planting:

1. Choose a turfgrass that fits your management style. For a good guide, look around at the lawns in your area and check with your regional Extension office.

2. Take a soil sample and have it tested for pH and fertility through your Extension office for recommendations on how much fertilizer or lime is needed.

3. Prepare the site by killing weeds with a non-selective herbicide such as Roundup® (glyphosate).

4. If you have heavy clay or very sandy soils, spread a 1- to 2-inch layer of organic matter such as compost over the soil.

5. Till the soil to a depth of 6 to 8 inches and thoroughly work in organic materials.

6. If lime is recommended by the soil test, mix it into the top 3 to 5 inches of soil.

7. Right before planting, broadcast fertilizer and lightly rake it in.

Lawns can be started for seed or sod; the choice is yours. Sodding provides an "instant" lawn while seeding is generally less expensive.

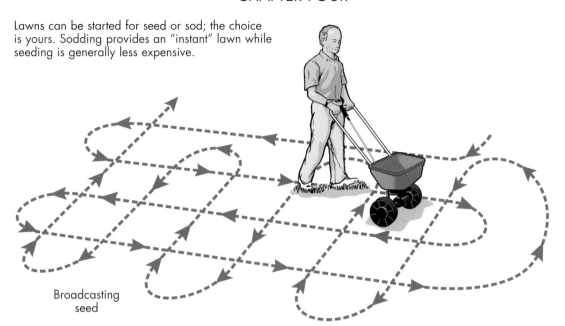

Broadcasting
seed

The best time for seeding cool-season grasses is September to mid-October. Warm-season common Bermudagrass can be seeded from April through July. Here's how to seed:

1. Apply the seed with a drop-type or rotary spreader to get uniform distribution. Sow the required amount in two directions at right angles (half in each direction) for good coverage.

2. Lightly rake the seeds into the top $1/4$ inch of soil. Then roll the seedbed with a lightweight or empty lawn roller (water-ballast roller) to ensure good seed-to-soil contact. You can rent these.

3. Mulch to prevent soil erosion, retain moisture, and prevent crusting of the soil surface. The most commonly used mulch is straw—it's important to use weed-free straw. Use enough weed-free straw so that one-half to three-quarters of the bare ground is covered. If it's not spread too thickly, straw can be left to decompose.

4. Water the lawn after seeding. Water lightly and often enough to keep the seedbed moist but not waterlogged until the plants can develop a sufficient root system. This may mean watering a few times a day for several weeks until the seedlings emerge and become established. As the seedlings mature and their root systems develop, water more deeply and less frequently.

5. Mow the lawn when the grass is one-third higher than the desired height. For example, if you want to maintain your lawn at 3 inches, mow the grass when it reaches a height of 4 inches.

Sodding gives you an instant lawn. The sod of cool-season grasses can be installed anytime during the year when the soil isn't frozen. Warm-season grasses are ideally sodded when temperatures remain above 55 degrees F. for sev-

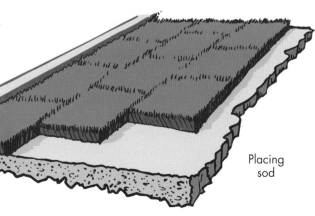

Placing
sod

eral weeks (usually April through September), but professional landscapers sometimes sow dormant grass in cooler weather. Sodding in the summer will require plenty of water and attention to help the sod cope with the stressful hot, humid weather. To avoid placing turf roots in contact with dry, hot soil, dampen the soil just before laying sod. Refer to March Planting p. 104 for the step-by-step approach.

Warm-season grasses can also be plugged or sprigged from April through July. Prepare the soil as you would for seeding. Plugging involves planting small pieces of sod—plugs—about 2 inches in diameter or larger on 6-inch or 1-foot centers. Plugs can be purchased in trays or cut from sod with a spade or axe. Centipedegrass, St. Augustinegrass, and zoysiagrass are sometimes plugged by digging a hole, putting in the plug, and then tamping it into place. You can even repair bare spots by cutting out plugs from your own lawn. Water immediately after planting to ensure rooting into the prepared soil. Water often enough so the plugs don't dry out. Deeper, thorough watering can then be done as the roots begin to penetrate the soil.

Sprigging is the planting of sprigs—aboveground and belowground grass parts called stolons and rhizomes. They can be purchased by the bushel or obtained by mechanically shredding or hand-shredding a piece of sod. In small areas the sprigs are planted in rows (called "space planting"); for larger areas, broadcast over the prepared area and cover lightly with soil. It's important that part of the sprig protrudes above the soil surface and part of it is buried or "set." Water lightly and frequently so the sprigs don't dry out. The goal is to water often enough to keep the seedbed moist but not waterlogged, until the plants can develop sufficient root systems to take advantage of deeper, less frequent watering. Weed control is a huge challenge with sprigs and plugs because weeds will sprout in the bare ground.

## WATERING

New lawns should be watered frequently to keep the top 1/2 inch of soil moist until it becomes established. Gradually cut back on the frequency of watering, but water longer to encourage deep

## Suggested Mowing Heights*

| Lawn Grass | Mowing Height (inches)+ |
| --- | --- |
| Common Bermudagrass | 1 to 2 |
| Hybrid Bermudagrass | 3/4 to 1 1/2 |
| Centipedegrass | 1 1/2 to 2 |
| Ryegrass (overseeded) | 1 1/2 to 2 1/2 |
| St. Augustinegrass | 2 1/2 to 4 |
| Semi-dwarf St. Augustinegrass | 1 1/2 to 2 1/2 |
| Tall Fescue | 2 1/2 to 4 |
| Zoysiagrass | 1 1/2 to 2 |

+Measure the height of the mower on a level surface and adjust it to the proper height. If you don't like to mow, choose zoysia or centipede, both of which grow slowly and won't need mowing other than once every 10 to 14 days.

rooting. A lawn is considered established when it's grown enough to need mowing three times.

Established lawns should be watered to a depth of 6 to 8 inches to encourage deep rooting. This can be accomplished by applying 1 inch of water per week to clay soils. (It takes 640 gallons of water to apply 1 inch of water to 1,000 square feet of lawn.) Since clay soils absorb water slowly, you may have to start and stop to allow the water to soak in. Wait a half-hour between waterings until you've applied the full inch. Refer to July Planning p. 112 to learn how to calibrate your sprinkler.

## FERTILIZING

The kind and amount of fertilizer you apply should be based on soil-test results. Although lawns require nitrogen, phosphorus, and potassium in the greatest quantities, the fertilizer recommendation is based on nitrogen, the nutrient that's most likely to be deficient in the soil.

Depending on the grass type, the level of maintenance, and overall lawn quality, apply either 1/2 or 1 pound of nitrogen per 1,000 square feet of lawn area. Rely on a trustworthy local garden center for the best formula for your lawn. Formulas will vary according to grass type. St. Augustine-grass formulas usually have lots of nitrogen and extra iron for good greening. Centipede formulas will by very low in phosphorus. Fescue will need fertilizer in the fall with plenty of nitrogen, but warm-season grasses like Bermuda will need low nitrogen and high potassium formulas to help winter hardiness.

Depending on your spreader and type of fertilizer, you may have to calibrate your spreader. Applying too much can be hazardous to your lawn and the environment. See February Planning p. 102 to learn how to calibrate your fertilizer spreader.

Apply the fertilizer uniformly with a drop-type or rotary spreader. Apply half of the total amount in one direction and the other half at right angles to the first to apply it uniformly. Keep a record of the total amount of fertilizer applied over the year.

## GENERAL FERTILIZER GUIDELINE

Suitable months for applying fertilizer to cool-season lawns are March, September, and November; for warm-season lawns, April through August, making the first application at least two or three weeks after the lawn greens up (according to soil-test results). The total yearly amount may be 1 to 3 pounds of nitrogen per 1,000 square feet—the higher rates are suited for lawn owners interested in higher quality and more maintenance. Centipede is the exception; this low-maintenance turfgrass does not respond well to excessive use of fertilizer, especially nitrogen. Apply no more than 2 pounds of nitrogen per 1,000 square feet per year.

## SUGGESTED MOWING HEIGHTS

Newly established lawns should be mowed when the grass is one-third higher than the desired height. For example, if you want to maintain your tall fescue lawn at 3 inches, mow the grass when it reaches a height of 4 inches. Measure the height of the mower on a level surface and adjust it to the proper height.

## PEST CONTROL

The secret to thwarting pests is to work with nature. Create conditions for the grass to thrive and resist invasion from weeds and attacks from insects and diseases. As they say: "An ounce of prevention is worth a pound of cure." If problems occur, identify the problem before taking action. If you need help, contact your Cooperative Extension Service.

# JANUARY
## LAWNS

### PLANNING

If you're planning on hiring a lawn-care service company, be realistic about what you expect from your lawn and from the company. Here are a few pointers:

1. Know what services you want. Get several estimates. Ask neighbors and friends for recommendations.

2. Obtain a written service agreement. Find out if the service is automatically renewed each year and request an annual written confirmation. Ask if there are penalties should you cancel your service agreement.

3. Ask if the company is licensed and insured. Don't be afraid to ask for proof.

4. Ask if the company is a member of a trade association, such as the Professional Lawn Care Association of America. Trade associations help keep their members informed of the latest technical information and the safe use of pesticides.

5. Pesticides and other lawn-care chemicals should be used only as needed. Ask the company what chemicals it plans to use.

6. A company should always provide advance notice of chemical applications so lawn furniture and toys can be removed.

7. Check with the Better Business Bureau to see if there have been any complaints lodged against the company. Ask the company for references from local customers.

### PLANTING

Sod of cool-season grasses can be installed anytime the soil isn't frozen. Delay planting warm-season grasses until the air temperature stays consistently above 60 degrees F.

### WATERING

Dormant and overseeded lawns may need watering if it's been dry, warm, and windy. See February for cool-season sod care.

### FERTILIZING

Do not fertilize this month.

### MOWING

If mowing is necessary, remove no more than one-third of the grass height with a sharp mower blade. Maintain **ryegrass-overseeded Bermudagrass** lawns at a height of 1 inch. Dormant lawns do not have to be mowed.

Plan to service your mower yourself or take it to a lawn repair shop this month or next. A few of the items to include:

- Air filter—clean or replace it if it's damaged.
- Spark plug—clean it or replace it if it's cracked.
- Oil—check to see that it's filled to the right level. Change the oil as recommended by the manufacturer.
- Mower blade—replace it if it's chipped, cracked, or bent. Maintain a sharp mower blade to cut the grass cleanly, which improves its look and ensures rapid healing and regrowth. A dull mower blade tears the grass. If the blades on your reel-type mower require special equipment to sharpen them (refer to your instruction manual), consider leaving this task to a professional.
- Tires—examine the tires for wear; replace them if necessary.
- Screws and bolts—check for loose screws and bolts on the handle controls and the motor now and throughout the season.

If you do-it-yourself, be safe. Disconnect the wire from the spark plug for safety and keep the manual within reach.

### PROBLEMS

Handpull winter annuals such as common chickweed and henbit. Pull wild garlic when the soil is moist to remove the entire plant. If you leave the bulb behind, it will resprout.

# THATCH CONTROL

If you cut a pie-shaped wedge of sod from your lawn, you may find a layer of thatch. Thatch is a dense, spongy collection of living and dead grass stems and roots lying between the soil surface and green grass leaves in established lawns. **St. Augustinegrass**, **hybrid Bermudagrass**, and **zoysiagrass** tend to develop thatch at a faster rate than **centipedegrass**.

Thatch originates from old stems, stolons (aboveground stems), roots, and rhizomes (belowground stems) shed by grasses as new plant parts grow. Unlike grass clippings, which decay quickly, these sloughed-off parts contain high levels of lignin (hard-to-decompose cell wall material) and decay very slowly, collecting on the soil surface faster than they decompose.

A shallow thatch layer (under $1/2$ inch) actually benefits the lawn.

• Thatch acts as a natural cushion, enabling the lawn to endure wear and tear.

• It works as a mulch, retaining moisture and insulating the soil from temperature extremes.

Unfortunately, thatch can become destructive, affecting the lawn's health, vigor, and appearance. It causes problems when it exceeds $1/2$ inch in thickness. The grass develops roots within the thatch, where it's unable to obtain adequate moisture and nutrients. The thatch also provides a habitat for destructive insects and diseases.

To remove thick thatch layers, use a dethatching rake for small areas or a vertical mower for larger lawns; you can rent these. A vertical mower with revolving, straight, fixed blades is a good choice. The blades cut into the thatch layer, lifting it to the surface where it can be raked up and added to the compost pile. This is done at the beginning of the growing season—fall for cool-season lawns and mid- to late spring for warm-season grasses. To reduce the accumulation of thatch, follow these practices:

• Fertilize according to soil-test recommendations and avoid applying excessive amounts of nitrogen.

• Mow your lawn at the proper height and mow frequently.

• Aerify your lawn with a machine that creates "pores" in the lawn with spoons or tines mounted on a drum or reel. As the machine rolls over the lawn, it removes cores of soil. The earthen cores are deposited on the lawn and contain microorganisms that help to break down the thatch. You can rent these aerators, too. Like dethatching, this is done at the beginning of the growing season to give grasses time to recuperate.

• Monitor the soil pH and keep it at the recommended level for your particular turfgrass. Acidic soils hamper the activity of earthworms, insects, and microbes involved in breaking down thatch.

• If you use pesticides, use them sparingly and locally to control specific pests, minimizing the destruction of earthworms and other thatch-decomposers.

• Do not burn thatch from dormant lawns. This can harm or kill the grass, and is a fire hazard.

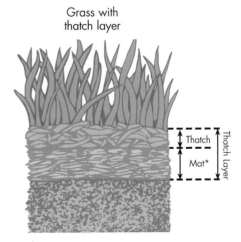

Grass with thatch layer

Thatch

Mat*

Thatch Layer

*Old thatch and soil

# FEBRUARY

## LAWNS

### PLANNING

Before you fertilize your lawn in the next few months, plan to calibrate your spreader. Calibrating your spreader enables you to apply the right amount of fertilizer to your lawn. It helps you avoid the mistake of applying too much, which can harm the plants and the environment, or too little and not achieve the results you expect.

### PLANTING

Sod of cool-season grasses can be installed whenever the soil is not frozen. Sodding gives you an instant lawn in the shortest time compared to seeding. See March Planting p. 104. Delay planting warm-season grasses until the daytime temperature stays consistently above 60 degrees F.

### WATERING

Moisten newly sodded areas of cool-season lawns so the sod will "knit" into the soil. Water immediately after sodding to wet the soil to a depth of 3 or 4 inches. Don't let the soil dry out until the sod has "knitted" or rooted into the soil. Observe established lawns for signs of drought stress and apply an inch of water per week (in the absence of precipitation).

For warm-season grasses, dormant and overseeded lawns may have to be watered if it's been dry, warm, and windy.

### FERTILIZING

Do not fertilize cool-season or dormant lawns at this time. Overseeded **Bermudagrass** and **zoysiagrass** lawns can be fertilized very lightly this month, but only if needed. Do not apply a fertilizer containing phosphorus if adequate levels are already present in the soil.

Rotary

There are basically
two types of spreaders—
rotary or drop.

### MOWING

Mow **tall fescue** between 2 and 3 inches high. Overseeded **ryegrass** lawns maintained at 1 inch should be mowed when the grass is 1 1/2 inches tall.

### PROBLEMS

Two basic lawn management practices that can "make or break" a lawn—opening it up to weed infestation—are mowing and fertilizing. Always mow with a sharp blade at the proper height for your lawn grass. Follow the rule of thumb of never mowing more than one-third the grass height at any one time. Proper fertilizing, the right amount at the right time, is another basic practice that is critical to lawn health.

Drop

# CALIBRATING A ROTARY OR CYCLONE SPREADER

The easiest way to spread the correct amount of fertilizer is to use a fertilizer and spreader of the same brand, so that the product directions are written with their specific spreader in mind and all the calibration is built into the directions. However, you can use any spreader and calibrate it yourself according to these steps for a rotary or cyclone spreader.

1. Gather these materials: rotary spreader (make sure parts are functional); bucket; hand-held calculator; tape measure at least 50 feet long; scale for determining weight; fertilizer.

2. Unlike a drop-type spreader that distributes a uniform amount of fertilizer across its width, a rotary spreader slings the fertilizer out in a wide, uneven pattern. More fertilizer falls in the center and less at the edges. About two-thirds of the application width—called the "effective width"—receive a uniform amount of fertilizer.

Here's how to measure the effective width of your spreader:

• Find a hard surface where you can measure the width of the fertilizer pattern.

• Place a small amount of fertilizer into the spreader's hopper.

• Walk a short distance at a regular pace and then stop.

• Measure the application width of the fertilizer band. Multiply the width by $2/3$ or 0.66. For example, if the fertilizer is cast out in a 12-foot-wide swathe, the effective width is 8 feet (0.66 x 12 feet). This 8-foot-wide band receives an even amount of fertilizer. An area 2 feet on either side of this band receives less fertilizer.

• Sweep up the fertilizer and return it to the bag.

Knowing the effective width of your spreader makes the rest of the calibration process easier.

3. When you're ready to fertilize your lawn, find a flat portion to calibrate the amount delivered by your spreader. Mark off an area that measures 1,000 square feet. In our example, the effective width is 8 feet—so the length must be 125 feet to create a 1,000-square-foot test area (1,000 square feet/8 feet).

4. To apply 1 pound of nitrogen per 1,000 square feet with a 16-4-8 fertilizer, you need to spread 6 pounds of fertilizer (100/16). To deliver it uniformly to avoid any skips, make two passes. Apply half the total amount in one direction and the other half at right angles to the first. Calibrate the spreader based on one-half the application rate or 3 pounds of 16-4-8 fertilizer.

5. Weigh some fertilizer, say about 10 pounds, and put it in the hopper with the spreader in the "closed" position.

6. Set your spreader according to the fertilizer label which may specify the setting. If it's not listed, start at a low setting to avoid applying too much.

7. Start walking about 10 feet behind the starting point you marked earlier. Open the spreader when you reach the starting line, walking at a "normal" pace.

8. Walk at a normal pace and close the hopper when you cross the finish line.

9. Weigh the remaining fertilizer in the spreader and subtract the final weight from the starting weight to determine how much fertilizer you applied over the 1,000-square-foot area. For example, if you poured in 10 pounds of fertilizer at the start and 8 pounds were left over, then you spread 2 pounds of fertilizer over the 1,000-square-foot area.

10. At the setting you tested, you applied less nitrogen than you need. So go back to step 6 and repeat the process with the spreader set at a higher setting. Move your calibration test site to another part of the lawn to avoid applying too much fertilizer to that area. Once you've found the correct setting that applies 3 pounds of 16-4-8 per 1,000 square feet, record it in your gardening journal for future reference.

To calibrate a drop-type spreader, follow the same steps. To make it easier, however, collect the fertilizer in a "catch pan" secured beneath the spreader openings. This catch pan is a V- or box-shaped trough made of cardboard or a piece of aluminum guttering. Weigh the fertilizer after the run to see how much was applied.

# MARCH

## LAWNS

## PLANNING

The first bagging mowers made their debut on American lawns in the early 1950s. But you should really plan to recycle your grass clippings as you mow by returning them to the lawn. This saves time, energy, and money, and is a way of fertilizing your lawn. Grass clippings contain about 4 percent nitrogen, $1/2$ to 1 percent phosphorus, 2 to 3 percent potassium, and smaller amounts of other essential plants nutrients. This is basically a 4-1-3 fertilizer.

## PLANTING

Wait until next month to plant warm-season grasses.

If you didn't seed thin or bare patches of cool-season grasses last fall, which is the best time to seed them, you can attempt to seed now; however, be prepared to accept some losses. Cool-season grasses prefer cool temperatures, especially for seed germination, and the longer you delay seeding, the less time the seedlings will have to become established before the arrival of summer's heat. And be mindful that what you do for your lawn grass seedlings will also benefit emerging weeds. Even if you get a fairly good stand, you'll have a

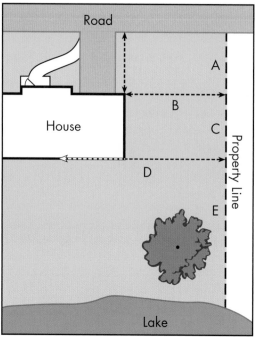

Road

House

A

B

C

D

E

Property Line

Lake

If you haven't measured your property, do so in order to estimate the amount of sod you'll need to order.

$A \times B = X$
$B \times C = Y$
$D \times E = Z$
$X + Y + Z =$

Total Square Feet

long road ahead to keep the young lawn alive during the summer months.

If you can justify the expense, install sod; you'll need plenty of water to help it through the summer. To sod a lawn, follow these steps:

1. Measure the area to be sodded and calculate the amount of sod you'll need. Rent a tiller and other needed equipment.

2. Schedule delivery only after you prepare the bed and are ready to install. Insist on prompt delivery after the sod is harvested.

3. Keep the sod in a shady place to prevent it from drying out. Lay it as soon as possible.

4. Start sodding from the longest straight edge such as a driveway, curb, or sidewalk.

Stagger the blocks or strips as if laying bricks. Butt the sod firmly and stretch each piece so it lies flat against the soil. In dry, hot weather, lightly wet the surface before laying and water each small area well immediately (within one hour) after laying. Use a knife, spade, or sharpened concrete trowel to trim the pieces.

5. On steep slopes, lay the sod across the angle of the slope; it may be necessary to peg the sod to the soil with homemade wooden stakes to keep it from sliding.

6. Immediately after laying the sod, tamp down the sod or roll the lawn perpendicular to the direction the sod was laid with a lawn roller (water-ballast roller), which can be rented. This eliminates any air spaces between

the soil and the sod and ensures good sod-to-soil contact.

7. Water immediately afterwards to wet the soil below to a depth of 3 or 4 inches. Don't let the soil dry out until the sod has "knitted" or rooted into the soil. More thorough watering can then be done as the roots begin to penetrate the soil.

8. Start mowing when the sod is firmly rooted, securely in place, and the grass has grown an inch taller than its recommended height.

## WATERING

Do not allow newly sodded cool-season lawns to dry out. When the sod has "knitted" or rooted into the soil, reduce the frequency of irrigation and water deeply as the roots begin to penetrate the soil.

Dormant warm-season lawns may need to be watered, especially if warm, windy weather prevails.

## FERTILIZING

Wait until next month to fertilize **hybrid Bermudagrass** and **zoysiagrass**. **Tall fescue** and cool-season mixes can be fertilized this month according to the results of a soil test. If the lawn has good color and vigor,

however, postpone any cool-season fertilizer applications until the fall.

## MOWING

There are two kinds of mowers: rotary mowers and reel mowers. Rotary mowers have a whirling blade that cuts the grass at high speeds. It can be used to mow lawns down to an inch. Reel mowers have a series of blades that cut the grass like scissors. The blades press against a bar at the bottom to slice the grass, giving the lawn a highly finished look. With either type of mower, follow the "proper mowing" described in May Planning p. 108.

## PROBLEMS

Mole crickets are serious lawn pests in the sandy soils along the coast. If you had mole crickets last year, look for areas where they may again be active. Their offspring will be vulnerable in June and July, when you can control the young nymphs with insecticides. If you delay, they are almost impossible to get rid of because the bigger, older mole crickets are hard to kill.

Brown patch attacks warm-season grasses in the spring as the lawn emerges from dormancy, or in the fall as they're

going dormant. Collect infected clippings and compost them. Avoid overfertilizing, especially with nitrogen during the fall or spring. Water during dry spells to keep the grass healthy, but avoid overwatering. If needed, fungicides can protect healthy grass from becoming infected.

Apply a "crabgrass preventer" or pre-emergent herbicide to control summer annuals such as crabgrass and goosegrass. A pre-emergent herbicide forms a barrier at or just below the soil surface and kills the emerging seedlings. Crabgrass seed germinates when the day temperatures reach 65 to 70 degrees F. for four or five days, coinciding with the time **forsythia** blooms. Goosegrass germinates about three or four weeks after crabgrass.

Prevent winter annuals such as common chickweed and henbit from going to seed by hand-pulling, mowing off the flowers, or spot-treating with a broadleaf herbicide. Identify weeds after they emerge to select an appropriate post-emergent herbicide. Post-emergent herbicides are most effective when the weeds are young and growing, with air temperatures between 65 and 85 degrees F. Be sure the herbicide is labeled for use on your lawn and your lawn has fully greened up and is actively growing.

# APRIL

## LAWNS

 **PLANNING**

Write in your journal when you fertilized the lawn and the amount you applied. Document insect, disease, or weed problems, and pesticide applications. Include your soil-test report. Your journal can become a teaching tool, especially when you need the assistance of a lawn-service company or County Extension agent to help you diagnose a problem.

 **PLANTING**

For warm-season lawns, repair bare patches or replant large areas when the average daytime temperatures stay above 60 degrees F. If the lawn is overrun with weeds or is beyond simple patching, you can renovate this month or in May.

Renovation is the step you should take before having to completely overhaul the lawn. Figure out how your lawn spiraled into decline, then follow these steps:

1. If your soil hasn't been tested in the past two or three years, submit a sample to your county Cooperative Extension Service office.

2. Eliminate undesirable weeds or lawn grasses. Handpull or use a herbicide. Some herbicides require a waiting period of four to six weeks before seeding, so plan accordingly if you are patching a cool-season lawn with seed or trying **common Bermuda** or **centipede** from seed. Do not apply a pre-emergence herbicide.

3. Mow the area at the lowest setting and collect the clippings. If a thick thatch layer is present (greater than $1/2$ inch in thickness), rake it out by hand. For large areas, rent a vertical mower. This machine has revolving blades that lift the thatch layer to the surface. Set the machine so the blades cut into the upper $1/4$ to $1/2$ inch of soil. Rake up the debris and compost it. Seeds falling into the furrows are more likely to germinate.

4. If the soil is compacted, use a power-driven aerifier or core aerator to improve air and water movement (see September Planning p. 116). Core in several directions. Use the vertical mower to break up the cores.

5. Seed the bare areas with a rotary or drop-type spreader, applying half the total amount in one direction and the other half at right angles to the first. Rake the seed into the soil to ensure good seed-to-soil contact. (See if your equipment rental dealer has a slit seeder—a machine that cuts furrows and deposits the seed in the soil.)

6. Cover the area with clean straw to conserve moisture and enhance germination.

7. Fertilize the lawn one month after renovating.

To renovate a cool-season lawn, if you can justify the expense, install sod; you'll need plenty of water to help it through the summer. Avoid seeding cool-season grass except areas where you are simply trying to thicken a thin lawn; then sow early in the month. Getting your lawn through the summer will be a challenge. If you can delay seeding until fall, then wait.

 **WATERING**

Newly seeded, plugged, or sodded lawns should be watered frequently. As the seedlings emerge and the sod "knits" into the soil, gradually water more deeply and less often.

Water established lawns as needed. One inch of water per week is adequate.

 **FERTILIZING**

Do not fertilize established cool-season lawns at this time.

Wait at least two or three weeks after your warm-season lawn has completely greened up before fertilizing according to soil test-recommendations.

# MOWING

Mow cool-season lawns frequently, removing no more than one-third of the lawn height at a time. Leave the clippings on the lawn.

Before **St. Augustinegrass** comes out of dormancy, lower the mowing height to remove the tops of the dead grass blades.

# PROBLEMS

Rust attacks **fescue**, causing leaves to turn yellow before turning brown and dying. Look for red, orange, or brown spores. Many grass varieties have good-to-moderate levels of resistance, so this disease shouldn't be much of a problem. Collect infected grass clippings to prevent spores from spreading. Water in the early morning to avoid keeping the grass wet for long periods.

Dollar spot attacks **fescue**, **Bermuda**, **zoysia**, and sometimes **centipedegrass** and **St. Augustinegrass**. It produces small circular areas of straw-colored grass from 1 to 6 inches across. Straw-colored lesions with reddish-brown borders sometimes extend across the leaf blade while the tip remains green. Early in the morning a spider web-like growth may extend

over the area. Maintain adequate levels of fertility, especially nitrogen, since this disease favors "hungry" lawns. Fungicides are generally unnecessary.

Spring dead spot is a fungal disease that primarily attacks **Bermudagrass**. Look for dead circular or doughnut-shaped patches, 2 or 3 feet across, in the spring as the **Bermudagrass** comes out of dormancy. Cut out the patches and mix the soil or remove the soil and replace with clean soil. To manage this disease, avoid excessive nitrogen applications in late summer and fall and aerify lawns to reduce thatch (see September Planning p. 116).

Florida betony (*Stachys floridana*) is a fast-spreading cool-season perennial weed called "rattlesnake weed" because it produces white, segmented tubers like a rattlesnake's tail. It emerges from seeds and tubers during the cool, moist months of fall. It grows and spreads rapidly throughout the winter months. From late spring to early summer Florida betony bears white to pink flowers. Growth stops at onset of high temperatures and the plant becomes nearly dormant.

Pull or dig out all plant parts, especially the tubers, when the soil is moist. Hoe or cut the top growth down to soil level repeatedly to "starve" the plant. Spot treat with a herbicide that notes Florida betony on the label as one of the targeted weeds and is also suitable for your grass type.

Florida betony is also known as "rattlesnake weed" because it produces white, tuberous growths that look like a rattlesnake's tail.

# MAY

## LAWNS

### PLANNING

Here are a few techniques to help you toughen up your lawn while reducing your water bill:

1. Encourage the development of a deep root system by watering only when the need arises. Look for signs of moisture stress: folded or curled leaves, a dull bluish-gray color, and footprints that remain in the grass long after you've walked over it. Water areas that exhibit these symptoms first. Irrigate only those areas that are important to your landscape.

2. Water late at night or early in the morning when dew has formed, which will not encourage disease. It will also save you money. At midday, in hot, dry, windy weather, 30 percent or more of the water evaporates. Watering at night or in early morning cuts evaporation in half, to 15 to 20 percent. Since it takes 640 gallons of water to irrigate 1,000 square feet with one inch of water, late-night and early-morning watering provides substantial savings.

3. Gradually raise the mowing height by one-quarter to one-half as the temperature climbs. A higher mowing height encourages deeper root growth and reduces heat stress.

4. Make sure that your mower blade is sharp. Grasses that are cut cleanly lose less water and heal more rapidly than leaves shredded by a dull mower blade.

5. Avoid a fast-food diet by using a slow-release fertilizer that contains $1/4$ to $1/2$ of its nitrogen in a "water insoluble" or "slowly available" form.

### PLANTING

Think twice before starting a cool-season lawn now from seed. The seedlings won't have time to get settled before the onset of hot weather. Consider installing sod, provided you're willing to keep it watered during its establishment and droughty periods this summer.

For warm-season lawns, see April.

### WATERING

Water your lawn on an as-needed basis. Keep newly seeded or sprigged areas moist. Rely on signs of moisture stress described in this month's Planning to determine which parts of the lawn need water.

### FERTILIZING

Wait until fall to fertilize your cool-season lawn.

**St. Augustinegrass** can be fertilized this month with a slow-release nitrogen fertilizer, which will help reduce chinch bug and gray leaf spot problems.

### MOWING

Refer to p. 98 for suggested mowing heights for cool-season lawns. Maintain a sharp mower blade and recycle the grass clippings by leaving them on the lawn.

Mow your warm-season lawn at the recommended height with a sharp blade (see p. 98). Avoid cutting more than one-third of the height or the plant may be stressed, exposing it to a weed invasion.

### PROBLEMS

In the southern parts of Alabama and Mississippi, look for tunneling and burrowing activity of mole crickets. Mark these areas for treatment with an insecticide in late June and July.

Southern chinch bugs are notorious pests of **St. Augustine-grass** that may also attack **Bermudagrass**, **centipedegrass**, and **zoysiagrass** but cause them less harm. Damage is mainly caused by the nymphs, which suck sap and inject a toxin that causes the leaves to turn yellow and die. As they feed, the dead areas slowly enlarge. Chinch bug damage is usually greatest during hot, dry weather, and in sunny areas rather than in shade. High levels of nitrogen and thick thatch layers predispose turfgrasses to chinch bug attacks.

Because chinch bug damage can be easily confused with drought, it's best to sample the patch. Here's how:

1. Cut out both ends of a coffee can and push one end into the yellowed grass at the edge of the damaged area.

2. Fill the can with water. If chinch bugs are present, adults and nymphs will float to the top within 10 minutes. Take action if you find 25 to 30 insects per square foot.

Chinch bugs can be controlled with an insecticide. To manage these pests, follow a balanced fertilization program according to a soil test. Use a slow-release nitrogen fertilizer and remove thatch layers that exceed $1/2$ inch in depth.

## HELPFUL HINTS FOR CENTIPEDEGRASS

"Centipedegrass decline" usually occurs in spring when parts of the lawn fail to come out of dormancy, or start to green-up then die in late spring and summer. Several factors cause centipedegrass decline—high soil pH, high amounts of nitrogen and phosphorus applied the previous year, heavy thatch buildup, nematodes, and diseases. Here are some controls:

1. Maintain a pH between 5.5 and 6.0.
2. Fertilize properly.
3. Control thatch.
4. Mow properly.
5. Renovate the lawn. Follow the renovation steps described in April Planting.

Brown patch can start appearing this month. See June Problems for more information. Look for gray leaf spot on **St. Augustine-grass**; collect infected clippings and compost them.

Slime molds are slimy-looking fungi that can be yellow, white, gray, red, violet, or other colors. They may be a few inches or up to several feet in diameter. You may even find them on your shrubs during warm weather, especially during or after heavy periods of rain. These fungi are not harmful to plants. They feed on bacteria, other fungi, and decayed organic matter. If you are bothered by it, hose or brush it off the lawn.

Pre-emergent herbicides to control crabgrass and goosegrass eventually lose their effectiveness. Therefore, a repeat application will be necessary for season-long control. Refer to the label to see when it has to be reapplied to control germinating weeds this summer.

Identify weeds after they emerge to select an appropriate post-emergent herbicide labeled for your lawn. Grassy summer annuals to watch out for include crabgrass, goosegrass, and sandbur. Dallisgrass and bahiagrass are perennial grasses that may be present.

Chinch bug (adult)

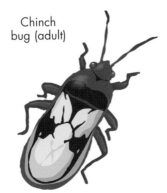

# JUNE
## LAWNS

### PLANNING

The best way to determine the fertilizer requirements of your lawn is by having your soil tested at least every three years through your local County Cooperative Extension Service office. Plan to have your soil tested this month or next so you can be ready for fall.

### PLANTING

Make sure you have plenty of water to help cool-season lawns get established and survive the summer.

Install sod or plant plugs or sprigs of warm-season grasses. There's still time to renovate warm-season lawns. If possible determine what led to the lawn's demise and correct any mistakes. See April Planting p. 106.

### WATERING

Water your lawn when it shows signs of stress: bluish-gray color; footprints that remain in the lawn after walking on it; wilted, folded, or curled leaves. During long, dry, hot spells, you have two choices when it comes to watering an established lawn:

1. Don't water. Let the lawn turn brown.

2. Water the grass to keep it green.

When a **tall fescue** lawn turns brown during a drought, you'd better water. Three weeks or more without rain in the summer can injure or kill **tall fescue**.

If your lawn is experiencing drought stress, apply about an inch of water per week. Set your irrigation system to apply the correct amount of water; too much will be wasteful and too little produces shallow-rooted plants.

Wether you choose to water or not to water, stick with it. Flip-flopping between the two can weaken your lawn.

### FERTILIZING

Do not fertilize **tall fescue** lawns at this time.

Fertilize **Bermudagrass** and **St. Augustine grass** this month with a nitrogen fertilizer. Remember, this application will encourage growth, which translates into higher maintenance. Also fertilize **zoysia** if it looks yellowish-green.

### MOWING

If the lawn grew so high that mowing it at the correct height would remove more than one-third its ideal height, raise the mower height so you will remove no more than one-third of the lawn height. Gradually reduce the mower height, with one or two days between mowings, until you reach the correct height. See Suggested Mowing Heights p. 98.

For the most attractive look, mow **Bermudagrass** and **zoysiagrass** with a reel-type mower. Allow the clippings to lie on the lawn.

### PROBLEMS

Beginning late this month, sample areas where you previously observed damage from mole crickets in the spring. Early in the morning or late in the afternoon, mix 2 tablespoons of liquid detergent in 1 gallon of water and pour it over a 1- to 2-foot-square area. The detergent solution irritates the mole crickets, forcing them to the surface. Newly hatched mole crickets are only about 1/4 inch long and tend to disappear quickly after coming to the surface, so watch very closely for two to three minutes. If small mole crickets appear, apply an insecticide according to the label directions. Irrigating dry soil twenty-four hours before applying the pesti-

It may not be how you want to spend your time but if your St. Augustine lawn is attacked by gray leaf spot, you must collect the clippings. Do not leave them on the lawn.

cide will cause mole crickets to move into the moist soil, making them easier targets.

Be on the lookout for nematodes. Nematodes are microscopic, soil-inhabiting, eel-like worms that feed on turfgrass roots. They are more commonly found in coarse-textured sandy soils than fine-textured clay soils. Nematode-infested roots cannot take up water or fertilizer as well as healthy ones. The infested lawn grass wilts easily and lacks normal green color. High nematode populations result in severe yellowing. The damage usually occurs in irregularly shaped or circular areas. **Centipedegrass** is especially susceptible to damage by ring nematodes. Lance nematodes are often found on **St. Augustinegrass**.

If you suspect nematodes, confirm your suspicions by having your soil analyzed. Contact your regional Extension office for instructions on how to collect samples and where to send them. If nematodes are a threat, the best defense is to keep your lawn healthy. The healthier the plant, the less susceptible it will be to light or moderate nematode attacks.

Brown patch, or Rhizoctonia blight, is a devastating disease that attacks most **fescue**. It's favored by high temperatures and high humidity. Look for circular, tan-colored dead patches several feet in diameter. Sometimes there's a tuft of green grass in the center creating a "doughnut." This disease is most severe on grasses receiving high levels of nitrogen in late spring or sum-

mer, which is a good reason to avoid fertilizing **tall fescue** in the spring. Collect and discard clippings from infected areas. Fungicides can be used to protect healthy grass from attack. Wait until fall to rake up dead areas and seed or sod.

Look for gray leaf spot on **St. Augustinegrass**. Infected leaves and stems have oblong tan lesions with purple borders. The gray spores can sometimes be seen during warm, wet weather. When severe, the entire lawn may look scorched. Collect the infected clippings while mowing, and compost them. Gray leaf spot can be controlled with fungicides. During the growing season use moderate amounts of nitrogen fertilizer, preferably one that contains $1/4$ to $1/2$ of the nitrogen in a slow-release form.

Apply post-emergent herbicides as needed to control summer annual and perennial broadleaf weeds such as knotweed, lespedeza, and spurge. Do not apply post-emergent herbicides unless weeds are present, grass is actively growing, and the lawn is not suffering from drought stress. Read label directions carefully and be careful not to apply them when the weather is hot—the label will note temperature warnings.

# JULY
## LAWNS

### PLANNING

Apply the correct amount of water each time you irrigate. To do this, you need to calibrate your irrigation system so you'll know how much water you apply per hour and exactly when to stop watering. Follow these steps:

1. For an in-ground home irrigation system, place several equal-sized coffee cans or other straight-sided, flat-bottomed containers randomly throughout the area to be irrigated. For aboveground, portable, hose-end sprinklers, containers should be arranged in a straight line away from the sprinklers to the edge of the water pattern.

2. Turn on the irrigation for 15 minutes.

3. Turn off the water, collect the cans, and pour all the water into one of the cans.

4. Measure the depth of water you collected.

5. Calculate the average depth of water by dividing the total amount of water in inches by the number of cans. For instance, if the total depth was 3 inches, and you used six containers, then the average depth would be $3/6$, or 0.5 inches.

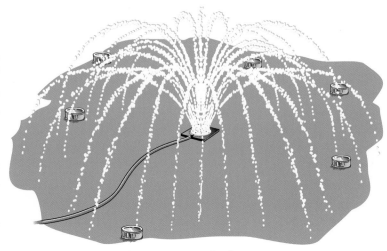

Measuring 1 inch of water

6. Multiply the average depth by four to determine the application rate in inches per hour. For example, $1/2$ inch multiplied by four equals 2 inches per hour. If you run the system for one hour, it will apply 2 inches of water; run it for half an hour, and it will apply 1 inch.

### PLANTING

Sod of warm-season grasses can be installed during hot weather as long as you provide sufficient water to keep the soil moist. Before laying the sod, moisten the soil to prevent the roots from coming into contact with excessively hot and dry soil. Water immediately afterwards to wet the soil below to a depth of 3 or 4 inches. See March p. 105.

### WATERING

New lawns cannot tolerate droughty conditions. Cool-season lawns established last fall by seed need attention to watering, too, as these lawns do not have an adequate roots to survive extended drought. At this stage of development, drought can kill the young crowns of turf. Look for signs of "thirst" and water accordingly or water by the calendar; during droughty periods apply 1 inch of water per week. If you choose not to water, repairing bare patches or renovation will be in order this fall. Do not discontinue watering cool-season lawns in midsummer—water dormant lawns every three weeks in the absence of rain.

## FERTILIZING

See May p. 108.

## MOWING

Start mowing a sodded lawn when it's firmly rooted, securely in place, and has grown 1 inch above the recommended height. If you haven't already done so, raise the cutting height of your mower a notch or two to put less stress on the turf. By increasing the height, you can also increase the depth of the root system.

## PROBLEMS

Sample areas where you have observed damage from mole crickets in the spring and treat accordingly. See June Problems p. 110.

Brown patch attacks **fescues** and is encouraged by overwatering and overfertilizing with nitrogen. Collect and discard clippings from infected areas. Fungicides can be used to protect healthy grass from attack. Wait until fall to rake dead areas and seed or sod.

## HELPFUL HINTS FOR WATERING

Here are some pointers to help you water efficiently:

1. If you have an in-ground, automatic sprinkler system, use the automatic position on the time clock when you are away from home for more than a few days. The system can be made more efficient by installing soil-moisture sensors in the lawn.

2. When you're at home, set the time clock to "off" and manually turn on the in-ground system when the lawn needs water.

3. While the irrigation system is on, check the sprinkler heads for an even spray pattern. Replace damaged or leaky heads and worn nozzles. Make sure the sprinklers are delivering water to the lawn instead of the driveway or road.

4. Fix leaky hoses, spigots, and valves. A lot of water is wasted through leaky hose connections and worn-out spigots. A fairly slow leak—a faucet dripping one drop per second—will leak 2 gallons of water or more per day.

Pythium blight is a "hot-weather" (80 to 95 degrees F.) fungal disease that rapidly gobbles up lawns. Infected leaves look water-soaked; are copper-colored, dark brown, or black; and feel greasy. Look for fungal strands during the evening or early-morning. Avoid spreading this disease when mowing. Collect the infected clippings and compost them. Fungicides are available.

To avoid pythium blight, water before dew forms at night or in the morning after sunrise. Do not fertilize cool-season (**fescue**) lawns in the summer months.

Watch for gray leaf spot on **St. Augustinegrass**. Collect infected clippings and compost them. Use a slow-release nitrogen fertilizer to reduce gray leaf spot problems.

During this time of the year it may seem as if the weeds are healthier and growing more vigorously than the lawn grass. See May Problems p. 109.

# AUGUST

## LAWNS

### PLANNING

Even the most shade-tolerant grasses need at least four hours of sunlight. If enough sunlight is available, consider shade-tolerant grasses. Fortunately, the one cool-season grass that is adapted to north Alabama and Mississippi is fairly shade-tolerant (**tall fescue**). **St. Augustinegrass** is the most shade-tolerant of the warm-season grasses, followed by **zoysiagrass**, **centipedegrass**, and **carpetgrass**; **Bermudagrass** is the least tolerant.

1. Mow grasses in the shade about 1/2 to 1 inch higher than normal. The shaded grass needs as much leaf surface area as possible to take advantage of available light.

2. Fertilize grasses growing in shade with only one-half to two-thirds as much nitrogen as grasses growing in sun.

3. Grasses in shady spots should be watered when they show signs of drought stress.

### PLANTING

Avoid seeding or sprigging warm-season grasses in late summer or early fall because they may be killed by cold weather and are sure to develop a weed problem. If you have to plant now, sod early this month to get the plants settled before they go dormant with the first frost.

### WATERING

Water dormant **fescue** lawns every three weeks in the absence of rain, or take your chances knowing that reseeding may be necessary in the fall.

Water only those areas that really need it.

### FERTILIZING

Avoid fertilizing **centipedegrass**, which can lead to centipede decline (see May Helpful Hints p. 109) as a result of excessive thatch.

### MOWING

Continue to mow your lawn regularly, removing no more than one-third of the grass height at each mowing. Mow **fescue** only if necessary.

### PROBLEMS

If your lawn looks wilted, even after watering; if it's been torn up by skunks, birds, and moles; or if parts have turned brown and feel spongy, check for a white grub infestation. White grubs are the larvae of scarab beetles, including Japanese beetles, masked chafers, and May and June beetles. They have plump, cream-colored bodies that rest in the shape of a "C" and have distinctive yellow to brown heads. Most have life cycles lasting from several months to three years.

The Japanese beetle white grub is common in northern parts of Alabama and Mississippi. Adult females lay their eggs in the soil around July. Two weeks later the grubs hatch and begin feeding on grass roots. The most serious damage occurs in September and October before hibernation and during April and May before the larvae pupate to become adults.

Make cuts on three sides of a 12-inch square of damaged area. Pry this flap back and examine the roots and upper 3 inches of soil. Count the number of grubs. Move on to another patch. After several samples, determine the average number of grubs. Most healthy lawns can tolerate five to seven Japanese beetle grubs per square foot. If your count is higher, an insecticide may be needed.

A biological approach is milky spore disease (Milky Spore Powder Japanese Beetle & Grub

Control®), a naturally occurring bacterium (*Bacillus popilliae*) that primarily infects Japanese beetle grubs; it will not work as well against other types of white grubs. To control other white grubs, use a granular or liquid drench grub control available at your local garden center. There are several available and the technology and active ingredients may change, so ask a good source at your favorite garden center. When the Japanese beetle grubs become infected with milky spore disease, they die, releasing spores into the soil to infect future generations. Ideal results are achieved when your neighbors also treat their lawns.

The best time to apply milky spore disease is now or in the spring. After three years milky disease becomes established and suppresses the grubs in your lawn. During its establishment period, do not treat the lawn with a chemical insecticide—the insecticide will keep the grub population at a low level, preventing the buildup of the bacteria.

Look for brown patch disease on **tall fescue**.

Check for gray leaf spot disease on **St. Augustinegrass**. Collect infected clippings and discard them. Use a slow-release nitrogen fertilizer to reduce gray leaf spot problems.

## HELPFUL HINTS FOR FIRE ANT CONTROL

The red imported fire ant was introduced into the U.S. as early as 1918. Because it's not native to this country, fire ants have no competitors, parasites, or predators. They produce unsightly mounds and their painful stings pose a health threat, particularly to young children and older people. If fire ants are in your landscape, control them with the "two-step method."

Step 1. Broadcast a fresh-bait insecticide over the entire landscape. While it can be used on individual mounds, it's best to distribute it widely. It's less expensive than individual mound treatments and controls colonies even when mounds aren't visible. Apply the bait when the workers are foraging for food. In the spring and fall, this is during the warmer daylight hours. In the summer, apply the bait in late afternoon or evening. Distribute the bait with a handheld seed spreader. Make one or two passes over the area at a normal walking speed. Most mounds that receive this slow-acting treatment will eventually be eliminated.

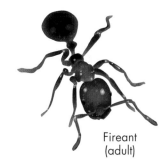

Fireant (adult)

Step 2. No sooner than seven days after applying the bait, treat only those mounds that pose a threat, located near walkways, play equipment, and other high-traffic areas. Use an approved fire ant insecticide following label directions. If you use a soluble powder, distribute it evenly over the mound. Liquid concentrates—chemical products diluted with water and then applied to the mound—must be used in sufficient volumes to penetrate the entire nest. Before using any of these pesticides, read and follow the label directions carefully. Alternatively, new granular insecticides are now available. These products are not baits, but can be broadcast over the entire area that is infested. They only control fire ants in the treated area.

Apply herbicides to your lawn for winter annual or perennial weeds that germinate or form rosettes in fall. Check herbicide labels before using.

If annual bluegrass and other winter weeds were a problem in spring, control them now. Apply a pre-emergence herbicide to prevent them from sprouting soon and appearing this fall.

# September

## LAWNS

### PLANNING

Lawns need air to breathe. When clay soil becomes compacted, closing up the air-filled spaces, the lawn declines. Compacted soil also reduces the movement of water and nutrients. Soon the grass weakens, making it less able to compete with weeds and slow to recuperate from injury. Eventually the lawn thins out, giving rise to goosegrass and prostrate knotweed—two notorious weeds that thrive in compacted soils. Make plans to help your lawn breathe easier this fall by aerifying your cool-season lawn.

A power-driven core aerator or aerifier can be rented at lawn-and-garden supply centers. These have spoon-shaped tines or hollow tubes. As the tubes are driven into the lawn, cores of soil are removed and strewn across the lawn. The holes that result increase air, water, and nutrient availability to roots.

Cool-season lawns should be aerified in the fall when there is less heat stress and danger of invasion by weedy annuals. Allow at least four weeks of good growing weather to help the plants recover. Warm-season lawns can be aerified in the spring.

### PLANTING

Seed thin, bare areas in cool-season lawns with a blend of **turf-type tall fescue**.

Overseed warm-season lawns with cool-season **perennial ryegrass** (*Lolium perenne*) or **annual ryegrass** (*Lolium multiflorum*) to provide green color during the winter months after warm-season grasses are brown and dormant. **Perennial ryegrass** is more expensive, but offers a higher-quality look. It's also more tolerant of cold, disease, and drought than **annual ryegrass**. However, these strengths allow **perennial ryegrass** to live longer than **annual ryegrass**, making it a burden in the spring when you want the warm-season lawn to overtake the **ryegrass**, so you may want to use **annual ryegrass** as your top choice for overseeding.

Never overseed turfgrasses in moderate to heavy shade—the **ryegrass** could linger into summer, competing with the turf awakening from dormancy, resulting in a thinned-out lawn easily invaded by weeds.

Overseeding is best done on a lush, healthy lawn. The best time is two or three weeks before the expected first frost or when the soil temperature drops below 75 degrees F. **Bermudagrass** lawns tolerate overseeding better than **centipedegrass**, **St. Augustinegrass**, or **zoysiagrass**. Here's how to overseed **Bermudagrass**:

1. Mow the lawn closely.

2. Use a power rake to remove excess thatch and open up the lawn for good seed-to-soil contact.

3. Use a rotary or drop-type spreader to apply 5 to 10 pounds of **ryegrass** seed per 1,000 square feet. Sow half the seed in one direction, the other half at right angles to the first.

4. After seeding, rake the ground with a stiff broom to make sure the seed is in contact with the soil. Follow-up by "top-dressing" (applying a shallow layer) with compost.

5. Water the lawn lightly two or three times a day until the seeds germinate.

6. When the lawn becomes established, water only when necessary.

7. After the second mowing, fertilize with 1 pound of nitrogen per 1,000 square feet, using a complete fertilizer, such as 16-4-8.

### WATERING

Water the lawn if necessary.

## FERTILIZING

By this time of year, potassium levels are often low, especially if you haven't fertilized since early summer. Now is the time to use a low-nitrogen, high-potassium formula such as 5-0-15 to help grasses with winter hardiness and drought tolerance. Recent research has shown that if adequate levels of potassium are present, additional applications can cause other nutrients (calcium and magnesium) to become deficient. So use a "winterizer" only if you've had your lawn on a low-maintenance schedule.

## MOWING

Don't retire the lawn mower—as long as the grass grows, it should be mowed.

## PROBLEMS

Sample several damaged areas to get an average number of white grubs per square foot to decide if control is necessary. Lawns can tolerate lower or higher numbers of grubs, depending on the health of the lawn and the kind of grub. Submit the grubs to your Cooperative Extension Service office for identification to help you decide if an insecticide is warranted.

Scout for adult mole crickets and treat if necessary.

Examine the yellowish to brownish spots in your **St. Augustinegrass** lawn for chinch bugs. Use the coffee can technique (see May Problems p. 109) to sample for them at the edge of the damaged area.

Dollar spot or brown patch may be present. Refer to March and April Problems pp. 105 and 107 to learn how to manage these fungal diseases.

If annual bluegrass (*Poa annua*) and other winter annuals have been a problem, apply a pre-emergent herbicide to control the germinating seeds before they appear. Annual bluegrass germinates in late summer and early fall when temperatures drop consistently into the mid-70s. A pre-emergent herbicide forms a barrier at or just below the soil surface and kills the emerging seedlings. Look for annual bluegrass in shady or moist areas.

Annual bluegrass can be thwarted by using a preemergent herbicide now.

# OCTOBER

## LAWNS

### PLANNING

As you rake up the fallen leaves from your lawn, recycle them as mulch or compost. For a fine-textured mulch, shred the leaves with a lawn mower or a leaf shredder. Finely cut leaves look more attractive and won't blow easily.

To compost leaves, researchers recommend building piles at least 4 feet in diameter and 3 feet high. To keep the piles a manageable size, make them no larger than 5 feet high and 10 feet wide. You can compost leaves by themselves, or add fresh vegetable peelings, grass clippings, or other kitchen or yard trimmings.

To speed up the composting process, shred the leaves before putting them into the pile. Avoid adding meat or grease, which may cause odors and attract pests. Pay particular attention to moisture and air: Keep the ingredients moist enough so you can squeeze water droplets from a handful of leaves, and supply air by turning the materials. Turn the pile once a month during warm weather. In cool weather turn it less frequently to prevent too much heat from escaping. To convert the leaves to compost fairly quickly requires adding a nitrogen-containing fertilizer such

as 10-10-10. Good natural substitutes for synthetic fertilizers include horse or cow manure, bloodmeal, or cottonseed meal.

Mix this crumbly, earthy-smelling "black gold" into heavy clay soil to improve drainage and make the soil easier to cultivate. Compost helps sandy soils retain water and nutrients.

### PLANTING

In northern parts of Alabama and Mississippi, there's still time to reseed bare areas of a cool-season lawn or start a new one, but hurry. Try to get it completed by mid-month. To fill in bare spots follow these steps:

1. Loosen the soil to a depth of 1/2 inch with a rake. If you can, use a shovel to break up the top 6 inches of soil.

2. Sow the seed and work it in lightly.

3. Gently water the newly seeded area. Keep it moist but not flooded.

4. Mulch lightly with weed-free straw to keep the area moist.

5. Keep the patch moist until the seedlings emerge.

6. After a month, fertilize the patch lightly to encourage growth.

If you want to overseed your warm-season lawn with **ryegrass**, start working on it early this month.

### WATERING

Newly seeded or sodded lawns should be watered frequently. As the seedlings emerge and the sod "knits" into the soil, gradually water less frequently but more deeply.

### FERTILIZING

Fertilize **tall fescue** according to a soil test. In the absence of soil-test recommendations, use a 3:1:2 analysis (such as 12-4-8 or 16-4-8) fertilizer on **fescue** where 1/4 to 1/2 of the nitrogen is slowly available (look for "water insoluble nitrogen" or "slowly available nitrogen" on the label). Apply 1/2 or 1 pound of nitrogen per 1,000 square feet of lawn. If you spread fertilizer on the sidewalk, driveway, or road, sweep it up and return it to the lawn.

### MOWING

Mow cool-season lawns often enough so that no more than one-third of the grass height is cut. Recycle grass clippings by leaving them on the lawn.

Remove tree leaves from the lawn to reduce lawn problems. Compost them or shred them to use as mulch around your flower or shrub border.

## PROBLEMS

If fire ants have cropped up in your lawn or landscape, control them with the "two-step method" described in August Problems p. 115.

Examine the yellowish to brownish spots in your **St. Augustinegrass** lawn for chinch bugs. Use the coffee can technique (see May Problems p. 109) to sample for them at the edge of the damaged area.

"Fairy rings" can be found in all types of grasses. They may appear as a ring of mushrooms or simply as a dark green ring of lush grass. The ring may vary from a few inches to several feet in diameter. Fairy rings are caused by soil-inhabiting fungi that feed on old roots, stumps, and thatch. Fairy-ring fungi are not plant parasites, but they can cause the lawn to dry out because their fungal bodies make the soil repel water. Grass inside the ring is usually in a state of decline. On young rings the grass on the inside of the ring may be dead. On old rings there may be a dead band of grass a few inches to several feet wide forming a partial or complete ring.

## HELPFUL HINTS FOR FILLING LOW SPOTS

Small low spots in the lawn can be raised by carefully removing the turf and filling in the low spots with soil. Use your spade to cut out the low spot, going down about 2 inches deep. Angle your blade under the sod to cut the roots cleanly. Lift up the sod and fill in the spot with soil. Replace the sod and keep it moist until it knits into the soil.

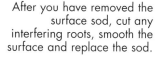

After you have removed the surface sod, cut any interfering roots, smooth the surface and replace the sod.

Fairy rings are difficult to control. You can be patient and allow them to disappear over time. Watering the ring to saturate the soil for several hours and over several days may help. As a last resort, you can replace the infested soil occupied by the fairy ring with clean soil.

Brown patch or Rhizoctonia blight is a devastating disease, especially on **St. Augustinegrass** in the fall. See November Problems p. 121.

Handpull or spot treat chickweed, henbit, and other winter annuals with a broadleaf herbicide. Use a herbicide labeled for your lawn grass and for the weeds you're trying to control.

Florida betony is a cool-season perennial weed that emerges from seeds and tubers during the cool, moist months of fall. Throughout the winter months it grows and spreads rapidly. Spot treat with herbicide while it's actively growing this month. See April Problems p. 107 for more information.

# NOVEMBER

## LAWNS

### PLANNING

"A rolling stone gathers no moss," but expect **moss** to collect in the moist, shaded areas of your lawn. In addition to shady places, **mosses** are especially fond of acidic (low pH) soils with low fertility, poorly drained or wet soils, or combinations of these. These primitive, nonflowering plants spread by dust-fine spores carried on the wind that alight on moist soil, rocks, bricks, or tree trunks. The spores germinate and form a network of green threads that develop into tiny matted plants. Most grow only 1/4 inch to 2 inches high.

Although **mosses** are harmless, folks either court them or hate them. I love the velvety, cushiony look and feel of **moss**. **Mosses** are cultivated as ornamentals in Japanese gardens. A famous 13th-century garden in Kyoto called Saiho-ji ("Moss Temple") has over forty species and varieties of rolling green **mosses** spread over 4 1/2 acres.

If you're planning to rid your lawn of **moss** by raking it out and then reseeding, be aware that in most cases, the **moss** will return. Only when you make the growing conditions less appealing to the **moss** and more favorable for the grass will you be able to halt the **moss's** advance.

Before you choose to fight a "turf war" with **moss**, figure out your chances of winning. If your moss-covered lawn gets less than four hours of sunlight a day, it will be too shady for turfgrasses. You're going to lose the battle unless you can improve sunlight penetration by selectively pruning tree limbs. If there's always going to be insufficient sunlight, your best bet is to forget about grass. If you really dislike **moss**, plant shade-tolerant ground covers or mulch with leaves, needles, or wood chips. Ideally, extend the mulch layer to the drip line or outermost branches of the tree.

If your lawn is receiving adequate sunlight but still seems to be losing ground to moss, follow these steps to improve the health, density, and appearance of your lawn:

- Test your soil at least every three years, and fertilize according to a soil test and at the proper time.
- Improve poorly drained areas by regrading to direct water away from the site.
- Cultivate compacted, heavy clay soils with a core aerifier—a machine that removes plugs of soil. You can rent, purchase, or contract this service through lawn care companies.
- Mow grasses growing in the shade at the top of their recommended mowing height range to promote deep rooting and to leave as much leaf area as possible to manufacture food.

### PLANTING

Install cool-season sod as long as the soil isn't frozen.

Postpone seeding, plugging, or sodding a warm-season lawn until next spring.

### WATERING

Do not allow new cool-season lawns to dry out. When the sod has "knitted" or rooted into the soil, reduce the frequency of irrigation and water deeply as the roots begin to penetrate the soil.

Dormant warm-season lawns may need to be watered to prevent them from drying out, especially when warm windy weather prevails. Water warm-season lawns overseeded with **ryegrass** as needed.

### FERTILIZING

Fertilize **tall fescue** and dormant, overseeded warm-season lawns according to the results of a soil test. Fertilizing in the fall promotes root development without excessive top growth. With a strong root system, your lawn will be better able to withstand drought conditions next summer. Do not apply a fertilizer containing phosphorus and potassium if adequate levels are already present in the soil. See September Fertilizing p. 117.

## PROBLEMS

Rust and dollar spot are fungal diseases that attack **fescue** lawns.

Rust causes grass leaves to turn yellow before turning brown and dying. Take a close look at the leaves for red, orange, or brown spores. Heavy infestations cause thinning. Many grass varieties have good-to-moderate levels of resistance to rust, so this disease shouldn't be much of a problem. Collect infected grass clippings to prevent the spores from spreading. Avoid keeping the grass wet for long periods by watering in the early morning.

## HELPFUL HINTS FOR WEED ASSESSMENT

If your lawn has a history of weed invasions, determine why the weeds invaded and correct the problem. Weeds are often found in lawns with a thin or weak stand of grass. The most common causes of a poor lawn are using a grass that's not adapted to your region or improper mowing, watering, and fertilizing. Other factors that affect the condition of the lawn include insects, diseases, compacted soil, and thatch.

Dollar spot produces small circular areas of straw-colored grass which range from 1 to 6 inches across. If you examine individual grass blades you'll find straw-colored lesions with reddish-brown borders. Sometimes the lesions will extend across the blade while the leaf tip remains green. Early in the morning you may be able to spot a spider web-like growth over the infected area. Dollar spot is more common during the spring and fall months. Maintain adequate levels of fertility, especially nitrogen, since this diseases favors "hungry" lawns. Fungicides are generally unnecessary.

Brown patch or Rhizoctonia blight is a devastating disease, especially on **St. Augustinegrass** in the fall. Look for circular, brown dead patches in the lawn. Take a close look at the infected grass plants at the edge of the dead area and you'll find rotting leaf sheaths near the crown at the soil surface. Rake up dead areas and remove the infected grass. Reduce the occurrence of this disease by not overfertilizing in the fall or spring when the disease is likely to appear.

Treat wild garlic with a broadleaf herbicide when the air temperature is above 50 degrees F. Handpull wild garlic when the soil is moist to remove the entire plant—bulb and all. If you leave the bulb behind, it will resprout. Pull young, emerged weeds now while the task is easier and the weather is comfortable. By eliminating the weeds before they set seeds, you'll also reduce next year's problem.

Dollar spot appears as straw-colored patches on fescue lawns

# December

## LAWNS

### PLANNING

Make plans to winterize the lawn mower before putting it away for the winter. Nothing could be more exasperating next spring than a lawn mower that won't start. The secret to getting it to start on the first (or second) pull next spring is to winterize it.

1. Run the engine until dry. Untreated gasoline stored for long periods can cause a gummy buildup in the carburetor that can make it impossible to start after a few months. Run the engine until it stalls. Alternatively, you can add a small amount of gasoline stabilizer to the fuel tank and run the engine for a few minutes to distribute it with the fuel.

2. Drain and replace the oil. Disconnect the wire from the spark plug for safety. Change the oil at least once a year (refer to your owner's manual) and check the oil level each time you use the machine. Recyle the used oil.

3. Clean the air filter. Foam-element air filters should be removed and cleaned with hot, soapy water. Before replacing it, pour a couple of tablespoons of clean engine oil onto it and distribute it by squeezing the foam.

4. Oil the spark plug. Remove the spark plug and pour a tablespoon of clean engine oil into the hole. Replace the spark plug and pull the starter cord a couple of times to crank the engine and distribute the oil. This will protect the engine from corrosion during the winter.

5. Clean and store the engine by brushing the cooling fins to make sure they're not plugged. Scrape off any dirt or grass clippings on the underside with a screwdriver, putty knife, or wire brush. If the blade is dull, remove and sharpen it or replace it.

### PLANTING

Sod of cool-season grass can be installed in north Alabama and Mississippi as long as the soil is not frozen.

Wait until next spring to seed, plug, or sod your warm-season lawn.

### WATERING

For cool-season grasses, if dry weather persists and the lawn shows signs of drought stress, apply an inch of water per week in the absence of precipitation. Newly seeded or sodded lawns should be watered frequently. As the seedlings emerge and the sod "knits" into the soil, gradually water less frequently but more deeply and less often.

For warm-season lawns, periodic watering may be necessary to prevent the grasses from drying out, especially when the weather is warm and windy.

### FERTILIZING

Do not fertilize the lawn at this time. Overseeded **Bermudagrass** lawns can be fertilized this month. Use a fertilizer recommended by soil-test results. Do not apply a fertilizer containing phosphorus and potassium if adequate levels are already present in the soil.

### MOWING

You may still have to mow your cool-season lawn this month. Continue practicing the "one-third rule": Do not remove any more than one-third of the height at each mowing.

Mow overseeded **Bermudagrass** lawns at 1 inch before the grass gets taller than 1¹/2 inches. Dormant **Bermudagrass** or any warm-season grass that has not been overseeded does not need mowing.

### PROBLEMS

Handpull or spot-treat chickweed, henbit, and other winter annuals with a broadleaf herbicide.

# PERENNIALS

Perennials are dependable and versatile. They come in every color imaginable and collectively have a flowering season that spans winter to fall. Best of all, well-adapted perennials grow fuller and more beautiful with each passing year.

Though often referred to simply as "perennials," technically these plants are "herbaceous perennials," so called because their soft and fleshy stems differentiate them from woody trees and shrubs. The top growth of most perennials is killed by freezing fall temperatures. The belowground portions—crown and roots—survive over the winter months and produce new growth in the spring. Although bulbs have a similar growth pattern, they are classified separately because of their unique system of storing food in thick, underground structures (the bulbs).

Unlike their cousins the annuals, perennials come back year after year. They have a shorter flowering period, however, generally lasting only three to five weeks (many annuals bloom for three to five months).

Before you flip back to the Annuals and Bulbs chapters or move on to Roses or Shrubs, be aware

that this shorter blooming period is not a short-coming. Perennials deliver more than just flowers: They offer an endless variety of leaf shapes and colors and interesting outlines and textures. They're constantly changing, too. You can expect a different look in each season before, during, and after flowering. Even in the winter months, perennials like maidenhair grass or coneflowers provide architectural interest with their leaves, stems, and seedheads.

## PLANNING

Picking the right perennials requires planning. Before you buy and plant perennials:

1. Know the growing conditions in your landscape.

2. Know the growing requirements of your perennials. Match their needs to the growing conditions in your landscape. Use these criteria to winnow the list of candidates to some really worthwhile selections.

**Hardiness:** Select perennials that are cold hardy in your area—able to survive the winter with little or no protection. See the cold-hardiness maps on pp. 278 and 279. Remember that these hardiness zones are only guidelines, since microclimates and soil drainage often determine how hardy and long-lived a perennial will be in any given landscape. Heat hardiness is also important. Plants native to climates that have cool summers will not tolerate hot, dry summers. Attempting to grow them in a landscape outside their "comfort zone" will result in disappointment.

**Soil conditions:** Generally, most perennials prefer soil that is well-drained. In fact, more perennials are killed during the winter by wet, poorly drained conditions than by cold temperatures. If the site is naturally wet and building a raised bed or improving drainage would be prohibitively expensive, then by all means cultivate moisture-loving perennials in that part of the garden.

**Sun exposure:** Determine the amount of sunlight an area receives and match perennials to those light levels.

3. Learn about the ornamental attributes of various perennials. Here are a few characteristics to look for.

**Eye-catching flowers, fruits and leaves:** Perennials are dynamic, ever-changing plants that are capable of offering more than one season of interest. In most cases, many cultivars of a given species are available, greatly extending the size and/or color range of the species.

**Time and length of bloom:** To create a season-long display of color, know when your perennials will flower—you will be able to create a parade of color from a variety of perennials throughout the season. If you're looking for long-flowering perennials, there's usually a catch: In order for them to bloom continuously, you'll have to dead-head them (remove the spent flowers) repeatedly or cut them back.

**Height and size of mature plants:** Knowing their eventual height and spread will help you select the right number of plants and to space them strategically to avoid an overcrowded or overplanted look.

4. Learn about the maintenance requirements of your perennials. If you prefer a low- maintenance approach, avoid perennials that require staking, frequent dividing, and regular deadheading, as well as those that are invasive.

5. Whenever possible, select plants that are resistant to or at least not bothered by serious pests that may wreak havoc in the garden.

Refer to mail-order catalogs, Internet resources, perennial plant encyclopedias, and gardening magazine articles to help you research your perennials. Your local Extension office and Master Gardener group are also good resources.

Prepare your site and then gently tap the container plant into your hand. Set it into a hole that is the same depth but slightly wider than the rootball.

However, because spring is when everyone shops, you'll usually find the best selection of perennials in spring. Gardeners faced with the prospect of a hot summer following closely on the heels of spring should plant early, then be prepared to coddle the plants with regular watering during the summer months.

Here's how to plant a container-grown perennial:

1. Hold your hand over the top of the pot with the plant stems between your fingers. Tip the pot over and gently tap the plant into your hand. If the roots are circling around the rootball, loosen them to encourage growth into the sur-

## SOIL PREPARATION

Because of their permanent nature, prepare the planting bed right the first time. Refer to Annuals, Preparing the Ground on p. 16 for details on good soil preparation.

## PLANTING

Purchase perennials in containers or as dormant bare-root plants. You can grow them from seed, but starting with established plants will give you quicker satisfaction.

You can plant container-grown perennials nearly year-round, but fall is the best time to plant because the plants have sufficient time to root and establish before the onset of hot, dry summer weather. For fall plantings, it's a good idea to plant at least six weeks before hard freezes.

Firm the soil slightly around the plant.

rounding soil. The tangled roots of large-rooted hostas and daylilies can be teased apart with your fingers. Use a knife, pruning shears, or sharp spade to score the sides of the rootballs of fine-rooted perennials; make three or four shallow cuts to encourage root growth along the length of the ball.

2. Dig a hole the same depth as the rootball and slightly wider.

3. Set the plant in the hole so the crown is at or slightly above ground level.

4. Cover and firm the soil lightly around the plant.

5. Water thoroughly to settle the soil around the roots. Depending on the weather and rainfall, you may need to water daily for the first few weeks. Mulch with a 2- to 3-inch layer of compost to conserve moisture and suppress weeds, spreading a 1/2-inch layer near the crown but not covering it.

6. During the next few weeks, keep the plants well watered to help them become quickly established. After that, begin cutting back on water, eventually watering on an "as-needed" basis. Test the soil and rootball to see if they're moist.

## FERTILIZING

If the soil is properly prepared at the start, supplemental fertilization may not be necessary for several years after planting. Let the perennial's growth rate and leaf color guide you in your fertilizing decisions—and rely on soil-test results. If the bed is already highly fertile, a soil test will save you from the undesirable results of overfertilizing, which leads to a lot of leafy growth at the expense of flowers.

In the absence of a soil test, use a complete balanced fertilizer that contains nitrogen, phosphorus, and potassium. Most fertilizer recommendations are based on nitrogen, which is an important element in plant growth and is often the one most likely to be deficient in the soil. Use a

slow-release fertilizer for flowers at the rate recommended on the label. If you are an organic gardener, work compost, bloodmeal, or cottonseed meal into the bed before planting.

Apply the slow-release fertilizer when the new shoots emerge and, if necessary, once or twice again during the growing season, depending on the formula.

Water the bed after application so the fertilizer enters the soil and is available to the plant. Wash any fertilizer off the foliage to prevent fertilizer burn.

## WATERING

Perennials vary in their watering needs, but most require an ample moisture supply at least when they are actively growing. Seedlings or newly planted perennials should be watered daily for the first few weeks, depending on the weather and rainfall. After that, begin cutting back, eventually reaching an "as-needed" basis.

When they become established, water less frequently. Established plants may need to be watered once a week in clay soils that hold more water than sandy soils. Sandy soils may need to be watered twice a week. Instead of following the calendar, water when the top 2 or 3 inches of soil feels dry. When you do water, water deeply to encourage deep rooting.

## DIVIDING

Perennials are divided to control their size, invigorate them, and to increase their numbers. Short-lived perennials or old perennials that have become crowded with sparse flowers can be kept vigorous and blooming through division. After dividing, the vigorous younger sections are replanted so they'll flower more prolifically.

A general rule-of-thumb is to divide spring- and summer-blooming perennials in the fall, and fall-flowering perennials in early spring when the new

Divide perennials to invigorate them and increase their numbers.

shoots have emerged. Exceptions to this rule are fleshy-rooted perennials such as peony (*Paeonia*) and oriental poppy (*Papaver orientale*), which should be divided in the fall.

Gardeners near the Tennessee line and in the higher elevations can wait until spring to divide, since the rigors of winter may kill the young divisions before they have time to become established. Gardeners in milder areas can divide through fall and into early winter. It is most important to divide the plants when they're not flowering.

## GROOMING

Pruning is not often associated with herbaceous perennials, but deadheading to remove spent flowers, pinching stems or buds, and cutting back leggy plants are all aspects of grooming. Grooming improves the appearance of the plants, extends their bloom period or encourages repeat-flowering, controls diseases by improving air movement, and increases the size and number of flowers.

## PROBLEMS

To manage pests, practice Integrated Pest Management or IPM. This commonsense method focuses on establishing and maintaining healthy plants and understanding pests. When pest control is necessary, start with the least-toxic solutions such as handpicking the pests or dislodging them from the plant with a strong spray of water. Potent chemical pesticides are a last resort to use when the pests threaten unacceptable levels of damage. You must decide if the plant or its show should be spared serious damage by a pesticide application, or possibly be composted. Follow this IPM approach to reduce or avoid pest damage:

• Select and properly plant well-adapted species and cultivars, especially those that have disease resistance.

• Maintain them properly by meeting their needs for light, water, and nutrients.

• Inspect for pests regularly. It's easier to control small outbreaks than wait to be surprised by full-scale attacks. If you have to, prune out affected plant parts or completely remove the plant from the bed.

Many disease problems can be prevented:

• Provide good soil drainage to prevent and control soilborne diseases that cause root and stem rots.

• To help reduce disease outbreaks, keep the leaves dry when watering and maintain enough room between plants for good air circulation.

• Clean up any fallen leaves and remove any spent flowers. They can harbor pests.

# JANUARY
## PERENNIALS

 PLANNING

As you design your garden, you can take the traditional route and use perennials in island beds or borders. An island bed can be viewed from all sides. A classic perennial border is often called a mixed border because it can include annuals, shrubs, and trees to create a variety of colors and textures. A classic border is usually backed up to a wall, fence, or hedge. It should be wide enough to accommodate a generous helping of plants; this means it is ideally at least 8 feet in width, including a 2-foot space in the back to allow for air movement and room for you to maintain the planting.

Perennials can also be used in other ways:

1) Pockets of color. Light up your landscape with long-blooming perennials. Tuck them in around your shrubs to add color and texture, and use them alone or in concert with annuals and bulbs to add some pizzazz to the front of your home, along walkways, or at the corners of your patio.

2) Ground covers. Evergreen **daylilies**, **hellebores**, and **wild gingers** (*Asarum*) can be used to cover large areas of ground.

3) Containers. Perennials can be grown with annuals and bulbs in containers to bring color where you want it—on the front porch, deck, patio, or near the swimming pool. Select compact, long-blooming perennials such as 'Stella de Oro' **daylily**, **gold-moss sedum** (*Sedum acre*), and the Galaxy series of **yarrow**.

 PLANTING

For the cost of a commercial packet of seed, you can produce hundreds of seedlings—less than the cost of a single potted transplant. Many cultivars will not come true from seed, which means that the offspring will not be identical to the parents and, in most cases, will be inferior to the parents. These cultivars must be propagated vegetatively—by stem or root cuttings or by division. There are some varieties, however, that will come true from seed (see the Helpful Hints on the following page).

In the warmer parts of Alabama and Mississippi, start perennials from seed late this month. Perennial seeds often require a specific chilling period before germination can occur. To learn about any special treatment required to overcome

dormancy and induce germination, follow the packet instructions prior to sowing the seeds. Starting perennial seeds indoors is similar to the seed-starting technique described in Annuals January Planting p. 18.

Some perennials will germinate readily—in one to two weeks or less than a month. Others, however, will germinate randomly over an extended period of time that can range from days to several weeks and sometimes several months. This most commonly occurs with perennial seeds that have very special germination requirements. Some seeds have thick seed coats (**wild blue indigo** and **perennial sweet pea**) and need to be soaked in water or scratched with a file so water can be absorbed or imbibed by the seed. Other seeds, particularly perennials from temperate regions, need to be stratified, or exposed to moist chilling conditions for a specified time period (check the seed packet for the length of cold exposure); otherwise, they will not germinate. Refer to the seed packet for instructions.

Seeds such as **bleeding heart** (*Dicentra*), **columbine** (*Aquilegia*), and **garden phlox** can be over-wintered outdoors in a cold frame (see October Planting p. 146 for more information). Seeds can also be stratified in the refrigerator. Here's how:

1. Fill a plastic bag with dampened milled sphagnum peat moss or vermiculite, and place the seeds in the bag. Label the bag with the date and the name of the seeds.

2. Place the bag in the refrigerator at 40 degrees F. for the required period of time, usually between six to eight weeks. After the required cold treatment, sow the seeds in trays or pots and move them to a cool location (less than 70 degrees F.), in bright, indirect light so that germination will occur.

## CARE

In northern parts of Alabama and Mississippi, inspect perennials to see if any have been heaved out by the freezing and thawing of the soil. Firmly press them back down into the soil to prevent them from freezing or drying out. To reduce frost-heaving, maintain a layer of mulch around your perennials to insulate the soil.

## HELPFUL HINTS

Many seed-propagated cultivars will not reproduce "true," which means the offspring will not be identical to the parents. There are a number of cultivars, however, that can be successfully propagated from seed. Here is a short list of some of these perennial cultivars:

- **Yarrow** (*Achillea* Summer Pastels Series)
- **Shasta daisies** (*Leucanthemum* x *superbum* 'Alaska' and 'Snow Lady')
- **Goldenrod** (*Solidago* 'Goldkind')
- **Speedwell** (*Veronica spicata* 'Blue Bouquet')
- **Tickseed** (Coeropsis *grandiflora* 'Early Sunrise', C. 'Sunray', and C. 'Sunburst')
- **Balloon flower** (*Platycodon grandiflorus* Fuji series, 'Sentimental Blue', and 'Shell Pink')
- **Butterfly weed** (*Asclepias tuberosa* 'Gay Butterflies')
- **Cardinal flower** (*Lobelia* 'Queen Victoria')

## WATERING

Determine the need for watering seed-propagated perennials by squeezing the top half-inch of medium between your thumb and forefinger. If water squeezes out easily, enough moisture is present. If the medium feels slightly moist but water is difficult to squeeze out, add water.

## FERTILIZING

Do not fertilize perennials now.

## GROOMING

**Ornamental grasses** don't have to be trimmed just yet. As long as they haven't been damaged by winter winds, ice, or snow, enjoy their glorious winter foliage.

## PROBLEMS

Damping off is a serious disease that attacks and kills seeds and seedlings. See Annuals February Problems p. 21.

# FEBRUARY

## PERENNIALS

 ### PLANNING

Design your garden on paper before planting—it's easier to move plants on paper with an eraser than in the garden with a trowel or shovel!

1. Make an outline of the bed on graph paper that has a grid of 1/4-inch squares, each square representing one foot. Divide and label the bed into three sections: "tall" on one end, "medium" in the center of the bed, and "short" in the front. To create a bed with spring, summer, and fall interest, use three sheets of tracing paper and start designing backwards: from fall to summer to spring, and from the back of the border to the front.

2. Label your first sheet "Fall" and use your pencil to plant fall-blooming perennials. Draw them as bubbles or blobs as much to scale as possible, accounting for their eventual mature spread. Since late-summer- and fall-blooming perennials are usually the tallest plants in the garden, reaching over 3 feet in height, focus on the "tall" section in the back first. Then intersperse a few "medium" and "short" growers in the middle and front of the bed. Identify

Keep seedlings moist (but not wet!) by misting—daily if needed.

each bubble with the name of the plant, and color it with the plant's predominant bloom color. Plant small perennials in groups of three for maximum impact.

Take a second sheet of tracing paper and label it "Summer." Most summer-blooming perennials are in the middle height range, between 2 to 3 feet tall. Plant a few taller ones in the back and some shorter ones in the front. Label and color the bubbles.

Take your last sheet of tracing paper and label it "Spring." Focus on the front of the border because a majority of these plants are low-growing, generally less than 2 feet. When you've created a spring-blooming pattern in the front, fill in the

center and back rows with other spring-flowering plants.

Finally, after you've moved your plants around and have arrived at the best design, draw up your master plan. Trace your Fall and Summer displays onto the Spring sheet, or transfer all of them to a fresh sheet of tracing paper. This final design will be your buying and planting plan.

You don't have to buy all of these plants at once. Over a period of two or three years you can start them from seed, buy transplants, or acquire them as trades or passalong plants. In the meantime, fill in the vacancies with annuals.

 ## PLANTING

Start perennials from seed. See January Planting p. 128 for detailed sowing instructions. Divide and replant summer- and fall-flowering perennials as their new growth emerges. These include **aster, chrysanthemum,** and **Shasta daisy**.

 ## CARE

Inspect perennials to see if any have been heaved out of the ground by alternating freezing and thawing. Firmly press them back down into the soil to prevent them from freezing or drying out. To reduce heaving, maintain a layer of mulch around your perennials to insulate the soil.

 ## WATERING

Do not allow the pot or flats to dry out. If they're uncovered, check them daily and water as needed.

 ## FERTILIZING

Seedlings growing in soilless mixes need to be fertilized when the first true leaves appear. Feed at every other watering with a water-soluble fertilizer in order to promote faster growth until the plants are ready to plant outdoors. Water between feedings with plain water.

 ## GROOMING

Cut shorter **ornamental grasses** to 4 to 6 inches in height and **pampas grass** from 6 to 12 inches in height. When pruning back the **pampas grass**, wear gloves and cinch the top-growth with rope to make removal easier.

Trim away any dead leaves or stems from **aster, coreopsis,** and **rudbeckia**. Avoid damaging the crown of new leaves at the base. Wait until new growth emerges before cutting back 'Miss Huff' **lantana** and **salvia**.

 ## PROBLEMS

Damping-off can be a problem on seedlings. See Annuals February Problems p. 21 for a description and controls.

Control any winter annual weeds such as bittercress, common chickweed, and henbit by handpulling. Suppress them with a shallow layer of mulch.

Cut most ornamental grasses 4 to 6 inches in height.

# MARCH
## PERENNIALS

### PLANNING

When designing a perennial garden, it's easy to go overboard and end up creating a complex border comprised of a multitude of plants. This can be a problem especially if you're faced with a shoestring budget. Try starting perennials from seed, trade plants with neighbors, purchase less expensive or smaller plants at the beginning, and grow perennials that are good reseeders.

### PLANTING

Plant perennials when they become available from local nurseries or when they arrive in the mail from catalog orders. Plant dormant bare-root plants soon after receiving them. Here's how:

1. Remove the plastic wrapping and shake the packing material loose from the roots. Soak the roots in a bucket of water at least an hour before planting.

2. Dig the planting hole wide enough to accommodate the roots when they're spread out.

3. Create a cone of soil in the bottom of the hole and tamp down the top firmly. This will prevent the plant from settling too deeply.

4. Set the plant over the cone and drape the roots evenly over the top.

5. Backfill the hole. Work the soil in among the roots with your fingers. If the perennial has settled too deeply, lift it gently to raise the crown to the proper level.

Dig up, divide, and replant established perennials if they've become too crowded and flowering has been sparse. Some fast-growing perennials need to be divided between one and three years after planting—these include **aster**, **astilbe**, **beebalm**, **boltonia**, **garden mum**, **garden phlox**, **rudbeckia**, **Shasta daisy**, and many others. To avoid interrupting flowering, dig up summer- and fall-blooming perennials when the new growth is a few inches high.

Divide **ornamental grasses** before new growth emerges. Cut back the old culms to within 4 to 6 inches of the ground and use a sharp shovel or large knife to slice one or more wedges out of the crown. Immediately plant them elsewhere.

Uncover the trays or pots overwintered outdoors and move them to a cold frame for protection from freezing temperatures. The perennial seedlings will emerge over a range of weeks (sometimes longer). Transplant tray-grown seedlings to individual pots after they've developed one or two sets of true leaves.

### CARE

Press back any perennials that may have frost-heaved over the winter. Maintain a 2-inch layer of mulch around your perennials. Keep the mulch away from the crowns to avoid rot.

### WATERING

Keep newly planted perennials moist (do not let them dry out).

### FERTILIZING

Most perennials benefit from a boost with fertilizer as new growth begins in the spring. Select a slow-release fertilizer according to soil-test results. Follow the label directions regarding the amount and frequency of application. Water the fertilizer in to make it available to the plants.

 GROOMING

As new growth emerges, prune away any dead, winter-killed leaves and shoots, and compost them or bury them in the vegetable garden.

Cut back **Mexican sage** (*Salvia leucantha*) and **cigar plant** (*Cuphea micropetala*), leaving 6 to 12 inches of woody stem. Pinch out the tips of the new growth that results, or cut it back by half when it reaches a foot in length to produce a denser, sturdier specimen.

Cut back the winter foliage of warm-season **ornamental grasses** within a few inches of the ground before the new shoots emerge. In northern parts of Alabama and Mississippi, cool-season grasses such as **blue fescue** (*Festuca glauca* 'Elijah Blue') and **blue lyme grass** (*Leymus arenarius*) can be sheared, generally removing no more than one-third of their height.

 PROBLEMS

Flower thrips damage **bellflower**, **daylily**, and **peony** flowers with their feeding. Remove and discard thrip-infested flowers.

## HELPFUL HINTS

How many perennials will you need to plant in a given area?
The following chart shows the number of plants per square foot for a given spacing:

| Spacing (inches) | Spacing Multiplier (# of Plants per Sq. Ft.) |
|---|---|
| 12 | 1.00 |
| 15 | 0.64 |
| 18 | 0.44 |
| 24 | 0.25 |
| 36 | 0.11 |

Assume the bed measures 48 square feet (8 feet long and 6 feet wide) and you want to plant the perennials 15 inches apart. To determine the number of plants needed for the bed, use this equation:

**Area of Bed x Spacing Multiplier = Total # of plants**

In our example, the perennials will be spaced 15 inches apart, so

**48 square feet x 0.64 = 31**

Space 31 perennials 15 inches apart to occupy a 48-square-foot bed.

Damping off can be triggered by sustained waterlogged conditions in the growing medium.

Avoid overwatering. Water your seedlings only when the surface of the medium feels dry.

Inspect the newly emerging leaves of your **daylilies** for reddish-brown streaks and browned-out spots. They could be afflicted with a disease called leaf-streak. This fungus overwinters in dead, infected leaves, so collect and discard diseased or dead leaves to reduce the chances of future outbreaks.

Handpull winter annuals such as henbit and common chickweed to prevent them from going to seed. Maintaining a 2-inch layer of mulch will suppress weeds.

In some cases you can rely on a preemergent herbicide to reduce the amount of handweeding required. See Vines and Ground Covers May Problems p. 237 for more information.

# APRIL
## PERENNIALS

 PLANNING

Some perennials become top-heavy and require support to prevent them from bending or toppling over. They include **Japanese anemone**, **boltonia** (*Boltonia asteroides* 'Snowbank'), **gaura**, **peony**, **sneezeweed**, **balloon flower**, **swamp sunflower**, and **Joe-pye weed**. Plan to support these plants early in their growth before they get too tall and floppy. There are a wide variety of materials you can use such as specially designed peony rings, tomato cages, and plastic or bamboo stakes.

If you love peonies, it's worth investing in peony rings. Place the ring over the plant in early spring; as the plant grows, raise the ring onto stakes to support the heavy flower heads.

Position the stakes so the plants will eventually hide the supports. When securing their stems, tie the soft twine into a figure eight to avoid binding a stem.

To avoid staking some perennials altogether, select compact, lower-growing cultivars or prune them (by pinching or cutting back) at least eight weeks before flowering to keep their height in check. See the Grooming section to learn more about this approach.

 PLANTING

Condition or harden-off the seedlings started indoors. Gradually expose them to outdoor conditions by moving them to a cold frame or a porch for at least a week before planting in the garden.

When planting **ornamental grasses**, follow this general rule of spacing: Place plants as far apart as their eventual height. This means that grasses that top out at 3 feet should be planted 3 feet apart from center to center.

Plant container-grown perennials as described in the Planting

section on p. 125 in the introduction to this chapter.

 CARE

Clean up plants and flower beds.

 WATERING

Keep newly planted perennials well-watered during the first few weeks to help them get quickly established.

 FERTILIZING

Apply a slow-release fertilizer when the new shoots emerge. Follow the label directions regarding the amount and frequency of application. Water afterwards to make the minerals available to the roots.

 GROOMING

Pinched perennials produce more but smaller flowers than plants that have not been pinched. Pinching will stagger the bloom period of plants, particularly **garden mums**, and will prevent them from growing tall and straggly. Plants that respond well to pinching include **aster**, **beebalm**, **garden mums**, **spotted Joe-pye weed** (*Eupatorium pur-*

*pureum* 'Gateway'), **pink turtle-head** (*Chelone lyonii*), **spike speedwell** (*Veronica spicata*), 'Autumn Joy' **sedum**, and others.

## PROBLEMS

Watch out for aphids and white-flies on **coreopsis, chrysanthe-mum, sedum, verbena**, and others (see p. 141). Snails and slugs may be a problem on **hosta, bear's breeches** (*Acanthus mollis*), and other perennials. See p. 286 for descriptions and controls.

Look for columbine leaf min-ers. The larvae tunnel between the upper and lower leaf sur-faces, producing telltale grayish-white serpentine trails. There are several generations of larvae and adults per year. Control leaf miners by crushing the larvae inside the leaf before they become too disfigured or by cut-ting off the leaf altogether and removing it from the garden. For heavy infestations, cut **columbines** to the ground after flowering. New growth will soon emerge.

At the end of the growing sea-son, remove any debris near the base of your plants to reduce next-year's overwintering off-spring. Not all **columbines** are equally susceptible to this pest. The native **American columbine** (*Aquilegia canadensis*), for

example, is reported to be less susceptible to leaf miner attack.

Botrytis blight (*Botrytis paeo-niae*) attacks **peony** buds, causing them to turn black and shrivel up. This fungal disease also attacks flowers stalks, leaves, and leaf petioles. Remove and dispose of infected plant parts as soon as you spot them. If neces-sary, apply a fungicide in the spring as new shoots emerge.

Handpull bittercress, chick-weed, henbit, and other winter annuals before they go to seed.

Pre-emergent herbicides are available for many of the more common perennials. These herbi-cides kill germinating weed seedlings before they appear. See Annuals March Problems p. 23 for tips on selecting a pre-emergent herbicide.

## HELPFUL HINTS FOR LONG-BLOOMING PERENNIALS

Some gardeners crave perennials that bloom longer than a month, which is the norm. Fortunately, there are a number of long-blooming perennials that can extend the flowering sea-son for several months. With periodic deadheading, the following perennials can be expected to bloom for two months or more:

- **Yarrow** (*Achillea* 'Coronation Gold' and 'Fire King')
- **Chrysanthemum** (*Chrysanthemum* 'Clara Curtis')
- **Coreopsis** (*Coreopsis verticillata* 'Moonbeam' and 'Zagreb')
- **Purple coneflower** (*Echinacea purpurea* 'Bright Star' and 'Magnus', among others)
- **Blanketflower** (*Gaillardia* x *grandiflora* 'Baby Cole')
- **Gaura** (*Gaura lindheimeri* 'Whirling Butterflies')
- **Reblooming daylilies**, (including *Hemerocallis* 'Bitsy', 'Stella de Oro', 'Black Stella de Oro', 'Black-eyed Stella', and 'Happy Returns')
- **Russian sage** (*Perovskia atriplicifolia*)
- **Garden phlox** (*Phlox paniculata*)
- **Black-eyed Susan** (*Rudbeckia fulgida* var. *sullivantii* 'Goldsturm')
- **Pincushion flower** (*Scabiosa* 'Butterfly Blue')
- **Longleaf veronica** (*Veronica* 'Sunny Border Blue')
- **Clump verbena** (*Verbena canadensis* 'Abbeville', 'Homestead Purple', and several others)
- **Speedwell** (*Veronica* 'Goodness Grows')

# MAY

## PERENNIALS

### PLANNING

If you're serious about growing perennials well, start a journal this month. It will document your observations, thoughts, and plans for the future. Some of the following items can be noted in your journal:

- Blooming dates for each variety
- Condition of the flowers, leaves, and overall health of your perennials
- Pest problems: insects, diseases, weeds
- Kinds of pesticides used and when they were applied
- Plants that need to be moved or replaced because they grew larger than you expected or were more demanding than you had planned

Your journal can become a teaching tool, especially when you need the assistance of a county Extension agent, Master Gardener, or a garden center staff person to help you diagnose a particular problem. The notes you took about weather conditions, fertilizing, watering, and any pest control applications are important clues that can help reveal the answer.

So start writing.

### PLANTING

It's not too late to plant perennials as long as you're willing to pamper them, helping with regular watering to speed up their establishment before hot summer weather arrives.

### CARE

Begin staking tall-growing plants when they reach one-third of their mature height. Place the stakes close to the plant, but take care to avoid damaging the root system. Secure the stems of the plants to stakes in several places with materials that will not cut into the stem. Tie the twine into a figure eight to avoid binding the stem. Summer- and fall-flowering perennials often require support. Some plants, however, can simply be pruned back lightly in midsummer to reduce their height and encourage branching and sturdiness. **Swamp sunflower** (*Helianthus angustifolius*) can be handled this way. See June Grooming for more information about this technique.

Other supports include hoops or stakes.

# WATERING

When watering, apply sufficient moisture to soak the soil deeply, wetting the root zone of your plants. Instead of following the calendar, water when the top 2 or 3 inches of soil feels dry.

# FERTILIZING

Evaluate your perennials for color and growth to determine the need for fertilizer. To encourage more growth, apply a slow-release fertilizer.

# GROOMING

In the spring, when new shoots in a clump of **garden phlox** reach 8 to 10 inches tall, thin out all but four or five of the well-spaced healthy ones to allow good air circulation. Thinning helps prevent disease (especially powdery mildew), improves the appearance of the plants, and produces sturdier stems.

Some spring-flowering perennials should be sheared after flowering, cutting them back by one-half. Among them are **cheddar pinks** (*Dianthus gratianopolitanus* 'Bath's Pink' and 'Firewitch'), **evergreen candytuft** (*Iberis sempervirens*), and **moss phlox** (*Phlox subulata*). **Garden chrysanthemum** can be sheared when the new growth reaches 4 to 6 inches in length. Shearing an inch off the top will delay flowering and encourage bushiness and the production of a lot of flower buds.

# PROBLEMS

Aphids, spider mites, and whiteflies can be a problem. Spider mites are especially fond of **chrysanthemum, coneflower, daylily,** and **phlox** (see July Problems p. 141).

Avoid leaf spot diseases by watering your perennials from below and limiting water on the leaves. Proper spacing with plenty of air movement will reduce fungal infections.

Handpull weeds when they're young. Try not to put off this chore until next weekend. Hoeing and maintaining a shallow mulch layer will also help.

## HELPFUL HINTS

Perennials that reseed themselves produce volunteers that can be transplanted to other parts of the garden or traded with friends and neighbors. Sometimes, they can produce more seedlings than you want, which makes them behave like weeds. The following perennials reseed freely so keep that in mind if you're going to introduce them into your garden. Deadheading them before they release their seeds is one way of reducing their offspring.

- **Blackberry lily** (*Belamcanda chinensis*)
- **Phlox** (*Phlox*)
- **Columbine** (*Aquilegia*)
- **Four-o-clock** (*Mirabilis jalapa*)
- **Hardy begonia** (*Begonia grandis*)
- **Lenten rose** (*Helleborus orientalis*)
- **Fountain grass** (*Pennisetum alopecuroides*)
- **Northern sea oats** (*Chasmanthium latifolium*)
- **Patrinia** (*Patrinia scabiosifolia*)
- **Purple coneflower** (*Echinacea purpurea*)
- **Shasta daisy** (*Leucanthemum* x *superbum*)
- **Hollyhock mallow** (*Malva sylvestris* 'Zebrina')

# JUNE
## PERENNIALS

### PLANNING

When you planned your garden, you probably chose perennials for their flowers, bloom time, and other features. But have you thought about selecting perennials for their ability to attract beneficial insects? Beneficial insect predators and parasites such as lady beetles, lacewings, syrphid flies, and tachinid flies prey on harmful insects including aphids, caterpillars, and mites. In general, the larvae feed on insects and mites while the adults feed on nectar and pollen—either exclusively or to supplement their diet when insects or mites are in short supply. Some of the perennials found by researchers to attract beneficial insects include: **fernleaf yarrow** (*Achillea filipendulina*), **basket-of-gold** (*Aurinia saxatilis*), **fever-few** (*Tanacetum parthenium*), **stonecrop** (*Sedum kamtschaticum*), **goldenrod** (*Solidago* 'Peter Pan'), and **spike speedwell** (*Veronica spicata*).

To keep beneficial insects in your landscape, plan to have flowering perennials in bloom all season long to provide them with a ready supply of nectar and pollen.

### PLANTING

Many perennials can be propagated by rooting softwood stem cuttings, including **balloon flower, beebalm, chrysanthemum, penstemon, phlox, salvia,** and **veronica**. (Softwood stems are mature and firm but not yet hardened and woody.) Here's how to do it:

1. Use a sharp knife or razor blade to take 3- to 6-inch-long cuttings of terminal growth. Make an angled cut just below a node—the point where the leaf joins the stem. Remove the lowest leaf or two.

2. Dip the cut end into a rooting hormone suited for herbaceous plants.

3. Fill a small pot with equal parts of peat moss and perlite. Use a pencil to poke a hole in the medium before inserting the cutting. This prevents the rooting powder from being scraped off.

4. When you have inserted all the cuttings, water them well, and place the pots in a plastic bag closed at the top with a twist-tie.

5. Set the pots in a bright location, but not in direct sunlight. When the cuttings have produced small new leaves, move them to the garden. Instead of transplanting them to their permanent homes, plant them in a "halfway house"—a makeshift nursery where they won't be neglected. After a few weeks, when they've grown large enough to hold their own, move them to their permanent spots.

Continue planting perennials; with the onset of hot, dry weather, however, be prepared to provide adequate water throughout their establishment period. Continue to move perennials outdoors that you grew from seed. Depending on their size, it may be better to transplant them to your home nursery. Better yet, transplant them in the fall when the weather becomes cooler and less stressful.

Plant **Shasta daisy, coreopsis,** and **coneflower** from seed. Sow them directly in the garden or in trays or pots. Seeds will take two to three weeks to emerge. When seedlings are 2 to 3 inches high, thin the plants to about 6 inches apart, or transplant them into individual containers.

## WATERING

Water recently planted perennials which are especially vulnerable to heat and drought stress. Water thoroughly to encourage deep rooting.

## FERTILIZING

If you used a slow-release fertilizer early in the season, check the label and evaluate the growth and appearance of your perennials to see if a second application is warranted.

## GROOMING

Pinch out the terminal growth of fall-blooming **garden chrysanthemum**. Repeat the pinching each time a lateral bud sends out a shoot—pinch as soon as the new shoot has about three sets of leaves. This will increase the number of blooms and produce bushier plants. To produce fewer but larger blooms, disbud **chrysanthemum** flowers—see August Grooming p. 142. **Sedum** 'Autumn Joy' tends to flop over in midseason, especially when sited in partial shade. Pinch out the growing tips or cut back the stems to a foot to encourage

branching and the production of lots of flowers.

Deadhead **achillea, bellflower, columbine, pincushion flower** (*Scabiosa* 'Butterfly Blue'), **spike speedwell** (*Veronica spicata*), and **salvia** to lateral or side buds. After the side buds finish flowering, cut the stems down to the basal leaves at the crown.

To avoid staking late-flowering plants such as **aster, Joe-pye weed**, or **heliopsis** (*Heliopsis helianthoides* 'Summer Sun'), prune them back to one-third their height. This will give them a fuller and more compact growth habit.

Pinch out the growing tips of other late-summer- and fall-flowering plants such as **boltonia, swamp sunflower** (*Helianthus angustifolius*), and **sneezeweed** (*Helenium autumnale*). They will produce many smaller flowers without any noticeable loss in height.

Cut back **amsonia** and **baptisia** after flowering by one-third to one-half their height; otherwise, they will continue to grow with abandon and will splay apart in late summer.

## PROBLEMS

Be on the lookout for aphids, slugs and snails, spider mites, and thrips. Handpick Japanese beetles and discard them in a jar of soapy water. Neem can be applied to the leaves to reduce feeding by the adults. Use other insecticides for heavy infestations.

Avoid overhead watering and remove spent flowers and dead or dying leaves. Look for signs of powdery mildew on **garden phlox** and **beebalm**. Infected leaves have a grayish-white powder on both sides. Heavy infestations can cause the leaves to curl and eventually yellow and die.

Remove infected plants and discard them. Thin out the plants to improve air movement. Fungicides can be applied when the symptoms appear and until they're gone. In the future, select varieties resistant to powdery mildew (see September Problems p. 145).

Handpull or hoe out any weeds to prevent them from stealing water and nutrients from your perennials. Suppress their emergence with a layer of mulch.

# JULY
## PERENNIALS

### PLANNING

If you haven't kept up with regular journal entries, record your observations of the performance of your plants, pest problems, control measures, and what needs to be done as summer closes and gives way to fall. Write down the plants that need to be composted or given away. And find some good regional books about perennials and learn more about the design of perennial borders.

### PLANTING

Any planting done now should be done with caution. Keep plants moist until they settle in. Divide **daylilies** after they finish blooming. Plants with fleshy roots—such as **butterfly weed** (*Asclepias*), **gas plant** (*Dictamnus albus*), and **bleeding heart** (*Dicentra spectabilis*)—can be propagated from root cuttings. Here's how to do it:

1. Rake the soil away from the crown to expose a few pencil-thick side roots. Cut these off cleanly with a knife and replace the soil. Do not remove more than a few roots from each crown.

2. Cut each root into 2- to 3-inch lengths and plant them horizontally in a flat containing moist sand or peat moss.

3. Cover the flat with a layer of clear plastic to keep the roots moist, and put the flat in a cool, shaded location. Callus tissue will form on the cut ends, and roots and shoots will develop from adventitious buds along the cuttings.

4. Several weeks after sprouting, transplant the young plants to a protected location.

The seeds of many perennials can be sown either in pots or directly in the garden. Although it may take seed-propagated perennials from two to three years to bloom, some will bloom in less than a year. Start the following perennials outdoors in a partially shaded location or indoors in trays or pots (next year you can sow a second crop indoors in early spring for flowering the same season):

- **Butterfly weed**
  (*Asclepias tuberosa*)
- **Large-flowered tickseed**
  (*Coreopsis grandiflora*)
- **Maltese cross**
  (*Lychnis chalcedonica*)
- **Purple coneflower**
  (*Echinacea purpurea*)
- **Red valerian**
  (*Centranthus ruber*)
- **Shasta daisy**
  (*Leucanthemum* x *superbum*)
- **Spike speedwell**
  (*Veronica spicata*)
- **Oxeye daisy**
  (*Heliopsis helianthoides*)
- **Violet sage**
  (*Salvia* x *superba*)
- **Yarrow**
  (*Achillea*)

### CARE

Stake tall-growing late-season bloomers before they topple over.

July is a good month to divide overgrown daylilies; use two shovels back to back to split the rootball.

140

## WATERING

During periods of low or no rainfall, water plants when they need it (especially new plantings or perennials that have been fertilized), and not by the calendar. When you water, do a thorough job so water penetrates the soil deeply. Wait until the soil becomes dry in the upper inch or so before watering again. To learn how to water efficiently, refer to Roses July Helpful Hints p. 167. Summer- and fall-flowering perennials such as **daylilies** need an ample supply of water to encourage flowering. Inspect the mulch in flower beds. If wind, rain, and natural decay have reduced its thickness to an inch or less, apply more mulch to raise the level to 2 to 3 inches—but leave only about a 1/2-inch-thick layer around the bases of the plants. Perennials that have been cut back heavily should be kept moist to support the emerging growth.

## FERTILIZING

After pinching or pruning your perennials, fertilize them to speed up their recovery. If you use a slow-release fertilizer, now is the time to make your second application of the season according to the label directions (your first application should have been applied in the spring at planting or when the new shoots emerged). Water afterwards to make the nutrients available to your plants.

## GROOMING

To ensure flowers this season, gardeners who've been shearing their **mums** should make their last cuts by the end of the month. Continue to deadhead spent flowers to improve appearance and prolong the blooming period of certain perennials such as **beebalm**, **black-eyed Susan**, **daylily**, **coreopsis**, **purple coneflower**, all **perennial salvias**, **spotted phlox** (*Phlox maculata*), **Stokes' aster**, **verbena**, and **yarrow**. Shear **threadleaf coreopsis** (*Coreopsis verticillata* 'Moonbeam') for a second bloom.

## PROBLEMS

Aphids, spider mites, and whiteflies continue to be on the prowl this month. They can be washed from plants with a strong stream of water. Insecticidal soap, insecticides, and miticides (for mites) will keep their numbers in check.

Watch for Japanese beetles this month. Their highest numbers occur in midsummer. Thankfully, there's only one generation a year.

Southern blight may attack a number of perennials, especially **artemisia**, **columbine**, **aster**, **coralbells**, **liatris**, **phlox**, **salvia**, and **Shasta daisy**. This soilborne disease occurs during periods of high temperatures (80 to 90 degrees F.) and in moist soils. The fungus attacks the stem at soil level and moves up rapidly, killing the tissues as it ascends. The leaves turn yellow and wilt, and eventually the entire plant collapses. Look on the infected stem for dozens of brown, mustard seed-sized sclerotia—the "seeds" of the fungus. Remove and discard infected plants. Leave the area fallow for six months or longer. Fungicidal soil drenches can be used to treat the soil when a shorter fallow period is used.

Leaf diseases may show up during wet weather. Trim away heavily infected leaves and compost them.

Continue handpulling weeds out of the flower beds. With proper spacing, your perennials should be able to shade out the soil naturally and keep the weeds at bay.

# AUGUST
## PERENNIALS

 PLANNING

This is a good month to make plans for improvements this fall and next year. What were the most troublesome insects and diseases this season? Perhaps you need to make plans to dig out some perennials and replace them this fall.

Think about the perennials that seemed to "take a lickin' and keep on tickin'." Take notes about perennials that looked attractive while requiring little attention. Did any of the perennials tolerate drought conditions better than others?

Over the past few months you may have saved newspaper and magazine clippings written by local garden writers who tout certain perennials. Perhaps you wrote down comments from friends, or saw high-performing perennials that grabbed your attention in private or public gardens. Find all the notes you wrote on the backs of credit card receipts, napkins, and road maps, and compile them into your gardening journal.

 PLANTING

Any planting done now should be followed with regular watering, keeping the soil moist in order to speed up establishment.

Pinching back the buds of mums (disbudding) forces the plant to become bushier and stronger, and delays blooming until the fall.

 CARE

If you're going on vacation this month, have someone take care of your flower beds while you're away. See Annuals July Planning p. 30 for some helpful suggestions.

 GROOMING

Deadhead **phlox** to prevent the flowers from going to seed. The seedlings do not come true to the color of the parent, and often their sheer numbers overtake a planting, giving you the impression that the flowers from the parents have magically changed color.

Disbud **chrysanthemums** to produce fewer but larger blooms. Most **mums**, except spray types, respond well to disbudding. To disbud, pinch off the side buds that form in the angles of the leaves along the main stems. Leave only the large top bud. The plant will channel its energy into this bud, which will develop into impressive proportions.

 WATERING

During periods of low or no rainfall, water plants—especially new plantings—when they need it, and not by the calendar. When you do water, do a thorough job so water penetrates the soil deeply. Wait until the soil becomes dry in the upper inch or so before watering again.

Avoid irrigating your perennials with an overhead sprinkler. In addition to wasting water and watering weeds, wetting the leaves will encourage diseases.

Container-grown flowers can dry out quickly, especially when located in full sun. Feel the soil in containers at least once a day to check for moisture. When water is necessary, apply it long enough so that it runs out the drainage holes. Keep in mind that clay pots, which allow water to be lost to evaporation from the walls of the pot, will need to be watered more often than plastic pots—and small pots will dry out faster than large planters.

Mulch to decrease weeds and conserve moisture. Inspect the mulch in flower beds. If wind, rain, and natural decay have reduced its thickness to an inch or less, apply more mulch to raise the level to 2 to 3 inches, but avoid piling it up around the base of the crown of the plants. Mulch conserves moisture, suppresses weed growth, and makes those weeds that do grow easier to pull out.

# FERTILIZING

Be cautious about fertilizing. Unless the leaves look pale or off-color, fertilizing won't be necessary. Avoid excessive fertilization. It produces the soft, succulent growth favored by pests.

Never skimp on building up the natural fertility of the soil with applications of organic mulches such as compost.

## HELPFUL HINTS

• If you have a friend who is new to gardening and is interested in trying perennials, introduce him or her to these "no fuss-no muss" beauties: 'Autumn Joy' **sedum, balloon flower, butterfly weed, daylily,** 'Goldsturm' **coneflower, hosta, Lenten rose, purple coneflower, southern shield fern,** and **threadleaf coreopsis.** They not only look terrific—they're great confidence-builders.

• Create a theme garden with perennials. It could be a single-color garden (such as a "white" garden with white-flowered plants); a butterfly and hummingbird garden; an evening garden with flowers and leaves that can be appreciated in the twilight hours; or a scented garden. Plans for these and other theme gardens can be found in perennial plant encyclopedias and other reference books. A number of reference books have sample designs for these gardens so you can make substitutions of plant materials to fit your design. Adapt the existing design and plant list to suit your site.

# PROBLEMS

Trim any dead, damaged, diseased, or insect-infested leaves.

To improve their appearance, deadhead the spent flowers from **garden phlox, obedient plant** (*Physostegia virginiana*), **perennial salvia, pincushion flower, purple coneflower,** and **sneezeweed**.

Nematodes are microscopic organisms that live in the soil and attack the roots of plants. They are commonly found in coarse-textured sandy soils. See Roses July Problems p. 167 for more information.

Be on the lookout for aphids and spider mites. Plants infested by spider mites have faded, stippled leaves. Remove these pests with a strong spray of water from the hose. Resort to a pesticide if their numbers are high and damage is great.

Fungal leaf spots, powdery mildew, and other diseases could be afflicting your perennials. Evaluate the extent of damage to determine if a fungicide application is necessary. Remove and discard heavily infested plants.

Control weeds by handpulling and maintaining a shallow layer of mulch. Prevent the weeds from going to seed by removing the flowers. Any seeds that can be eliminated now will not have to be dealt with next year.

# SEPTEMBER

## PERENNIALS

### PLANNING

As the transition from summer to fall approaches and you feel as bedraggled as your garden, you can gain inspiration from fall-flowering perennials. **Garden mums** (*Chrysanthemum* x *morifolium*) have long been the mainstay of the fall garden and are available in a wide array of heights, flower forms, and colors. But there's more than **mums**. Consider **aster** (*Aster* x *frikartii* 'Monch'), **ironweed** (*Vernonia noveboracensis*), **sedum** (*Sedum* 'Autumn Joy'), **Confederate rose** (*Hibiscus mutabilis*), **Joe-pye weed** (*Eupatorium purpureum*), **goldenrod** (*Solidago* 'Golden Thumb' and 'Peter Pan'), **swamp sunflower** (*Helianthus angustifolius*), **blue anise sage** (*Salvia guaranitica*), **Japanese anemone** (*Anemone hupehensis*), **Mexican sage** (*Salvia leucantha*), **cigar plant** (*Cuphea micropetala*), **azure sage** (*Salvia azurea*), and **Philippine violet** (*Barleria cristata*).

**Ornamental grasses** also make great choices for the fall and winter garden with their plumes of flowers and shimmering leaves. Some great choices include **maidenhair grass** (*Miscanthus sinensis* 'Morning Light'), **pink muhly grass** (*Muhlenbergia capillaris*), **feather reed grass** (*Calamagrostis* x *acutiflora* 'Karl Foerster'), and **switch grass** (*Panicum virgatum* 'Heavy Metal'). Learn more about these and other late-season flowering plants that will thrive in your corner of Alabama or Mississippi. Look for them in your garden center or mail-order catalogs, and plan to weave them into your landscape.

### PLANTING

Establish new perennial flower beds: Begin digging, dividing, and replanting overcrowded beds of **beebalm, daylily, cheddar pinks, Shasta daisy,** and **threadleaf coreopsis**. This can continue throughout fall. Spread a liberal amount of organic matter over the area and mix it into the soil at least 6 to 8 inches deep. Space divisions at least 1 foot apart in all directions so that root competition will not be a problem for several years.

Plant cool-season **ornamental grasses** now to take advantage of the cool temperatures, allowing the roots to become established before spring's burst of growth.

**Astilbe** is not a long-lived perennial, so divide it every three or four years to maintain vigor. When replanting divisions, leave three or four "eyes" in each section, and replant so the eyes are about $1/2$ inch below the soil surface.

Now is the time to move perennial plants started from seed in midsummer to the home nursery row or to their permanent spot in the garden. Follow these general guidelines for spacing plants: Small plants under 1 foot tall or front-of-the-border plants should be spaced about 12 to 18 inches apart; plants of intermediate size (1 to $2^{1}/_{2}$ feet tall) should be placed at least 18 to 24 inches apart (three or four plants per 10 square feet); and larger plants should be spaced roughly 3 feet apart.

### CARE

Pull out stakes and remove cages as plants finish for the year. Clean the stakes and cages and store them where you can locate them next spring.

### WATERING

Fall is the driest season in Alabama and Mississippi. Keep newly set-out transplants well watered to help them establish quickly.

# HELPFUL HINTS FOR CHOOSING PEONIES

Herbaceous **peonies** are long-lived plants (even outliving gardeners!) that sport gorgeous flowers in white, pink, or red in double, semi-double, or single forms (depending on the cultivar). Even when out of flower, their attractive leaves command attention. **Peonies** can't be grown throughout Alabama and Mississippi, however, because of their need for cold temperatures and disdain of extended hot and humid conditions. Depending on the cultivar, **peonies** require a certain number of hours of temperatures below 40 degrees F. to come out of dormancy, grow, and bloom normally.

To cultivate **peonies** at the edge of their heat hardiness in Zone 7b and the northern half of 8a, select early- to mid-season cultivars and single or Japanese flower forms. Early-blooming cultivars enable you to avoid warm, humid weather and accompanying diseases, particularly gray mold or botrytis blight. Late-flowering semidoubles and doubles with their thick collection of petals tend to hold moisture, which fosters fungal infection.

Some herbaceous **peonies** that have performed well in Zone 7b include the double-flowering 'Red Charm', 'Félix Crousse', and 'Highlight'. Double pink-flowered **peonies** include 'Raspberry Sundae', 'Sarah Bernhardt', 'Mrs. Franklin D. Roosevelt', 'Mons. Jules Elie', and 'Gene Wild'. Double white **peonies** include 'Carolina Moon', 'Festiva Maxima', 'Shirley Temple', 'Duchesse de Nemours', and 'Gardenia'. Some good single-flowered performers include 'Mikado' (red), 'Westerner' (pink), and 'Jan van Leeuwen' (white).

 FERTILIZING

Fertilizing is not necessary this late in the season. Allow the perennials to go dormant so they can tolerate the winter weather.

 GROOMING

Continue deadheading long-blooming perennials to encourage a flush of fall bloom.

 PROBLEMS

Check for evidence of snails and slugs. Set out baits or traps for them as the weather turns cooler and wetter.

Remove infected leaves and clean up fallen leaves and discard them. Fungicides may not be warranted this late in the season. Make a note in your gardening journal about varieties that were highly susceptible to powdery mildew, and consider replacing them with more resistant cultivars next year. Powdery mildew-resistant **garden phlox** cultivars include 'Bright Eyes', 'David', 'Eva Cullum', 'Franz Schubert', 'Natascha', 'Robert Poore', and 'Starfire'. The following **beebalm** cultivars are less prone to infection by powdery mildew: 'Claire Grace', 'Colrain Red', 'Elsie's Lavender', 'Jacob Cline', 'Vintage Wine' 'Raspberry Wine', and 'Marshall's Delight'.

Don't turn your back on the weeds in your flower beds. Summer annual weeds like crabgrass and goosegrass have matured and are going to seed. Winter annual weeds like annual bluegrass, chickweed, and Carolina geranium are germinating. Hoe them out or handpull them now.

# OCTOBER

## PERENNIALS

### PLANNING

With the onset of cooler temperatures, expand old beds, create new ones, or rearrange plants. When starting new beds, have the soil tested through your Cooperative Extension Service office. Test old flower beds every three years.

### PLANTING

Herbaceous **peonies** can remain undisturbed for many years. When they become overcrowded, however, and blooms are few and far between, they will have to be divided. Divide them when the leaves and shoots are killed by frost. Gardeners in the northernmost parts of Alabama and Mississippi should be aware that **peonies** need six to eight weeks to develop roots before the ground freezes, so don't drag your feet.

1. Cut the foliage to within 4 inches of the ground. Then use a spading fork to gently lift each clump.

2. Set the clumps on a tarp or piece of newspaper and allow them to air-dry for an hour or so. This will make it easier to brush the soil off the root and crown.

3. Examine each plant carefully before dividing it with a sharp knife. Your goal is to make divisions that have at least three stout roots and three to five dark-red "eyes" or growth buds each. Smaller divisions will take longer to bloom. The outer edges of the clump typically yield better divisions than the woody center.

4. Allow the divisions to cure in a warm, dry place for a day or two. Plant the cured divisions in a well-drained fertile bed, allowing 3 feet between plants. Dig each hole 2 feet wide and 18 inches deep, and mix compost or well-rotted manure into the bottom. Position the division and backfill the hole so the eyes are no more than $1/2$ to 1 inch below the surface. **Peonies** planted too deeply will never bloom.

5. Water the newly planted divisions well, and mulch lightly with compost or shredded leaves.

**Ferns** can be planted or transplanted in fall. **Hardy ferns** are best divided in early fall or very early spring before new growth emerges. **Ferns** such as **hay-scented fern** (*Dennstaedtia punctilobula*) and **ostrich fern** (*Matteuccia struthiopteris*) have branching rhizomes on or near the soil surface. These can simply be cut; make sure, however, that you have a growing tip and one or two intact fronds. Replant the divisions at the same level.

Other species such as **cinnamon fern** (*Osmunda cinnamomea*) develop a tangle of rhizomes and roots—you will have to dig up the whole clump and do your best to separate individual plants. Occasionally **ferns** develop multiple crowns that can be cut apart. The important thing is not to cover the crowns of the new transplants with more than $1/2$ inch of soil, and to keep them well watered until they are established. A shallow layer of mulch throughout the growing season will help retain moisture in the soil.

Cinnamon fern is a spectacular addition to your garden. To divide, you must dig up the entire plant and then separate into clumps.

There's still time to dig, divide, and replant crowded perennials. Look for perennials that have grown out-of-bounds or have declined due to overcrowding and have developed a ring of growth with an empty center.

## CARE

Before the first freeze, take cuttings of **Confederate rose** (*Hibiscus mutabilis*), a fall-blooming perennial that's marginally hardy in Zone 7b, where the top growth will get winter-killed and resprout from the crown the following spring. The flowers can be either single or double, depending on the cultivar. The peony-like flowers go through subtle color changes from light pink to red, or white, to pink, to crimson.

If you're concerned that the plant will not survive the upcoming winter, or if you choose to share this plant with friends, it roots very easily in water from cuttings taken in the fall. Pot up rooted cuttings and transplant them outside after the last freeze in spring to an area in full sun or partial shade.

## HELPFUL HINTS

• As you divide your perennials and replant them, don't forget the passalong features of plants, which means you can give them to a friend or swap for another desirable plant.

• Some perennials, such as **butterfly weed**, **euphorbia**, and **gas plant** (*Dictamnus albus*), resent division. **Hellebores** are difficult to move when they're more than a few years old; fortunately, they reseed with abandon, allowing you to transplant or share the offspring with friends.

## WATERING

Add mulch to your perennial border. A 2-inch layer of weed-free straw or chopped leaves will help conserve soil moisture, protect root systems, and reduce plant loss from soil heaving during the winter. Keep new plantings watered if the weather is dry. Established gardens may need water as well so they won't go into winter with insufficient moisture.

## FERTILIZING

Do not fertilize this late in the season. Allow the perennials to go dormant so they can tolerate the winter weather.

## GROOMING

Cut back **iris** and **peonies** hard after the first frost and compost the trimmings to reduce the chances of disease outbreaks.

Prune perennials when their tops are nipped by cold. Some perennials produce seeds that are attractive to birds. Leave these plants standing as long as there are still seeds in them.

## PROBLEMS

Clean up the dead leaves from around your perennial flowers. If left on the ground, leaves and stems can harbor diseases and provide convenient places for pests to spend the winter.

Hoe or handpull any weeds in the beds to prevent them from going to seed, and to prevent the younger weeds from settling in for the winter. Mulch with a shallow layer to suppress emerging weeds.

# NOVEMBER

## PERENNIALS

### PLANNING

You can keep your garden looking good while nourishing birds with perennials that offer attractive leaves, stems, and seedheads. **Ornamental grasses** are at the top of the list with their beautiful seedheads and leaves that turn yellow, orange, red, or purple with the onset of cooler winter temperatures.

### PLANTING

Continue to set out perennials if good selections are available from garden centers. Gardeners in the northernmost parts of Alabama and Mississippi should be aware that transplants should be set out at least four to six weeks before the ground is expected to freeze. Occasional freezing and thawing is hard on new plants because it pushes them up out of the ground. Late-planted perennials will benefit from a 3- to 5-inch layer of mulch after the ground freezes to protect them from being lifted by the freezing and thawing of the soil.

Start perennial seeds that need to be stratified or exposed to moist chilling conditions (check the seed packet for the length of cold exposure); otherwise, they won't germinate. Stratification is

a survival mechanism that prevents seeds from germinating in the fall when they can be killed by harsh winter temperatures. Only after being exposed to conditions that mimic winter can they overcome the seed's internal mechanism that inhibits it from germinating. Seeds such as **amsonia** (*Amsonia taberrnaemontana*), **gas plant** (*Dictamnus albus*), and **turtlehead** (*Chelone* spp.) can be stratified in a cold frame. Here's how:

1. Sow the seeds in pots or trays. Label each container with the plant's name and the date of sowing.

2. Move the pots and trays to an unheated porch, garage, or cold frame where they can be exposed to outdoor temperatures but protected from snow, wind, and rain. Cover the pots or trays with plastic wrap to prevent the potting medium from drying out. They should be exposed to cold temperatures of less than 40 degrees F. for four to eight weeks.

3. As springlike weather gets here, the seeds will start sprouting, usually when the temperatures are between 45 and 60 degrees F. Different species will germinate at different times. Some may appear in very early spring, others in late spring, while a few may take up to a year or more. Once the seedlings emerge, remove the plastic,

and water them to keep them from wilting.

4. As seedlings sprout, move the pots to a cool location (below 70 degrees) with bright indirect sunlight.

5. When the seedlings have grown a second set of true leaves, thin or transplant them to prevent overcrowding. If you don't need many plants, thin to one seedling per pot by cutting off extras with scissors. If you want a lot, transplant the seedlings one per container into 2¹/₄- or 3-inch-wide plastic pots filled with a moist, peat-based potting mix. Use a fork to gently lift seedlings out of containers and tease them apart. Handle seedlings by the leaves to avoid damaging their stems.

6. Water the seedlings and place them out of direct sun for a few days to recover. After a week, put them in a place that receives morning sun. Begin feeding the seedlings once a week with a dilute (half-strength) liquid fertilizer.

7. Plant in the garden by late summer or early fall. Some slower-growing species may not be large enough to move yet. Keep them in a cold frame over the winter, and set them out the following spring.

Plant **peonies** now in the northern halves of Alabama and Mississippi. For best results, choose a variety that blooms in early to mid-season. **Peonies** are long-lived, reliable, and extremely cold-hardy plants (Zones 3 to 7) that produce magnificent flowers in spring and early summer and attractive compound leaves throughout the season. Gardeners who want to grow **peonies** in the warmer parts of Zones 7 and 8a should refer to the September Helpful Hints p. 145. Plant dormant bare-root herbaceous **peonies** so the "eyes" or buds on the division are covered by no more than $1/2$ to 1 inch of soil. **Peonies**

planted too deeply will never bloom. Plant container-grown **peonies** so the top of the rootball is less than an inch below the soil surface.

## CARE

There's still time to dig, divide, and replant crowded perennials. Look for perennials that have grown out-of-bounds or have declined due to overcrowding and have developed a ring of growth with an empty center. Divide **peonies** when the leaves die back (see October Planting p. 146).

## WATERING

Keep newly planted transplants well watered to help them get established.

## FERTILIZING

Fertilizer is not needed at this time of year.

Once you've dug up the peony you wish to divide, cut it into sections or divisions containing at least three or four "eyes" or buds. Replant them so the eyes are about $1/2$ inch below the soil surface.

## GROOMING

Reduce peony botrytis blight and powdery mildew on **beebalm** and **phlox** by trimming away and disposing of old, dead stems.

Avoid pruning **Monch's aster**, **ferns**, **salvias**, **mums**, and other marginally hardy plants so the crowns will be insulated during cold weather. Prune them when new growth emerges in the spring. Plants such as **leadwort** (*Ceratostigma plumbaginoides*) that also emerge late in the spring should not be pruned; the old stems and leaves will let you know where they are so you won't damage them by digging.

Perennials with winter interest should not be pruned until winter takes its toll.

## PROBLEMS

See October Problems p. 147 for advice on diseases.

Handpull any young winter annuals, or cover them with a shallow layer of compost. Weeding is never fun, but the cooler temperatures can make it more bearable.

# DECEMBER

## PERENNIALS

 PLANNING

As you pore over catalogs or read gardening magazines, jot down the names of perennials that are worth growing in your garden. Start a "wish list" of perennials in your gardening journal. Some information that should be included:

- Name (common name and botanical name) and cultivar
- Expected bloom time (for example, early spring, midsummer, early fall)
- Cold/heat hardiness
- Flower color
- Ornamental characteristics (flowers, leaves, seedheads)
- Height and spread
- Pest problems
- Additional comments (self-sows, requires staking, needs regular deadheading, etc.)

Cut out pictures of perennials from catalogs and paste them in your journal of favorites. This will help you identify perennials and quickly visualize them.

Add perennials to your Christmas wish list. A gift certificate from your local garden center or favorite mail-order source might be in order.

## HELPFUL HINTS

Join a garden club, become a Master Gardener with the Cooperative Extension Service, or volunteer at a local botanical garden or arboretum. Share your gardening experiences with others and refine your gardening skills with other supercharged gardeners. It's also a good way of sharing your excesses with like-minded gardeners who are willing to share their bounty.

 PLANTING

Seeds that need an exposure to cold temperatures can be sown this month and set outdoors.

 CARE

Late-planted perennials in the colder parts of Alabama and Mississippi, where the soil may freeze, should be mulched to insulate the soil and reduce the occurrence of frost-heaving.

 WATERING

Keep newly planted transplants well watered to help them get established.

 FERTILIZING

Do not fertilize your perennials at this time.

 GROOMING

Continue to cut back dead, damaged, or dying perennial top growth that offers no winter ornamental interest or food for birds. Cut down to within 2 to 3 inches of ground level or just above the new foliage at the base.

Perennials such as **coneflower**, **heliopsis**, and **black-eyed Susan**, whose seedheads offer food for birds, are best left unpruned until late winter.

 PROBLEMS

Diseases can be carried over the winter on plant parts and infect the plants in spring. Remove all fallen leaves and dead stems from the perennials before mulching.

# ROSES

Most of us love to give roses and we love to receive them; we're divided, however, on the issue of growing them in our gardens.

Some gardeners will grow roses with the thought that beauty has its price ("no pain, no gain"). They devotedly dust, spray, deadhead, prune, feed, mulch, and otherwise defend and nurture these garden bluebloods. Other gardeners avoid roses for this very reason, seeing them as fussy and temperamental, unable to flourish without human support. However, not all roses are so fussy. Any gardener can enjoy some member of this royal family if choices are made knowledgeably:

• The high-maintenance/high-performance types demand a certain level of doting that includes preventative pesticide applications, regular feeding, and primping. Your efforts will be rewarded with blemish-free leaves and exquisite flowers.

• The easy-care types are suitable for gardeners who love roses but aren't interested in intensive management. These include not only the eye-catching old garden roses discovered in cemeteries and abandoned homesteads but also some modern hybrid teas, grandifloras, and climbers. They are vigorous and more tolerant of pests than other kinds of roses. Though less demanding, they can still produce magnificent flowers.

## PLANNING

Roses have three basic requirements:

1. At least six hours of direct sunlight each day: An ideal location receives full sun in the morning and shade from the late-afternoon sun. Sunlight is important for the production of flowers; the flowers can quickly fade, however, if exposed to sun all day.

2. A well drained, fertile location: See January Planting p. 154.

3. Room to grow: Whether you plant them in groups or among flowers or shrubs, give roses room to spread their stems and roots. Avoid shoehorning them into overcrowded plantings—airflow is critical for keeping rose leaves dry to discourage diseases.

Once you've found the right spot, the next step is to pick the right roses for your garden. More than 20,000 cultivars of roses have been divided into three groups by the American Rose Society: old garden roses, modern roses, and species roses. These are further subdivided into classes. How you want to use these roses in your landscape—in flower borders, hedges, or on trellises—will dictate the classes of roses you'll select. But don't forget to choose for flower color, fragrance, and durability, too.

Your local rose society or Master Gardener group will be a good source to recommend favorite local cultivars.

## PLANTING

Plant bare-root and potted roses in the spring or fall. The selection is usually best in the spring.

Whether you buy your roses at a garden center or from a mail-order company, always select a grade No. 1 rose. Look for the grade on the tag. Cheaper roses are no bargain.

Plant bare-root roses soon after buying them or receiving them in the mail. Unwrap and soak the roots in a bucket of water for a few hours, then follow the steps on their label or these planting steps:

1. Dig the planting hole about 12 inches deep and at least 2 feet wide for hybrid teas and other large rosebushes.

2. To prevent the rose from settling too deeply, create a cone of soil in the bottom of the hole and tamp down the top.

3. Set the plant over the cone and drape the roots evenly over the top. If the rose is grafted, the bud union should be about an inch above the soil

surface. Lay your shovel handle across the hole to help gauge the correct depth.

4. Backfill the hole. Work the soil in among the roots with your fingers. If the rose has settled too deeply and the bud union is below soil level, grasp the canes close to the crown and lift it gently to raise it to the proper level.

5. To protect the canes from losing too much moisture as the roots are developing, hill up dry mulching materials like pine straw or shredded leaves over the top of the plant so only a few inches of the canes are showing. Once the new shoots begin to emerge, remove the mulch from the canes.

Potted roses are typically bare-root plants that have been potted up by the nursery. They can be set in as late as summer, but it's best to plant them in the garden as early as possible so that they will be established before summer's heat and humidity arrive. Follow these steps:

1. Dig a hole as deep as the container and at least three times the diameter of the pot. If soil at the bottom of the hole is loose, firm it with your hand.

2. Adjust the depth of the rose so the graft union is at least 1 inch above the soil surface. The graft union is the knobby swollen knot where a bud from the flowering variety was grafted or, more accurately, budded onto a rootstock of another variety.

3. Remove the plant by cutting away the bottom and sides of the container if it's a "plantable" pot.

4. If the roots are growing around the rootball, use a sharp knife to score the rootball shallowly in three or four places. Cut from the top down to the bottom.

5. Backfill the hole and water to settle the soil.

Whether planting a potted rose or a bare-root rose, apply a shallow 2- to 3-inch layer of mulch to conserve moisture, suppress weeds, and cool the soil.

## WATERING

To speed up establishment, water newly planted roses often enough to keep the roots moist during

the first few weeks. Gradually reduce the frequency but not the depth of watering: Water your roses deeply to encourage deep rooting.

## FERTILIZING

Take the guesswork out of fertilizing your roses—rely on a soil test. Follow soil test results to see what nutrients and micronutrients (elements needed in small quantities such as iron, manganese, zinc, and others) are lacking. With that in mind, you can make a sound decision when searching for the right fertilizer for your roses.

## PRUNING

Roses have to be pruned. But before you flip to the next chapter, understand the reasons why:

• To keep them healthy. Remove dead, damaged, or diseased growth when discovered, at any time of year.

• To shape and direct their growth. Climbing and rambling roses must be pruned so their canes can be secured to trellises or arbors. Roses with a bush-type habit benefit from having their shoots directed away from the center of the plant.

• To encourage more blooms. Pruning repeat-blooming roses such as hybrid teas that produce flowers on current-season's shoots encourages flushes of growth on which flowers are produced.

• To keep them confined to their allotted space. Some roses can be given 3 feet, but in a short time they'll scramble for more room. Pruning keeps them in their place so they won't crowd their neighbors.

Pruning can be intimidating, not only because of the thorns but also because of the uncertainty of what and where to cut. It's really not a complicated process. Pruning roses involves three basic cuts:

• Thinning is the removal of a shoot at its point of origin on the stem, back to another side branch, or at the base. These cuts open up the plant to improve air movement and sunlight penetration.

• Cutting back or heading back is pruning back to a bud on the stem. This cut encourages branch-

ing by stimulating a few buds behind the cut to grow.

• Shearing is an intense form of heading back where multiple cuts are made to produce dense growth. Miniature roses and floribundas grown as hedges are commonly sheared.

Although pruning methods vary among different classes of roses, they all follow these general rules:

• Use sharp tools to make clean cuts for rapid healing of wounds.

• Always begin by pruning out dead, damaged, and diseased wood (the "3 D's"). Head or cut back the canes to at least an inch below darkened or discolored areas, making sure you cut back to healthy green wood. Examine the pith or center of the cane. If it's brown, continue pruning back until the pith looks white.

• Angle each cut. Point your shears at a 45-degree angle towards the center of the shrub, sloping the cut downward from the bud. The dormant bud should be at the top of the angle.

• Make pruning cuts above a bud or branch that faces away from the center of the plant.

• Remove the lower of any crisscrossing canes that rub together. Rubbing produces wounds that are open invitations to pests.

• Prune out suckers—growths that emerge from below the bud union on grafted roses—at their attachment on the rootstock.

• Thin out any spindly, weak branches and any canes growing into the center of the bush.

• Allow the natural habit of the plant to guide your cuts.

## PROBLEMS

Roses are troubled by a wide range of pests; some varieties, however, are more susceptible than others. To manage rose pests, learn to identify them and follow an Integrated Pest Management approach to deal with them (see Problems in the introduction to the Shrubs chapter p. 180).

# JANUARY
## ROSES

### PLANNING

Whether you plan to sprinkle a few roses amongst your perennials and shrubs or dream of an everblooming rose border, sit down and take the time to select the right roses for your purpose. Aside from saving you time, money, and sleep, choosing roses that match your site and your management style will pay big dividends in beauty. Unless you're willing to commit to a regular pesticide program, select durable, easy-care roses.

As you swoon over the colorful catalogs, compile a list of roses that you "just gotta have." Before you mail in your order, compare your list with varieties recommended by a local rose society. Take a look at the *Handbook for Selecting Roses*, published yearly by the American Rose Society (American Rose Society, P.O. Box 30,000, Shreveport, Louisiana 71130-0030; 318-938-5402; http://**www.ars.org**). It covers both **old garden** and **modern roses** that are evaluated by rosarians across the country. The scores will give a clue to how your choices measure up against others in their class. If it turns out some varieties you have picked have not been tested by the rosarians in the your area, you may enjoy taking it upon

yourself to give it a trial in your own garden.

Consider All-America roses as well. All-America Rose Selections, Inc. (AARS) is a nonprofit research organization founded in 1938 for the purpose of evaluating and identifying roses that stand head-and-shoulders above others. Six types of roses can vie for the All-America title each year: **hybrid tea**, **floribunda**, **grandiflora**, **miniature**, **climber**, and **landscape rose**. AARS roses are evaluated in test gardens throughout the U.S. by commercial rose producers. They are scored on such characteristics as vigor, growth habit, hardiness, disease resistance, and flower production.

Before you order, make sure you've got enough room in your garden. Order the plants early and they will arrive at the right time for your area.

You can also contact consulting rosarians in your area through the ARS website.

### PLANTING

It's time to prepare the site for your roses:

1. For individuals or groups of roses, dig and work the soil thoroughly over as large an area as possible. Before digging, make sure the soil is dry enough to

work. If soil sticks to the shovel or your shoes, wait a few days to allow the soil to dry. Digging wet clay soil can ruin soil structure, making it more suitable for making bricks than growing roses.

2. Spread a 2- to 4-inch layer of organic matter such as compost on the soil surface. Add limestone to increase the soil pH of acidic soils or sulfur to decrease the pH of alkaline soils as recommended by the soil-test results. Roses can tolerate a soil

Digging and preparing a proper planting site is well worth the investment of your time.

pH between 5.5 and 7.0; a pH of 6.2 to 6.8, however, would be ideal. Mix the amendments into the bed 8 to 12 inches deep. Allow the bed to settle for a few days before planting.

3. Coastal gardeners can select and plant bare-root roses at the middle of the month or later. When selecting a bare-root rose, look for these features:

• Three or more sturdy canes that show no signs of shriveling or discoloration.

• Healthy-looking roots that are well distributed around the plants.

• Dormant, leafless canes. A bare-root rose that has leafed out is in jeopardy, because the leaves are demanding sustenance from the roots. If you choose to purchase plants in this state, plant them immediately if the conditions are good, or pot them up and transplant them later when more favorable conditions exist.

Remember that a grade No. 1 rose will be a better investment than lower grades (which are indicated by higher numbers).

Along the coast, roses grafted on fortuniana rootstock will be more vigorous, live longer, and resist nematodes.

Plant bare-root roses as discussed in the Planting section in the introduction p. 152.

Space plants according to their growth habit and mature spread. Follow these general spacing guidelines: **hybrid tea** and **grandiflora**, 3 to 4 feet apart; **floribunda**, 2 to 3 feet. **Climbers** need 8 to 12 feet between plants, and **miniatures** between 18 and 24 inches. **Species**, **shrub**, and **old garden roses** can be spaced 5 to 6 feet apart.

Coastal gardeners can move roses to other spots in the garden now. Unless the conditions are dry enough so you can work the soil without damaging its structure, wait until next month elsewhere in Alabama or Mississippi.

## CARE

Check the winter protection of any roses you might have covered. If the mulch has been scattered or blown away to expose the crown of the plant, particularly at the bud union, put it back in place.

If you have **miniature roses** indoors as gift plants, they need bright light. Move them to a south-facing window or place them under fluorescent lights.

## PROBLEMS

Mites can be a problem on **miniature roses** growing indoors. Use insecticidal soap to get rid of them. Before doing so, check the label to see if roses are listed. You may have to test a small area first for signs of injury. It may take seven to ten days for injury symptoms to appear. If your rose shows sensitivity to insecticidal soap, rinse the soap off once the mites are killed.

Apply dormant horticultural oil in late winter or early spring before bud-break to smother overwintering insects and their eggs. Read the label for cautions on high and low temperature limits at the time of application.

## HELPFUL HINTS

Finding disease-resistant roses requires careful study and observation. Speak to consulting rosarians with your local rose society. Reach them through the American Rose Society or Master Gardener organization. Ask your County Cooperative Extension agent about university-based rose trials. Finally, monitor other gardens for disease-free varieties that remain healthy and vigorous all season long without being sprayed. These are the ones likely to be resistant to local diseases.

# FEBRUARY

## ROSES

### PLANNING

Winter-blooming annuals and spring-flowering bulbs can fill in around the stark-looking canes of roses that are dormant or easing into growth. During the growing season, roses can bloom at the same time as perennials to create an eye-catching display. When roses have finished bearing their first round of flowers and are gearing up for another flush, low-growing, flowering perennials can fill in those voids so your bed or border will always be in bloom.

### PLANTING

Plant bare-root roses as discussed in the Planting section in the introduction on p. 152.

If you have to delay planting for a week, store the plants in a cool (above-freezing), dark location such as a refrigerator or garage. Keep the roots moist with sawdust, compost, or peat moss.

To store them temporarily for more than a week, "heel-in" (cover the roots of dormant plants with soil for a short period) the roses in the garden. Pick a well-drained spot and dig a trench about 12 inches deep and wide enough to accommodate the roots. Lay the rose down at a 45-degree angle, and cover the roots and most of their canes with soil.

Greenhouse-grown **miniatures** should be protected from frost and planted after the weather has warmed and the chance of freeze injury is past.

### CARE

Cut and divide outdoor-growing **miniature roses** when they're dormant in the central and southern parts of Alabama and Mississippi. Wait until March farther north. See March Care p. 158.

### WATERING

Water newly set plants at planting. Keep the soil moist but avoid excessive watering, which can inhibit root growth.

### PRUNING

Prune roses that produce flowers on current-season's growth before new growth begins. Valentine's Day is often the recommended pruning time for south Alabama and Mississippi. In central Alabama and Mississippi, wait until the end of the month; early March is okay in northern parts of Alabama and Mississippi. Others prune when the **forsythia** is in full bloom. I wait for the rosebuds to start swelling before pruning. The idea is to prune before plants leaf out.

Do not prune **climbers** or any roses that bloom in early to midspring; these bloom on old wood and pruning now will remove their buds.

To prevent a bare-root rose from setting too deeply, drape the roots over a soil "cone" in the bottom of the planting hole.

**Hybrid teas** produce single flowers on long stems, while **grandifloras** send up clusters of large flowers on strong, straight stems. Prune both classes to outward facing buds to develop an open, bowl-shaped habit.

1. Select three to six of the most vigorous, well-spaced canes (pencil size in diameter or thicker) from **hybrid teas**, and up to eight from **grandifloras**.

2. Remove the older canes that are brown or gray at the base.

3. Reduce the length of the canes by one-third or one-half. Generally, do not cut them back lower than 18 inches unless they've been damaged by pests or cold. Alternate the height of these final cuts to outward-growing buds to give your rose an informal look rather than an unnatural-looking "flat top."

**Floribundas** and **polyanthas** are grown for their grand display of flower clusters. They need a lighter-handed approach that will encourage the production of gobs of flowers all season long.

1. Lightly head back the canes either just below where they flowered or down to one-third their length. Cut back twiggy clusters to a strong bud. When grown as a hedge they can be sheared with hedge clippers to remove one-third to one-half of their height.

2. Thin out the twiggy growth or dead stems on the inside of the plant.

3. Remove a few of the spindly canes at the base to make room for the remaining canes. To produce the maximum number of flowers, leave more canes than you would for **hybrid teas** and **grandifloras**.

Repeat-blooming **old garden roses**, **species**, and **shrub roses** that flower on current-season's wood should be pruned right before growth begins in late winter or early spring. They can be tip-pruned throughout the growing season to encourage the production of flower-bearing side shoots.

## PROBLEMS

Apply dormant oil spray as described in January Problems p. 155. Cane-boring insects such as square-headed wasps and small carpenter bees bore into the pith of cut rose stems, leaving a telltale hole in the tip. The attacked cane wilts and dies back. Control them only when high numbers are present. After pruning your roses, paint the cuts on stems larger than $1/4$ inch in diameter with wood glue or shellac to block borers from entering.

Remove any of last year's leaves that remain after pruning.

Overwintering leaves could harbor disease spores. Apply a fresh layer of compost over the old mulch.

To control blackspot on susceptible roses, apply fungicide after pruning. Powdery mildew-susceptible varieties can be treated with a fungicide (Neem oil, lime-sulfur, or others) at the first sign of the disease.

Cankers are dark areas on canes caused by fungi. These dead areas often encircle the cane completely and kill all growth above the canker. Sometimes they elongate and extend down to the crown, killing the entire plant. These fungi enter healthy canes through wounds caused by winter injury or improper pruning cuts.

Use sharp tools for clean cuts that will heal rapidly. Prune infected canes, cutting back to healthy tissue. Look at the pith or center of the cane and continue pruning back until the pith looks white. If you cut into diseased canes, disinfect your pruning shears with Lysol®, which is less corrosive than the traditional mixture of water and household bleach (4 parts water to 1 part sodium hypochlorite). This will prevent diseases from spreading to other canes.

# MARCH

## ROSES

### PLANNING

If you have little room for roses in your landscape, plan to go vertical with **climbing roses**. Use existing structures in your landscape such as lampposts, clothesline posts, or porch columns. You can even sink an 8-foot pressure-treated 4 x 4 about 18 inches into the ground and train a **climber** onto it. Or link two or three posts together with chain or heavy rope to create a garland.

### PLANTING

Plant potted roses when they become available. Plant them as early as possible to get them settled in before summer's heat and humidity arrive. In the northern parts of Alabama and Mississippi, you can still plant dormant bare-root roses about four weeks before the last expected freeze.

### CARE

Remove the winter coverings from your roses when the **forsythia** is in full bloom. But be prepared to protect your roses if an unexpected cold-air mass moves in. Get indoor-grown **miniature roses** ready for planting outdoors. Acclimate them gradu-ally to the outside air. After the last freeze, plant them in the garden or in outdoor containers.

Divide dormant **miniature rosebushes** that have produced a lot of woody, unproductive growth. Dig them up; then gently twist or cut apart the clumps. Trim any old woody growth and replant the divisions like new bushes.

### WATERING

Water newly planted roses often enough to keep the roots moist during their first few weeks. Gradually reduce the frequency but not the depth of watering—deep watering promotes deep rooting.

### FERTILIZING

Fertilize roses after pruning and before they leaf out. Fertilize **once-blooming roses** in early spring before growth begins. Follow soil-test results to supply the necessary nutrients. Use a slow-release fertilizer that contains at least one-third of its total nitrogen in a slowly-available form.

### PRUNING

**Miniature roses** are dense, low-growing roses with small stems, leaves, and flowers range in height from 6 to 18 inches. Use a hedge clipper to trim the tops to about a foot above the soil (height will vary according to variety). Afterwards, use pruning shears to remove any twiggy growth from the center to increase air movement.

Despite their name, **climbing roses** cannot climb but rather lean, relying on their sharp thorns to give them a foothold and to secure their canes to the support. The goal for pruning and training **climbing roses** is to produce a "skeleton" or basic framework of upright canes or "trunks" with flower-bearing side shoots. Create this framework by training the shoots onto a support during the first few years. Keep the shoots spaced far apart to allow air movement and sunlight penetration. When training a **climbing rose** onto a support, orient the shoots horizontally so they will produce flowers along their length. Follow these guidelines when pruning **climbing roses**:

1. Allow **climbers** to become established during the first few years so they produce long, sturdy canes. Don't prune them back too heavily or you can

cause **climbing sports** to revert back to their bush form. Secure the canes with soft twine or green tie-tape. Tie the twine into a figure eight to avoid binding the stem.

2. In early spring before new growth emerges in **everblooming climbers**, shorten lateral or side shoots to two or three buds.

3. After flowering, examine the framework of vertical canes. Thin out thick, brown woody canes that bear few flowers and have less growth compared to the other canes. Try not to remove more than one of the skeletal canes a year. You can also cut back one of the oldest canes to a new side branch to encourage further growth from the base. Fill each vacancy with a flexible new shoot that's growing from the crown at or just above the bud union.

4. On **once-blooming climbers** that produce their heaviest crop of flowers on previous season's growth, deadhead the faded flower stems to three or four pairs of leaves. Remove some of the oldest wood at the base as well, provided that you have enough younger canes to replace it.

5. To encourage repeat flowering on **everblooming climbers**, head back the side shoots that have flowered to the lowest pair of five-leaflet leaves close to the main stem.

In many cases, **ground cover roses** are just **climbers** in disguise. Instead of being trained upright, they grow along the ground. The objective is to encourage as much ground-covering growth as possible. Tip-prune the ends of the shoots before new growth begins on **everblooming roses** and after the major flush of bloom from **once-bloomers** and most of the **old-fashioned roses**. Thin out bushy types of **ground cover roses** to prevent the plants from being choked with branches.

## PROBLEMS

Handpull winter annuals such as henbit and common chickweed to prevent them from going to seed. Maintain a 2- to 3-inch layer of mulch to suppress weeds.

Watch out for aphids and spider mites. Look for aphids clustered near the tips of new shoots and flower buds. Treat with a spray of hydrophobic extract of Neem oil, a botanical pesticide that controls aphids, mites, blackspot, and powdery mildew. It's a rose gardener's dream.

If your roses are plagued by blackspot and powdery mildew, either follow a weekly fungicide

spray program with the spray described above or plant the most disease-resistant roses you can find. Although these roses may still get diseases, they are usually vigorous enough to outgrow infections. The new Knock-out **landscape roses** are proving among the best so far.

Flower buds and flowers covered with grayish-brown fuzz might be infected with gray mold, a springtime fungal disease that's active in cool, wet weather. It also attacks new shoots. Collect and discard the infected flowers and prune out discolored canes back to healthy tissue. After pruning, treat plants with a recommended fungicide to protect the wounds.

Climbing roses need a support, which can be of many different types.

# APRIL

## ROSES

### PLANNING

If you're serious about growing roses, start a journal this month. Document your observations, thoughts, and plans for the future. Some of the following items can be noted:

- Bloom dates for each variety
- Condition of the flowers, leaves, and overall health
- Problems such as insects, diseases, and weeds
- Pesticides used and when they were applied
- Plants that need to be moved or replaced because they turned out to be "a lotta-care" roses

Your journal can become a teaching tool, especially when you need the assistance of a County Extension agent or a consulting rosarian to help you diagnose a problem. The notes you took about weather conditions, fertilizing, watering, and pest control applications are important clues.

So start writing.

### PLANTING

When planting **climbing roses** next to a wall, place them at least 2 feet away from it. Plant potted roses when the soil is dry enough to be worked (not soggy).

Roses can be rooted by taking softwood cuttings in late spring and summer from the current-season's growth:

1. Fill a 6-inch pot with equal parts of moist peat moss and perlite.

2. Remove a stem that has just flowered and is about the diameter of a straw.

3. Count upward two or three pairs of leaves from the bottom of this cutting, and make a cut 1/4 inch above the topmost bud.

4. Wound the bottom end of the stem with a razor blade or sharp knife by making a 1/2- to 1-inch vertical slit through the bark on the side opposite the top bud. Roots will emerge from along the edges of the wound.

5. Dip the lower end in a rooting hormone (contains indolebutyric acid or IBA) to encourage uniform rooting. Tap off the excess.

6. Using a pencil, make a hole in the rooting medium and insert the cutting. Remove leaves that may be buried in the medium. Firm the medium around it and settle them in with a fine spray of water.

7. Put the pot in a plastic bag and move it to a shaded location outside against the north wall of your house or under a tree. Alternatively, you can sink the pot in the ground in a shaded location and cover the cuttings with a clear plastic 2-liter soda

bottle whose bottom has been removed. Water to prevent the cuttings from drying out.

8. Open up your mini-hothouse occasionally if there's too much condensation inside. You can unscrew the cap of the soda bottle.

9. The cuttings should root in a month and will send out new leaves if you've been successful. To see if they've rooted, give the stem a gentle tug. If it resists, it has rooted. Remove the bag. Pot up the cuttings in individual pots and keep them moist and shaded. Gradually expose the rooted cuttings to stronger light to harden them off. After a couple of weeks, transplant them.

### CARE

Loosely tie **climbing roses** to trellises with broad strips of material such as soft twine or nylon. Use a figure-eight tie between the cane and the trellis so that the tie won't put pressure on or otherwise injure the cane. Do not use wires; they can damage canes.

Last year's mulch may contain fungal disease spores that can infect your rosebushes. If you haven't done so already, apply fresh mulch to blanket the old mulch. Keep the layer between 2 and 3 inches thick. If you prefer to remove the old mulch, apply it to other areas of the landscape not occupied by roses, or compost it.

## WATERING

To prevent water from running off, it is helpful to create a temporary berm, or dike, around newly planted roses. Remove the berm when the roses become established. Whenever you irrigate, keep the leaves dry to reduce the growth and spread of diseases.

Water at ground level. Of course, the easiest way to do this is with a soaker hose or by using a drip irrigation system.

## FERTILIZING

Fertilize all roses if you didn't do it last month. A slow-release fertilizer is best. When using a fast-release fertilizer, time your application after each flush of bloom. Only one or two applications may be necessary during the season if you use a slow-release fertilizer. Refer to the fertilizer label for the rate and frequency of application. Water afterwards to make the nutrients available to the rose.

## PRUNING

Do not prune **climbers** or **early-blooming roses** yet. Wait until

Aphids like to cluster near new buds; you can actually see and feel their soft bodies if you touch your fingers to the rose stem.

after they bloom. Ideally, pruning should be done by now, but if you're late, prune to buds and shoots that point outward. Chances are that by now the canes are sprouting and the new shoots may be several inches long. Opening the center of the plant encourages good air and sunlight penetration. Dark-colored canes indicate dead wood. Cut back an inch below these darkened areas. If the center of the cane is discolored, cut back further until your see white pith. If there are no live buds, remove the entire cane or branch.

Remove suckers arising from below the graft union of roses. Cut them off where they attach to the rootstock. If you're not sure of the extent of winter injury, wait until the buds "break" (new growth emerges). Remove any dead wood above a bud.

## PROBLEMS

Inspect your roses for rose aphids and spider mites. See March Problems on p. 159 for controls.

Nematodes are microscopic organisms that live in the soil and attack the roots of plants. They are commonly found in coarse-textured sandy soils more often than fine-textured clay soils. The best way to deal with them is to buy roses grafted onto *fortuniana* rootstock whenever possible. This rootstock is vigorous and resists nematodes. If this is not an option because plants aren't available in your area, you can probably order from a mail-order source.

# MAY
## ROSES

 PLANNING

Water your roses efficiently this summer when hot weather arrives. The general recommendation is to apply 1 to 2 inches of water on a weekly basis. One inch of water is equivalent to applying 5 to 6 gallons of water to a 3-foot-square area with the rosebush in the center. With clay soils, which hold more water than sandy soils, apply this amount once a week; with sandy soils, however, it's best to split it into two applications of 3 gallons, each spaced a few days apart. Adjust the amount to account for rainfall and prevailing weather conditions. If the weather has been cloudy and rains have been adequate, watering may not be necessary. Rely on common sense and observation:

• Check the soil. A sandy soil that's dry to a depth of 2 to 4 inches indicates a need for water. In clay soil, simply not being able to dig easily down to 2 to 4 inches is enough to know that it's dry.

• Look at your roses. If the leaves are grayish-green in color and slightly wilted, moisture could be lacking. Waiting until the roses are completely wilted before watering can affect their health and survival.

Always water at ground level when watering roses to avoid wetting the leaves.

 PLANTING

A potted rose makes a great gift for Mother's Day. Refer to the Planting section of the introduction p. 152 for details.

 WATERING

See April Watering on p. 161.

FERTILIZING

See April Fertilizing on p. 161.

 PRUNING

**Old garden roses**, **species**, and **shrub roses** come in a wide range of sizes and shapes. Generally, allow the natural shape of the plant to guide your pruning cuts. Hold off on pruning them until after they've bloomed and then only if they've achieved a decent size, perhaps after the second or third growing season. Here are a few pruning tips:

• Shorten long, vigorous canes by up to one-third to encourage production of flower-bearing side shoots.

• Tip-prune last year's lateral or side shoots to 6 inches in length.

• On established plants, remove one or two of the oldest canes that produce few, if any, flowers, maintaining a balance between old and new growths.

To avoid pruning flower buds, remember that one-time bloomers or roses that produce their heaviest flush on old wood should be pruned after flowering in the spring. For **shrub roses** that produce attractive hips, or rose fruits, such as hybrid **rugosa roses**, prune only some of the shoots, preserving some of the hip-bearing branches.

As befits their name, **ramblers** (forerunners of today's large-flowered **climbers**) will ramble and scramble hither and yon if allowed. They'll do it beautifully, however, even though they generally bloom only once in early summer. Pruning and training a **rambler** is akin to housebreaking a pet: Start early and be consistent or you'll be left with a mess.

1. When the flowers fade, deadhead the flowering shoots by cutting them back to three or four leaf pairs.

2. **Ramblers** tend to sprout more new canes than most **climbers**, and it's the one-year-old canes that produce flowers. So make room for new canes by taking out one-third of the oldest canes—provided that you have enough young replacements. Before removing any of the old-est canes, take a look at the new ones. Some canes will emerge from the base, but others will sprout higher up on older wood. Prune out the oldest wood that has little or no new growth.

3. Tie the vigorous new canes to their supports. Since **ramblers** have long flexible canes, try spiraling them around arches or pillars, or festoon them through chains. Bend them sideways to encourage flowering along their length.

4. Finally, cut back any wayward limbs that have outgrown their space.

Once-blooming climbers produce their heaviest crop of flowers on last-year's growth, so prune them after flowering:

1. Deadhead the faded flower stems to three or four pairs of leaves.

Deadheading means snipping off the dead flowers. It improves a rose's appearance, removes potential harboring sites for diseases, and encourages more flowers on repeat-flowering varieties. To deadhead, remove the flower stem by making a diagonal cut $1/4$ inch above the first compound leaf that has five leaflets, otherwise known as a "five." (Roses produce compound leaves containing three, five, and seven leaflets.) On young, newly planted roses, this may remove too much of the cane, so cut back to a three-leaflet leaf. (In following years, cut down to a five-leaflet leaf with a leaf bud facing outward. When the bud breaks, the new shoot will be growing out and away from the rose to keep an open habit.)

2. Examine the framework of vertical canes. Thin out thick, brown, woody canes that bore few flowers and had less growth compared to the other canes. Before doing so, make sure you have enough younger canes to replace the ones you remove.

3. Tie in younger canes growing from the crown at or just above the bud union.

 PROBLEMS

Be on the lookout for damage caused by rose aphids, spider mites, and flower thrips. If needed, spray with Neem oil as described under Problems on p. 159.

Leaves attacked by blackspot and powdery mildew should be picked up and discarded. To improve the effectiveness of fungicide sprays, practice good sanitation: Clean up any fallen leaves and faded blooms, prune out dead, damaged, and diseased canes, and replace mulch each spring.

# JUNE
## ROSES

### PLANNING

As part of your summer vacation, find some time to visit private and public gardens that feature roses. Seeing those extraordinary roses that you've glimpsed only in catalogs can be inspiring.

Some notable rose gardens are the All-America Rose Selections Public Gardens. These accredited gardens showcase those three or four exceptional roses selected from thousands each year. Winners of this coveted title are chosen from six types of roses: **hybrid tea, floribunda, grandiflora, miniature, climber**, and **landscape rose**. Here are the AARS gardens in Alabama and Mississippi:

• Battleship Memorial Park in Mobile, AL

• Bellingrath Gardens Rose Garden in Theodore, AL

• Dunn Formal Rose Garden in Birmingham, AL

• Fairhope City Rose Garden in Fairhope, AL

• Hattiesburg Area Rose Society Garden in Hattiesburg, MS

• Mississippi Agriculture Museum in Jackson, MS

You can check updates to this list and learn more about All-America Rose Selections at **www.rose.org**.

### PLANTING

If you happen to see a variety that you like in your local nursery or garden center, buy it—but be careful. Although container-grown roses can be transplanted this month, you need to pay careful attention to watering and mulching. Such roses are under a lot of stress from heat and humidity and can easily be forgotten when stuck somewhere in the landscape. It may be better to keep it in the container close to the house so that it can get the attention it needs. Plant it in the fall when weather becomes more favorable.

### CARE

**Climbing roses** may not produce canes near the base after a period of years. If removing some of the oldest canes doesn't spark any growth, try notching. Make a cut above a bud near the base of the plant by slicing one-third of the way through a stem. This tends to force that bud into growth.

### WATERING

Keep the following "ground rules" in mind when watering your roses this summer:

• Newly planted roses need to be watered often enough to prevent the soil from drying out as they settle into their new surrounding. Reduce the frequency of watering gradually, but continue to water deeply to encourage the development of a deep, extensive root system. See May Planning p. 162.

• Roses in sandy soils will require more-frequent watering than roses in clay soils.

• Roses will need more water when the temperatures are high than when they're cool.

• Water deeply and infrequently, wetting as much of the root zone as possible. Roots may extend to a depth of 6 to 12 inches. The goal is to produce deeply rooted plants. Shallow, frequent sprinklings on established plants encourage shallow roots.

• Keep the leaves dry by applying water to the soil surface. Fungal diseases such as blackspot rely on moisture to infect and spread.

• Mulch your roses with a 2- to 3-inch layer. Organic mulches—compost, pine needles ("pine straw"), shredded leaves, and wood chips—conserve moisture, suppress weeds, and supply nutrients as they decompose. Keep the mulch a few inches away from the crown.

## FERTILIZING

Avoid excessive fertilization. It produces the soft, succulent growth favored by pests. Try to grow your roses on the "lean and mean" side. Evaluate the quality and quantity of flowers and shoots produced by your roses, and decide if a boost of fertilizer is warranted. Never skimp on building up the natural fertility of the soil with applications of organic mulches such as compost. If you used a slow-release fertilizer early in the year, check the label and evaluate the growth and appearance of your **everblooming roses** to see if a second application is warranted. Supplement mulch with well-rotted horse or cow manure to add nutrients.

## PRUNING

Cut few if any flowers during the first blooming season. By removing only flowers and not stems you will encourage plants to develop into large bushes by fall, at which time some flowers and stems may be cut. Deadhead flowers as soon as they have passed their peak. If allowed to remain on the plant, the flower heads will develop seedpods (also called hips) that draw heavily on the plant's food supply. Always use sharp pruning shears and cut on a downward slant from the bud.

Remove any spindly shoots or suckers originating below the graft union, or any damaged, diseased, or dead canes. To produce specimen flowers on **hybrid tea** or **old garden roses**, remove flower buds that have developed on shoots other than the main one. Allow only one flower bud to develop and mature on each main shoot.

If you haven't already done so, prune **once-flowering climbers** and **ramblers** that bloom on last year's growth. Thin out any of the oldest canes to make room for new ones from the base.

Long canes that have to be removed should be cut out in a piecemeal manner. Cut the cane into 8- to 12-inch sections and remove them one at a time. It's far easier to deal with the cane in short bites than to wrestle all of its length out at once. Head back any wayward canes to keep them confined to their support. Refer to May Pruning p. 163 for more details.

## PROBLEMS

Pests to watch for include rose aphids, spider mites, thrips, and Japanese beetles. Handpick Japanese beetles and discard them in a jar of soapy water. Neem can be applied to the leaves to reduce feeding by adults. Use other insecticides for heavy infestations.

Be on the watch for blackspot and powdery mildew. To avoid resistance to controls by the disease organisms, when using synthetic fungicides, switch back and forth between different kinds.

Handpull weeds when they're young and easier to remove. Suppress their growth with a shallow layer of compost.

# JULY
## ROSES

 PLANNING

This is the perfect month to find a comfortable chair, a cool drink, and another good book (besides this one). Kick back and enjoy the fruits of your labors. You might select a book about the lore of roses. The beautiful flowers, the exquisite fragrances, the nutritious rose hips, all set among vicious thorns, is the stuff of poetry. Much has been written since roses were first cultivated during the Shen Nung dynasty in China (2737-2697 B.C.). Use these summer doldrums to learn more about the less-strenuous side of roses. Also, visit the website of the American Rose Society at **www.ars.org**, and visit the Gulf District local societies in Mississippi and the Deep South District local societies in Alabama.

 PLANTING

If you must plant potted roses now, water them thoroughly. Keep them well watered to speed up their establishment. If you can, delay the project until fall, when the temperatures are cooler and less stressful for the rose and you.

 CARE

Roses may take a rest, as you should, when the daytime temperatures ease into the 90s. Plants in full summer sun are especially affected. Unless you're willing to push them with adequate water and fertilizer, give 'em a break.

Do not fertilize unless the plants are growing vigorously and showing "hunger" signs. Prune off faded flowers and cut back any weak canes to prepare the plant for a long blooming spell in the fall.

 WATERING

See May Planning p. 162.

 FERTILIZING

Do not fertilize your roses unless you are willing to support their growth with regular watering. Water is necessary to making the fertilizer available to the roots, but it is important to keep that new growth healthy and alive. In the hotter parts of Alabama and Mississippi, roses can rest this month. When the cooler fall temperatures arrive, you can resume feeding and water them for a fabulous fall display.

 PROBLEMS

Several insects are active now. Japanese beetles skeletonize leaves and feed on flower buds and flowers; rose aphids occur in clusters near the tips of shoots and their feeding causes leaves to become wrinkled, sticky, and sometimes coasted with a black sooty mold; spider mites cause yellow or bronze stippling on the leaf surface; thrips damage flower buds, creating streaks or spots on the open blooms and brown edges on flower buds that fail to open.

Nematodes are microscopic organisms that live in the soil and attack roots. They are more commonly found in coarse-textured sandy soils than in fine-textured clay soils. One type, the root-knot nematode, produces small galls or swellings on the roots. Nematode-infested roots cannot take up water or fertilizer as well as healthy ones. The plants may be weak-looking, stunted, and wilted. Their leaves turn yellow or off-color and drop off earlier than normal.

# HELPFUL HINTS

Follow these steps to conserve water by using it more efficiently while maximizing its effectiveness:

1. Amend the soil prior to planting. Use organic matter such as shredded leaves, compost, and well-rotted manure to help the soil hold moisture, especially in sandy soils, and to improve aeration of clay soils. Work the soil as deeply as possible to encourage deep rooting.

2. Mulch. Apply a 2- to 3-inch layer of organic materials to reduce water evaporation from the soil. Use whatever is inexpensive and available such as compost, pine needles or "pine straw," shredded leaves, bark, or wood chips.

3. Fertilize moderately. Fertilization requires watering to make the nutrients available to the plant. It also encourages growth which, in turn, needs to be supported by more water. Consider using slow-release fertilizers that produce moderate growth. Fertilize according to soil-test results. Use natural fertilizers with "slowly available" or "water-insoluble" nitrogen and synthetic fertilizers containing slow-release technology—usually in the form of a polymer coating that releases nutrients gradually. These are usually labeled as 3-month, 6-month, or 9-month formulas. Under hot-weather conditions and in the presence of lots of water, they may not last quite as long as the package says, but they last much longer than cheap agriculture-grade, fast-release fertilizers. The nitrogen in these types of fertilizer does not quickly wash away, and it provides green color without excessive leaf growth.

4. Use drip irrigation for efficient watering. These systems use emitters, drip collars, or drip tubing to apply water right to the soil surface. Another advantage is that they keep the leaves dry and thus avoid foliar diseases. On clay soils, where run-off can occur when watering with a hose, this waste of water is greatly reduced. Coastal gardeners who have saline water will benefit from drip-irrigation systems. They use less water to moisten the root zones of your plants, putting less salt in the soil. Planting in raised beds will also make it easier to flush out accumulated salts with irrigation water and rainfall.

5. Water deeply. Encourage the growth of deep, extensive roots by watering to a depth of 6 to 12 inches.

6. In addition to relying on rain gauges and weather forecasts, serious water-conservationists may want to invest in devices that measure moisture tension—the amount of force holding water to the soil particles. As the soil dries, the moisture tension increases, making it more difficult for the plant to absorb water. These devices detect when a critical level is reached beyond which the plant will become stressed. With this information, you can irrigate and avoid the crisis. Among these instruments are tensiometers, gypsum moisture blocks, and neutron probes.

If you suspect nematodes, have your soil assayed by submitting samples through your regional Extension office. If nematodes are a threat, the best defense is to keep the plants healthy. Add organic matter such as compost, composted pine bark, or peat moss to improve soil structure and moisture retention in sandy soils. This not only makes a better growing environment for the plant but also creates a favorable environment for the growth of natural predators of the nematode.

# AUGUST

## ROSES

 PLANNING

The cool early mornings and evenings during the "dog days of August" are a fitting time to plan on renovating beds and preparing new ones. Plan—don't plant, unless you're working in the early morning and the temperature is inviting enough to work the beds. If it's dry, clay soils may require a pickaxe this month; wait until it rains before getting to work. If your roses were planted in low spots and aren't thriving, now is the time to consider where you can move them in the coming winter when they're dormant. Also, plan where and how to build raised beds or install drainage tiles to carry away excess water. Mark roses to be transplanted with colorful tape.

 PLANTING

Don't!

 CARE

Late this month, jump-start **everbloomers** into growth for a fall-flowering display. See Fertilizing.

 WATERING

See May Planning p. 162.

 FERTILIZING

Depending on the fertility of your soil, **everblooming roses** may require a little boost from a fast-release fertilizer. Follow label directions to determine the amount to apply.

 PRUNING

Remember the "3 d's" when visiting the garden: damaged, diseased, or dead twigs must go.

Remove any suckers from the rootstocks of grafted plants. The leaves on these shoots will look different from the grafted variety.

 PROBLEMS

Inspect your roses for Japanese beetles, rose aphids, and spider mites. Evaluate the extent of injury and decide on the level of control. Should you resort to handpicking Japanese beetles? Or is the infestation bad enough that you should cover the roses

with cheesecloth or netting? Are they present in such high numbers that chemical control is the best course of action?

Watch out for blackspot and powdery mildew. Warm, humid days and cool night temperatures favor the growth of powdery mildew.

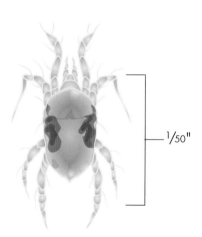

1/50"

Spider mite

Rose mosaic virus is the most common viral disease of roses. Symptoms usually occur on new growth: crinkly deformed leaves; misshapen buds and flowers; leaves with blotches of yellow, ring patterns of light green, yellow lines, or a mottling of different shades of green. Rose mosaic virus makes a rose less vigorous, reduces the size and number of flowers, and sometimes deforms them. The plant is stunted and the bud graft may fail, killing the top variety and leaving the rootstock.

Rose mosaic is systemic, meaning that it can be found in all parts of the plant except the few cells at the tips of the growing points. Infected plants may decline in vigor and become stunted so your only course of action is to remove them. Pruning away the afflicted parts will not remove the virus from your rose. There are no chemicals that cure a virus-infected plant or any that protect plants from becoming infected. This particular virus spreads through the propagation of infected plants, as when virus-infected

plant material is budded or grafted to a healthy plant. Since there is little natural spread of rose mosaic viruses, plants that develop mosaic symptoms in the rose garden do not need to be replaced as long as their growth is acceptable.

The only control for viruses is prevention: Avoid purchasing plants showing mosaic symptoms. The industry is taking steps to rid rose cultivars of viruses. The plants are extensively tested to be sure that the virus is not detected in the treated material. Plants that pass the test are used to propagate virus-free stock.

Handpull grassy and broadleaf weeds from your rose beds. Maintain a shallow mulch layer to suppress their growth.

---

## HELPFUL HINTS

A simple way of propagating roses, particularly **shrub roses** that have long, pliable stems, is by layering anytime from April through September:

1. Bend one of the lowest stems to the ground.
2. Wind the underside of the stem and cover it with soil. Hold it in place with a piece of wire bent to a hairpin shape and pushed into the ground. Do not bury the shoot tip.

If you layer now, the shoots will usually be rooted by the end of the growing season. Then you can sever the new plant from the parent and transplant. Shoots layered later in the summer should be left through the winter and separated in the spring.

---

Certain roses are subject to myriad insects and diseases, including blackspot. Our warm humid days and nights favor its spread.

# SEPTEMBER

## ROSES

 **PLANNING**

Order roses for delivery in December on the Coast, and early next year elsewhere. Select roses for their flowers, fragrance, and ability to withstand the rigors of summer heat and humidity. Disease resistance should be as important as the appearance of the plant. Refer to your gardening journal to help you make the right selections. Some companies have deadlines for accepting orders, so once you've ogled the photographs, start ordering and make a notation in your calendar.

 **PLANTING**

It is a good time to plant roses. Look for roses that you can purchase as replacements, or other good roses that deserve to be in your garden.

 **CARE**

Continue tying up the canes of **climbing roses**, securing them sideways to encourage horizontal growth.

 **WATERING**

Fall is the driest season in Alabama and Mississippi. Whenever you water, keep the rose leaves dry to reduce the growth and spread of diseases.

 **FERTILIZING**

Stop fertilizing roses six weeks before the average first freeze date in your area to allow the new growth to harden off, preparing the roses for their winter rest.

If you didn't do so last month, fertilize **everblooming roses** with a fast-release fertilizer if necessary. Water afterwards to make the nutrients available to the roses.

 **PRUNING**

Deadhead and prune to encourage new growth now that the cooler temperatures of fall are on the way. Later after fall flowering, stop deadheading roses so the seedpods, or rose hips, will mature. The colorful hips add an attractive feature to the winter garden. Producing them also encourages the rose to focus its energy on "hardening off," in anticipation of winter dormancy.

 **PROBLEMS**

Rose aphids and spider mites may still be active. Evaluate the extent of injury and decide if pest control measures are warranted. Use a water wand to wash mites off of plants on a weekly basis, preferably early in the morning.

Clean up fallen rose leaves. They can harbor diseases and insect pests over the winter if allowed to remain on the ground. Keep the rose plants clean, and the area around their feet tidy and free of debris. During the growing season, pick up and remove fallen leaves.

Keep the area around the roses free of weeds to eliminate any overwintering hide-outs for two-spotted spider mites.

# HELPFUL HINTS

Growing roses near walkways or front porches creates a hazardous situation for passersby who may find themselves pierced by thorns. Fortunately, not all roses are equipped with thorns. Botanically, they're not thorns, they're prickles—but they hurt anyway. For these situations, consider thornless or nearly thornless roses. Your children will be out of harm's way, and weeding won't be a bloody venture. Roses that have smooth or nearly thornless canes are: **Lady Banks' rose (species**; white and yellow-flowered varieties); **swamp rose** (*R. palustris*); **prairie rose** (*R. setigera* var. *serena*); 'Zephirine Drouhin' (**bourbon**; cerise pink); 'Paul Neyron' (**hybrid perpetual**; pink); and 'Marie Pavié' (**polyantha**; creamy-white). Thorny roses do have their place in your landscape. They can be used as barriers to prevent people from taking shortcuts through your garden, or to keep your neighbor's roaming dog on his side of the hedge. Unfortunately, deer are unfazed.

If you've become a rose aficionado, try growing a rose using seed from the hips that you find on your plants in the fall. Just be aware that the seedlings, especially those of hybrid roses, will not be identical to the rose from which you collected the seed. You may get lucky and end up with your own new, highly sought-after rose. Here's how to collect and sow the seeds:

1. Harvest the ripe hips soon after they turn color. Though the color varies according to species and cultivar, expect the hips to change to red, yellow, or orange. Collect them soon after they color up: The longer you allow them to ripen, the more dormant the seeds will become, further delaying germination.

2. Slice each hip from top to bottom in two or three places with a knife; peel each section open to expose the seeds. Soak the seeds in water for twelve to twenty-four hours. Drain the seeds, then mix them with equal parts of moistened sphagnum peat moss and vermiculite in a plastic bag. Seal the bag and place it in your refrigerator crisper for about three months, which is usually adequate for hybrid rose seeds. This exposure to cool temperatures is called moist-chilling or stratification and is necessary to encourage uniform germination.

3. After this conditioning, take the seeds out of the refrigerator and sow them in a seed flat, which is basically a shallow wooden, plastic, or aluminum container with drainage holes. Use the same medium you used for stratification. Move the flat to a sunny location offering bright indirect sunlight. This can be a room maintained at 65 to 70 degrees F., outdoors on the north side of your house, or in a cold frame. The seedlings can be transplanted when they develop two or three sets of true leaves (the leaves that follow the first "seed leaves" or cotyledons). Use 3-inch pots and treat them as potted roses.

During the first few months, the seedlings often produce tiny flowers. You will have to wait until the roses mature to see the true size and form of the flowers. You may want to cull out some of the seedlings on the basis of flower color alone. The seedling roses can be transplanted outdoors.

Lady Banks rose is an old-fashioned favorite in Alabama and Mississippi— and it's nearly thornless, too!

# OCTOBER

## ROSES

### PLANNING

Identify beds whose soil needs to be tested. Soil testing is best done every two or three years. Contact your Cooperative Extension Service office for soil-testing materials. You can take samples this month or wait until the cooler fall weather arrives. This is also a good month to think about creating new beds, keeping in mind the three basic requirements of roses: 1) Six hours of direct sunlight per day; 2) a well-drained, fertile location; and 3) room to grow.

Create narrow beds, about 4 to 5 feet wide, so you can reach the plants from both sides. This will make chores like deadheading, watering, fertilizing, and pest control easier. Having access from the sides will also prevent you from walking inside the bed and compacting the soil.

In northern parts of the states where the temperatures can drop to 10 degrees F. or lower, plan to put grafted and the least-hardy roses to sleep under protective blankets of soil or mulch. This will also protect any rose—even the hardiest—from freezing temperatures and the seesaw weather patterns of winter, which can tease a dormant bud into waking up too early. Find and stockpile dry mulching materials such as wood chips, shredded leaves, and evergreen branches.

### PLANTING

Fall is a good season for planting in the milder areas of Alabama and Mississippi. Coastal gardeners and those in warmer parts of central Mississippi can even plant throughout late fall and into winter if temperatures are mild. The welcome cooler temperatures are important to us and the roses. It lets them concentrate on producing roots and settle in as the tops slow down and become dormant. Follow the steps in the Planting section of the introduction on p. 152.

Now is a good time to begin moving roses that have outgrown their location. You can do this through winter if the weather and soil conditions allow. Here's how to do it:

1. Cut out all dead wood and twiggy undergrowth.

2. With soft twine such as jute, slowly draw the canes together into a bundle. You can cut them back, but if it has taken many years to produce this growth, you may want to save it.

3. Use a spade to cut the roots, starting 1 or 2 feet from the center of the rose, getting as much of the rootball as possible. The size of the rootball will depend on how much you or a friend can physically manage. Drive the spade as deep as it will go.

4. Using a spading fork (it has four straight prongs), lift up the rose. Cut any stubborn roots with pruning shears or your spade.

5. Slide the rootball onto a tarp that's about 6 square feet, or large enough to allow you to wrap up the rootball to prevent it from falling apart. If the rose is dormant and the temperatures are cool, you can remove some of the soil (in most cases all of it) and treat the plant like a large bare-root rose.

6. Transplant the rose into its new location as soon as possible. If you take the bare-root approach, protect the roots from drying out. Moisten them with water or cover them with wet newspaper during the move.

The site should be prepared as discussed in the introduction. After planting, water to settle the soil and apply a 2- to 3-inch layer of mulch. You can keep the canes secured with twine for protection from damaging winter winds, or the twine can be removed.

## CARE

If your **climbing roses** are in an exposed location, tie them up firmly with broad strips of rags so that the wind will not whip them against the trellis and bruise the bark. Roses grown in containers need to be put in the ground, container and all, in a protected area of the landscape. Mulch with a layer of compost.

## WATERING

Water newly planted roses if there's insufficient rain. Fall can be dry time. Water deeply and only when needed.

## FERTILIZING

Stop fertilizing your roses six weeks before your expected first freeze.

## PRUNING

Stop deadheading spent flowers. Remove petals with your hand to allow the rose hips to form, which helps trigger winter dormancy.

## HELPFUL HINTS

Because plant labels and stakes disappear shortly after putting them in the landscape, create a simple map of your rose garden on an $8^1/_2$ x 11-inch sheet of paper. Sketch each bed and mark the location of each of your roses with circles. Include the names of surrounding plants. You can even add information such as the planting date and any remarks about culture or performance in your garden. (If you're apt to misplace this piece of paper, you can choose from a wide variety of landscape design programs that will allow you to computerize and access it whenever you like—barring any unforeseen "crashes," that is.)

This handy map will serve as another educational tool to help you in renovating your garden, making new purchases, or counseling friends who are interested in growing one of the beautiful roses in your garden.

## PROBLEMS

Spider mites make a strong comeback in dry fall weather. The good news is that since your roses will shed their leaves soon, immediate control may not be necessary. However, controlling the overwintering eggs with a spray of dormant horticultural oil later this fall when the rose goes dormant, but before freezing weather, may be all that's needed.

Rake and clean up the garden to get rid of blackspot spores that can overwinter on the leaves. If powdery mildew is a problem, control may not be necessary, since we're approaching the end of the season and leaves will be shed.

For those areas that experience freezing temperatures, mound soil or mulch for winter protection.

# November

## ROSES

 PLANNING

Update your gardening journal and plan for improvements next year. What were the most troublesome insects and diseases this season? Were there problems with the pest control measures you selected? Perhaps you need to dig out some roses and replace them early next year.

Think about the roses that seemed to "take a lickin' and keep on tickin'." Was it the rose itself, or could its performance also be attributed to the growing environment—plenty of air circulation, diligent removal of infected leaves, adequate water and fertility? Spend some time pondering these factors, along with others, and document them in your journal.

 PLANTING

There is still time to plant and move roses. Water them thoroughly and mulch to keep them from freezing.

 CARE

Prepare your roses for winter by allowing rose hips to form. If you haven't done so already, have a soil test done of your rose beds. At least every two or three years, have your soil tested through your Cooperative Extension Service to determine soil pH and fertility levels. **Miniature roses** need lots of light to bloom indoors. Give them at least four hours of direct sunlight from a south-facing window, or put them under cool-white fluorescent lights to receive at least sixteen hours of light daily. The tops of the plants should be 2 to 4 inches below the lights.

 WATERING

As cold weather sets in, reduce water, but do not allow roses, especially those that have recently been planted, to dry out completely. Plants need water during dry spells, even during the winter months.

 FERTILIZING

Do not fertilize at this time of the year.

**Miniature roses** growing indoors under artificial lights can be fertilized with a liquid water-soluble fertilizer to encourage flowering.

 PRUNING

Allow the hips to signal dormancy. It's not necessary to prune back roses to make them attractive in winter. If you do this before a freeze, you may awaken dormant buds, which will produce new growth that will only be killed by freezing temperatures. Even gardeners along the warmer coast should wait until January (at the earliest) to begin pruning roses. If a rose's height will put it in peril of being damaged by strong winter winds, prune back only after a freeze.

 PROBLEMS

Spider mites are a serious pest of **miniature roses**, especially indoors. To reduce their numbers, bathe each plant once a week under running water, washing the undersides of leaves as well as the tops. Their population can also be checked with applications of insecticidal soap.

Clean up rose beds. Rake fallen leaves and compost them, or bury them in the vegetable garden.

# HELPFUL HINTS ABOUT ROSE CARE

## TO HELP YOUR ROSES SURVIVE THE WINTER

Gardeners, particularly in north Alabama and Mississippi, need to keep in mind:

• The plants should go into the winter in a vigorous state. Plants stressed by drought or lack of fertility, or those defoliated by pests, are more inclined to succumb to cold than robust plants are.

• Roses should be grown in a well-drained location. Roses will not tolerate "wet feet," especially during the winter months.

• Winter winds can dry out the canes of exposed roses, loosen a rose's footing, or bruise canes as they're jostled by the wind. You can plant roses near walls or fences or erect temporary windbreaks of burlap, or the canes may benefit from staking or being tied down. Plant the roses at a distance that is at least four to six times their mature height from the windbreak.

• The freezing and thawing of the soil, frost-heaving, can lift up plants, causing them to dry out. Carefully push down any plants and maintain a mulch layer to moderate soil temperatures.

## OWN-ROOTED ROSES

Own-rooted roses are varieties grown from cuttings. **Old garden roses** are typically grown on their own roots, as are some modern roses. Own-rooted roses offer an advantage in the areas where winters are very cold. If the top is lost to winter cold, but the rootstock survives, the variety won't be lost. New growth will arise from the roots. When you lose the top of a grafted rose, what's left is a rootstock that is durable but not beautiful.

## TOOLS NEEDED FOR PRUNING

Pruning will begin early next year. Assemble your pruning tools and equipment. If you need any tools, put them on your Christmas wish list. Pruning tools needed are:

• *Pruning shears.* The proper tool for most pruning is a sharp set of bypass pruners with curved blades that cut with a scissorlike action and give the cleanest cut. Pruning shears cut canes up to $1/4$ inch in diameter. The bypass types are preferred over anvil pruners. These have a single cutting blade that, when cutting, presses the stem against a flat piece of metal (anvil). They should not be used for roses because they crush the stem.

• *Long-handled lopping shears* (12- to 18-inch-long handles) to cut out thick canes up to one-half-inch in diameter. Select bypass types with lightweight metal alloy handles.

• *A keyhole saw* about 7 to 8 inches long with a thin pointed tip allows you to maneuver into tight corners. It can be used to cut very large canes ($1/2$ inch diameter or greater) near the crown. Remove large stubs close to the bud union.

• *Thorn-proof gloves* with gauntlet-type cuffs to protect your hands and forearms when pruning.

• *Hedge shears* to prune miniature roses or floribunda hedges.

• *Spray bottle of Lysol®.* Use it to disinfect tools when cutting into cankers or canes infected with crown gall disease. It's less corrosive than bleach.

# DECEMBER

## ROSES

### PLANNING

Look at this month as a time of reflection. Review what happened during this past year. If this was your first year growing roses and you've been pleased by your performance and theirs, make plans to get better. Add favorite roses to your Christmas list as gifts or to receive.

### PLANTING

Weather permitting, you can plant bare-root roses or move roses to other parts of the landscape. Most garden centers will not get their roses in until next month, so check with them if there are any specific ones that you'd like.

### CARE

Roses that are newly planted in the fall will benefit from winter protection in areas where on-again/off-again cold weather causes early budding. Late-summer and early fall-planted roses also need to be protected. Tender roses such as **tea**, **China**, and **Noisette** should be protected with mulch to protect their roots and aboveground canes:

1. Prune out any dead or diseased canes.

2. Mound the plant with dry materials like wood chips, leaves, or pine needles 1 to 2 feet high and as wide at the base of the plant. Carefully shake the mulch into the center of the plant around each cane.

3. To keep the mulch contained, surround the shrub with chicken wire that's been staked into place and fill this cylinder with mulch.

When the buds of **miniature roses** have started to open, bring them into living areas to enjoy. After the flowers fade, return them to a bright location receiving at least four hours of direct sunlight, or position them beneath artificial lights. Shear away dead flowers and allow about six weeks for a new flush of flowers to develop.

### WATERING

Keep **miniature roses** well watered to encourage the production of new shoots and flowers.

### FERTILIZING

Do not fertilize roses this month. **Miniature roses** growing indoors can be fed with a liquid houseplant fertilizer.

### PRUNING

Winter winds can aggravate tall-growing **hybrid teas**, breaking their canes and injuring their roots as they're tossed about by the wind. Wait until they're dormant to cut them back to 3 feet, thereby lessening their chances of getting tousled by the wind.

### PROBLEMS

Watch out for spider mites on indoor **miniature roses**. Use insecticidal soap to control them. Heavily infested roses should be quarantined to prevent the mites from infesting other plants.

Apply dormant oil spray early in the month, before new growth emerges, to control overwintering insect and spider mite eggs. Read the label and watch for temperature warnings.

Blackspot overwinters on fallen leaves and canes. Rake out the leaves and compost them or bury them in the flower border or vegetable garden away from any roses.

Handpull any young winter annual weeds, or cover them with mulch. Weeding is never fun, but the cooler temperatures can make it more bearable.

# SHRUBS

Shrubs are a gardener's best friends. For starters, they come in a dizzying array of shapes, sizes, forms, and colors. Some have soft, naturally billowy forms, others sport showy, fragrant flowers or brightly colored berries, and still others deliver stunning fall color.

Some shrubs can be used as ground covers with their wide-spreading branches and low growth habit, while other, taller-growing shrubs can be pruned to look like small trees.

Shrubs can be used in a variety of ways: foundation plantings, flower borders, screens, hedges, and stand-alone "look-at-me" accent plants. They also lend themselves to being sheared and clipped into geometrical, sometimes whimsical shapes.

Like best friends, shrubs are there through each changing season. For year-round appeal, unite shrubs and other plants in your landscape—small trees, ground covers, perennials, and annuals—to match and contrast leaf colors and textures, forms, and flowers.

## PLANNING

Once you've determined where you need shrubs for ground cover, screening, background, accents—whatever—select ones that match the conditions in your location. Pay attention to the following factors.

**Light requirements:** Does the area have full sun, partial sun, or shade? What do the shrubs prefer?

**Drainage:** In general, plants prefer well-drained soils. Plants like azaleas and boxwoods will wilt and die in a constantly damp low spot faster than you can say *Phytophthora* (that's the root rot that preys on plants intolerant of "wet feet"). If you have such "hog wallows," choose shrubs that are adapted to boggy conditions. These include anise-tree (*Illicium*), Virginia sweetspire (*Itea virginica*), and summersweet (*Clethra alnifolia*).

**Temperature:** Will the shrubs be exposed to freezing temperatures or extreme heat? Be sure that you select species that withstand it.

**Space limitations:** What is the eventual mature height and spread of the shrub? How fast will it grow? In limited spaces, select smaller, more compact shrubs over the vigorous growers that soon engulf windows and porches.

**Function:** Shrubs can be used in a variety of ways.

- screen, hedge, focal point, mixed border, or ground cover
- ornamental interest—flowers, leaves, and fruit
- food for wildlife—berries, acorns, seeds, and nectar

**Low maintenance:** Several qualities can mean a plant does not require a lot of maintenance.

- drought tolerance
- pest resistance
- slow growth rate

Consider native shrubs (and their domesticated cultivars), whose ability to thrive in your area for centuries gives them reason enough to be part of a low-maintenance landscape.

## PLANTING

To learn how to plant shrubs, refer to Planting in the introduction to the Trees chapter p. 206.

## FERTILIZING

Newly planted shrubs can be fertilized after they've become established. That may take months

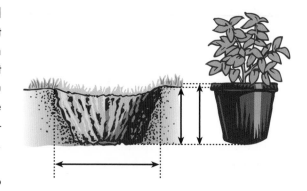

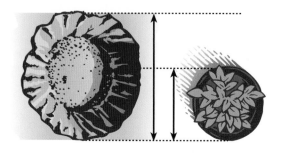

When planting shrubs, prepare a hole that is the same depth as the rootball, and at least two to three times as wide.

or longer, depending on their size. Once established, fertilizer applications can stimulate growth and help shrubs fill their allotted space in the landscape.

Shrubs that have already "filled-in" won't have to be fertilized on a regular basis. Replenishing the mulch at their roots with compost or other "recyclable" organic materials will provide them with a steady diet of minerals. If your shrubs are growing in a lawn that is fertilized, do not add additional fertilizer.

Apply fertilizer when it will be readily absorbed by the roots of your shrubs and when the soil is moist, which can be any time from late spring after new growth emerges up to early fall. However, if water is unavailable or when the shrubs are stressed by drought during the summer months, do not fertilize at all because their roots will be unable to absorb the nutrients.

## CHAPTER SEVEN

Fertilize based on the shrub's appearance (see March Fertilizing p. 186) and according to soil-test results. Most fertilizer recommendations are based on nitrogen, which is an important element in plant growth and often the one that's most likely to be deficient in the soil. Apply 1 pound of a good slow-release nitrogen per thousand square feet of root zone area. Up to 2 pounds can be applied with a slow-release fertilizer.

In the absence of a soil test, use a complete fertilizer with a ratio of 3-1-2 or 3-1-3, such as 12-4-8 or 15-5-15. Palms benefit from fertilizers that also contain magnesium and other micronutrients, such as manganese, particularly palms growing in sandy coastal areas, where micronutrient deficiencies are common.

Apply fertilizer to the shrub's root zone area (area occupied by nutrient and water-absorbing roots), which can extend beyond the drip line or outermost branches. See Fertilizing in the Trees chapter introduction p. 206 for more information.

Since most of a shrub's roots are in the top foot of soil, evenly broadcast the fertilizer with a hand-held spreader or a rotary or cyclone spreader over this root zone area. Sweep any fertilizer off the branches and water afterwards to make the nutrients available to the roots. If the shrub's root zone area is confined by a sidewalk or driveway, reduce the root zone area in your calculations accordingly.

## WATERING

Not all established shrubs have to be watered during hot, dry summer months. Drought-tolerant shrubs can withstand long periods without rain or irrigation.

See the ground rules for proper watering in the Watering section in the Introduction to this book p. 9.

Refer to May Planning p. 190 to learn more about efficient watering methods.

## HOW MUCH FERTILIZER?

If your shrubs are growing in a bed, follow the steps outlined in Fertilizing in Vines and Ground Covers introduction pp. 234 and 235, to determine the right amount of fertilizer to apply.

## PRUNING

Pruning is a basic maintenance requirement for shrubs; it improves their health and appearance and keeps them in bounds. Not all shrubs have to be pruned, however. Barberry, cotoneaster, Indian hawthorn, gardenia, mahonia, and pittosporum rarely need to be pruned if given enough space to develop their natural size. Some multistemmed shrubs such as deutzia, forsythia, plumbago, lantana, and nandina must have their older stems removed entirely, a few at a time each year. This keeps them youthful and vigorous. Others, such as mountain laurel, ligustrum, rose-of-Sharon, and viburnum already have an attractive natural shape that may require the occasional removal of wayward branches that detract from their beauty.

There are two basic pruning cuts: Heading or heading back involves removing a portion of a branch back to a bud or branch. Heading stimulates a flush of new shoots just below the cut making the plant look more dense. When you shear your yaupon holly or boxwood hedges, you're making a bunch of heading cuts.

A thinning cut is the removal of a branch back to where it joins the limb or trunk. Thinning opens up the center of the shrub to sunlight and reduces the number of new shoots that sprout along the branches. A lot of growth can be removed by thinning without dramatically changing the shrub's natural appearance or growth habit and giving it the "just-pruned" look.

When you prune, follow two basic rules:

1. Spring-flowering plants that bloom before June 1 can be pruned right after flowering; they

bloom on last year's growth. So pruning shrubs such as forsythia, quince, and azalea right after they bloom will then give them time to develop new flower buds for next year. There are a few exceptions to this rule, such as oakleaf hydrangea and certain azalea cultivars that bloom after June 1, even into July, but on last year's wood. Reblooming hydrangeas that produce flowers on current season's growth, including 'Bailmer' (Endless Summer), 'David Ramsey', 'Decatur Blue', 'Luvumama', 'Madame Emile Mouillere', 'Oak Hill', and 'Penny Mac', are among the mopheads, and the lacecap 'Lilacina' can be pruned in late winter by removing no more than one-third of the oldest shoots at the base to encourage the production of new shoots.

2. Summer-flowering shrubs produce flower buds on current-season's shoots. They can be pruned in late winter before new growth emerges. A few of these summer-flowering shrubs are beautyberry, butterfly bush, and glossy abelia.

Prune out dead, damaged, or diseased wood at any time of year.

## PROBLEMS

Experts have developed a commonsense approach to pest management. It brings Mother Nature into the battle on the gardener's side by integrating smart plant selection with good planting and maintenance practices and an understanding of pests and their habits. It starts with growing strong, healthy plants that by themselves can prosper with minimal help from you. As in nature, an acceptable level of pests is accommodated. Control is the goal, rather than elimination. This is called Integrated Pest Management, or IPM for short. And it can work for you. It can be summarized in these steps:

1. Select shrubs that are adapted to your region and that have few pest problems. Visit local nurseries and garden centers, and consult with your regional Cooperative Extension Service agent.

2. Start with healthy, high quality, pest-free plants.

3. Select the right location.

4. Properly plant, fertilize, mulch, and water the plants. Avoid overfertilizing, which encourages a lot of succulent growth that is attractive to insects and susceptible to disease. Overfertilization can also contaminate streams, lakes, and ground-water.

*At right:* There are many types of hydrangeas, but the oak leaf hydrangea is a favorite native hydrangea for multiseason interest.

CHAPTER SEVEN

# SUITABLE SHRUBS FOR ALABAMA AND MISSISSIPPI

**Deciduous Shrubs**
- Bottlebrush buckeye (*Aesculus parviflora*)
- Butterfly bush (*Buddleia davidii*)
- Chastetree (*Vitex agnus-castus*)
- Deciduous hollies (*Ilex* spp. and hybrids)
- Dwarf fothergilla (*Fothergilla gardenia*)
- Hydrangea (Hydrangea spp.)
- Native azalea (*Rhododendron* spp. and hybrids)
- Old-fashioned weigela (*Wiegela florida*)
- Rose-of-Sharon (*Hibiscus syriacus*)
- Spirea (*Spiraea* spp.)
- Sweet pepperbush (*Clethra alnifolia*)

**Evergreen Shrubs**
- Anisetree (*Illicium* spp.)
- Azalea (*Rhododendron* spp. and hybrids)
- Boxwood (*Buxus* spp.)

- Camellia (*Camellia japonica, C. sasanqua*)
- Chinese fringe-flower (*Loropetalum chinense*)
- Chinese juniper (*Juniperus chinensis*)
- Chinese podocarpus (*Podocarpus macrophyllus* var. *maki*)
- Glossy abelia (*Abelia* x *grandiflora*)
- Heavenly bamboo (*Nandina domestica*)
- Holly (*Ilex* spp.)
- Indian or Yeddo hawthorn (*Rhaphiolepsis umbellata*)
- Japanese cleyera (*Ternstroemia gymnanthera*)
- Japanese pittosporum (*Pittosporum tobira*)
- Jasmine (*Jasminum* spp.)
- Needle palm (*Rhapidophyllum hystrix*)
- Oleander (*Nerium oleander*)
- Osmanthus (*Osmanthus* spp.)
- Southern wax myrtle (*Myrica cerifera*)

# JANUARY
## SHRUBS

## PLANNING

As you examine the gardening magazines and catalogs arriving this month, make entries in your gardening journal. As you look at the gorgeous photographs of attractive shrubs, check to see if they come with the added bonus of pest resistance. Try to avoid adding another plant to your landscape that will result in a battle with pests during the hot, humid summer months! Have you forgotten about your fights with euonymus scales, *Entomosporium* leaf spot on red tips, and lace bugs on **azaleas** and **cotoneasters**? You can always practice "tough love" gardening by getting rid of the infested plants, but this can quickly become an expensive practice. Use catalogs as a starting point, and continue your search for pest-resistant plants in magazines and reference books, and during visits to local nurseries and garden centers.

## PLANTING

Set out container-grown and balled-and-burlapped shrubs when the soil is not frozen. Follow the step-by-step planting instructions outlined in the introduction to Trees p. 206. If you were unable to move established shrubs last fall, you can transplant them now while they are dormant.

## HELPFUL HINTS IN CASE OF ICE OR SNOW

Ice damage to woody plants occurs when high winds break heavily iced branches. Evergreens are more susceptible to snow damage than are deciduous plants because they have more leaf surface for accumulating snow. Ice and snow can damage your evergreens by their weight or if they are removed carelessly. A branch that breaks or becomes damaged by bending downward can be invaded by canker-producing fungi, leading to the death of the limb the following season.

Shrubs that would collapse beneath heavy snow loads can be protected. Place a crate or a wooden box with slats over the plants to catch any accumulating snowfall. During the winter, lift off snow with an upward sweep of a broom. When removing snow from walks and driveways, avoid piling the snow around the root zone areas of plants, which can produce waterlogged conditions when the snow melts.

Ice can be more troublesome than snow because it cannot be easily brushed off without damaging the limbs. Allow ice to melt naturally.

The limbs of valuable plants can be protected from ice breakage with flexible supports. Consider looping a bicycle tire inner tube around the trunk and branches. Or you can create horizontal supports by securing bungee cords throughout the framework of the shrub and attaching their ends to bamboo poles or posts oriented on the outside of the plant.

At the end of winter, examine your plants and prune out any broken or dead limbs.

Before you prune out a limb that looks dead, scrape the bark with your thumbnail and look at the underlying tissue. A green layer indicates living tissue. A brown layer indicates a dead limb.

Cut back or thin out any damaged shoots by pruning within 1/4 inch above a live bud or just outside the branch collar.

## CARE

Protect newly planted evergreens from winterburn by shading

them on the south and southwest sides with temporary burlap screens or snow fences. Established evergreens may also require similar sun and wind protection to prevent the leaves from turning brown and scorching. This is especially important in areas where the soil can freeze and remain frozen on sunny days. When this happens, the leaves continue to transpire or lose water, but the roots cannot replace the lost moisture from the frozen soil. Winterburn can also occur when the sun thaws the leaves, which then refreeze rapidly when the sun is blocked or at sunset when the leaf temperature drops quickly.

## WATERING

During winter thaws, water fall-planted and established evergreens, especially those on the south and west sides of the house. Mulch newly planted shrubs with a 2- to 4-inch layer of compost, and keep them well-watered.

## FERTILIZING

Do not fertilize at this time.

## PRUNING

Remove any broken storm-damaged limbs. Use pruning shears, loppers, or a saw to make clean cuts. Any major pruning should be reserved for next month or after the coldest part of winter has passed.

Delay pruning or removing cold-damaged plants. Sometimes they'll sprout from the stems or the roots, depending on the plant and the extent of injury. Be patient. It may take until May or June before new leaves sprout from the seemingly lifeless branches.

Summer-flowering plants that can be pruned later this month, after the coldest part of winter has passed, include **butterfly bush**, **glossy abelia** (*Abelia* x *grandiflora*), **fragrant tea olive** (*Osmanthus fragrans*), **smooth hydrangea** (*Hydrangea arborescens*), and others. They produce flowers on current-season's growth.

## PROBLEMS

Apply dormant horticultural oil sprays on small landscape trees to smother overwintering insect eggs, aphids, mites, and scale insects. Be sure to spray the trunk, branches, stems, and both sides of the leaves thoroughly. Read the label for any precautions regarding the recommended high and low temperature limits at the time of application. Special equipment (or a professional) may be needed to treat large tree-sized shrubs.

# FEBRUARY

## SHRUBS

### PLANNING

In the colder areas of Alabama and Mississippi, bring a touch of springtime indoors. Spring-flowering woody plants (whose flower buds were produced on last year's growth) can be forced into early bloom indoors once their dormancy requirements have been met. Though the time varies between species, at least eight weeks of temperatures below 40 degrees F. is generally sufficient.

Branches from shrubs are easier to force than those from trees, and the nearer the time is to the shrub's normal blooming, the more rapidly the forced branches will bloom.

Some readily forced branches include those of **border forsythia** (*Forsythia x intermedia*), **bridal-wreath spirea** (*Spiraea prunifolia*), **Corneliancherry dogwood** (*Cornus mas*), **honeysuckle** (*Lonicera*), **serviceberry** (*Amelanchier*), and **spicebush** (*Lindera benzoin*).

*Follow these steps:*

1. Cut the branches on a day when the temperature is above freezing, being careful not to disfigure the plant.

2. Cut the branches 6 to 18 inches long; longer branches are easier to use in floral bouquets.

3. Bring the branches indoors and make a second cut on a slant just above the previous cut. Make several 1-inch-long slits in the end of each stem as well.

4. Place the stems in a container to which a floral preservative has been added, covering up one-third of the stems. You can make your own by mixing 2 tablespoons of fresh lemon or lime juice, 1 tablespoon of sugar, and 1/2 tablespoon of household bleach in a quart of water. Place the container in a cool, dark location.

5. When the buds begin to show color, move the branches to the light, but keep them away from direct sunlight. Cool temperatures will prolong the life of the flowers when they appear.

### PLANTING

Bare-root deciduous shrubs can be planted while they're dormant, about a month before the last average freeze in your area. See Trees February Planting p. 210.

Plant container-grown and balled-and-burlapped shrubs anytime, except when the soil is frozen and when severely cold weather prevails.

### CARE

Watch for signs of heaving among your small shrubs; the freezing and thawing of the ground can force shallow-rooted plants out of the soil. Replant any that have been heaved and mulch with 3 to 4 inches of organic material to reduce fluctuations in soil temperature.

### FERTILIZING

Don't be too hasty to fertilize your shrubs. Wait until at least budbreak—when new growth emerges.

### WATERING

Water newly planted shrubs. Keep the soil moist but avoid overwatering, which can inhibit root growth.

If severe cold is forecast for your area, water evergreens before the soil freezes. The roots are not able to take up moisture when the soil is frozen.

### PRUNING

Shrubs can get a new look or be renewed when they have outgrown their location (perhaps they were mistakenly planted along the foundation of a house and have begun to engulf the windows), have been seriously damaged or neglected, or have become "leggy" with most of their leaves clustered at the op, revealing bare or leafless stems below. There are two approaches.

1. The drastic approach is to cut back the plant to within 6 to 12 inches of the ground before spring growth begins. Most broadleaf shrubs, including **Japanese cleyera**, **holly**, **azalea**, **privet**, and **gardenia** respond well to this treatment. When the new shoots emerge, pinch out the tips and thin out some of the shoots to make some room and begin developing a strong framework.

2. A milder tactic is to stretch renewal pruning over a period of three years. This works well for multiple-stemmed plants such as **forsythia**, **leucothoe**, **nandina**, **glossy abelia**, and **spirea**. In the first year, remove one-third of the oldest stems. In the following year, take out one-half of the remaining old stems. If needed, head back long shoots that grew from the previous pruning cuts. In the third year, remove the remaining old wood and, if needed, head back the long new shoots.

Summer-flowering shrubs such as **butterfly bush** and **beauty-berry** can be cut back to within 6 inches or a foot since they bloom on current-season's growth. Wait to prune spring-flowering shrubs until after they bloom.

## PROBLEMS

Use dormant oil sprays on landscape plants to smother overwintering insects and mites before the plants leaf out. See January Problems p. 183.

Camellia flower blight is a fungal disease that attacks only the flowers of **Japanese camellia** (*Camellia japonica*). Follow these steps to manage this disease: 1) Pull off all affected flowers and discard them. At the end of the flowering season, rake up and destroy all fallen blossoms and other plant debris.

2) This disease requires community-wide attention. Fungal spores are produced over the length of the **Japanese camellia** flowering season in late winter and spring and can travel one-half mile or more from the source. Educate your neighbors about this disease and encourage them to pick up and discard or destroy diseased flowers.

3) A fungicidal drench can offer some degree of control, but it will be futile if your neighbors are not controlling this disease in their own gardens.

Control any winter annual weeds such as bittercress, common chickweed, and henbit by handpulling. Suppress them with a shallow layer of mulch.

Use scissors to cut away the container around potted shrubs before planting.

# MARCH

## SHRUBS

### PLANNING

Take a look at the shrubs near the foundation of your house and in your landscape. Dense shrubs should not be planted close to the foundation or siding, or in front of foundation vents because they can obstruct air flow around and beneath your home, which can lead to moisture problems. Make plans to prune these shrubs or move them to another area in the landscape. If you move them to south- or west-facing walls to insulate your house from summer's heat, keep them away from foundation vents and at least 4 feet from the foundation.

Be sure to keep shrubs away from the compressor on your split-system air conditioner. While the shade cast by the shrubs can reduce energy consumption, they should be planted far enough away so they won't obstruct air flow or service.

### PLANTING

Plant balled-and-burlapped or container-grown shrubs. Follow the step-by-step instructions in the Trees introduction p. 206.

Ground-layering is a simple way to propagate shrubs that have long pliable stems (such as **forsythia**, **indica azalea**, and

**winter jasmine**) or difficult-to-root plants (such as **rhododendron**). Here's how to do it:

1. Before growth begins, bend one or two young, healthy stems to the ground.

2. Wind the underside of the stem and cover it with soil. Hold it in place with a piece of wire bent to a hairpin shape and pushed into the ground. Do not bury the shoot tip.

3. If you layer now, the shoots will usually be rooted by the end of the growing season. Then you can sever the new plant from the parent and transplant it. Shoots layered later in the summer should be left through the winter and separated in spring.

### WATERING

Water newly planted shrubs every few weeks in dry weather. Check the moisture in the root-ball and surrounding soil before watering (see Trees October Watering p. 226).

### FERTILIZING

Evaluate the growth and appearance of your shrubs to decide if fertilizing is necessary. Look for these signs of "hunger" or mineral deficiency: stunted growth, smaller than normal leaves, poor leaf color, early leaf drop. Be

aware that these same symptoms of poor growth can be the result of the following causes: heavily compacted soil; stresses induced by insects, diseases, and weeds; or adverse weather conditions. Before you fertilize, determine the cause of the problem and correct it. Having your soil tested is one way of getting to the "root" of the problem. Rely on soil-test results to supply the minerals that are deficient in the soil.

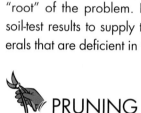

### PRUNING

To create a hedge, start shearing plants during their early years to encourage compact growth.

1. Prune young one- to two-year-old plants to within a foot of the ground.

2. During the growing season, head back the tips of the shoots to encourage branching below the cuts.

3. Once a hedge reaches the desired height, choose an informal or formal look. An informal-looking hedge requires little care; you simply maintain the natural growth habit of the hedge. Prune only to remove dead, diseased, or damaged wood, and occasionally head back the shoots to maintain the desired height and width if needed.

The formal look requires regular shearing during the growing

Pruning a hedge is a two-step process beginning with cutting stems back to within a foot of the ground followed by heading back the tips during the season to encourage branching.

season. When maintaining a formal hedge, follow these two rules-of-thumb:

1. Clip the hedges when new growth is green and succulent.

2. Shape the plants so the base of the hedge is wider than the top. A hedge with a narrow base becomes "leggy" over time because the top shades out the bottom, causing the stems to lose their lower leaves and show their knees.

Prune summer-flowering shrubs before new growth starts. Wait until spring-flowering shrubs bloom before pruning them.

## PROBLEMS

Early this month, apply a dormant horticultural oil spray on dormant landscape plants. See January Problems p. 183.

Watch out for the "cool-weather" mites: southern red mites which attack **Japanese** and **American hollies**; **azalea**, **camellia**, and **rhododendron** and spruce spider mites which feed on **arborvitae**, **false cypress**, **juniper**, and other conifers.

They attack in the spring and fall. See p. 286 for controls.

Look for small cone-shaped objects hanging from the branches of your **arborvitae**, **cedar**, **juniper**, and **Leyland cypress**. These are the nests of bagworms, which contain from 500 to 1,000 eggs that will hatch next month and into June. Remove the bags and discard them.

Handpull winter annuals such as bittercress, common chickweed, and henbit to prevent them from going to seed. Maintain a 2- to 4-inch layer of mulch to suppress weeds.

A pre-emergent herbicide can reduce the amount of hand weeding required. Pre-emergent herbicides kill germinating weed seedlings before they appear. See Annuals March Problems p. 23 for tips on selecting a pre-emergent herbicide.

## HELPFUL HINTS

To calculate the correct spacing for shrubs, add the ultimate spread of two of them and divide by two. The result will tell you the proper distance between them from center to center at planting time. If plants at first appear to be too far apart, you can interplant these permanent plantings with temporary "filler" plants. Bulbs such as **daffodils**, **alliums**, **lilies**, and **glads** or annual bedding plants can be used to fill in the gaps.

# APRIL

## SHRUBS

 PLANNING

Look for shrubs that bear edible fruits like **fig**, **pomegranate** (*Punica granatum* 'Wonderful') and **pineapple guava** (*Feijoa sellowiana*). My favorite shrub for year-round beauty is the **blueberry** with creamy-white or pink flowers in spring; delicious deep-blue fruit in summer; red, orange, and yellow fall color; and rosy-pink stems in winter.

**Rabbiteye** and **southern highbush blueberries** can be grown throughout Alabama and Mississippi. **Highbush blueberry** and its hybrids, which are more cold hardy, are also suited for the coldest regions of the states because they can survive cold winter temperatures of 10 degrees F. and lower. **Blueberries** are acid-loving shrubs that can be grown like **azaleas** and **rhododendrons**. Use them in borders and hedges. Plant at least two varieties of **rabbiteyes** that bloom at the same time so that the plants will cross-pollinate, or you won't get many berries. Your regional Extension agent will have a list of which are good matches for your area.

 PLANTING

Continue planting container-grown shrubs, following the step-by-step instructions in the Trees chapter p. 206. Pay strict attention to watering to help them get established.

 CARE

Do not be too quick to pull out shrubs that are damaged by cold. Cut back dead branches above the ground, but leave the roots in place until June. Sometimes it takes a few weeks of warm weather for the new shoots to be jump-started into growth. Check mulched areas and replace or replenish where needed.

 WATERING

To prevent water from running off, create a temporary berm, or dike, of piled up soil around newly planted shrubs in clay soil. Smooth out the berm when the plants become established.

 FERTILIZING

For blue flowers on your **mophead** and **lacecap** or **French hydrangeas**, maintain a soil pH between 5 and 5.5. An acid soil increases the availability of aluminum, which turns the flowers blue. Apply aluminum sulfate or sulfur to reduce the pH to this ideal range when you see new growth emerging. To avoid having to adjust the pH, grow a blue-flowered **hydrangea** cultivar such as 'All Summer Beauty', 'Blue Wave', or 'Nikko Blue'.

Fertilize **palms** with a slow-release fertilizer that has a 3-1-2 analysis (such as 18-6-12) and that contains micronutrients for a deep green color. Broadcast or scatter the fertilizer under the canopy.

 PRUNING

If you aren't sure of the extent of winter injury, wait until growth begins before removing dead

Lacecap hydranagea

wood. **Plumbago**, **lantana**, and **jasmine** are among the last shrubs to leaf out—often not until late April or May. Prune spring-flowering shrubs as their blossoms fade. Prune out dead, damaged, or pest-ridden branches first. Avoid using heading cuts to prune them into "mushrooms" or "meatballs." Rather, use thinning cuts to remove renegade limbs and to accentuate their natural shapes.

To prune **forsythia**, **quince**, **sweet mockorange**, **nandina**, and other multistemmed shrubs, cut off a few of the older central stems at ground level so new ones can spring up and take over.

Prune **azaleas** only if they need it. Thin wayward branches. Cut back branches that have just a ring of leaves at the top.

## PROBLEMS

Watch for aphids, whiteflies, and spider mites. See Pest Control on pp. 283 to 285 for descriptions and controls. Azalea lace bugs suck sap from the undersides of **azalea** leaves, creating stippled or blanched areas. The underside of the leaf will be covered with splattered, brown or black, varnish-like patches of fecal material. The leaves will turn pale green or yellow and fall off. Expect two or three generations. Damage from this pest is most serious on **azaleas** growing in sunny locations. If yours are growing in full sun, try moving them to a location that receives only filtered sunlight or afternoon shade.

If you use an insecticide, start early in the season to destroy the first generation of nymphs. You can apply insecticidal soap or pyrethrin at three- to four-day intervals for a minimum of three applications, making sure to spray the undersides of the leaves. (If there is no rain to wash the leaves, don't exceed three applications or you may damage the plants.)

Look for tea scales on the undersides of **camellia** and **holly** leaves. They look like white waxy or cottony oval specks. Scale insects suck plant sap and exude a sticky honeydew that's often colonized by a sooty mold fungus. The young scale insects are called "crawlers" and are about the size of the period at the end of this sentence. They scurry about, then settle and produce a protective shell or cover. Heavy infestations cause leaf-drop. Light infestations can be scraped off the plant. Control with summer horticultural oil sprays and other pesticides.

Azalea leaf gall is a fungal disease that infects newly emerging leaves and flowers of **azaleas**. The fleshy galls begin as light green to pink thickened areas on the leaves and turn chalky white as the spores are produced. Camellia leaf gall infects **sasanqua camellias** more than **Japanese camellias**. The gall containing the fungus eventually ruptures and disperses the spores to other plants. Handpick the galls and discard them. Fungicides are available.

*Entomosporium* leaf spot is a disease that attacks **red tips** (*Photinia* x *fraseri*) and **Indian hawthorn** (*Raphiolepis indica*), causing leaf drop. To prevent its spread, follow these steps:

1. Prune only in the winter before growth begins. (Summer pruning encourages flushes of new growth, which are susceptible to attack.)

2. Remove infected twigs and leaves and rake up and discard fallen leaves.

3. Space plants far enough apart to encourage rapid drying of the leaves after rainfall; avoid wetting the leaves, since the fungus is spread by splashing water.

4. As a last resort, protect the new leaves with a fungicide. Because **photinia** produces several growth flushes a season, expect fungicide applications to be a regular gardening chore. It's a good idea to avoid planting **red tips**.

# MAY

## SHRUBS

### PLANNING

With summer around the corner, take some time this month to consider which irrigation method is best suited to your situation.

If you're going to handwater, find a nozzle that breaks the water into rain-size droplets that won't wash the soil away. If you choose to automate, think about an irrigation system.

Some install-it-yourself systems allow you to turn the water on and off yourself or automatically, in various patterns, and for any length of time. The simplest is a soaker hose, a fibrous tube that "sweats" or allows water to seep out along its length. It is suitable for dense plantings.

A soaker hose (and a rain guage) is a great aid in the fight against drought.

Some systems have nozzles that deliver the water in a low, horizontal pattern that wets the root zone but keeps the plants dry.

The most efficient watering method is drip or trickle irrigation. Such systems use short tubes, called emitters, which come off a main water-supply hose and go directly to the base of the plant. This is generally the most expensive form of irrigation and the most complex to set up, but it has advantages. The weeds in the area are not watered, and evaporation from the soil is minimized. Drip systems can have problems with clogging from soil particles and/or mineral salts suspended in water taken from springs or wells. New designs address this problem: Some include filters and self-flushing emitters. All these systems can work on a timer.

Purchase all of these at garden centers or shop the Internet.

### PLANTING

Although shrubs are best planted in the fall, container-grown plants can be planted throughout the summer months as long as you pay careful attention to watering. When the flowers fade on your Mother's Day **hydran-**

**geas**, don't throw them out. Plant them in the garden where they'll get morning sun and afternoon shade.

### CARE

To prevent damage to shrubs while mowing, surround them with a ring of mulch. Apply the mulch as far as the dripline or outermost branches.

### WATERING

Avoid watering your shrubs with a sprinkler. In addition to wasting water and watering weeds, wetting the leaves will encourage disease outbreaks.

### FERTILIZING

Evaluate your shrubs for leaf color and growth to determine the need for fertilizer. To encourage more growth, fertilize with a slow-release fertilizer. Water well immediately afterwards.

Avoid excessive fertilization. High levels of nutrients, particularly nitrogen, will encourage leafy shoot growth at the expense of flower buds. Overfed shrubs produce a lot of growth that can be attacked by insects or diseases. Sometimes it has to be pruned to keep the shrub confined to its allotted space in the landscape.

## PRUNING

As **French** or **lacecap hydrangeas** age, renew the plants to encourage new shoots. Remove no more than one-third of the oldest shoots at the base immediately after flowering. They will be replaced by more-vigorous younger shoots, which will flower the following season.

Continue pruning spring-flowering shrubs as their flowers fade. The new growth that develops will mature over the summer and fall and produce flowers next spring.

Generally, **azaleas** shouldn't be pruned, but if they've overgrown their location or have dead branches, they will benefit from careful trimming. Take out individual branches with thinning cuts, removing the oldest branches at the base.

To control height on **aucuba**, don't trim across the top. Prune away the tallest branches by cutting them back to their point of origin.

## PROBLEMS

Be on the lookout for damage caused by aphids and spider mites. Take necessary action if their feeding is more than you or your shrubs can tolerate. Blast these critters off with a strong spray of water from the hose. Get underneath the leaves to dislodge spider mites.

Boxwood leafminer is the most serious pest of **boxwoods**, with heaviest infestations occurring on **common box** (*Buxus sempervirens*), **littleleaf boxwood** (*B. microphylla*), and **Harland boxwood** (*B. harlandii*). The larvae feed inside the leaves, resulting in splotchy, yellow, puckered or blistered areas on the undersides of the leaves. Heavily infested leaves often drop prematurely. Severe attacks can weaken the plant, resulting in twig dieback and exposing the plant to diseases and winterkill in colder regions.

The best way to suppress infestations of boxwood leafminers is to apply a systemic insecticide to kill the young larvae inside the leaves. Alternatively, your susceptible **boxwood** hedge could be replaced with certain cultivars of **common box** (*Buxus sempervirens*), such as 'Suffruticosa' (**English boxwood**) and 'Argenteovariegata,' that escape serious attacks, or the **Japanese boxwood** (*B. microphylla* var. *japonica*) cultivars 'Morris Midget' and 'Morris Dwarf'.

Euonymus scale is a common pest of **euonymus**. These oyster-shaped brown or white, scaly insects suck plant sap from the leaves and stems. Heavy infestations cause the leaves to turn yellow and fall off. Eventually, entire branches may be covered, finally killing the plant. Expect two or three generations of euonymus scale per year. Prune out heavily infested branches. Control the offspring called "crawlers" in April, May, and June with an insecticide. 'Acutus' **wintercreeper euonymus** (*Euonymus fortunei* 'Acutus') is resistant.

Watch for Japanese beetles in the northern parts of Alabama and Mississippi.

During long, wet springs, **azaleas** and **camellias** may be attacked by the leaf gall fungus, which causes the new leaves to become thick and fleshy. See April Problems p. 189.

Fireblight is a bacterial disease that attacks **cotoneaster**, **flowering quince**, and **pyracantha**. The new shoots suddenly wilt, turn brown, turn black, and die. Prune out the diseased branches several inches below the infection. Grow fireblight-resistant **pyracantha** cultivars such as 'Apache', 'Fiery Cascade', 'Mohave', 'Navaho', 'Pueblo', 'Rutgers', 'Shawnee', and 'Teton'.

See Trees May Problems p. 217 for poison ivy information.

# JUNE
## SHRUBS

 PLANNING

As part of your summer vacation plans, why not find some time to visit private and public gardens? These gardens can be inspirational and educational. Refer to Public Gardens on pp. 288 to 291 for their addresses. Don't forget your camera and gardening journal. Enjoy!

 PLANTING

With the availability of container-grown plants, the planting season is limited only by extremely hot weather, frozen soil in winter, and your ability to water regularly. With the onset of hot, dry weather, you can plant, but be prepared to be on call with adequate water throughout the establishment period of your shrubs.

June and July is an ideal time to take semi-hardwood cuttings when the new green growth begins to harden and turn brown. When you snap the twig, the bark often clings to the stem.

Some of the plants that can be rooted now include broadleaf evergreens such as **camellia**, **banana shrub** (*Michelia figo*), **azalea**, **osmanthus**, **magnolia**, **nandina**, **coniferous evergreens** like **Japanese plum yew** (*Cephalotaxus* spp.), **podocarpus**, and many others. Here are some simple propagating steps:

1. Remove a strip of bark $1/2$ to 1 inch long on one side of each cutting. Dip them in a rooting hormone suited for woody plants (available at most garden centers).

2. Stick them in a container of equal parts peat and perlite or coarse sand. First make a small hole with a pencil in the moist medium. Then put the cutting into the hole, making sure it's deep enough in the medium to hide the wound.

3. Enclose the container in a zip-top plastic bag or one that can be twist-tied at the top. Or use a clear 2-liter soft-drink bottle with its bottom removed over the cuttings.

The process of rooting semi-hardwood cuttings is basically the same as rooting other cuttings.

4. Place the pot in a shaded location. Keep the cuttings moist. Check the cuttings for roots by gently tugging at a few of them. When you feel resistance, it means they have rooted and you can safely remove the top of the bottle.

5. Remove the plastic bag and repot them in a medium composed of equal parts potting soil and peat moss.

6. Gradually expose the rooted cutting to stronger light to harden them off. After a couple of weeks, transplant them into the garden.

 WATERING

Water the shrubs planted within the past year, which are especially vulnerable to heat and drought stress. Water thoroughly to encourage deep rooting. Avoid irrigating your shrubs with an overhead sprinkler. Besides wasting water and watering weeds, wetting the leaves encourages disease outbreaks.

 FERTILIZING

If necessary, fertilize your palms with a slow-release nitrogen fertilizer as described in April. The goal is to maintain growth. If the soil is low in magnesium as determined by a soil test, apply the recommended amount of Epsom salts.

Pink flowers occur on **French** and **lacecap hydrangeas** with a soil pH between 6.0 and 6.5. In this pH range, aluminum becomes "tied up" or rendered unavailable in the soil and so is absent from the flowers. Use lime to increase the soil pH to this desirable range. To avoid having to maintain this pH, grow pink-flowering cultivars such as 'Forever Pink' and 'Pia'. For blue flowers on your **French hydrangeas**, maintain a soil pH between 5 and 5.5. Apply aluminum sulfate or sulfur to reduce the pH to this ideal range. To avoid having to adjust the pH, grow a blue-flowered **hydrangea** cultivar such as 'All Summer Beauty', 'Blue Wave', or 'Nikko Blue'.

Fertilize shrubs that are not yet to the size that you intend (if you did not do this in May). Use a slow-release fertilizer according to label directions.

# PRUNING

Prune out dead, damaged, or pest-ridden branches. When shearing your hedges, shape the plants so the base of the hedge is wider than the top. This will expose the entire hedge to create a dense screen of leaves. See March Pruning p. 186.

If you shear your **boxwoods**, it's important that you thin out some of the interior branches to admit sunlight and air movement. Light encourages growth on the inner stems, and air circulation reduces the occurrence of fungal diseases.

# PROBLEMS

Pests to watch for include aphids, euonymus scale, spider mites, and Japanese beetles.

Two-spotted spider mites (pale yellow, sometimes green, brown, or red) are "hot-weather" mites, becoming active during the heat of summer. They attack a wide variety of shrubs. Evaluate the extent of injury and decide if pest-control measures are warranted.

**Gardenia** and whiteflies go together like peanut butter and jelly. These tiny mothlike insects are a common pest. Whiteflies feed by sucking plant sap from the leaves. Lightly infested leaves develop a mottled appearance while higher populations cause leaves to yellow, shrivel, and die prematurely. Heavy infestations result in sticky leaves covered with a thin black film of sooty mold, a fungus which feeds on the honeydew excreted by the whiteflies. See p. 285 for controls.

Azalea stem borers infest **azalea**, **rhododendron**, **blueberry**, and **mountain laurel**. Prune out the wilted twigs and discard them. Plants attacked year after year can be protected with an insecticide.

Nematodes are microscopic, soil-inhabiting eel-like worms that damage roots. They are more commonly found in coarse-textured sandy soils than fine-textured clay soils. See Roses July Problems p. 166 for a description and controls.

Be on the lookout for root rot caused by the fungus *Phytophthora*, which means plant destroyer. See July for a description and controls.

When some gardeners find lichens growing on their shrubs, they often panic, thinking that their plants are under siege. Relax. See Trees June Helpful Hints p. 219.

Handpull, or use a herbicide to spot-treat water- and nutrient-stealing weeds from your shrub beds and borders. A makeshift cardboard shield can be used to protect your shrubs from accidental contact with the herbicide. Suppress their emergence with a layer of mulch.

# JULY
## SHRUBS

 PLANNING

Learn more about the tremendous diversity of shrubs that can be cultivated in your landscape. Each year, there are more cultivars introduced that offer variety in color, size, and form. **Sky pencil boxwood** is a good example. Its narrow, Italian-cypress-like form is a far cry from the typical chubby **boxwood**.

Don't forget native "American-made" shrubs that deserve a place in the landscape. These plants were growing in North America when the Europeans first arrived and are still here, which is proof of their longevity and ability to adapt readily to our climate, soils, and pests. Besides, they make terrific plants for attracting songbirds, butterflies, beneficial insects, and other wildlife. Look for cultivars of native plants that will fit perfectly into your landscape.

 PLANTING

If your summer vacation is the only time you can plant, then go ahead and install container-grown shrubs. Keep the rootball and surrounding soil moist until winter rains begin doing it for you. Roots need a year to thoroughly establish.

 WATERING

Water recently planted shrubs, which are especially vulnerable to heat and drought. Water thoroughly to encourage deep rooting. Check the rootball and soil before watering instead of relying on the calendar. Avoid overwatering which can suffocate the plant roots, causing the leaves to wilt. It can also expose the shrub to attack from root rot, a deadly fungal disease that prevails in waterlogged conditions and attacks susceptible plants.

Established, drought-tolerant shrubs may not require water; other shrubs, however, may need to be watered during prolonged dry periods. These shrubs will benefit from an application of 1 inch of water per week.

 FERTILIZING

If your healthy-looking shrubs already fit into their allotted space, there's no reason to encourage any further growth with fertilizer.

If your shrubs are experiencing drought stress, water is what they need most. Wait until late fall to fertilize them when they'll be more receptive.

 PRUNING

Remove diseased, dead, or broken branches at any time.

 PROBLEMS

Be on the lookout for damage caused by aphids and spider mites. Take necessary action if their feeding is more than you or your shrubs can tolerate. Blast these critters off with a strong spray of water from the hose. Get underneath the leaves to dislodge spider mites.

The second generation of azalea lace bugs occurs in late July through September. The adults and nymphs have piercing-sucking mouth parts for sucking sap from the undersides of the leaves. Injury by their feeding results in stippled or blanched areas on the upper leaf surface. They also deposit black, tarlike feces (frass) and the skins of molting nymphs on the undersides of the leaves. Heavy infestations cause the leaves to turn pale green or yellow and fall off.

A scuffle hoe may be the perfect solution to weeding around shrubs.

Damage from this pest is most serious on **azaleas** growing in sunny locations. If yours are growing in full sun, try moving them to a location that receives only filtered sunlight or afternoon shade. This tactic should reduce the lace bug populations.

Apply an insecticidal soap at three- to four-day intervals for a minimum of three applications, making sure to spray the undersides of the leaves. If there is no rain to wash off the leaves, then do not exceed three applications or you may damage the plants. Other insecticides are available.

If you prefer not to use insecticides and find that you can't maintain your **azaleas** without them, consider replacing them with lace bug–resistant **azaleas** such as 'Cavalier', 'Dawn', 'Dream', 'Elsie Lee', 'Eureka', 'Macrantha', 'Marilee', 'Pink Fancy', 'Pink Star', 'Red Wing', 'Salmon Pink', 'Seigai', and 'Sunglow'.

In the northern parts of Alabama and Mississippi, watch for Japanese beetles this month. These big slow-flying bugs, metallic green with bronze wing covers, skeletonize leaves, leaving only a lacy network of leaf veins after their feeding. They also feed on flowers. Pick them off and discard them into a jar of soapy water. Neem can be applied to the leaves to reduce feeding by the adults. Other insecticides can be used for heavy infestations. If you choose to use Japanese beetle traps, place them far away from your susceptible shrubs. Thankfully, there's only one generation a year.

This is a tough month for **rhododendrons**, which are tricky even in the northern parts of Alabama and Mississippi. Look for shoot blight, which is where the terminal bud and leaves turn brown, roll up, and drop. Prune out affected branches. Fungicides can be applied at the first sign of disease. There is no cure for infested plants.

If your plants suddenly wilt and die, it may be *Phytophthora* root rot, a devastating fungal disease that attacks a wide variety of plants. Scrape the bark near the crown and look for a reddish-brown discoloration where the fungus has moved into the stem. Examine the roots as well. The "outer skin" or cortex of the root can be slipped off easily like the paper covering from a straw. When you slice it open, a root rot-infected root is reddish-brown inside instead of a healthy white in color. When symptoms are evident, chemical fungicides are often ineffective in controlling this disease. Remove the infected plant and replant in the same spot. Make certain the new location has perfect drainage.

Control weeds by handpulling and maintaining a shallow layer of mulch. Prevent the weeds from going to seed by removing the flowers.

# AUGUST

## SHRUBS

### PLANNING

Take advantage of the cool temperatures inside to catch up on writing in your garden journal and reading about shrubs. If you haven't kept up with regular entries, plan some time this month to sit down and record your observations on the performance of your plants, any pest problems, control measures, and thoughts about what should to be done as summer closes and gives way to fall. Write down any plants that need to be transplanted or given away.

### PLANTING

This is the most challenging month to plant shrubs, but if you want to take advantage of special prices, it is usually the time when you will find nurseries discounting perfectly good stock to make room for fall items. If you shop now, keep your new plants well watered and in the shade. After planting, thoroughly water again and keep watering regularly.

### WATERING

Continue watering any plantings made within the last year.

Along the coast, anyone with saline water will benefit from a drip-irrigation system. Drip systems use less water to moisten the root zones of your plants, thus putting less salt in the soil. Planting your shrubs in raised beds will also make it easier for nature to flush out accumulated salts with rainfall.

### FERTILIZING

If you want to fertilize your young shrubs now, use a slow-release fertilizer to avoid encouraging the rapid, succulent growth which can be killed by early fall freezes. Look for a low-nitrogen "winterizer" or "fall feed" formula. Otherwise, wait until next spring when new growth begins.

### PRUNING

Remove diseased, damaged, or dead branches from shrubs. Avoid severe pruning.

### PROBLEMS

Spider mites are very active during hot, dry weather. Their feeding injury results in discolored, bronze-colored leaves. Check for mites by tapping a branch onto a white sheet of paper and looking for moving specks. Natural predators can control spider mite populations. You can wash off mites with a strong stream of water. If this doesn't work, especially on needle-leafed evergreens, try spraying Neem, a botanical pesticide.

Redheaded azalea caterpillars devour entire leaves and completely defoliate branches. You can identify this caterpillar by its red head and yellow stripes. When disturbed, it curls backward in a defensive posture. Handpick the caterpillars and discard them in a jar of soapy water. *Bacillus thuringiensis* (Bt) is a biological insecticide that will control young caterpillars. Other insecticides are available and can be applied to control heavy infestations.

Remove the silken-needle-covered bags of bagworms on **pine**, **juniper**, **hemlock**, **arborvitae**, and other evergreens.

Weak-looking, stunted plants may be infested with nematodes. Because some shrubs are susceptible to certain kinds of nematodes and resistant to others, determine the identity of the nematodes attacking your plants. You may be able to outsmart them by growing resistant shrubs. See Roses July Problems p. 166 for a description and controls.

Wilted, dying plants may be a symptom of *Phytophthora* root rot. See July Problems p. 195 for a description and controls. Although this fungal disease is often found in wet or poorly drained sites, it will attack plants in fairly dry sites if they are planted too deeply. Over-watering plants also favors attacks by this disease. Here are some tips to avoid root rot:

1. Avoid planting in poorly drained sites.

2. Improve drainage in heavy clay soil by planting in slightly raised beds, or add organic matter such as composted pine bark to as large a planting area as possible.

3. Use plants that are highly resistant to root rot. **Azaleas** resistant to *Phytophthora* root rot include 'Corrine', 'Fakir', 'Fred Cochran', 'Glacier', 'Hampton Beauty', 'Higasa', 'Merlin', 'Polar Seas', and 'Rose Greely'. Grafting can also be used to thwart *Phytophthora* root rot. For example, susceptible **Japanese camellia** cultivars can be grafted onto rot-resistant **sasanqua camellia** rootstock.

See July p. 195 for weed control tips.

# HELPFUL HINTS
# FOR EXTREME CONDITIONS

Gulf Coast landscapes expose plants to challenging, often inhospitable growing conditions. Few inland plants can survive the salt spray, sand, and battering winds.

Select native coastal plants that are indigenous to the area. Plant them on the windward side of your property. Not only will they prosper in these natural conditions, they'll also keep your landscape in harmony with its surroundings. Hardy exotic plants that can set the stage for the less-conspicuous natives include **Japanese black pine**, **Indian hawthorn**, and **Japanese pittosporum**.

Tender plants can be planted on the leeward side of your home or in protected microclimates created by gazebos, arbors, and fences. These microclimates can provide shade and protection from the seaside elements. Here's a sample of shrubs that can be grown in these exposed, oceanfront environments:

| Shrub | Hardiness Zone |
| --- | --- |
| **Common oleander** (*Nerium oleander*) | (7b)8 to 10 |
| **Dwarf palmetto** (*Sabal minor*) | 8b to 11 |
| **Dwarf pittosporum** (*Pittosporum tobira* 'Wheeler's Dwarf') | 8a to 11 |
| **Dwarf yaupon holly** (*Ilex vomitoria* 'Nana') | 7a to 9b |
| **Groundselbush** (*Baccharis halimifolia*) | 5 to 9 |
| **Indian hawthorn** (*Raphiolepsis indica*) | 7b to 10 |
| **Japanese cleyera** (*Ternstroemia gymnanthera*) | 7 to 10 |
| **Wax myrtle** (*Myrica cerifera*) | 7b to 11 |

• If you're looking for plants that tolerate acid soil, consider **azalea**, **rhododendron**, **blueberry**, all members of the heath family, and **camellia**—all thrive at a pH of 4.5 to 6.0. Other shrubs include **fothergilla** (*Fothergilla gardenii* and *F. major*), **New Jersey tea** (*Ceanothus americanus*), **serviceberry** (*Amelanchier*), **summersweet** (*Clethra alnifolia*), and **sweet bay** (*Magnolia virginiana*).

# September

## SHRUBS

### PLANNING

As summer's heat and humidity finally yield to the shorter, cooler days of autumn, pay a visit to those far corners of the garden that haven't seen a gardener's eye since the 4th of July. Begin a wholesale evaluation of your landscape and make notes about tasks that need to be completed this month. Look for plants that may be in decline and will have to be replaced.

If you need some new ideas for plants, look at the plant introduction programs of various southern states. These plants have been selected for their outstanding landscape attributes and their adaptability to the south.

Examples include the Mississippi Medallion (**www.msnla.org**) winners. These award-winnning recipients include shrubs, which are selected for outstanding multiseason features such as summer flowers, colorful leaves, durability, and adaptability to various soil types and climates; they are easy to grow, have few pest problems, and require minimal care.

Be adventurous by selecting a few new and delectable shrubs from the menu.

### PLANTING

Fall is the prime-time planting season. Select healthy container-grown or balled-and-burlapped shrubs and plant them properly in the right location in your landscape.

### CARE

As the leaves fall, rake them up, shred them, and use them as a mulch around your shrubs.

### WATERING

Don't let the cooler temperatures deceive you. Fall is the driest season. Continue watering regularly and remember that it's better to water established shrubs deeply once a week than lightly every day. Water newly planted shrubs to provide sufficient moisture and encourage rapid establishment.

### FERTILIZING

If your shrubs have produced sufficient growth this year, fertilizing may not be necessary. If you choose to fertilize, rely on soil test results to apply the nutrients required by your shrubs.

### PRUNING

Prune out only branches that are dead, diseased, or broken. Hold off on major pruning such as rejuvenation until late winter. Pruning now will only stimulate tender, new growth, which can be killed by our first freeze.

### PROBLEMS

Aphids and spider mites may still be active. Evaluate the extent of injury and decide if pest control measures are warranted. Use a water wand to wash mites off plants on a weekly basis, preferably early in the morning.

Clean up fallen leaves, which can harbor disease and insect pests over the winter if allowed to remain on the ground.

Don't turn your back on the weeds in your shrub beds. Summer annual weeds like crabgrass and goosegrass have matured and are going to seed. Winter annual weeds like annual bluegrass, chickweed, and Carolina geranium are germinating. Hoe them out or handpull them now.

Geotextile or landscape fabrics are synthetic mulch underliners that are used to suppress weeds on a long-term basis. When placed on the soil surface

# HELPFUL HINTS FOR EARLIER BLOOMING CAMELLIAS

Generally, most **Japanese camellia** (*Camellia japonica*) cultivars bloom throughout the winter and early spring months. They can be coerced into bloom earlier, however, around October, through a simple technique called "gibbing."

Gibbing involves the application of the natural plant hormone gibberellic acid to **camellia** flowers. This growth regulator "awakens" the flower buds, releasing them from their state of dormancy. As a result, the treated flower buds swell and open up earlier than normal.

For more than twenty-five years, **camellia** enthusiasts have gibbed buds. Gibbing allows you to hasten flowering, especially on cultivars that tend to flower during the winter months. And gardeners who battle camellia flower blight, a diseases that kills **camellia** flowers in the spring (see February Problems p. 185), can avoid the disease by coercing their camellias to bloom earlier when the fungus is still dormant.

Giberellic acid can be purchased from the American Camellia Society (100 Massee Lane, Fort Valley, GA 31030; (478) 967-2358). A one-gram package will treat 1,000 flowers.

To gib your **camellia** flowers, look for plump, round flower buds at the tips of the branches. Next to the flower bud should be a smaller, pointed vegetative or growth bud (it produces leaves and stems). Twist out the growth bud, leaving its base or "cup" intact. Then apply one drop of gibberellic acid to the cup. Now move on to the next flower bud. You can expect blooms to open three to twelve weeks following the treatment. Obviously, early-flowering **camellia** cultivars will respond faster than the later-blooming ones. Start gibbing the first of September and treat a few buds on each **camellia** at weekly intervals so flowers will be produced throughout the season. One gibbing rule of thumb: Treat no more than $1/4$ of the buds on young **camellia** plants. (On older plants, gib as many you like.)

You can learn more about **camellias** and the camellia society at their website, **www.camellias-aes.com**. The site also includes a list of **camellia** clubs by state.

and covered with mulch, they enhance the ability of the mulch to suppress weeds. See Vines and Ground Covers November Problems p. 255 for more information about these weed barriers.

Rabbits and deer can be a problem. Various commercially available mammal repellents can be applied to your shrubs. See October Problems p. 201 for a homemade repellent recipe.

Camellia 'Guilo Nuccio'

# OCTOBER

## SHRUBS

### PLANNING

Late-season flowering plants could be considered the "Rodney Dangerfields" of the plant kingdom. They don't get any respect. How can they? During the spring months when gardeners break cabin fever and are looking for a floral feast, they skip over these late bloomers for the sumptuous and immediate flowers of **azaleas** and a multitude of other spring bloomers.

Even when they reach their peak in late summer and fall, late-season flowering plants sometimes still go unappreciated because everyone is focused on leaves (or football). But give these late-summer treats a second look either for color or a great fragrance:

**Holly tea olive** (*Osmanthus heterophyllus*), **Fortune's osmanthus** (*Osmanthus x fortunei*), **senna** (*Cassia corymbosa*), **sasanqua camellia** (*Camellia sasanqua*), and **tea-oil camellia** (*C. oleifera*) are standard fare. **Japanese fatsia** (*Fatsia japonica*) is another fall-flowering choice. Learn more about these and other late-season flowering plants that will thrive in your corner of Alabama or Mississippi.

### PLANTING

Fall is a perfect season for planting. Gardeners in the southern and central parts of the states can even plant throughout late fall and into winter. The cooler temperatures allow the shrubs to settle in comfortably and concentrate on producing roots. Follow the steps in the Planting section of the Trees introduction p. 206.

To minimize the look of open spaces between newly planted shrubs, plant cool-season annuals or perennial low-growing ground covers.

Now is a good time to move shrubs that have outgrown their location. Shrubs normally transplant more readily than trees. Small plants transplant more successfully than do large ones of the same species.

You can postpone any moves until next month or December, depending on how mild the weather is. Be mindful of this transplanting rule-of-thumb: Allow at least four weeks of soil temperatures above 40 degrees F. after planting to give the shrub some time to settle in before cold winter temperatures. See November Planting p. 202 to learn the step-by-step transplanting approach.

The foliage of fatsia is interesting and as an added bonus, they bloom in fall!

## WATERING

Fall is dry in Alabama and Mississippi, so don't rely on Mother Nature to water newly planted shrubs. Water frequently, checking the soil and rootball before watering.

## FERTILIZING

To add nutrients, supplement mulch with well-rotted horse or cow manure.

## PRUNING

Don't shear now, it's too late. You'll have brown-edged leaves all winter and you may spark tender new growth that will be killed by the first freeze. If there are a few wayward branches, cut them back by hand. Wait until spring to do any major shaping. Continue to prune out dead, damaged, and diseased branches.

## PROBLEMS

Spider mites can still be active. Control the overwintering eggs with a dormant horticultural oil later this fall when the shrubs go dormant (see January Problems p. 183).

---

## HELPFUL HINTS FOR COLD-HARDY CAMELLIAS

While the two commonly grown species of **camellia** (*C. japonica* and *C. sasanqua*) are hardy only in Zones 7, 8, and 9, the Ackerman hybrids have *C. oleifera* in their parentage, making them extra cold hardy. They are the result of the work of Dr. William Ackerman, a research horticulturist at the U. S. National Arboretum. According to him, the hardiest of the group are the fall-blooming 'Winter's Rose' (miniature, shell pink, formal double), 'Winter's Interlude' (miniature, pink, anemone form), 'Winter's Beauty' (medium, lavender pink, peony form), and 'Winter's Waterlily' (medium, white, anemone to formal double). These have successfully weathered temperatures to -10 degrees F. If you've had trouble with cold damage to **camellia** shrubs (not flowers), you might try these.

They should be planted in a well-drained location with northern or western exposure, ideally with an overstory of shade trees to offer protection from sun and winter winds. Mulch well with a 2- to 3-inch layer of pine needles or other organic matter.

---

Prune out infected limbs and rake up dead leaves to remove any overwintering fungal diseases.

Keep the area around your shrubs free of weeds to eliminate any overwintering hideouts for two-spotted spider mites.

If you'd like to make your own repellent, mix 2 tablespoons of homemade hot pepper sauce per gallon of water or blend 2 or 3 rotten eggs in a gallon of water and spray it on your plants. Dried ground red peppers, ground black pepper, or chili powder are other repellents that can be dusted on or near flowers. To be effective, they will have to be reapplied after rain or heavy dew, and quite often to new plant growth.

Be aware that some of the repellents designed for mammals may kill non-targeted, beneficial insects. Before choosing a course of action, weigh the benefits of the treatment versus the level of acceptable damage.

# NOVEMBER

## SHRUBS

### PLANNING

Identify shrub beds and borders whose soil will have to be tested. Soil testing is best done every two or three years. Contact your Cooperative Extension Service agent for soil-testing materials.

### PLANTING

This is a good month to plant and move shrubs. Mulch with compost, shredded bark, or shredded leaves soon after planting. In areas where the ground might freeze, it keeps the ground warmer, which helps roots establish. Now is a good time to move shrubs that have outgrown their location. Here's how to move a shrub:

1. Tie up the branches of wide, low-spreading shrubs with soft twine.

2. Use a ribbon to mark the side of the shrub that faces north so it can be properly oriented when replanting.

3. Create a good-sized rootball. Deciduous shrubs less than 3 feet in height can be moved bare root. Bare root means that most or all of the soil is removed from the roots after digging the plant. Bare-root plants should be moved when they're dormant.

Shrubs greater than 1 inch in trunk diameter and all broadleaf and narrowleaf evergreens should be moved with the soil attached. The size of the ball should be large enough in diameter and depth to include as much of the fibrous and feeding roots as possible. It also depends on how much you or a friend can physically manage.

1. With your shovel, dig a trench around the shrub to create a rootball that's 12 to 14 inches wide. This will be adequate for deciduous shrubs up to 2 feet tall and sprawling evergreens with a spread of two feet.

Mulch is a critical component of gardening and there are many types of mulch including chopped. leaves, pine straw, grass clippings, and straw.

2. Use a sharpshooter, or transplanting spade, to dig under the shrub. Undercut all around the plant with the long blade before rocking it.

3. Once the rootball is free, tip the shrub to one side and slide a tarp beneath it as far as possible. Then lay down the shrub in the opposite direction and pull the tarp all the way under the plant. Now slide the shrub out of the hole.

4. Use a shovel handle to measure the depth and width of the rootball to determine how wide to make the hole.

5. Plant the shrub so the rootball is a few inches higher than the surrounding soil.

6. Backfill around the plant, and tamp down the soil lightly with the end of your shovel handle to settle the soil around the roots.

7. Water the plant thoroughly, making sure the rootball and surrounding soil are completely wet.

8. Water it in to settle the soil, and follow up with a 2- to 4-inch layer of mulch.

## CARE

Rake up and compost fallen leaves and fruit around shrubs because this litter offers overwintering places for insects and diseases.

Broadleaved and tender evergreens exposed to drying winds and sun may need to be shaded on the south and southwest sides to reduce moisture loss and leaf injury. Enclose your evergreens in these exposed locations with a burlap screen.

## WATERING

If fall rains have been scarce in areas where it's cold and windy, or where the ground may freeze, keep broadleaf evergreens such as **hollies** and **rhododendrons** well watered. Give them a deep watering once every two weeks. Evergreens continue to lose moisture from their leaves all winter, but if the ground freezes, they'll be unable to take up enough water to replace it. Sending them into winter well watered reduces the potential for damaged foliage.

## FERTILIZING

Do not fertilize shrubs that are displaying their fall colors—wait until next year.

## PRUNING

Limit any pruning to the removal of diseased, damaged, or broken branches. Wait until after the coldest part of winter has passed next year before pruning summer-flowering shrubs.

## PROBLEMS

Those small cone-shaped bags aren't the fruits of your **arborvitae** or **juniper**. They house the eggs of bagworms which have been feeding on your conifers. Remove and destroy bagworm bags on narrow-leaved evergreens. Eggs overwinter in the bags produced by the females and will hatch out next spring.

If there is any evidence of scale on shrubs, spray with dormant oil in late fall and again in early spring. See January Problems p. 183.

To protect young shrubs against deer damage, there are a number of deterrents you can try. Remember, deer will become accustomed to any object, so alternating items will help. Hang bars of strong-scented soap, mesh bags filled with human hair, paper bags of dried blood (bloodmeal), or strips cut from white plastic bags on shrubs that are likely to be attacked. Chemical deer repellents also can be applied. Be sure to reapply any chemicals after two to three weeks of normal weathering.

# December

## SHRUBS

 PLANNING

The best way to prevent winter damage to shrubs is to select hardy species. As you tinker with your landscape over the winter, plan to consult publications containing information on the climatic zones for the shrubs you are interested in planting. It is better to select cold-hardy species in the first place rather than attempt to protect tender plants later.

 PLANTING

Continue planting container-grown and balled-and-burlapped shrubs. Take hardwood stem cuttings of evergreens such as **boxwood**, **camellia**, **holly**, and **juniper** this month, and root them in a cool greenhouse or cold frame.

 CARE

In the case of a rare ice storm or snow, protect prized **boxwoods** and other evergreens. Drive four wooden stakes around the shrub, wrap it with burlap, and staple the burlap to the stakes.

### HELPFUL HINTS FOR FRUITFUL HOLLIES

**Hollies** are either male or female. The males produce pollen while the female hollies produce fruit. Although some female **hollies** such as Burford will produce fruit without requiring pollination, other **hollies** need pollen from a male shrub. Generally, the best pollinator for a female **holly** is a male of the same species. Distinguishing between male and female **holly** (*Ilex*) plants is pretty straightforward once the plants begin to flower next spring.

Male plants produce profuse numbers of whitish flowers, each with four prominent stamens that stick up between the petals. When the anthers ripen and split open, you can see the sticky yellow pollen.

Female **hollies**, by contrast, produce fewer blooms, and each bloom has in its center a green, pealike pistil, which will develop into the berry, surrounded by four poorly developed, nonfunctional stamens.

Because **hollies** are insect-pollinated, it's possible to get fruit from a pair spaced as far apart as 1/8 mile. But you will improve your berry set by locating the two sexes closer together. If this is not possible, place flowering male branches in a container of water and set them at the foot of a flowering female plant.

Tie a piece of heavy boxboard or put plywood over the stakes to create a "roof" to catch the snow or ice.

 WATERING

Make sure newly planted shrubs are well watered.

 FERTILIZING

Do not fertilize shrubs this month.

 PRUNING

When cutting branches from **hollies** or other evergreen shrubs for indoor decoration, maintain the natural form and beauty of the plant.

Limit pruning of other shrubs to the removal of damaged or dead branches.

# TREES

We're fortunate to be able to grow a wide variety of native and adapted trees. They grow more magnificent with each passing year and offer so much to our landscapes. They shade us during the summer, offer privacy, and hide unsightly views. They surround us with the seasonal beauty of their leaves and flowers, and their attractive bark and branch architecture.

There's something for the energy-conscious, too. Trees save energy and money. Deciduous trees (leafless in winter) can shade your home in the summer, then let in sun to warm it in the winter. The afternoon shade of trees planted on the southeastern and western sides can reduce temperatures inside the home by 8 to 10 degrees. Trees also provide food, shelter, and nesting for wildlife. Pollen and nectar for hummingbirds, butterflies, and bees are added bonuses. Fruit trees, of course, provide tasty figs, apples, pears, peaches, and persimmons.

Trees are permanent plants, so pay particular attention to their selection and proper placement in your landscape.

## PLANNING

Once you've determined where you want your trees, select ones that match the conditions in your landscape. Here are a few suggestions to help you select the right ones:

• Look for trees well suited to the growing conditions in your landscape. Sun-loving trees should be sited in full sun; understory types should be located in partial shade.

• Know the ultimate size and growth rate of the tree, in order to select the right location.

• Select trees for shade and multiseason interest. Look for those that excel in several seasons, offering flowers, fruit, attractive bark, and fall color.

• Look for trees that have few insect or disease problems.

## PLANTING

Most trees are available in containers or as field-grown balled-and-burlapped plants. Follow these steps to ensure a good start for your new tree:

1. Match the tree to its location. In addition to light levels, be aware of drainage, salt spray, and other factors that can affect the tree's growth.

2. Have your soil tested through your County Cooperative Extension Service office.

3. Dig a wide, shallow hole at least two or three times bigger than the diameter of the rootball, but no deeper than the height of the ball. By making the hole as wide as possible, the roots will grow quickly into the loosened soil, thereby speeding up the plant's establishment in its new home.

4. Slip the plant out of the pot and examine the rootball. Shrubs or trees growing in containers may have roots circling around the outside of the rootball. If you plant it as is, roots will grow from the bottom of the rootball. You should encourage roots to grow along the entire length of the rootball. Take a knife, pruning shears, or the end of a sharp spade and score the rootball in three or four places. Make shallow cuts from the top to the bottom. Gently tease the sides of the rootball apart. Now this "doctored" plant will produce new roots from these cuts all around the rootball.

5. Remove wire or twine from balled-and-burlapped plants and cut away as much wrapping material as possible after placing it in the hole.

Remove synthetic burlap entirely; it won't break down and will ultimately strangle the roots.

6. Plant even with or slightly above the surrounding soil. Place the tree in the hole for fit. Lay your shovel across the hole. The rootball should be level with or slightly above the handle. If, in your zeal, you've gone too deep, shovel some soil back in. Compact it with your feet. You want a firm footing for the rootball so it won't later sink below the level of the surrounding grade. That can cause roots to suffocate. In slowly draining soils, set the rootball an inch or two higher than the surrounding soil and cover it with mulch.

7. Start backfilling—returning the soil to the planting hole. Tamp the soil lightly as you go, but don't compact it. When half the rootball is covered, add some water to settle out any air pockets and remoisten the rootball. Finish backfilling and water again. Do not cover the top of the rootball with soil.

8. Mulch. Apply 2 to 4 inches of organic mulch such as compost, leaf litter, shredded wood, or pine straw. Extend it to the outermost reaches of the branches (the drip line). Leave a space of 3 inches or more around the trunk to keep the bark dry.

9. Depending on weather and rainfall, you may need to water daily for the first few weeks. After that, begin cutting back, eventually reaching an "as needed" basis by testing the soil and rootball for moisture. See October Watering p. 226 for details.

## WATERING

Not all established trees have to be watered during hot, dry summer months. Drought-tolerant trees can withstand long periods without rain or irrigation.

## FERTILIZING

Newly planted trees can be fertilized after they become established, which may take months or longer, depending on their size. Once established, fertilizing can stimulate growth and help them fill into their allotted height and space in the landscape.

## CHAPTER EIGHT

Older, established trees shouldn't be fertilized on a regular basis. Replenishing the mulch over their roots with compost or other "recyclable" organic materials provides them a steady diet of minerals. If your trees are growing in a lawn that is fertilized, do not add additional fertilizer.

For trees that you are encouraging to grow and fill out as quickly as possible, fertilize when it will be readily absorbed by the roots and when the soil is moist, which can be anytime from late spring after new growth emerges to early fall. However, if water is unavailable or when the trees are stressed by drought during the summer months, do not fertilize at all because their roots will be unable to absorb the nutrients.

Fertilize based on the tree's appearance (see May Fertilizing p. 216) and soil-test results. Most fertilizer recommendations are based on nitrogen: apply 1 pound of nitrogen per 1,000 square feet of root zone area; up to 2 pounds can be applied with a slow-release fertilizer.

Apply the fertilizer to the area occupied by the tree's roots, which is called the root zone area. It's roughly a circular area that extends out to the drip line or outermost branches with the tree in the center. The radius of the circle is the distance from the trunk to the drip line. A majority of the fine "feeder" or mineral-absorbing are located in this circular area.

The root zone area of tree cultivars with naturally narrow crowns, or trees pruned into unusual shapes, must be determined differently. Calculate the fertilizer application area based on the trunk diameter measured in inches at 4.5 feet above the ground. Multiply it by either 1 or 1.5 to get a number expressed in feet. This number expressed in feet is the radius measurement for the fertilization area. For example, if the diameter of the tree is 8 inches, then the radius of the circular fertilization area will be 8 to 12 feet, depending on the multiplication factor that you used.

Root Zone Area = 3 x (root zone radius) x (root zone radius)

For example, if the root zone radius measures 10 ft., then the Root Zone Area is:

$$3 \times 10 \text{ ft.} \times 10 \text{ ft.} = 300 \text{ sq. ft.}$$

Assuming you have a 16-4-8 fertilizer, determine the amount of fertilizer required to apply 1 pound of nitrogen per 1,000 square feet using this equation:

Root Zone Area or 1,000 square feet divided by the %N in the fertilizer bag equals the amount of fertilizer to apply over the tree's root zone area.

$$\frac{300 \text{ sq. ft.} \div 1,000 \text{ sq. ft.}}{16\%*} = 2$$

Broadcast 2 lbs. (or 4 cups) of 16-4-8 evenly over the root zone area.

*16% = 0.16

## PRUNING

Trees are pruned to improve their health and their branching structure. The goal of pruning young trees is to create a strong structure of trunk and limbs to support future growth. The main reason for pruning mature trees (usually by professionals) is to remove weak limbs to focus the tree's resources on the stronger remaining branches. See January Planning p. 208 for more information.

## PROBLEMS

Insects and diseases can be serious threats to many trees, especially any weakened by unfavorable growing conditions; they are less able to tolerate pest attacks. Select better-adapted plants and match them to the site, or concentrate on pest-resistant cultivars.

Even so, some pest-resistant trees that are correctly located can still be attacked by pests. It's just nature. A tree ought to be able to support a few insects or diseased leaves if it is kept healthy and vigorous.

When pests strike, follow an Integrated Pest Management approach to their control (see p. 11).

# JANUARY

## TREES

### PLANNING

Now is the time to prune small trees that need a little help. Pruning large trees should be done by a professional, preferably a certified arborist. To find a certified arborist near you, try **www.treesaregood.com**.

Follow these steps:

1. Thin out dying, dead, or pest-ridden twigs and branches. Thinning is a term that describes the removal of a branch where it joins the limb or trunk. Thinning opens up the center of the tree to sunlight and reduces the number of new shoots that sprout along the branches. A lot of growth can be removed by thinning without dramatically changing the tree's natural appearance or growth habit and giving it the "just-pruned" look.

Heading cuts are usually reserved for shrubs (see Shrubs Pruning p. 179) and are generally undesirable on mature trees. Young trees can be headed back to encourage branching on long leggy branches.

Never let a tree service head back or "top" the limbs of mature trees—their structure is weakened or lost with the production of numerous snake-like sprouts, and the stubs that result are exposed to attack from insects and diseases.

January is a good month to prune crossing branches. It's easier to see the branch structure in winter.

2. Remove one of any two branches that are rubbing or crossing over each other. Wounds develop on rubbing branches, creating entryways for invading insects and diseases.

3. Remove branches that form a narrow, V-shaped angle with the trunk. Branches that form an angle less than 45 degrees F. from the trunk (10 and 2 o'clock) are weakly attached.

4. Remove upright-growing side limbs that are growing taller than the main trunk.

5. Do not coat the wounds with pruning-wound paints. There is no scientific evidence that dressing wounds prevents decay.

### PLANTING

If you purchased a live Christmas tree, plant it outdoors as soon as possible, especially if it has already been in the house for longer than three days.

### CARE

If you staked your newly planted tree last fall, check the rubber straps and stakes. Make sure they're secured at the lowest point on the trunk to give it a little room to move back and forth (encouraging the development of a strong, thick trunk). Make a note in your journal to remove the straps in the spring after growth has started.

### WATERING

During mild winter spells, water fall-planted and established evergreens, if the weather is dry.

Pay particular attention to trees planted on the southern and western sides of your home. Mulch newly planted trees with a 2- to 3-inch layer of compost and keep them well watered.

## FERTILIZING

Don't be too hasty to fertilize your trees. Wait until at least budbreak—when new growth emerges in the spring. See May Fertilizing p. 216 to determine if fertilizing is necessary.

## PRUNING

Remove small limbs hitting gutters or other problem places if the weather allows. You can do this now or wait until next month or March.

## PROBLEMS

Apply dormant horticultural oil sprays on small landscape trees that have been attacked by aphids, mites, or scale in the past. Do this now or anytime before growth begins to smother insect eggs, aphids, mites, and scale insects that overwinter in cracks and crevices of the bark. Special equipment or a professional service is required to treat large trees.

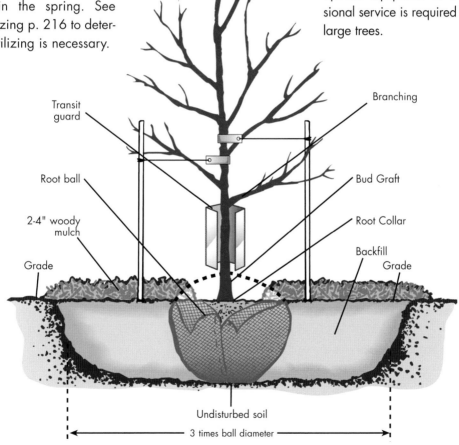

Transit guard

Branching

Root ball

Bud Graft

2-4" woody mulch

Root Collar

Grade

Backfill

Grade

Undisturbed soil

3 times ball diameter

It's not impossible to plant a tree outdoors after the holidays, especially if you prepared the site ahead of time.

# FEBRUARY

## TREES

### PLANNING

Order fruit trees, or look for them in garden centers and nurseries. Before you shop, do your homework. Be familiar with their growing requirements. In addition to full sun and a well-drained location, certain fruit trees need regular pruning, watering, and pest control to realize a full, blemish-free crop.

Fruit trees such as **peaches** require a certain number of chilling hours—hours at temperatures between 33 and 45 degrees F.— for the dormant flower and leaf buds to awaken and develop normally. In the coastal counties, varieties that need 500 to 600 chilling hours are ideal. In the central parts of Alabama and Mississippi, it is best to plant varieties with 750-hour chill requirement. Farther north, you should select varieties that need 850 hours or more. Your regional Extension agent is the best source to recommend local varieties.

For smaller landscapes, consider **apple** trees grafted onto size-controlling rootstocks. A grafted tree has the scion, or fruiting part, joined to a rootstock. These dwarfing rootstocks encourage earlier bearing on trees and also reduce their ultimate height. For example, a standard **apple** tree growing on its own roots will usually reach a mature height of 30 feet. If grafted onto a dwarfing rootstock, however, the same variety may reach only 6 feet. This means that the trees can be planted closer together and can be pruned and picked without the use of ladders.

Various rootstocks offer widely different degrees of dwarfing. In catalogs the word "dwarf" is generally used to describe trees that are 50 percent or less of normal size, and semidwarf for those that are larger but less than full-size. To be sure of the rootstock you're getting, call the company for more details. Also check with your County Extension office for recommended dwarf varieties.

### PLANTING

Bare-root, deciduous trees can be planted while they're dormant, about a month before the last freeze. Plant them as soon as possible after obtaining them. Unwrap and soak the roots in a bucket of water at least twelve hours before planting. Broken roots should be pruned back cleanly to behind the break. Follow these steps for planting:

1. Dig the planting hole wide enough so the roots can be spread out. Don't break or bend the roots to make them fit.

2. Create a cone of soil in the bottom of the hole and tamp down the top firmly. This will prevent the tree from settling too deeply.

3. Set the plant on top of the cone. Drape the roots evenly over the top. The topmost root should be positioned so it's just under the soil surface. Lay your shovel handle across the hole to help gauge the correct depth.

4. Work the soil in among the roots with your fingers. Backfill the hole halfway with soil, and water it in. Add the remaining soil and water again. If the tree has settled too deeply, grasp the trunk and lift it gently to raise it to the proper level.

5. Mulch with a 2- to 3-inch layer of compost, pine straw, or shredded wood.

### CARE

By the end of the month, begin cutting old dead fronds from **palms** if they are hanging down on the trunk and looking messy. Leave any that may be near the center to protect the bud from possible late cold.

## WATERING

Water newly planted trees. Keep the soil moist but avoid overwatering, which can inhibit root growth. If severe cold is forecast for your area, water evergreens. The roots are not able to take up moisture if the soil should freeze. A severely dry, cold wind can scorch leaves even if the soil doesn't freeze.

## FERTILIZING

Don't be too hasty to fertilize your trees. Wait until at least budbreak, when new growth emerges in the spring. See May Fertilizing p. 216 to determine if fertilizing is necessary.

## PRUNING

Begin pruning when the coldest part of winter has passed and before new growth begins. When pruning limbs too large for loppers, use a tree saw; follow the three-cut approach to prevent the branch from stripping bark away as it falls.

1. Make the first upward cut about a foot from the trunk and one-third of the way through the bottom of the limb.

2. Make the second downward cut from the top of the branch a couple of inches away from the first cut, farther away from the trunk. As the branch falls, the undercut causes the limb to break away cleanly.

3. Finally, remove the stub by making the last cut outside of the branch collar (a swollen area at the base of the branch). The collar region is the boundary between the trunk and the branch that acts as a natural barrier to decay-causing organisms. Never leave a stub. Stubs usually die and are entry points for decay-causing fungi.

Avoid making "hat racks" out of your **crapemyrtles**. Follow these steps to produce a natural-looking tree form that accentuates the flowers, beautiful bark, and elegant structure:

1. Remove all broken and diseased limbs.

2. Next, thin out all of the side branches one-third to one-half the way up the height of the plant.

3. Remove rubbing and crossing branches and shoots growing into the center of the canopy or upper part of the **crapemyrtle**. Make your cuts to a side branch or close to the trunk.

4. Head-back wayward and unbranched limbs. Make each cut above an outward-facing bud. This will encourage the development of branches behind the cut and make them fuller.

5. Remove dried-up seed clusters within reach. This will give the tree a more uniform appearance and look neater. A pole pruner makes relatively easy work of this.

## PROBLEMS

See January Problems p. 209 for advice on mites and insects.

Examine your **arborvitae**, **Leyland cypress**, and **juniper** for the pine cone-shaped nests of overwintering bagworms. Pick off the egg-containing "bags" and discard them.

Inspect your arborvitae and other evergreens for bagworm; simply pick them off and dispose of them.

# MARCH

## TREES

### PLANNING

Make plans to plant a tree or support an organization that does.

### PLANTING

Plant balled-and-burlapped or container-grown trees. See Planting instructions in the introduction p. 206. Deciduous trees such as **river birch**, **black gum**, **dogwood**, **maple**, **fringetree**, **redbud**, **cherry**, and **oak** are best moved and planted in early spring before new leaves appear. Evergreens such as **magnolia**, **holly**, **cypress**, and **arborvitae** are, too.

### CARE

Check the supports on newly planted trees. Support and anchor stakes are only temporary and should be removed within a year after planting. Allow some slack in the support so the trunk can move slightly, encouraging the development of a strong, thick trunk.

Mulch as far out as the drip line or outermost branches, but leave 6 inches between the trunk and the mulch to keep the bark dry.

### WATERING

Newly planted shrubs need watering every few weeks if the weather becomes dry. Check the moisture in the rootball and surrounding soil before watering. Gradually reduce the frequency but not the depth of watering: Deep watering encourages deep rooting.

### FERTILIZING

Fertilize newly planted and young trees after they leaf out. Use a slow-release fertilizer that contains one-half of the nitrogen in a slowly available, water-insoluble form or a long-lasting 6- or 9-month polymer-coated formula.

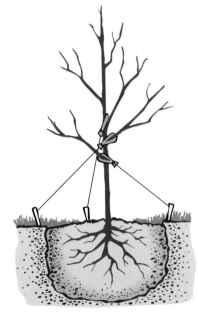

Supports are only temporary, so remove them within a year of planting.

### PRUNING

**Pines**, most **junipers**, and **spruces** should not be pruned back to older, bare sections of branches because they will not produce new growth; the needleless branch usually dies. Young **arborvitae**, **Leyland cypress**, **false cypress** (*Chamaecyparis*), and **yew**, however, can be cut back when they're dormant to one- or two-year-old wood that lacks foliage; dormant buds will sprout and fill in.

Trees that "bleed" or excrete sap profusely should not be pruned at this time. Although the bleeding is not harmful, it's unsightly. To minimize bleeding, prune after the leaves green-up in the summer and the shoots stop growing. Some arborists have found that fall pruning minimizes bleeding, but this must be weighed against the possibility of making the trees susceptible to winter injury. The following trees "bleed" when pruned shortly before budbreak: **birch** (*Betula*), **elm** (*Ulmus*), **dogwood** (*Cornus*), **European hornbeam** (*Carpinus*), **honeylocust** (*Gleditsia*), **magnolia** (*Magnolia*), **maple** (*Acer*), **silverbell** (*Halesia*), and **yellowwood** (*Cladrastis*).

If your **crapemyrtle** grows too large and only heavy pruning will reduce it to the size you want, consider replacing it with a lower-growing **crapemyrtle**. **Crapemyrtles** that mature between 5 and 10 feet include 'Acoma' (white flowers), 'Pecos' (pink), and 'Tonto' (red). These are also resistant to powdery mildew, a grayish-white fuzzy fungus that attacks and distorts leaves. If these are still too tall, try 'Hopi' (white), 'Ozark Spring' (lavender), and 'Victor' (dark red). They're only 3 to 5 feet in height. Unfortunately, they are extremely susceptible to powdery mildew. For a mature height of less than 3 feet, try the slow-growing 'Chickasaw' (pink-lavender), which reaches a height of 2 feet.

Some trees such as **Bradford pear** produce a lot of upright branches that grow too close together on the trunk. As a result, they often split apart during snow-, ice-, and windstorms. To help prevent this, thin out the branches on young trees to give them more room. Shorten upright-growing limbs to prevent all of them from growing to the same size at one point on the trunk. **Bradford pear** trees have turned out to be disappointments because of limb breakage, so avoid them the second time around.

## HELPFUL HINTS FOR PRUNING FRUIT

Fruit trees require specialized training and pruning, which will vary according to the type, age, and variety of the fruit. The objective is the same: producing a strong framework of fruit-bearing limbs and shoots. Fruit trees need attention, otherwise you'll be left with an untrained, unruly tree with tangled masses of shoots and branches which produce little or no fruit and serve as a haven for insects and diseases. Consider the following tips when training and pruning fruit crops:

1. Before training or pruning, visualize the results. Training mistakes may be easily corrected, but once a branch is pruned or removed it cannot be replaced.

2. Train as much as possible and remove as little as possible. Bending and tying shoots instead of cutting them, especially on **apple** and **pear** trees, can induce early fruit production.

3. Use sharp pruning tools to make clean cuts.

4. Discard pruned-out shoots and branches. These plant parts will serve as dwelling sites for insects and diseases and should be removed from the area to reduce pest populations.

Light pruning can be performed throughout the growing season to remove broken, injured, or diseased branches and to improve air circulation to control leaf diseases. Major removal of twigs and branches should be done during the dormant season, preferably before active growth begins in the spring.

 PROBLEMS

Apply a dormant horticultural oil spray on dormant landscape plants to control overwintering insects and mites. See January Problems p. 209.

Look for the grayish-white webs or "tents" of eastern tent caterpillars in the crotches of trees. They feed on the leaves of **crabapple**, **wild cherry**, and **apple**, but when these trees are scarce, you'll find them in **ash**, **willow**, **maple**, and **oak** trees. Trees are rarely killed, but the damage is unsightly. To control them, wait until evening and wipe out the nests with a gloved hand, or wrap the nest around a stick and drop the whole nest into a container of soapy water. A forceful spray of the bacterial insecticide Bt (*Bacillus thuringiensis*) can be used to control the caterpillars when they are small.

# APRIL
## TREES

### PLANNING

Variety is the spice of life—which also applies to the landscape. Find time to increase your tree vocabulary by learning about a few trees this month. Research native trees that have grown in the area longer than we can know. Their longevity and ability to adapt to this climate, soils, and pests is a tremendous asset in the landscape.

Visit parks and preserves to see native plants in their natural habitats. You'll see **hawthorn, redbud, plum, dogwood, bald cypress, fringetree,** and many other excellent landscape trees. Take photographs of the plants that you like and show them to knowledgeable people to help you identify them, or use a good field guide with color photos. Visit your local library and bookstores to find reference books on native trees. Become a member of a local native plant society. The members often swap plants and seeds and are knowledgeable about what grows best in your area.

When you have found some favorites, look for good local nursery sources. Also, be on the lookout for plant digs on property that is about to be developed. Of course, never dig elsewhere; there are ethical, legal, and ecological consequences to this practice. It's better to purchase nursery-propagated natives from nurseries or mail-order catalogs.

### PLANTING

It's not too late to plant container-grown and balled-and-burlapped plants. Pay careful attention to watering during their first year.

### CARE

Avoid bumping into tree trunks with your lawn mower or whipping them with a nylon string trimmer. The resulting wounds can girdle the tree and cut off circulation from the roots. They can also be colonized by fungal diseases or infested by borers, which can eventually kill the tree.

### WATERING

Sometimes it's necessary to create a temporary berm or dike around newly planted trees in clay soil to prevent water from running off when watering. Remove the berm when the plants become established (see May Watering p. 216).

### FERTILIZING

Fertilize **palms** with a slow-release fertilizer having a 3:1:2 analysis such as 18-6-12 or 15-5-10 that also contains magnesium and iron and other micronutrients. **Palms** benefit from fertilizers that also contain other micronutrients such as manganese. Apply according to label directions. This is particularly true of **palms** growing along the coast where micronutrient deficiencies are common. Broadcast or scatter the fertilizer under the canopy or over the bed area.

### PRUNING

Prune **cherry, crabapple, dogwood,** and other spring-flowering trees after they bloom and only if needed to control low-hanging or wayward branches. Of course, remove dead or diseased branches, too.

## HELPFUL HINTS FOR TRAINING YOUNG TREES

Start training young trees and larger treelike shrubs after they've had a full season of growth in their new location. If you didn't plant a high-quality tree with a strong trunk and well-spaced branches, you may have to prune regularly at first to improve its structure. Follow these proper pruning rules:

1. Cut the branch, but not the branch collar. The collar is a swollen area at the base of a branch just before it enters the trunk. It acts as a natural barrier to decay-causing organisms.

2. Do not make "flush cuts" in line with the trunk. These cuts create wounds to trunk tissue, which lead to decay. Instead, cut the branch just beyond the branch collar, which will leave a little rise or unevenness with the trunk.

3. Never leave a stub. Stubs usually die and are entry points for decay-causing fungi.

## PROBLEMS

Watch out for the "cool-weather" mites: southern red mites which attack **holly** and **spruce**, and spider mites which feed on **arborvitae**, **juniper**, **spruce**, and other conifers. They attack in the spring and fall.

Dogwood anthracnose is a devastating fungal disease of **flowering dogwoods** (*Cornus florida*). It produces leaf spots and cankers on the twigs and trunk, eventually killing the tree. Fungicides can control this disease. **Dogwoods** that are resistant to dogwood anthracnose include *Cornus kousa* 'Steeple' and the Stellar® hybrids (hybrids between **flowering dogwood** and **kousa dogwood**), Stardust®, Stellar Pink®, and Celestial™.

Many leaf diseases become active as the trees begin to leaf out. For example, apple scab will attack **apple** and **crabapple** trees as they come out of winter dormancy. It also affects flower stems, blossoms, and fruit, but is most noticeable on the leaves and fruit. Velvety brown to olive spots develop on the undersides of the leaves as they emerge in the spring. Eventually the spots turn black and the leaf dies. While apple scab will not kill your **crabapple**, severe leaf-drop two or three years in a row can weaken your tree and make it susceptible to injury from freezing temperatures.

As with all diseases, reduce future infections by collecting and disposing of fallen leaves. Selectively thin out a few of the interior limbs to improve air movement and sunlight penetration to dry off the leaves quickly.

Fungicides can be applied to your **crabapple** to prevent future infections. These sprays should be applied in early spring after the last flower petals have dropped and the green tips of leaf buds are showing. If you are unwilling to take on this battle or if your **crabapples** continue to languish and die, consider planting cultivars that are resistant to scab and other diseases such as fireblight, cedar-apple rust, and powdery mildew. A few of these cultivars are 'Autumn Treasure', 'Adirondack', 'Centurion', 'Callaway', 'Donald Wyman', 'Indian Summer', 'Molten Lava', and 'Tina'.

# MAY

## TREES

### PLANNING

Update your gardening journal, noting spring-flowering trees, their peak bloom periods, and pest problems. Use this information to add trees, rearrange or replace, and correct any problems. Keep a record of the varieties you grow. By knowing the specific names, you can ask for that variety next season if you like it, or avoid it if it wasn't up to par.

### PLANTING

Trees are best planted during cooler seasons when the top-growth has little demand for moisture. Container-grown plants, however, can be successfully planted now if you water them regularly during their establishment period.

**Palms** transplant best in spring and summer when they're actively growing. (When it's time to plant **tomatoes**, it's time to plant **palms**.) They prefer a well-drained, fertile, slightly acidic to neutral soil. Cold-sensitive **palms** should be placed within 8 to 10 feet of the warm, southwest side of a brick wall for a few extra degrees of protection in the winter. Tender **palms** should not be planted in exposed areas where

they can be harmed by dry, cold winter winds.

### CARE

To prevent mower and string trimmer damage to tree trunks, keep a 3-foot circle clear of grass around the trunk. Mulch with bark or pine straw. Clean up under **Southern magnolias** as they drop old leaves. This leaf drop is normal as new leaves emerge.

### WATERING

Water newly planted trees. Research shows that the establishment period for trees is 3 months per inch of trunk caliper (trunk diameter measured 6 inches above the ground) in hardiness Zone 9, 6 months in Zones 7 and 8, and 12 months in cooler regions. Water on a weekly or "as-needed" basis by testing the soil and rootball for moisture (see October Watering p. 226).

### FERTILIZING

Look for these signs of plants that are deficient in minerals: stunted growth, smaller-than-normal leaves, poor leaf color, early leaf drop. If you want to encourage more growth, fertil-

Mulching is important, but avoid "volcano" mulching. It leads to bark decay, which opens the door to pests and diseases.

ize with a slow-release fertilizer. Water well immediately afterwards.

### PRUNING

Remove dead or diseased wood at any time. If you cut into diseased wood, disinfect your pruning shears with Lysol®, which is less corrosive than the traditional mixture of water and household bleach (sodium hypochlorite: 4 parts water to 1 part bleach). This can prevent the spread of disease to other branches.

**Palm** leaves die naturally and new leaves are produced from the growing point or "head" of the **palm**. Prune old, dead **palm** fronds to tidy up the tree. Leave the leaf base attached to the trunk so the fibers of the trunk won't be torn away. Do not injure the growing point or the entire tree will die.

# PROBLEMS

Aphids are soft-bodied insects often found clustered at the ends of tender new growth. They suck plant sap with their piercing-sucking mouth parts, causing the leaves to curl and become malformed. Aphids have many natural predators, including ladybird beetles, lacewings, and syrphid fly larvae. Crapemyrtle aphids can be controlled with summer horticultural oil, insecticidal soap, and other insecticides; specialized equipment may be required to treat **crapemyrtles**. The *L. faurei* hybrids (hybrids between the Chinese *Lagerstroemia indica* and the Japanese *L. fauriei*), developed by Dr. Donald Egolf of the U. S. National Arboretum, have moderate resistance to aphids. A few of these hybrids are 'Acoma', 'Biloxi', 'Caddo', 'Choctaw, 'Natchez'', 'Muskogee', and 'Tuscarora'.

The adult dogwood borer is a clearwing moth that resembles a slender bee. The moth is attracted to weakened, stressed trees where it lays eggs on wounds, cankers, or pruning cuts. When the eggs hatch, the caterpillars bore into the bark and begin tunneling.

**Dogwoods** can be protected from attack with a pesticide application in late spring or early summer. As with all borers, timing is very important. The insecticide must be on the bark to intercept the newly hatched larvae before they burrow into the tree. Only wounded and cankered areas on the bark should be treated. There's no need to spray the healthy portions of the tree.

Watch for bagworms on **arborvitae**, **juniper**, **hemlock**, and **Leyland cypress**. Bagworms also feed on many broadleaf shrubs and trees including **rose**, **sycamore**, **maple**, **elm**, and **black locust**. See p. 286 for a descriptions and controls.

Watch for Japanese beetles in the northern parts of Alabama and Mississippi.

Look for powdery mildew on **flowering dogwoods** (*Cornus florida*), a white powdery growth on infected leaves which may cause them to drop. Most powdery mildews of landscape trees occur in late summer and do not pose any harm since they will be shedding their leaves shortly; **dogwoods**, however, become infected in early summer. Fungicides can control this disease. **Dogwoods** that are resistant to powdery mildew include the **kousa dogwood** cultivars 'Big Apple', 'China Girl', 'Gay Head', 'Greensleeves', 'Julian', 'Milky Way Select', and 'Temple Jewel.' The Stellar hybrids Aurora®, Celestial™, and Stellar Pink® are also resistant to powdery mildew.

Poison ivy is dangerous year-round. You can develop an irritation from exposure to the leaves, roots, berries, and even smoke when burning the vines. Learn to identify this deciduous vine with compound leaves comprised of three leaflets, hairy aerial roots along its stem, and clusters of white waxy fruit in late summer. Don't confuse it with **Virginia creeper** (*Parthenocissus quinquefolia*), which has five leaflets and climbs by tendrils with adhesive disks at its tips. Remember, "Leaflets three, let it be."

If you think you may have come in contact with poison ivy, wash immediately with soap and water and remove any clothes that may have the oil on them.

You can try killing poison ivy with Roundup, but it will take several applications over the year. Fall is an especially good time to spray (before leaf drop) because sap is moving down to the roots where the Roundup can be most effective.

# JUNE
## TREES

### PLANNING

As part of your summer vacation plans, why not find some time to visit private and public gardens around the region? These gardens can be inspirational and educational. Refer to pp. 288 to 291 for their names and phone numbers. Don't forget your camera and gardening journal. Enjoy!

### PLANTING

With the availability of container-grown trees, the planting season is limited only by extremely hot weather, frozen soil in winter, and your ability to water regularly. With the onset of hot, dry weather, you can plant, but be prepared to be on call with adequate water throughout the establishment period of your trees. Unless you're willing to put in the time, wait until fall when the odds of successful establishment are in your favor.

### CARE

If distance and mulch don't protect the bark of young trees from string trimmer or mower damage, especially by a mowing service that may come while you're away, resort to putting up stakes or guards. Do not tolerate this kind of damage because it will ruin your tree.

### WATERING

Water recently planted trees which are especially vulnerable to heat and drought. Water thoroughly to encourage deep rooting. Mulch with a 2- to 3-inch layer of compost to conserve moisture, suppress weeds, and moderate soil temperatures. Extend the mulch layer out to the drip line (outermost branches of the tree).

### FERTILIZING

Fertilize trees based on need. If the trees are growing in a fertilized lawn, fertilizing may not be necessary. Time the application for the appropriate time for the grass. This is especially important for warm-season grasses, which may be subject to winterkill if they're fertilized late in the fall or early in the spring. Since most of a tree's roots can be found in the top 12 inches of soil, the simplest way to fertilize them is with a rotary or cyclone spreader according to soil-test results.

### PRUNING

When dead or damaged branches are found on shade trees, prune them out immediately. Summer storms can seriously damage trees in the landscape. Storm-damaged trees should be repaired when needed, rather than waiting for the dormant season. Hire certified arborists to remove large damaged limbs.

### PROBLEMS

Be on the lookout for aphids, scale insects, spider mites, and dogwood borers. Monitor trees for Japanese beetles. Adults lay eggs in July and August and continually migrate to susceptible hosts. If only a few are present, pick them off by hand and discard them in a jar of soapy water. Neem can be applied to the leaves to reduce feeding by the adults. Use other insecticides for heavy infestations.

Keep bagworms at bay by applying the bacterial insecticide Bt (*Bacillus thuringiensis*) as the larvae begin to feed and construct their bags. Heavy infestations may require an application of a systemic insecticide later in the season. Light infestations of bagworms can also be controlled by handpicking. Remove the bags with scissors or a knife, and dispose of them by dropping them into a container of soapy water. Birds and parasitic wasps will work in concert with your efforts, and low winter temperatures can damage overwintering insect pest eggs.

Fireblight is a bacterial disease that attacks **apple**, **loquat**, **pear**, and other trees. Prune out the diseased branches several inches below the infection. If you cut into a diseased branch, disinfect your pruning shears with Lysol®, which is less corrosive than the traditional mixture of water and household bleach (sodium hypochlorite: 4 parts water to 1 part bleach). This can prevent the spread of fireblight to other branches or trees.

Powdery mildew is a grayish-white fungal disease that attacks the leaves, flowers, and shoots of older cultivars of **crapemyrtle**. Prune out heavily infested shoots. Fungicides are available; however, specialized equipment may be needed to treat large **crapemyrtles**. Instead, consider growing the *L. faurei* hybrids—crosses between the Chinese *Lagerstroemia indica* and the Japanese *L. fauriei* developed by Dr. Donald Egolf of the U. S. National Arboretum: They are resistant to powdery mildew. They include 'Acoma', 'Biloxi', 'Apalachee', 'Hopi', 'Lipan', 'Choctaw', 'Comanche', 'Miami',

---

## HELPFUL HINTS ABOUT LICHENS AND SPANISH MOSS

When some gardeners find **lichens** or **Spanish moss** on their trees, they often panic, thinking that their trees are under siege. Relax. **Lichens** are ominous-looking but harmless organisms that consist of a fungus and green or blue-green algae, which live in association with each other, looking like a single plant. **Lichens** often appear leafy or crusty and are colored gray, green, yellow, or white. They are typically found on dead or declining trees, on rocks, or on the ground. Their presence on failing trees is a sign, but never the cause, of poor plant health—the reduction of plant vigor has resulted in a more open canopy, which increases sunlight penetration and subsequent **lichen** growth.

You can remove the **lichens** from your tree with a stiff brush, but they will probably reappear if you do not determine the cause and correct it. Restoring the vigor of your tree should increase the size and number of leaves and eventually lead to the gradual disappearance of lichens.

The gray strands of **Spanish moss** (*Tillandsia usneoides*) draping the limbs of **live oaks**, **pecans**, and **pines** pose no harm to the trees. **Spanish moss** is an epiphyte, which means that it's simply growing on the tree and using it for support as it collects minerals and water from the air. It's not stealing water or nutrients from the tree—rather, it gives the tree an unmistakably Southern, genteel look.

---

'Prairie Lace', 'Sioux', 'Osage', 'Pecos', 'Tonto', 'Tuskeegee', 'Wichita', 'Zuma', and 'Zuni'.

Handpull or use a herbicide to spot-treat water- and nutrient-stealing weeds growing at the base of newly planted trees. Suppress their emergence with a layer of mulch.

Crapemyrtles are beautiful ornamental trees; select the right cultivar for the right location.

# JULY

## TREES

### PLANNING

This is an appropriate time of year to learn about a landscape approach that combines water conservation techniques with good old-fashioned common-sense gardening. It's called *xeriscaping*, which means "dry landscaping." Although the idea originated in the western United States, the same water-saving principles can be used anywhere. Here are its seven basic principles:

1. Careful planning and design. Divide the landscape into "hydrozones" (areas within the design that receive low, moderate, or high amounts of water).

2. Reducing lawn areas to functional spaces and growing drought-tolerant lawn grasses.

3. Preparing the soil well by using organic matter such as compost to improve soil structure. Organic matter improves air and water movement and the ability of our soils to retain moisture and nutrients.

4. Appropriate plant selection and grouping plants with similar water needs. Because xeriscapes have low-, medium-, and high-water-use hydrozones, you can grow a wide variety of trees, shrubs, and flowers. These include drought-tolerant plants that can cope with extended periods of dry weather after they've become established. A xeriscape also has room for high-water-use annuals or vegetables that need water to keep them blooming.

5. Efficient watering methods such as drip and micro-sprinkler systems to help conserve water.

6. Mulching. Blanket the soil around trees and shrubs, and in plant beds with mulch to conserve moisture, suppress weeds, and enhance plant growth.

7. Proper landscape maintenance. Fertilize, prune, mow, and water the right way to produce healthy plants.

Research indicates that incorporating these principles into the landscape reduces water consumption by 30 to 60 percent or more. Thus xeriscaping lowers maintenance costs and increases the survival rate of landscape plants during droughty periods.

### PLANTING

If your summer vacation is the only time you can plant, go ahead and install container-grown trees. Keep the rootballs and surrounding soil moist until winter rains begin doing it for you.

Root semi-hardwood cuttings of favorite trees to "passalong" to a friend. To take semi-hardwood cuttings, notice when the current season's shoots begin to harden and turn brown. When you snap the twig, the bark often clings to the stem. Here's how to take semi-hardwood cuttings of your favorite trees:

1. Remove a strip of bark about 1 inch long from one side of each cutting.

2. Dip each cutting in a rooting hormone for woody plants.

3. Stick the cuttings in a container filled with equal parts peat moss and coarse sand. Each cutting should be deep enough in the medium to hide the wound.

4. Finally, enclose the container in a polyethylene bag, tie the bag at the top, and place the cuttings in a shaded location.

5. After a few weeks, check the cuttings for roots by gently tugging at a few of them. When you feel resistance, it means they have rooted. Now you can safely remove the plastic bag and repot the young plants in individual pots in a mix of equal parts potting soil and peat.

6. Gradually expose the rooted cuttings to stronger light to harden them off. After a couple of weeks, transplant them into the garden.

### WATERING

Water recently planted trees, which are especially vulnerable to heat and drought. Check the rootball and soil before watering instead of relying on the calendar. Avoid overwatering, which can suffocate plant roots, causing leaves to wilt. Excess water can also expose the tree to root rot, a deadly fungal disease that prevails in waterlogged conditions and attacks susceptible plants (see September Problems p. 225).

## FERTILIZING

Do not fertilize at this time unless you've established a need for it, and only if you're willing to irrigate regularly afterwards to sustain the new growth.

## PRUNING

Remove diseased, dead, or broken limbs at any time.

## PROBLEMS

Japanese beetles are highly attracted to some trees. A long-term solution is to replace Japanese beetle-prone trees with less palatable ones. Here are a few attractive ornamentals from a long list of resistant trees: **arborvitae**, **ash**, **Chinese redbud**, **cryptomeria**, **dogwood**, **ginkgo**, **hazelnut**, **Japanese pagodatree**, **hollies**, **hemlock**, **hickory**, **mag-**nolia, **maples**, **oaks** other than **chestnut** and **pin**, **smoketree**, **spruce**, **sweetgum**, **tamarisk**, **tuliptree**, and **yew**.

Spines of sawdust an inch or more long sticking out of the trunk are a sure sign of the Asian ambrosia beetle. This aggressive pest first appeared in this country in 1974 in Summerville, South Carolina, and has now spread to other southeastern states where it attacks more than 100 species of trees. The $1/8$-inch-long reddish-brown beetles typically invade young trees less than a foot in diameter. Because nearly the entire life cycle of the beetle is spent inside the wood, ambrosia beetles are difficult to control with insecticides. There are typically two generations per year, and for trees younger than three years old, infestations are likely to be fatal. Spraying trunks and limbs with an insecticide in late February or March will help reduce infestations, but the only guaranteed way to kill all of the beetles is to dig up and destroy an infested tree. Older trees are likely to survive an attack, however, particularly if they are growing vigorously.

Remove bagworms with scissors or a sharp knife. Bagworms are parasitized by several kinds of parasitic wasps and insecticides are effective, if applied when the bagworms are small.

If you'd rather switch than fight, a Japanese cryptomeria is both ornamental and resists Japanese beetles.

Powdery mildew attacks the leaves and shoots of the older **crapemyrtle** cultivars. See June Problems p. 219.

Handpull any weeds. Use a shallow layer of mulch to suppress them.

# AUGUST

## TREES

### PLANNING

Start planning for fall-planting. Keep in mind the xeriscape principle, appropriate use of plant materials. Choose your plants thoughtfully and plant them in an environment that matches the plant's native habitat. There are plants that are highly adaptable and will perform well in a variety of situations. For example, **river birch** and **bald cypress** (*Taxodium distichum*) are native to low, wet areas, but they can be grown successfully on high ground.

Coastal residents will have a challenging time finding appropriate plants that will tolerate salt-laden ocean breezes near the beach. The challenge is especially great on the beaches where plants have to contend with poor sandy soils that have little ability to retain water or nutrients. A good solution is to rely on native plants. Examine the local habitat to see which indigenous plants can be used in the landscape. Native coastal plants not only perform better than most exotics but also keep the garden in harmony with its surroundings. However, not all of a coastal garden's plants have to be native. Hardy exotic plants can set the stage for the less-conspicuous natives.

### PLANTING

This is a difficult time to establish new trees because the need for water is so great in the heat. However, it's a good time to buy from a good local nursery that takes care of their plants well, but is clearing out spring stock to make room for fall items. Keep plants in shade and well watered until you're ready to get them in the ground.

### WATERING

Inspect the soil moisture of newly planted shrubs and trees. If the soil is dry near the rootball, give them a good soaking to wet the soil deeply. According to research findings, mulch promotes faster growth of trees and shrubs than does grass or ground covers.

### FERTILIZING

Do not fertilize at this time unless you've established a need for fertilizing and you're willing to provide adequate moisture for roots to grow and absorb the applied minerals.

### PRUNING

Prune out dead, diseased, or broken wood. Hold off on major pruning until late winter. Major pruning now will only stimulate tender, new growth, which can be killed by our first freeze.

### PROBLEMS

To have an insect identified, visit your local garden center or Cooperative Extension Service office. Put the insect in a pill bottle and mail it or take it directly to the Extension office. Dropping it into a small vial of isopropyl alcohol will preserve the insect, making identification easier.

Spider mites are very active during hot, dry weather, especially on **junipers**, **hollies**, and many other ornamentals. Feeding injury results in discolored, bronzy leaves. Check for mites by tapping a branch onto a white sheet of paper and looking for moving specks. Natural predators can control spider mite populations. A strong spray of water from the hose applied to the undersides of the leaves will dislodge the adults during the growing season. An insecticidal soap, Neem oil, or a miticide will also be effective, although repeated applications may be necessary.

# HELPFUL HINTS FOR NOISE REDUCTION

Plants can be used to reduce road noise. Solid barriers tall enough to screen the noise source from view are the best way to reduce the noise from high-speed car and truck traffic, like that on interstates. Plantings of trees and shrubs will mitigate the noise from moderate-speed automobiles, found in suburban locations. Plants are better at absorbing high-frequency sounds, which are most bothersome to human ears, than they are at absorbing low-frequency sounds.

You will need to plant two or three rows of plants. Shrubs should be located adjacent to the traffic and be backed by taller trees. The planting must be sufficiently dense to screen the traffic from view. For year-round noise reduction, evergreens are the best choice. A mixture of plants—such as **arborvitae**, **spruce**, and **juniper**, as well as broad-leaved **holly**, **Southern magnolia**, and **boxwood**—will ensure against a total loss if there is a disease or insect outbreak. If you plant fast growers for an "instant screen," be aware that many of these are weak-wooded and short-lived. Interplantings of longer-lived species will fill in the vacant spots when the fast growers die or have to be removed.

Recent research has shown greater noise reduction is obtained from a combination of trees and shrubs planted atop an earthen berm. Such combinations produce a noise reduction of 6 to 15 decibels immediately behind them, which the human ear will perceive as one-third as loud.

---

The leaves on deciduous trees will be falling in the next few months, so infected leaves may not require attention at this time since they're going to be shed soon.

Powdery mildew diseases attack a great many ornamentals, most often in late summer when the days are warm and nights are cool. Prevention is the first defense.

1. Grow powdery mildew-resistant varieties.

2. Prune plant to improve air circulation and sunlight penetration.

3. Reduce fertilizer applications to avoid excessive, late-season growth.

Cercospora leaf spot is a common disease of **crapemyrtles** that becomes noticeable this month and next. Diseased leaves have brown lesions that eventually turn yellow to red in color and then are quickly shed. Select resistant **crapemyrtles**.

The following cultivars are resistant to powdery mildew and Cercospora leaf spot: 'Tuscarora', 'Tuskegee', 'Tonto', and 'Fantasy' **Japanese crapemyrtle**.

Here's a sample of trees that can tolerate exposed, Gulf Coast environments:

| Common Name/(Botanical Name) | Hardiness Zone |
| --- | --- |
| **Cabbage palmetto** (Sabal palmetto) | 8b to 11 |
| **Darlington's oak** (Quercus hemisphaerica) | 6 to 10 |
| **Live oak** (Quercus virginiana) | 7b to 11 |
| **Red cedar** (Juniperus virginiana) | 2a to 10b |
| **Southern magnolia** (Magnolia grandiflora) | 6b to 10a |
| **Southern red cedar** (Juniperus virginiana var. silicicola) | 8a to 10b |
| **Windmill palm** (Trachycarpus fortunei) | 8a to 10b |
| **Yaupon holly** (Ilex vomitoria) | 7a to 9b |

# SEPTEMBER

## TREES

### PLANNING

This fall recycle your fallen leaves into mulch or compost. For a fine-textured mulch, shred the leaves with a lawn mower or a leaf shredder. Finely cut leaves look more attractive and tend to stay where you put them.

To compost leaves, researchers recommend building piles at least 4 feet in diameter and 3 feet in height. To keep them manageable, make the piles no larger than 5 feet high and 10 feet wide. Compost leaves by themselves or add fresh vegetable peelings, grass clippings, or other kitchen or yard trimmings.

To speed up the composting process, shred the leaves before putting them into the pile. Avoid adding meat or grease, which may cause odors and attract pests. Pay particular attention to moisture and air. Keep the ingredients moist enough that you can squeeze water droplets from a handful of leaves. Aerate or supply air to the pile by turning the materials. During warm weather, turn the pile once a month; in cool weather, turn it less frequently to prevent too much heat from escaping. To convert the leaves to compost fairly quickly, add nitrogen to the pile. Add a nitrogen-containing fertilizer such as 10-10-10 or a natural substitute such as horse or cow manure, bloodmeal, or cottonseed meal. Mix this crumbly, earthy-smelling "black gold" into heavy clay soil to improve drainage and make the soil easier to cultivate. Compost helps sandy soils retain water and nutrients.

### PLANTING

Fall is the prime planting season. The tops of trees stop growing, thus making fewer demands on the root system. Also, the ground is warm, encouraging roots to grow. So if you want to plant a tree, September, October, and even November are great times to do so.

### WATERING

Fall can be a very warm and dry month. Water newly planted trees. Check moisture in the rootball prior to watering.

### FERTILIZING

If your trees have produced sufficient growth this year, fertilizing may not be necessary. If you choose to fertilize, rely on soil-test results to apply the nutrients required by your trees. If they're showing their fall colors, wait until next year.

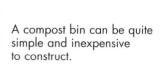

A compost bin can be quite simple and inexpensive to construct.

## PRUNING

Prune out dead or diseased wood from trees. Hold off on major pruning until mid- to late winter or even early spring before growth begins. Major pruning now will only stimulate tender, new growth, which can be killed by our first freeze. Any storm damage to large trees should be repaired by a certified arborist.

Wait until next year to prune your **crapemyrtles**. Research shows that late-summer, fall, and early-winter pruning may predispose woody ornamental plants, especially **crapemyrtles**, to cold injury. Delay pruning until late winter or early spring before budbreak.

## PROBLEMS

Fall webworm is a North American native insect that attacks more than 100 species of deciduous trees and shrubs. Unlike the eastern tent caterpillar, which constructs similar nests, the fall webworm does not become conspicuous until late summer and early fall. Two generations hatch each year, the second being more conspicuous. Fall webworms are a cosmetic nuisance. The defoliation typically involves only a few branches and occurs late in the season (by which time the tree is ready to shed its leaves naturally).

In most years, a large number of natural predators and parasitoids keep fall webworms in check. The bacterial insecticide *Bacillus thuringiensis* (Bt) can be applied in June when the caterpillars are small and sprayed onto leaves next to the nest, on which the caterpillars will soon feed. Nests that are easy to reach can be pruned off or torn apart with a stick and the caterpillars dislodged with a strong stream of water. The simplest course of action, however, is to do nothing in the confidence that the fall webworms aren't doing your plants any real harm.

Root rot caused by *Phytophthora*, which means "plant destroyer," attacks a wide variety of plants including **dogwood**, **deodar cedar**, **white pine**, and many others. Look for wilted, dying plants. Scrape the bark near the crown and look for a reddish-brown discoloration where the fungus has moved into the stem. These fungi are often found in wet or poorly drained sites. They'll attack plants in moderate to dry sites if they're planted too deeply. Overwatering plants in moderate to dry sites also favors these fungi. When symptoms are evident, fungicides are often ineffective in controlling this disease. Here are some tips to avoid root rot disease:

1. Avoid planting in poorly drained sites unless you are using trees adapted to soggy soil.

2. Improve drainage in heavy clay soil by planting in slightly raised beds, or add organic matter such as composted pine bark.

3. Use plants that are highly resistant to root rot.

Prepare now to protect your trees from deer and rodents. Protect trees from deer with fencing or repellents. Rabbits can be deterred by installing wire or plastic guards around the trunks of young shade trees and fruit trees. To discourage voles, pull the mulch away from the trunk about a foot.

Rabbits and voles will feed on the thin bark of young trees. To protect trees, shrubs, and ornamentals, use hardware cloth cylinders to keep voles away. First use a shovel to cut the ground around the plant just enough to insert a wire cylinder. Then add the hardware cloth. The bottom edge of the cylinder should be buried at least 6 inches below the ground. If kept in place permanently, the mesh will girdle the tree's roots. To avoid injury, remove it after one or two years or bury it further away from the trunk without harming the feeder roots.

# OCTOBER

## TREES

### PLANNING

Deciduous trees light up the autumn skies with an assortment of fiery reds, oranges, and yellows. These colors result from the interaction of several pigments, including yellow xanthophylls, orange carotenoids, and red anthocyanins. The anthocyanins are manufactured by the conversion of sugars in the fall; the other pigments have been there all along but are not visible until the masking green chlorophyll has disappeared.

Okay, so maybe it's not that important to know where these brilliant colors came from. But it's good to know the names and cultivars of trees whose fall color would make an important addition to your landcape. Some good ones include **ginkgo**, **red maple**, **Japanese maple**, certain **crapemyrtles**, **black gum**, **sweet gum**, and **Chinese pistache**.

### PLANTING

Now and next month are excellent times to plant trees during the cooler temperatures of fall. In warmer areas, planting can continue into December. Trees planted in the fall can establish before warm summer temperatures draw moisture from roots to stress the trees.

Chinese pistache foliage becomes a brilliant red in fall.

Remember to make the planting hole only as deep as the rootball. You can make it as wide as you like, but at least two to three times the diameter of the rootball. Purchase a high-quality tree with a strong trunk and well-spaced branches to avoid costly "training" by pruning.

### CARE

Do not become alarmed if your **yews**, **pines**, **arborvitae**, and **junipers** begin to shed their interior needles. It is natural for them to do so at this time of year.

### WATERING

Water evergreens thoroughly before the ground freezes. Evergreens continue to lose water by transpiring during the winter, but when the ground is frozen they cannot replenish the water.

In fall and early winter, don't forget to water newly planted trees to help them become established. A few weeks after planting, start reducing watering to every few days or longer, especially with cloudy, rainy, or cool weather. Eventually, you can water on an "as-needed" basis by testing the soil and rootball for moisture. Here's how:

1. Dig a small hole in the loosened backfill soil just outside the rootball.

2. Squeeze a handful of the soil from the top and another from the bottom of the hole. If water drips between your fingers or the soil feels sticky, the soil is too wet. If it crumbles and falls

from your hand as you open your fingers, you need to add water. If the soil stays together in your hand as you open your fingers, the moisture in the backfill is just right. But you'll still need to test the rootball.

3. Insert your fingers into the rootball. If it's dry, go ahead and water.

## FERTILIZING

See September p. 224.

## PRUNING

While you can still identify them easily, prune dead and diseased branches from trees and shrubs.

## PROBLEMS

Remove and destroy bagworm bags on narrow-leaved evergreens. Eggs overwinter in the bags produced by the females and will hatch-out next spring.

Old, fallen leaves contain the disease spores for next year's plant infections. If you have diseased plants, prune out infected branches in the late fall and winter when the disease-causing organism is inactive. Remove any infected debris from around the plant's base and dispose of it.

To protect young trees against white-tail deer damage, there are a number of deterrents you can try. Remember, deer will become accustomed to any object, so alternating items will help. Hang bars of strong-scented soap or mesh bags filled with human hair on the outer branches with no more than 3 feet between them. Chemical deer repellents also can be applied. To be effective, repellents will have to be reapplied if there is rain or heavy dew; they will have to be applied often to new plant growth.

The only technique that ensures safety from deer is fencing. Both woven wire fences and multi-strand electric fencing will do the job, but their construction can be elaborate and expensive. An alternative fencing material— $7^1/2$-foot black plastic mesh—is nearly invisible and can be used to completely surround your plantings. To learn more about these and other techniques for keeping deer at bay, contact your local Cooperative Extension Service.

## HELPFUL HINTS FOR PROTECTING TREES

• Over the course of their lives, trees sometimes develop holes in their trunks. Depending on the size of the cavity and the extent of decay, you may want to consult a certified arborist for advice. In general, cavities are no longer routinely filled now that it's known trees compartmentalize wounds by creating chemical and physical barriers to contain the spread of infection. Over time, wounded wood formed by callus tissue will develop along the edges of the cavity, forming a "callus roll" and strengthening the damaged trunk. Nevertheless, an arborist may decide to fill the cavity withurethane foam to prevent rainwater from accumulating. This soft, flexible foam forms a better bond with wood than the concrete that was used in the past. A piece of sheet metal can be tacked over the foam for cosmetic purposes if desired.

• Young trees can be inexpensively protected from rodents, string trimmers, and mowers with short, plastic tube-shaped tree guards. Each protector should be 6 to 12 inches tall and long enough to wrap around the entire trunk. Alternatively, you can purchase trimmer guards or make your own out of corrugated plastic drainpipe.

# NOVEMBER

## TREES

### PLANNING

When planning to include trees in your landscape, take advantage of their winter interest. Bark, branches, and architectural forms give deciduous trees character. Look at the peeling or exfoliating bark of a wide variety of trees such as **crapemyrtle**, particularly 'Natchez' and 'Fantasy' **Japanese crapemyrtle** (*Lagerstroemia faurei* 'Fantasy').

### PLANTING

Fall is the best time of year for moving trees. To ensure success, transplant trees when they're dormant. Where circumstances necessitate very late planting of trees, remember to mulch the area heavily to keep the ground thawed so roots can become established.

If you're planning on having a live balled-and-burlapped Christmas tree, you might consider digging the planting hole now before the Christmas craziness arrives. It will make it easier to plant later.

### CARE

Protect tender **palms** with tall, solitary trunks during the winter by tying up their leaves and wrapping the trunk with insulating blankets. Small specimens can be enclosed in a wire circle and buried with pine straw. Check guy wires around newly planted trees to be sure hose sections still cover the supporting wires or ropes so they will not damage the trunks in windy weather. Mulch plantings to protect against winter cold.

### WATERING

Newly planted trees may require watering, especially in areas where the cold wind can dry out evergreens.

If fall rains have been scarce, water landscape evergreens thoroughly once every week or so until the ground freezes. Evergreens continue to lose moisture from their foliage all winter, but if the ground should freeze, they'll be unable to take up enough water to replace it. Sending them into winter well watered reduces the potential for damaged foliage.

### FERTILIZING

Do not fertilize trees now.

### PRUNING

Do not be in a hurry to prune trees. Wait until next year after the coldest part of winter has passed.

### PROBLEMS

Remove all mummified fruit from fruit trees, and rake up and destroy those on the ground. Rake and dispose of dropped **apple** and **cherry** leaves. Good sanitation practices reduce reinfestation of insects and diseases the following season.

Inspect trees and shrubs for bagworm capsules and the silvery egg masses of tent caterpillars. Remove and destroy them to reduce next year's pest population. If there is any evidence of scale on trees and shrubs, spray with dormant oil in late fall and again in early spring.

For animal pests, see December p. 230.

Mistletoe is a cherished Christmas decoration, but when you find it growing on your **oaks**, thoughts about kissing under the mistletoe on Christmas Eve last month are forgotten, and you will want to get rid of it. It is a pest that is half-parasitic: it has leaves to produce its own food, but it steals water and nutrients from its host. It can affect the growth and vigor of its host, exposing the tree to attacks by diseases and insects. In some instances, mistletoe can cause branches to die back, and heavy, shrubby mistletoes can break entire limbs. In other situations, mistletoe is simply a cosmetic problem, which affects only the appearance of the tree.

The only effective way to rid your tree of a mistletoe infestation is by pruning. Cut the infected limb 1 to 2 feet below the mistletoe because its "roots" may extend up to a foot on either side of the point of attachment. Breaking off the tops (similar to plucking off the leaves of dandelions or wild garlic in the lawn) only encourages regrowth. Pruning out mistletoe clumps from the uppermost reaches of trees should be left in the hands of certified arborists. Haphazard cuts can harm the tree. Growth hormone sprays interrupt flowering or cause the shoots to fall off, but the mistletoe eventually resprouts and needs to be treated again.

## HELPFUL HINTS FOR A LIVING CHRISTMAS TREE

If you want to purchase a live Christmas tree, choose one that will thrive in your area, and make sure you know where you're going to plant it. Here are some choices: **Arizona cypress** (*Cupressus arizonica* var. *arizonica*), **deodar cedar** (*Cedrus deodara*), **red cedar**, **Virginia pine**, and **Leyland cypress**. Follow these steps to choose the right live tree this holiday season:

1. Choose a balled-and-burlapped tree with a firm rootball. Grab the trunk and push it back and forth once or twice. If the root system is healthy and unbroken, the tree will bend along its length. It's damaged if it rocks at its base before it bends.

2. Store the tree in a shaded protected location before bringing it inside. Cover the root-ball with pine straw to protect it from cold.

3. Once you bring the tree indoors, keep it inside for no more than five to seven days. Keep the tree away from heating vents, fireplaces, and other heat sources.

4. Place the rootball in a large tub and water from the top. Check the rootball daily and water often enough to keep the soil moist.

5. After the holiday, plant your tree immediately. The rootball will be very heavy, so enlist the help of any holiday guests to help you carry it outside.

6. Plant the tree in a sunny well-drained location with plenty of room to spread out. We hope you heeded our advice and scouted the perfect spot before you purchased the tree!

7. Dig the hole as deep as the rootball and at least twice the rootball diameter. Place the tree in the hole, stand it straight, and fill in with soil. Water thoroughly and mulch with 2 to 4 inches of compost, shredded bark, or pine straw. Keep the tree well watered during the winter months to help it become established.

# December

## TREES

 PLANNING

Trees can be planted this month as long as the weather is mild and the soil is not too soggy or possibly frozen. Visit your favorite garden center to try something new. Just as you may feel comfortable with a particular entrée at a restaurant but sometimes want something different, get adventurous—*Carpe diem*—and try something new.

 PLANTING

For good establishment, transplant at least four weeks before the soil temperature goes below 40 degrees F. Newly planted trees should be watered immediately after planting. Continue to water them during the winter months. Don't keep them waterlogged, however.

Root hardwood stem cuttings of coniferous evergreens such as **juniper**, **cypress** (*Cupressus*), **falsecypress** (*Chamaecyparis*), and **cryptomeria**. Some broadleaf evergreens that can be propagated now are **holly** and **arborvitae**.

 CARE

Check the water in your Christmas tree stand on a daily basis and replenish it so it won't go dry. Remember to limit a live Christmas tree to five to seven days indoors. Keep the rootball moist.

 WATERING

Water newly planted trees. Drain garden hoses and store them where you can get to them in midwinter if you need to water. Cover outdoor spigots with foam housing to protect them from freezing.

Never allow the reservoir of your Christmas tree holder to go dry; an air lock can form in the trunk that can keep the tree from absorbing any more water. Research has shown that plain water is best.

 PRUNING

Wait until after the coldest part of winter has passed before doing any major structural pruning that would remove large limbs. That may encourage new growth or make the tree susceptible to winter injury.

 PROBLEMS

If scale insects and mites have been a problem this past season, apply a dormant horticultural oil when the plants go dormant. Be sure to spray the trunk, branches, and stems and both sides of the leaves thoroughly. Read the label for precautions regarding the high and low temperature limits at the time of application.

Check your plants for the spindle-shaped bags of bagworms which contain 500 to 1,000 eggs that will hatch next spring.

Take precautions against deer and rodents. Protect trees from deer with fencing or repellents. Rabbits can be deterred by installing wire or plastic guards around the trunks of young shade trees and fruit trees. To discourage voles, pull the mulch away from the trunk about a foot. Refer to p. 285 for more information about controlling voles.

CHAPTER NINE

# VINES & GROUND COVERS

Vines and ground covers are more than just drab workhorses—they can be bold and colorful living screens or blankets. Some gardeners have shied away from vines and ground covers because of what they've seen running amok in the countryside: Oriental bittersweet (*Celastrus orbiculatus*) swallowing up trees; and kudzu (*Pueraria lobata*)—"the vine that ate the South"—engulfing trees, utility poles, abandoned houses, and everything else in its path. But these invasive bullies have well-mannered cousins that can be introduced into the landscape.

Vines can be used to hide ugly views or for other important functions, or simply as accent plants or attention-grabbers with bold and attractive leaves, beautiful fragrant flowers, and decorative fruits and seedheads. Many offer brilliant fall color and provide shelter for wildlife. Flowering annual vines, many of which are native to tropical regions, hold up well in our hot and humid summers, blooming well until the first frost.

Ground covers can be functional as well as ornamental. Ranging in height from 2 inches to 2 feet, ground covers can be low-growing and spreading evergreen or deciduous shrubs, perennials, or even vines. Some have colorful flowers, while others have showy leaves splashed with pink, silver, white, or yellow. When they're used

to fill in gaps around shrubs and trees they create interesting patterns and textures that unite the individual plants into a single, solid-looking planting.

When vines and ground covers are used together they offer your landscape the dimensions of height and breadth, uniting function with beauty.

## PLANNING

Before selecting vines and ground covers for your landscape, become familiar with the environmental conditions of the site: light exposure (full sun, partial shade, or dense shade), soil moisture, and drainage. Most flowering vines perform best in full sunlight to partial shade. Along the coast, you need to select vines that tolerate salt spray. Always match the plant to the site rather then attempting to change the environment to accommodate the plant.

Before purchasing vines for your landscape, become familiar with the way they climb so you'll know the kind of support to select for them and how to maintain them. If you already have a support, select a vine that will be able to climb it with ease.

Twining vines twist their stems around supports. With a little coaxing, mandevilla (*Mandevilla splendens*), Carolina yellow jessamine (*Gelsemium sempervirens*) Confederate jasmine (*Trachelospermum jasminoides*), and swamp jessamine (*Gelsemium rankinii*) happily wrap themselves around mailbox posts, lampposts, and railings.

Some vines use tendrils to cling to objects. Morning glory (*Ipomoea*), passionflower (*Passiflora*), and sweet pea (*Lathyrus odoratus*) need thin wire or string supports for the tendrils to grasp.

Finally, some vines use specialized structures to give them a foothold. Crossvine (*Bignonia capreolata*), climbing fig (*Ficus pumila*), Japanese hydrangea-vine (*Schizophragma hydrangeoides*), climbing hydrangea, English ivy, Virginia creeper (*Parthenocissus quinquefolia*), and trumpet creeper (*Campsis radicans*) produce rootlets along their stems that have adhesive, suction cup-like disks at their tips for attaching to surfaces.

Keep vines off wooden walls—they trap moisture and slow the drying of wood, which can encourage decay. When shading brick or masonry walls with clinging vines that have aerial rootlets or adhesive disks (like English and Boston ivies and climbing hydrangea), think twice before allowing them to cling to the walls. Once you allow them to climb on the walls, they're very difficult to remove. After you tear down the vine you're left with rootlets and disks that can only be removed with a stiff scrub brush.

If you're planning on using ground covers on steep slopes, select evergreen ground covers, especially those that form a dense blanket of leaves and branches to shade the soil and suppress weeds year-round.

If you have large areas that allow plants to roam freely, select aggressive ground covers that spread above- and belowground. A handful of blue periwinkle (*Vinca minor*) or creeping liriope (*Liriope spicata*) can be used to fill an area in short time. Vines such as Asiatic jasmine (*Trachelospermum asiaticum*), ivy, or Carolina jessamine will run along the top, sometimes rooting as they go to form a dense impenetrable mat.

For smaller areas with a mixed planting use clumping plants such as bordergrass lilyturf (*Liriope muscari*), hosta, or Lenten rose (*Helleborus orientalis*). These plants need to be planted close together to create a ground cover. Although it means buying more plants, you won't have to struggle to keep them in bounds.

## PLANTING

A few weeks before planting, select the area to receive the vines or ground covers and till it to a depth of 8 to 12 inches. Spread a 2- to 4-inch

layer of organic matter such as compost or composted pine bark mulch over the bed, and work it to a depth of 4 to 6 inches. Test the soil for pH and fertility levels. Add lime or sulfur and any nutrients as recommended by soil-test results.

When planting ground covers on slopes, dig individual planting holes since cultivating the area could increase the chances for soil erosion.

1. Dig a hole that is at least two to three times the diameter of the rootball but no deeper than the height of the rootball. Roots will grow quickly into the loosened soil and will speed up the plant's establishment into its new home.

In heavy clay soils, dig the hole so the rootball will be 1 to 2 inches higher than the surrounding soil. It's always better to err on the side of planting higher than the surrounding soil. Never place the plant so the top of the rootball is below the soil surface. When planting high, cover the exposed rootball with mulch.

2. Slip the plant out of the pot or pack and examine the rootball. Vines or ground covers growing in plastic or other hard-sided containers may have roots circling around the outside of the rootball. Encourage roots to grow along the entire length of the rootball by lightly scoring the rootball in three or four places with a knife, pruning shears, or the end of a sharp spade. Make shallow cuts from the top to the bottom of the rootball. Gently tease the sides apart. Now this "doctored" plant will produce new roots from the cuts all around the rootball.

3. Plant even with or slightly above the surrounding soil. Place the vine or ground cover into the hole and measure the height of the rootball against the surrounding soil. With large plants, lay your shovel across the hole to see that the rootball is even or slightly above the handle. If the hole is too deep, put some soil on the bottom of the hole, tamp it down with your feet to give the plant some solid footing, and put the plant back in the hole.

4. Loosen and break up any clods of soil before backfilling half the hole. Never add any organic matter or sand into the backfill soil when digging individual planting holes—doing so will create problems with water movement and root growth between the rootball and soil.

5. Lightly tamp down the soil with your feet or hands, but not so heavily that you compact the soil. Water when half the rootball is covered, to settle out any air pockets and to remoisten the soil in the rootball. Finish backfilling and water again.

6. Mulch. Apply a 2- to 3-inch layer of organic mulch such as compost, leaf litter, shredded wood, or pine straw.

## WATERING

Water newly planted vines and ground covers frequently until they become established. Water—not fertilizer—is the most important ingredient for helping them get established in the landscape. Keep the soil moist, but not sopping wet.

Refer to Trees October Watering p. 226 to learn how to water on an "as-needed" basis by testing the soil and rootball for moisture.

## FERTILIZING

Once newly planted vines and ground covers become established in the landscape, they can benefit from fertilizer applications from late spring to early fall which will stimulate growth and help them fill in their allotted space in the landscape.

To take the guesswork out of fertilizing your vines and ground covers, rely on a soil test. In the absence of a soil test, use a complete fertilizer with a ratio of 3:1:2 or 3:1:3 (for example, 16-4-8). The rule of thumb is to apply 1 pound

# HELPFUL HINTS FOR MAILBOXES AND FENCEPOSTS

Mailboxes and fence posts make good supports for certain vines that don't get very heavy and can be easily pruned if they get too long. A few good choices of annual vines that can be grown from seed are cypress vine (*Ipomoea quamoclit*), morning-glory (*Ipomoea* spp.), and scarlet runner bean (*Phaseolus coccineus*). These will need a little cutting back to keep them in bounds.

Showy tropical vines include allamanda (*Allamanda cathartica*) and mandevilla (*Mandevilla splendens*).

Perennial deciduous vines include goldflame honeysuckle (*Lonicera* x *heckrottii*) and clematis, notably 'Gravetye Beauty', 'Duchess of Albany', and 'Etoile Rose'. Confederate jasmine (*Trachelospermum jasminoides* 'Madison') is a fragrant twining evergreen vine.

of nitrogen per 1,000 square feet of bed area. To simplify, you can use a good-quality, polymer-coated, timed-release fertilizer at the rate recommended on the label. However, it's good to know the following so that you can always figure how much fertilizer to apply over a ground cover bed.

1. Assume the bed is 20 feet long and 10 feet wide. The bed area = length x width; 20 ft. x 10 ft. = 200 sq. ft.

2. Because fertilizer recommendations are given on a 1,000-sq.-ft. basis, divide the area of the bed by 1,000.

So 200 sq. ft. /1000 sq. ft. = 0.2

3. Determine the amount of 16-4-8 fertilizer needed to apply 1 lb. of nitrogen per 1,000 sq. ft. 100 = 6.25 lb. of 16-4-8 per 1000 sq. ft.

4. To determine the amount of fertilizer required in the 200-sq.-ft. bed, make this calculation: 0.2 x 6.25 lb. = 1.25 lb. of 16-4-8. Therefore, 1 1/4 lb.* of 16-4-8 spread evenly over the bed will supply the appropriate amount.

*2 cups of a synthetic inorganic fertilizer is equivalent to 1 lb. of fertilizer.

## PRUNING

Vines and ground covers require little pruning except to keep them confined to their allotted space and to keep vines on their supports. Woody vines that produce flowers on last-year's growth, such as Confederate jasmine, should be pruned after they flower. Some ground covers, such as liriope, should be pruned annually in the spring before new growth emerges, removing winterkilled shoots and tattered leaves.

## PROBLEMS

Select vines and ground covers that have few, if any, pest problems. Meeting their growing conditions and keeping them healthy should help them avoid confrontations with insects and diseases.

# JANUARY
## VINES & GROUND COVERS

 PLANNING

As the gardening catalogs arrive this month, scan them for unique and interesting vines and ground covers that will complement your landscape. Think about some troublesome areas that would benefit from a colorful vine or ground cover. Look for multi-season ornamental characteristics in the plants. The leaves of evergreens offer year-round interest. Deciduous plants can offer attractive leaves and fall color that can enhance the architectural features of a trellis or latticework. Don't forget about fragrant flowers, colorful fruit, and unique seedpods.

As you compile your list of favorites, remember the importance of matching the vine or ground cover to the site. Avoid the disappointment you will have if you try to force a vine or ground cover to grow where it just doesn't belong.

 PLANTING

In the warmer parts of Alabama and Mississippi, plant vines and ground covers now when the soil can be worked. Before you dig, test the soil for moisture by squeezing a handful. Soil that can be dug is lightly moist and will loosely hold its shape after you squeeze it. If the soil forms a sticky ball in your hand, it's too wet to work. If you dig in a wet soil you can ruin its structure, creating large clods that will dry out and become rock-hard with few pore spaces for air and water. At the other extreme is very dry soil, which also should not be worked. If a handful of soil when squeezed turns to dust, wait for a rain shower a day or two before digging to prevent the topsoil from eroding away.

 CARE

Check the condition of the vines growing on trellises or supports and see that they're still attached.

 WATERING

Water fall-planted vines and ground covers, especially evergreen types, if the soil is dry.

 FERTILIZING

Do not fertilize at this time.

 PRUNING

Wait until next month after the coldest part of winter is over before pruning ground covers and vines.

 PROBLEMS

To control overwintering insects and spider mite eggs, apply a dormant oil spray before new growth emerges. Read the label for cautions regarding the limits of high and low temperatures at the time of application.

As ground covers are settling in, fill the open areas with mulch. An alternative to mulching is interplanting with annuals. Use transplants for small areas and direct-sow large areas. A couple of points to consider when interplanting with annuals:

1. When using a pre-emergent herbicide, you cannot seed with annuals—they will be prevented from germinating by the herbicide.

2. Select well-behaved varieties of annuals and don't plant them so densely that they'll shade or crowd out ground covers or compete for light or nutrients. As the ground cover plants spread, fewer annuals can safely be planted without encroaching on the permanent plantings.

# FEBRUARY
## VINES & GROUND COVERS

 PLANNING

There are some vines that are just plain frightening. When kudzu made its American debut at the United States Centennial Exposition's Japanese Pavilion in Philadelphia in 1876, little did the organizers and visitors know that this lovely "porch vine" would eventually be billed as the world's fastest-growing vine, growing a foot a day and up to 100 feet in a single season. The rest is history.

Vines like **Japanese wisteria** can become botanical pythons, strangling trees and pergolas with their sheer weight. Some vines raise concern because of their rampant free-wheeling nature, not only in the garden but also in nature where they have escaped. These include **English ivy** (*Hedera helix*), **Hall's Japanese honeysuckle** (*Lonicera japonica* 'Halliana'), **Oriental bittersweet** (*Celastrus orbiculatus*), and **porcelainberry** (*Ampelopsis brevipedunculata*).

Do some research at a nearby library. Read local gardening columns in newspapers and gardening magazine articles, and visit private and public gardens to see these vines in action in the landscape. Speak to the gardeners and get their opinions. These background checks will alert you to any landscape surprises.

 PLANTING

For those heavily shaded areas where grass won't grow, try ground covers. **Mondo grass, liriope, pachysandra, English ivy** and **periwinkle** are excellent choices for shaded areas.

If you didn't plant **sweet peas** last October or November, plant them outdoors this month. You can even start the seed indoors in peat pots four to five weeks before setting them out, giving them a head start before the temperatures get too hot. Refer to the October Planting p. 252 to learn how.

Dig up, divide, and replant overgrown clumps of **liriope** that you'd like to share with friends or expand for more ground cover. Replant the **liriope** divisions about a foot apart.

 CARE

In colder areas, some shallow-rooted ground covers may have been heaved out of the ground by freezing and thawing soil. Once the soil is not frozen and is fairly dry, gently press the plants back into the ground to prevent them from drying out.

 WATERING

Keep newly planted ground covers and vines well watered to help them establish quickly.

 FERTILIZING

Fertilize ground covers and vines based on need. It's best to rely on soil-test results when you are going to replace any nutrients that are deficient in the soil. Don't be too hasty to fertilize your vines and ground covers. Fertilize when new growth begins.

 PRUNING

Vines that have outgrown their spaces can be cut back now. Prune other vines that bloom on current-season's growth now. Avoid pruning vines that will be blooming in the spring on last year's growth. After the coldest part of winter has passed, prune summer-flowering vines such as **Confederate jasmine** (*Trachelospermum jasminoides*), **trumpet-creeper** (*Campsis x tagliabuana* 'Madame Galen'), and **Japanese hydrangea vine** (*Schizophragma hydrangeoides*).

# HELPFUL HINTS TO THE TIMING OF CLEMATIS PRUNING

The key to determining when to prune your **clematis** is to know whether it flowers on last year's wood, this year's wood, or both. Experts divide the genus into three groups: Group I contains all the early-spring-flowering evergreen clematis and early- and mid-flowering species. This group includes *Clematis alpina*, **Armand's clematis** (*C. armandii*), **downy clematis** (*C. macropetala*), and **anemone clematis** (*C. montana*). These **clematis** flower on last year's wood and should be pruned after the flowers fade but no later than July. The only pruning really needed is to remove weak or dead stems and to confine the plant to its allotted space.

Group II consists of **clematis** that also flower on last year's growth but will produce a second flush of bloom on new growth. Included are mid-season large-flowered cultivars such as 'Bees' Jubilee', 'Henryi', 'Nelly Moser', and 'Vyvyan Pennell'. Remove all dead and weak stems in late winter or early spring, and cut the remaining stems back to a pair of strong buds which will produce the first blooms. Occasional pinching after flowering will stimulate branching.

Group III consists of late-flowering cultivars and species that flower on this season's growth such as **golden clematis** (*C. flammula*), **solitary clematis** (*C. integrifolia*), *C. 'Jackmanii'*, **Italian clematis** (*C. viticella*), **golden clematis** (*C. tangutica*), **scarlet clematis** (*C. texensis*), and the herbaceous species. These can also be pruned in late winter or early spring. For the first two or three years they may be cut back to a foot from the ground. Later, cut them back to 2 feet. If not cut regularly, this group can become very leggy and overgrown.

The boundaries between these three groups are not absolute. Certain Group III **clematis**, for example, can be treated as Group II to produce early blooms on previous year's wood. The groups serve as a rough guide to keeping your **clematis** vines within bounds.

Cut **liriope** back to within 3 to 4 inches of the ground using clippers, a string trimmer, or a mower set at its highest setting. If you wait, you'll have to do it carefully by hand to avoid nipping the new growth which will be left with brown edges on the leaves throughout the season.

**Dwarf mondo grass** (*Ophiopogon japonicus* 'Nana') grows more slowly than **liriope** and usually requires cutting back every two or three years. If the leaves look unsightly, trim it lightly to encourage the production of new leaves.

## PROBLEMS

See January p. 235 for advice on controlling insects and mites.

Weed control is critical early in the establishment of ground covers. Handpull young weeds, use pre-emergent herbicide, and suppress weed growth with mulch. Once the planting fills in, it should outcompete weeds and stay relatively weed-free.

Apply a pre-emergent herbicide to control summer annuals such as crabgrass and goosegrass (the application is made when they germinate but before they emerge). Wait until later this month to do this in the central and northern parts of Alabama and Mississippi.

# MARCH
## VINES & GROUND COVERS

 PLANNING

**Strawberries** make an uncommon ground cover for edging walkways or flower beds in full sun or part shade. **Alpine strawberries** (*Fragaria vesca*) are attractive ground-hugging choices, particularly 'Improved Rugen' and 'Semperflorens'. But when you want luscious **strawberries** on your morning cereal, you need to grow the cultivated **strawberry** (*F. x ananassa*). Although not as compact or as contained as **alpine strawberry**, each plant can be expected to bear a quart of berries.

Select **strawberry** varieties that are June-bearers or "single-croppers." These plants develop flower buds in the short days of the fall and produce a heavy crop in April in the Coastal Plain and May farther north in Alabama and Mississippi. ("June-bearer" is a bit of a misnomer in the South.) During the long days of summer they produce aboveground runners called stolons.

You can plant June-bearers from November to March whenever they are available at your favorite garden center. Plan to purchase June-bearing varieties for early, mid-, and late-season harvests. Contact your County Cooperative Extension Service office for the recommended varieties for your area. **Strawberries** are not permanent ground covers because they have to be replaced every two or three years, but they do add a whole new edible dimension to ground cover plantings.

 PLANTING

Plant container-grown ground covers and vines this month. Refer to p. 232 for step-by-step instructions. Plant them as early in the season as possible to help them get established before the heat of summer.

 CARE

If you've overwintered your **mandevilla** indoors, wait until late winter or early spring before growth begins to prune out old, crowded stems and to shorten others.

 WATERING

Spring is rarely dry, so newly established plants may not need frequent irrigation. Check the soil, however, to make sure the roots are moist during their first few weeks.

Check mulched areas and replenish where needed. Organic mulches such as compost, pine needles ("pine straw"), and shredded leaves or composted wood conserve moisture, reduce weed growth, prevent soil compaction, and supply nutrients as they decompose.

 FERTILIZING

Ground covers can be fertilized when new growth begins. Sweep any fertilizer from the leaves to avoid burning them.

 PRUNING

Mow your **liriope** beds before the new growth emerges in the spring. Browned or unsightly leaves of **mondo grass** can also be cut back at this time.

Cut back the winterscorched or winterkilled leaves and shoots

Vines aren't just for inground plantings; you can grow some, like strawberries, in pots!

# HELPFUL HINTS FOR CALCULATING NUMBER OF GROUND COVER PLANTS

To determine how many ground cover plants you'll need, refer to the following plant spacing table:

| Area (sq. feet) | Square Spacing* | | | | | | | |
|---|---|---|---|---|---|---|---|---|
| | 4 in. | 6 in. | 8 in. | 10 in. | 12 in. | 15 in. | 18 in. | 24 in. |
| 25 | 225 | 100 | 56 | 36 | 25 | 16 | 11 | 6 |
| 50 | 450 | 200 | 113 | 72 | 50 | 32 | 22 | 12 |
| 100 | 900 | 400 | 225 | 144 | 100 | 64 | 44 | 25 |
| 200 | 1,800 | 800 | 450 | 288 | 200 | 128 | 89 | 50 |
| 300 | 2,700 | 1,200 | 675 | 432 | 300 | 192 | 133 | 75 |
| 1,000 | 9,000 | 4,000 | 2,250 | 1,440 | 1,000 | 641 | 444 | 250 |
| Spacing Multiplier | 9 | 4 | 2.25 | 1.44 | 1 | 0.64 | 0.44 | 0.25 |

*"on center" spacing (plants are spaced from the center of one plant to the center of the next one)
For an area not found in the chart, use the following formula:
area in square feet x spacing multiplier = number of plants needed
OR use this simple formula: $N = \dfrac{A}{D^2}$

Where  N = the number of plants in a given bed;
       A = the area of the bed in square inches, and
       D = the distance in inches between plants in the row and between rows.

of **St. John's-wort** before new growth begins, using a pair of pruning shears or a nylon string trimmer.

Spring-flowering vines such as **Carolina jessamine, Armand clematis**, and **crossvine** should be pruned as necessary after flowering. Remove any dead or damaged shoots and cut back others to keep the vine in bounds.

Thin out the congested shoots of fall-flowering vines such as **sweet autumn clematis** (C. terniflora) before growth begins since it flowers on current-season's shoots.

## PROBLEMS

Early this month, apply an oil spray before new growth emerges as described in January. Use a dormant oil if the plant is still dormant; if not, use a summer oil.

Sanitation is a cost-effective way to reduce disease problems. Rake out dead leaves from ground covers and prune out any dead, diseased, or broken limbs from vines. Before treating with a fungicide, identify the disease and determine if chemical control is warranted.

Ground cover beds should be kept relatively free of weeds until they are dense enough to crowd them out. Instead of handpulling or mulching, you can control weeds with a pre-emergent herbicide, which kills germinating weeds before they appear. See p. 23 for pointers on selecting a pre-emergent herbicide.

# APRIL
## VINES & GROUND COVERS

### PLANNING

Take pictures of various views to see where vines and ground covers can be used to bring color to otherwise nondescript areas. Use variegated plants to add the illusion of light to a dark area. Shade-loving ground covers such as **hosta**, **ivy**, **variegated liriope**, **variegated pachysandra**, **wild ginger**, and **variegated Asian jasmine** can be suitable choices. Take a look at the color of your home, fences, and paving to see if any ground covers can be used to unite and harmonize these features with the landscape.

### PLANTING

Sow seeds of tender summer-flowering annual vines in the garden after the last expected freeze; they will flower in mid-summer to fall.

Some seeds require special treatment prior to sowing to encourage germination. The seeds of **morning glory** and **moonflower** (*Ipomoea alba*) should be nicked with a knife or file and then soaked overnight to allow water to be absorbed by the seed for germination to occur.

### CARE

A few weeks after the last area freeze, bring your **mandevilla**, **allamanda**, **Queens wreath**, and other tropical vines outdoors. Before planting, set them in a shaded location for about a week or two; move it to a partially shaded location the following week. Then, plant them in a partially shaded location out of the hot afternoon sun. Fertilize every other month from spring through fall with a soluble houseplant fertilizer such as 20-20-20. To make overwintering easier, you can keep the plants growing in their black nursery pot and bury the whole thing so it's easier to lift the plant in the fall.

### WATERING

Water any newly planted vines or ground covers. Check the soil in the rootball regularly and water it when necessary.

### FERTILIZING

Fertilize ground covers and vines based on need. Vines may not need fertilizer if they look robust and are vigorously growing. Excessive fertilizer may encourage leafy growth at the expense of flowers, and vigorous vines may become unmanageable and require excessive pruning.

Hostas can be beautiful ground-covers, alone or in beds such as under this crapemyrtle.

# HELPFUL HINTS FOR MANAGING WISTERIA

A common question asked by exasperated gardeners is: "Why doesn't my **wisteria** bloom?" First of all, bear in mind that **Chinese** and **Japanese wisterias** in general may require five or six years before flowering. If your plant was seed-propagated or is an unnamed cultivar, you may have to keep waiting—perhaps for several more years. 'Amethyst Falls' **American wisteria** is an exception. It blooms the first year from cuttings and sporadically throughout the summer. My best advice is to plant 'Amythyst Falls' **American wisteria**.

**Wisteria** can be encouraged to bloom by meeting certain cultural requirements. It should be planted in full sun and in a fertile, well-drained site. Fertilize only when necessary. Excessive fertilization, especially with nitrogen, triggers leafy shoot growth at the expense of flowers.

Superphosphate is often touted as an elixir for flowering. If adequate levels of phosphorus are already present in the soil as determined by the results of a soil test, additional amounts are wasteful.

Prune properly. Avoid indiscriminate hacking, which inspires vigorous vegetative growth and further delays flowering. Instead, aim to restrict growth to spurlike shoots that produce the flowers. Flower buds form on previous-year's wood. In midsummer, cut the lateral shoots in half or just beyond the sixth or seventh leaf. New shoots may break from buds behind the cut; wait until they have developed one or two leaves, then cut them back beyond this point as well. In late winter before bud-break, shorten the side shoots coming off the main framework branches to three or four buds. Over time, these shoots will be converted to short, flowering spurs. Head back the main branches to three or four buds.

Remove dead, dying, or diseased branches as soon as you notice them. Thin out branches which are not growing in the direction you want. In addition to pruning the top, pruning the roots in the fall may further coerce your **wisteria** to bloom. Root-prune as if you were going to transplant the vine. Divide the root zone area into four quadrants. Select two quadrants on opposite sides of the rootball and excavate a trench 8 to 12 inches deep. Slice the roots cleanly with a sharp spade (pruning shears may be necessary for thick roots), and then backfill.

Water your **wisteria** during dry periods if the foliage begins to wilt. Once it finally flowers, expect it to bloom in subsequent years.

 ## PRUNING

Prune **Carolina jessamine, wisteria**, and other spring-flowering vines after flowers have faded.

If you want to cut **sweet pea** flowers, collect them when at least one flower in a cluster has fully opened and the others are just beginning to unfurl. They can last up to ten days in a vase.

 ## PROBLEMS

Watch out for aphids, whiteflies, spider mites, and euonymus scale. Evaluate the injury and decide if pest control measures are warranted.

Large-flowered **clematis** is highly susceptible to a notorious fungal disease called clematis wilt. See May Problems p. 243 for description and controls.

Handpull bittercress, chickweed, henbit, and other winter annuals before they go to seed. Weeds can be hoed out, but lightly, so as not to disturb the ground covers. Grassy weeds can be controlled with a selective post-emergent grass herbicide.

# MAY

## VINES & GROUND COVERS

 PLANNING

This month, keep an eye out for troubling spots in the landscape. If you've been struggling to grow turfgrass in an area that receives less than four hours of sunlight and you choose not to thin out the tree canopy to admit more sunlight, consider evergreen shade-loving ground covers. Some shade-loving ground covers that can be used in place of turf are **English ivy**, **liriope**, **pachysandra** (northern areas), **mondo grass**, **periwinkle** (*Vinca minor*), **Asian jasmine** (southern areas), and **carpet bugleweed** (*Ajuga*).

English ivy can be an excellent substitute for turf.

 PLANTING

It's a good time to dig and divide those crowded **liriope** borders. You may be able to find enough neighbors to share the bounty. Plant container-grown vines and ground covers, but be careful—they'll need attention after planting until they get established. Make sure you're familiar with the plant's site preferences prior to planting. Plant seeds or seedlings of annual vines like **morning glory**, **moonflower**, and **scarlet runner bean**. Plant the summer annuals you sowed indoors into the garden after the last freeze in your area.

 CARE

Mulch vines and ground covers to suppress weeds and to conserve moisture. Organic mulches will break down and enrich the soil with nutrients. Create supports for annual vines before they become a tangled mess. Use strings, trellises, or other supports, making sure that they will be strong enough to support the weight of the vines. Train newly planted vines onto their vertical supports by securing one end of the string to the support and the other end to a rock or a stick driven next to the vine. As the vine grows, use soft twine or nylon to tie the vine to the support until it begins to twine or cling.

 WATERING

May can be a dry month. Water newly planted vines and ground covers.

 FERTILIZING

Ground cover plants can be fertilized to encourage their spread. If vines need to be fertilized, avoid adding too much, which can make them produce a lot of leaves at the expense of flowers.

 PRUNING

Limit pruning to plants that have already finished flowering.

## PROBLEMS

Aphids, Japanese beetles, and spider mites can be a problem. Look for spider mites on **juniper**, **pachysandra**, and other ground covers (see Shrubs p. 194).

Watch out for snails and slugs on your ground covers. See p. 286 for descriptions and controls.

Several fungi cause leaf spots on **English**, **Algerian**, and other **ivies**. A bacterial disease called bacterial spot and canker is more serious because it attacks the leaves and produces cankers—discolored areas of dead tissue—on the stems, which result in dieback. Clip off infected leaves. Prune out and discard dead or dying plants. Identify the particular disease before seeking control with a fungicide.

Leaf and stem blight is a serious pest of **pachysandra**—brown blotches appear on the leaves and spread to the stems. Remove and discard infected plants. To avoid this blight, rake up and compost any leaves in the fall. Fallen leaves create moist conditions that favor the growth and spread of disease.

Scale insects are often associated with leaf and stem blight. Control them with a horticultural oil or other insecticide.

Large-flowered **clematis** are highly susceptible to a notorious fungal disease called clematis wilt. The disease strikes in early summer, often when plants are on the verge of flowering. Although wilted leaves and stems that droop and turn black are the first signs, the fungus initially attacks the stem close to the soil line, invading cracked, damaged, or weak tissue. Lesions or discolored areas associated with the fungus girdling the stem can usually be seen below the first pair of wilted leaves.

Despite its devastating appearance, clematis wilt is rarely fatal. Even when all topgrowth is killed, new healthy shoots can emerge from basal buds below the soil surface. This is the reason for the recommendation that clematis be planted with the crown at a depth of 2½ inches below soil level.

Prune back infected stems to healthy tissue and discard the trimmings. Fertilize and water to encourage regrowth. To encourage the production of woody tissue on the lower stem, pinch out the tips of new shoots when they reach 2 to 3 inches in length. Carefully tie the shoots that emerge from below the pinch to avoid damage from wind and rain.

At present there is no registered fungicide for controlling clematis wilt. You may want to plant some of the smaller-flowered **clematis** such as C. alpina, C. macropetala, C. viticella, and their hybrids, which are less susceptible to clematis wilt.

Juniper tip blight, caused by a fungus called Phomopsis, attacks the tips of **shore** and **creeping junipers** and others in the spring. The dead branches gradually turn gray. Tiny black dots on recently killed needles are the fruiting bodies of the fungus. Prune out infected plant parts and discard them, since this fungus survives in dead and decaying plant material.

Handpull weeds when they're young. Try not to put off this chore until next weekend. Hoeing and maintaining a shallow mulch layer will also help. If you use a nonselective herbicide containing glyphosate (Roundup®), glufosinate (Finale®), or one containing potassium salts of fatty acids (Sharpshooter®), use a piece of cardboard to shield your desirable plants from any accidental contact with the herbicide. Apply the herbicide according to label directions in the early morning or late evening when the air is still (to reduce the chances of drift).

# JUNE
## VINES & GROUND COVERS

### PLANNING

Take notes on your vines and ground covers this month and over the next few months and record your observations in your gardening journal. Take notes on bloom times, ornamental features, growth rates, and pest problems. Use this information to begin making plans to correct any problems or to make arrangements to replace some of the poorly performing plants.

### PLANTING

You can still plant container-grown vines and ground covers from nurseries and garden centers. Get them into the ground as soon as possible and water faithfully.

### CARE

Train the new growth of **clematis, Confederate jasmine, swamp jessamine, trumpet honeysuckle,** and other twining vines to guide them onto the trellis. Use soft twine to give the new shoots a start. Keep the "feet" of your **clematis** cool by creating shade with shrubs or planting a ground cover or perennial that will not be invasive. Some good **clematis**

companions are **hardy geranium** (*Geranium*), **candytuft, creeping phlox, coral bells, lamb's ear,** and most **veronicas**.

### WATERING

Apply water as needed to keep newly planted ground covers and vines from wilting. Use soaker hoses to water ground covers on slopes; this will reduce water runoff and soil erosion. If you have an automated irrigation system, water for short periods rather than all at once, reducing the chance of runoff. Keep ground covers and vines mulched with compost, pine straw, or shredded wood.

### FERTILIZING

Follow soil-test results when fertilizing your vines and ground covers. Supplement mulch with well-rotted horse or cow manure to add nutrients.

### PRUNING

Limit your pruning to vines that have already flowered on last year's growth.

### PROBLEMS

Look for the telltale signs of these pests: beetles chew holes in leaves and feed on flower buds and flowers; aphids occur in clusters near the tips of shoots and their feeding causes leaves to become wrinkled, sticky, and sometimes coated with a black sooty mold; spider mites cause yellow or bronze stippling on the leaf surface; thrips damage flower buds, creating streaks or spots on the open blooms and brown edges on flower buds that fail to open.

Avoid overhead watering and remove spent flowers and dead or dying leaves. Keeping plants clean will reduce the chances of infection. Crown rot is the only serious pest of **ajuga** or **carpet bugleweed** (*Ajuga reptans*). Look for a roughly circular patch of dead or dying plants with blackened leaves. A "cottony" fungus may be visible in damp, shady areas. The roots of affected plants are often discolored and rotted and can be easily lifted from the ground. Remove dead and dying plants. In the future, provide good, well-drained conditions and avoid excess watering. Infested areas can be treated with a fungicide prior to replanting. Avoid replanting if you can't improve drainage.

## HELPFUL HINTS FOR PROPAGATING CLEMATIS

A simple way to propagate vines is by layering. Here's how to layer a **clematis** vine:

1. In the spring select one or two dormant shoots of last year's wood.

2. With a sharp knife, start about $1/2$ inch away from a node (the point of attachment of the leaves and buds) and make an angled cut halfway into the underside of the stem toward the node.

3. To encourage rooting, dust the wound with a rooting hormone, bend the stem over, and bury that portion of the stem 2 inches deep. A stiff U-shaped wire can be used to peg the stem into the ground so that it doesn't pop up.

4. Secure the growing tip to a cane or pole so it can grow upward.

5. Lightly mulch the layered stem and keep the soil moist.

6. Every month or two, check the stem for any roots. Give the stem a tug, and if it feels well rooted, sever it from the parent plant.

Vigorous vines may form roots in a few weeks, while others may be rooted by the end of the growing season.

Clematis (here 'Madame Julia Correvon') flower best when trained to a support.

Choose another plant such as **liriope** that is more tolerant.

Handpull or hoe out any weeds to prevent them from stealing water and nutrients. Suppress their emergence with a layer of mulch over any bare ground. Sheets of newspaper camouflaged with grass clippings or other organic matter will suppress subsequent weed seed sprouting.

# JULY
## VINES & GROUND COVERS

 PLANNING

If you're going on vacation during this month, plan on finding someone to take care of your plants while you're gone. Not only does this keep up the appearance of the plants, it also makes it look as if someone is home. If you'll be gone for an extended time, these tasks will need attention:

• Water newly planted ground covers and vines.

• Edge the ground cover beds

• Trim vines that are escaping from their allotted space.

 PLANTING

Has the lawn beneath your trees disappeared? Extend the mulch area out to or beyond the drip line of your trees, or try planting **ajuga**, **ivy**, **liriope**, **vinca**, or other shade-tolerant ground covers beneath the trees (this chore can wait until fall).

**Clematis** can be propagated by seed, but the seedlings will not be identical to the parent; this method is usually reserved for species and not cultivars. Here's how to start **clematis** from seed:

1. When the seedheads have turned brown, you can collect the seeds. Select the swollen ones.

2. In general, **clematis** seeds require cold stratification at 40 degrees F. To stratify the seeds, fill a plastic bag with equal parts damp peat moss and perlite. Remove the long feathery "tails" (the styles) from the seeds before mixing them with the medium.

3. Place the bag in the refrigerator for three months.

4. Sow the seeds in a flat filled with the same mix, covering them lightly. Move the flat to a location in bright, indirect sunlight and water as needed.

5. Seeds can take from three weeks to several months or longer to sprout. When the seedlings have developed at least one pair of true leaves, transplant them into 3-inch pots filled with standard potting mix.

 CARE

Use compost, shredded bark, or pine straw to mulch around ground covers and vines. You can also use shredded wood, especially if you've got piles of it from stumps that have been ground. However, you must let shredded wood age for several months before using; fresh wood will rob the soil of nitrogen.

Sprinkle the wood with a few shovelsful of soil to introduce organisms to promote decomposition and also sprinkle with fertilizer containing nitrogen to feed the bacteria.

 WATERING

See June p. 244.

 FERTILIZING

Fertilize your vines and ground covers if you are still working on getting them to fill in. Otherwise, there is no need to feed now unless plants look malnourished. Water is necessary to make the fertilizer available to the plant roots, and it's also important to keep the new growth healthy and alive.

 PRUNING

Ground covers that have become overgrown need to be pruned back into shape. Make thinning cuts down in the plant so the cuts will be hidden. Use sharp pruning shears to make clean cuts that will heal rapidly. Dead, broken, or diseased limbs and shoots should be removed any time during the growing season.

A good, sharp pair of pruners is invaluable.

Your **wisteria** may need to be pruned to encourage the production of spurs, which will provide next year's floral display. Cut the lateral shoots in half or just beyond the sixth or seventh leaf. New shoots may break from buds behind the cut; wait until they have developed one or two leaves, then cut them back beyond this point as well.

## PROBLEMS

Pests to watch for include aphids, spider mites, and beetles. Aphids and spider mites can be washed from plants with a strong stream of water. Use insecticidal soap and insecticides for aphids and miticides to keep mites in check.

In northern parts of Alabama and Mississippi, watch out for Japanese beetles this month. These big slow-flying bugs, metallic green with bronze wing covers, skeletonize leaves, leaving only a lacy network of leaf veins after their feeding. They also feed on flowers. Pick them off and discard them into a jar of soapy water. Neem can be applied to the leaves to reduce feeding by the adults. Other insecticides can be used for heavy infestations. If you choose to use Japanese beetle traps, place them far away from your susceptible shrubs. Thankfully, there's only one generation a year.

Kabatina blight is a disease that attacks the tips of **shore** and **creeping junipers** and others in the summer. Prune out infected plant parts and discard them, since this fungus survives in dead and decaying plant material.

Start pulling weeds out of ground cover beds. Maintain a shallow layer of mulch to suppress them. The weeds are competing with the ground covers for light, water, and nutrients. Eventually the ground covers will fill in and shade the soil, naturally preventing weed seeds from germinating. Apply a pre-emergent herbicide to young plantings to prevent weeds from sprouting on top of mulch in spaces between plants.

# AUGUST
## VINES & GROUND COVERS

 PLANNING

Summer takes its toll on plants. High nighttime heat and humidity, pests, and storms with high winds are a few natural problems faced in the Deep South. Since the cool temperatures of fall are ideal for planting new vines and ground covers or transplanting established plants, spend some time in the early morning or late afternoon evaluating your landscape. Make plans to replace your annual flowering vines with something more vigorous or tolerant of the summertime conditions. If you've tired of pruning a highly vigorous specimen, make plans to remove it this fall, giving it to a friend who's willing to take it on. For ground cover plantings that haven't filled out very much, determine why they didn't and make plans to fertilize them. Keep them well watered and mulched during their establishment period. Take along your gardening journal and jot down notes for things to do next month.

 PLANTING

You can still plant container-grown vines and ground covers. This is a very stressful time, however, and unless there is sufficient water available you may want to wait until September or October when the temperatures are more favorable for planting.

 CARE

Collect seeds from annual vines and store them for planting next year. Actively growing vines may need to be secured to their moorings. Vines that do not have tendrils will have to be tied with soft twine. Check the fastenings on other shoots to see that the stems aren't being girdled.

 WATERING

Apply water as needed to vines and ground covers to prevent them from wilting. Check the soil before watering and look at the plant to see if water is necessary. When you water, water deeply, and thoroughly wet the soil.

 FERTILIZING

If your vines and ground covers need to be fertilized, water afterwards to make the nutrients available to the plants. Otherwise, wait until next spring when new growth begins.

 PRUNING

Remove dead, damaged, or infested shoots or limbs. Trim renegade shoots from tangled vines.

 PROBLEMS

Inspect your vines and ground covers for aphids and spider mites. Evaluate the extent of injury and take action if the health of the vine or ground cover is in jeopardy.

Nematodes are microscopic organisms that live in the soil and attack the roots of plants. They are more commonly found in coarse-textured sandy soils than in fine-textured clay soils. See Roses July Problems p. 166 for more information.

Watch out for leaf spot diseases. Infected leaves can be trimmed out and discarded. Severe infections can be treated with a fungicide. If fungicides are required on a regular basis, plan on replacing the vine.

See July p. 247 for advice on controlling weeds.

## HELPFUL HINTS

• If the flowers in your perennial garden are quickly fading in the hot summer sun, think about creating a trellis and covering it with vines. This will protect the flowers from the hot afternoon sun and make them last a little longer.

• To cover large areas inexpensively with a ground cover such as **liriope** or **lily turf** (*Liriope muscari*) or **mondo grass** (*Ophiopogon japonicus*), purchase large pots and tease apart the clumps. Plant individual plants at the appropriate spacing.

• Erect a trellis on the south-facing side of your house a few feet away to shade the house from the sun. If you have an attractive trellis, you can even use deciduous or annual vines that will allow sunlight to warm your home during the winter months yet shade it in the summer. Keeping the vine away from the house will keep it away from siding or shingles.

To protect nearby plantings from drift, you can cut out the bottom of a plastic gallon milk jug; the sides form a shield.

# SEPTEMBER
## VINES & GROUND COVERS

### PLANNING

For something completely different, grow well-behaved vines on some your shrubs and trees. Draping vines on other plants allows you to create eye-catching combinations. Use flowers and leaves to create contrasting colors and textures, extending the flowering display of a tree with flowering vines, and dressing up otherwise boring plants with a feather boa of vines. Annual vines good for this purpose include **black-eyed-Susan vine**, **love-in-a-puff** (*Cardiospermum halicacabum*), and **moonvine**. Some choice perennial vines are **clematis**, 'Tangerine Beauty' **cross vine**, **potato vine** (*Solanum jasminoides*), and **hairy Virginia creeper** (*Parthenocissus quinquefolia* var. *hirsuta*). To select the right vine-shrub/tree associations, keep these points in mind:

1. The vine should not be too small compared to the shrub, or so vigorous that it completely engulfs the shrub.

2. Both vine and shrub or tree should share the same preferences for soil, water, and light.

3. Dabble with mixing and matching flower colors, leaf textures, and bloom times.

To help vines that need a little structural help in starting their ascent, use fishing line, twigs, or the black plastic bird netting used for protecting fruit trees.

### PLANTING

Fall is prime-time planting season. Plant container-grown vines and ground covers this month. Water the plants well following planting and until they become established. It's a good time to transplant ground covers to fill in bare areas. Some ground covers such as **euonymus** and **English ivy** already have visible roots. Prune a stem and bury the shoots. Roots will form and you can start another ground cover bed.

### CARE

**Mandevilla** is a common "mailbox vine" that blooms all summer long. This native of tropical South America should not be exposed to freezing temperatures. If you want to overwinter your **mandevilla** indoors and replant it outside next spring, there are two ways of doing this. The first approach is to root stem cuttings before the first expected freeze:

1. Take 4- to 6-inch-long cuttings that include a "heel" or portion of the bark and stem.

2. Dip the bottom of each stem in a rooting hormone and insert the stems in a sterile well-drained medium such as equal parts peat and perlite.

3. Water them and enclose the pot inside a clear plastic bag. Move the pot to a warm spot receiving bright, indirect light.

4. After the cuttings have sufficiently rooted—usually in eight to twelve weeks—take the pot out of the bag and repot the cuttings into larger pots, using your favorite houseplant potting mix. Gradually expose the rooted **mandevillas** to brighter light. Eventually move them to a window that receives bright light. A spot on your fluorescent light table where the **mandevillas** can receive light fourteen to sixteen hours a day would be ideal.

The second approach is to rescue the entire plant and bring it indoors:

1. Prune back the plant to a manageable height of about 2 feet, then lift it out of the ground with as much of the intact root system as possible. Shake off some of the soil and pot it up. Any houseplant potting soil may be used, as long as it allows good drainage and is heavy enough to support the plant.

2. Quarantine the plant for several days before moving it indoors. If you see any insects that may have hitched a ride,

take action and control them immediately to prevent them from attacking other plants. When you're confident that your **mandevilla** is pest-free, move it to a window that receives bright, direct sunlight.

3. Water the **mandevilla** often enough to keep the soil from drying out. In the fall and winter, locate the plant in a cool room with a night temperature of 60 to 65 degrees F. (although temperatures as low as 45 to 50 degrees can be tolerated). Water sparingly and cease fertilizing.

4. In late winter or early spring before growth begins, prune out old, crowded stems and shorten others. Flowers are produced on the current season's growth. Next year, a few weeks after the last freeze in your area, bring your **mandevilla** outdoors.

5. Before planting it in its permanent location, acclimatize the vine to the outdoors. First set it in a shaded location for about a week; move it to a partially shaded location the following week. Finally, plant it in its permanent location in full sun.

## WATERING

Water all newly planted vines and ground covers thoroughly until they become established.

## FERTILIZING

If your vines and ground covers have produced sufficient growth this year, fertilizing may not be necessary. If you choose to fertilize, rely on soil test results to apply the nutrients required by your plants. See pp. 233 to 234. If they are showing their fall colors, wait until next year.

## PRUNING

Any major pruning should be saved until late winter or early spring. Remove dead, damaged, insect-infested, diseased, and stray shoots now.

## PROBLEMS

Aphids and spider mites may still be active. Evaluate the extent of injury and decide if pest control measures are warranted.

Clean up fallen leaves. They can harbor diseases and insect pests over the winter if allowed to remain on the ground.

Watch out for germinating winter annuals such as annual bluegrass, chickweed, and henbit. Remove them now while they're young and easy to remove. Don't wait until spring when they'll be well established

Some people allow ivy to climb trees, but it's really not well-behaved enough to do so.

and poised to go to seed. In northern parts of Alabama and Mississippi, you may still be able to prevent some sprouting with a pre-emergent herbicide. The earlier you use it, the better.

# OCTOBER
## VINES & GROUND COVERS

### PLANNING

If you have a steep slope that is dangerous to mow, plan a few low-maintenance solutions:

1. Cover it with some good slope-stabilizing ground covers. These include **Asian star jasmine, daylily, juniper, liriope, periwinkle** (*Vinca minor*), **willowleaf cotoneaster** (*Cotoneaster salicifolius*), and **winter jasmine** (*Jasminum nudiflorum*). Be sure to choose hardy ground covers adapted to your region and match their preferences for sunlight or shade with the site.

2. On very steep slopes, build a retaining wall to reduce the height of the slope. Above and below the wall create usable gardening space. If the wall is less than 1 1/2 feet in height, it could be a do-it-yourself project.

3. Long and steep slopes can be terraced with a series of walls to create several layers of gardening space.

### PLANTING

Interplant spring-flowering bulbs with your ground covers for splashes of color next year. Start planting vines and ground covers this month so they will become established by next summer. Planting can continue through winter if weather allows.

Certain types of cotoneaster are excellent ground covers for slopes or other hard-to-mow areas.

The keys to growing **sweet peas** are cool weather, full sun, and fertile soil. Here's how to plant them:

1. Select a well-drained site in full sun. Prepare the bed by adding generous amounts of organic matter such as compost. Add ground limestone if the soil is acid; **sweet peas** prefer a nearly neutral soil pH.

2. Sow seed now or next month, or wait until very early spring of next year as early as the soil can be worked. Consider cultivating **sweet peas** that combine colorful flowers with a heady aroma—included in this group are 'Firecrest', 'Maggie May', and 'White Supreme'. Improve germination by soaking the seeds in warm water for a couple of days.

Alternatively, you can sandpaper the seeds just enough to make a hole in the seed coat.

3. Space the seeds 4 to 6 inches apart and plant them 2 inches deep. Expect the seeds to germinate in two to three weeks.

4. When the seedlings reach 4 inches in height, sidedress with a complete fertilizer such as 10-10-10 at a rate of 3 tablespoons per 10 feet of row.

5. Mulch the seedlings with a 2-inch layer of mulch to conserve moisture.

6. Support the climbing types with wire fencing or string. When the plants flower, remove the faded flower stalks to encourage repeat flowering and provide plenty of moisture during the growing season.

## CARE

Dig up **sweet potato** tubers of 'Blackie', 'Margarita', 'Pink Frost', and others, and store them in a cool, dry location for replanting next year. The tubers have eyes that will sprout once they're back in the ground.

Refresh mulch on newly planted vines and ground covers. Annual vines that have been killed with the first freeze should be cut back from their supports and composted or buried in the vegetable garden.

## HELPFUL HINTS FOR STEEP SLOPES

When planting a ground cover on a steep slope, reduce the need for handweeding by using a geotextile or landscape fabric which will curb weed growth. Follow these steps for installing landscape fabric:

1. Kill the existing vegetation with a clear plastic sheet or a nonselective herbicide. (See p. 85; solarizing is generally done in hot weather.)

2. When the vegetation has been killed, lay down the fabric, making sure you overlap the pieces of fabric and tack them down tightly with U-shaped nails.

3. Place the potted ground covers on top of the fabric in staggered rows. Stagger the plants across the slope to reduce the occurrence of soil erosion from water runoff (and to keep them from looking like rows of soldiers when you're finished).

4. Cut an "x" through the fabric and dig a planting hole. Avoid spilling any soil on top of the fabric because it may contain weed seeds.

5. Fold the x back down after planting. Try to avoid leaving any large gaps which can be invaded by weeds.

6. Apply a 2- to 3-inch layer of pine straw over the fabric.

## WATERING

See September p. 250.

## FERTILIZING

Do not fertilize vines and ground covers when they or other plants are displaying their fall colors—wait until next year.

## PRUNING

Limit pruning to the removal of dead, damaged, or diseased branches and wayward shoots.

## PROBLEMS

Spider mites can still be active. Controlling the overwintering eggs with a dormant horticultural oil this fall when the plants go dormant may be all that's needed to kill the eggs and any active mites that may be present.

Clean up plantings to get rid of diseased leaves.

Weeds continue to germinate and emerge. Handpull them while they're young and suppress their growth with mulch.

# NOVEMBER
## VINES & GROUND COVERS

## PLANNING

Throughout history gardeners have showcased their vines on structures that ranged from the simple to the elegant. You can buy ready-made fan-shaped or rectangular trellises at garden centers. Make sure they are sturdy enough for the vines you

This goldflame honeysuckle is being trained through the lattice of this fence.

choose. If you're a do-it-your-selfer, you can plan to build your own this month after you decide on the kinds of vines you're going to support. Twining vines with long flexible stems—**hyacinth bean**, **morning glory**, **moonvine**, and **trumpet honeysuckle**—need to wrap them- selves around something like a string, wire, or trellis. They climb best on narrow, vertically-oriented supports.

Climbing vines that use tendrils need a support that's small enough for their threadlike "fin-gers" to grasp. Fine lattice work or a structure that includes wire, string, or plastic mesh is suitable for **passionflower** (*Passiflora*) and **sweet pea** (*Lathyrus odora-tus*). Chicken wire can be wrapped around a freestanding pole or pillar to give the vines something to hold onto. A tripod is a simple way of mixing these climbers into borders of annual and perennials.

Use your gardening journal to record any observations about the expected vigor and eventual weight of these vines. If you're going to be growing a heavy-weight like **Japanese** (*Wisteria floribunda*) or **Chinese wisteria** (*W. sinensis*), be prepared to build a sturdy structure and foundation. Arbors need to have 6x6 posts set in concrete with 4x4 cross members. **American**

**wisteria** isn't as heavy and does not require an arbor of this magnitude.

## PLANTING

Plant container-grown vines and ground covers. In the colder areas, mulch with oak leaves, composted wood chips, shredded bark, pine needles, or shredded leaves to moderate soil temperature.

## CARE

Don't hesitate to tie uncoopera-tive vines in place with twine or twist ties. This will help your **clematis**, **climbing hydrangea**, and **Confederate jasmine** find their way across arbors.

## WATERING

Fall is usually dry, so don't rely on Mother Nature to water newly planted vines and ground covers. A few weeks after plant-ing, start cutting back on water-ing to every few days or longer, especially with cloudy, rainy, or cool weather. Eventually you can water on a weekly or "as-needed" basis, testing the soil and rootball for moisture. Estab-lished plants, especially evergreens, should be watered during the winter months so they won't go into the winter on the dry side.

## FERTILIZING

Do not fertilize vines and ground covers at this time. Wait until next year. Keep in mind that if they have already filled in their allotted space and have grown vigorously this past year, fertilizing may not be necessary. In fact, it can result in a lot of excess, junglelike growth that would have to be removed with a machete.

## PRUNING

Limit any removal to dead, damaged, or overly long branches.

## PROBLEMS

If there is any evidence of scale on vines and ground covers, spray with dormant oil in late fall and again in early spring when the plants are dormant.

Rake up fallen leaves from your ground covers and compost them or bury them in the vegetable garden. See the Helpful Hints.

## HELPFUL HINTS FOR COLLECTING FALLEN LEAVES

When growing ground covers beneath trees such as **maples** and **oaks**, it's a chore to remove fallen leaves from the ground cover beds. (The leaves should be removed because they can smother the ground cover plants.) There are several ways of managing these leaves:

• Blow off the leaves into long piles and shred them with a lawn mower. Then return them to the bed as an attractive mulch. Shredding the leaves beforehand reduces their volume, increases surface area to speed-up decomposition, and keeps them secured to the soil surface.

• Use netting to capture the leaves. Buy large plastic bird netting sold for protecting fruit trees and stretch it over the ground cover in the fall. It won't be noticeable from a distance and it won't crush the ground cover. After the leaves have collected on the net, drag it off or roll it up and move the leaves to an area where they can be shredded with the lawn mower and composted or used as mulch and sifted back into the ground cover.

• If harvesting and shredding the leaves proves to be a daunting chore, transplant the ground covers and allow the leaves to fall naturally in place. If you want to convince your neighbors that not raking your leaves is a conscious decision, border this area with timbers, stones, or turf to impart a natural, forested design to your landscape.

Geotextile or landscape fabrics are synthetic mulch underliners that are used to suppress weeds on a long-term basis. When placed on the soil surface and covered with mulch, they enhance the ability of the mulch to suppress weeds. Geotextiles are woven and nonwoven fabrics of polypropylene or polyester that have been developed to replace black plastic. Black plastic, a solid polyethylene material, has been used underneath mulches to provide excellent control of annual weeds and suppress perennial weeds; black plastic isn't porous, however, and doesn't allow for air and water movement. Geotextiles overcome this disadvantage by admitting air and water. They should not be used in plantings where the fabric would inhibit rooting and spreading of the ground cover.

# DECEMBER
## VINES & GROUND COVERS

 PLANNING

Update your gardening journal this month and make plans for improvements next year. See if you've cured any of your trouble spots with vines and ground covers. Are there any other areas in the landscape that need to be fixed with a ground cover? Perhaps you'll have to replace the annual vines with perennial woody types to give you year-round privacy. Were pests a problem this season? Make plans to learn more about controlling the most troublesome insects and diseases by refining your pest control techniques or simply replacing the pest-prone plants with more resistant ones.

During the year you may have saved newspaper and magazine clippings of articles from local garden writers who touted certain ground covers and vines. Perhaps you wrote down comments from friends and others regarding some aspect of their gardening or the names of a few plants. Compile these notes and plan on acting on them next growing season.

 PLANTING

You can still plant vines and ground covers, especially in the warmer areas or anywhere the weather and soil conditions allow.

 CARE

Keep vines off wooden walls—the vines trap moisture and slow the drying of wood, which can encourage decay. When shading brick or masonry walls with clinging vines that have aerial rootlets or adhesive disks such as **English** and **Boston ivies** and **climbing hydrangea**, think twice before allowing them to cling to the walls. Once you allow them to climb on the walls, they're very difficult to remove. After you tear down the vine you're left with rootlets and disks that can only be removed with a stiff scrub brush.

Give **English ivy** a trim and pull it off house walls or trees. Ivy which grows up into a tree may eventually cover too much of the crown and cause the tree to die. Heavy infestations have been known to break tree limbs. Once **ivy** climbs it also flowers and sets seeds, leading to seedlings that can be a nuisance.

 WATERING

Pay special attention to watering newly planted vines and ground covers.

 FERTILIZING

Wait until spring when new growth begins before fertilizing vines and ground covers.

 PRUNING

Remove damaged branches and those overly long shoots that are being whipped around by the wind.

 PROBLEMS

Apply a dormant oil spray early in the month before new growth emerges to control overwintering insect and spider mite eggs. Read the label for cautions regarding the limits of high and low temperatures at the time of application.

Rake out the leaves and dispose of them in the compost pile, or bury them in the vegetable garden to reduce the amount of fungal spores next year.

Handpull any young winter annuals or cover them with a shallow layer of compost. Weeding is never fun, but the cooler temperatures can make it more bearable.

# WATER GARDENING

Compared to "terrestrial" gardening, water and bog gardening offers a different set of challenges and experiences. You'll be introduced to a whole new range of unique plants that don't mind "wet feet" or poorly drained soils.

You can introduce fish into your garden. Eventually you'll find that your simple water garden has become a complex ecosystem with dragonflies, tadpoles, frogs, toads, turtles, and birds.

## PLANNING

Before you start digging, you should plan. An underground water feature cannot be moved so easily. Choose the right location.

1. The plants need at least six hours of sun a day.

2. A spot near your home makes a good place to enjoy your water garden.

3. Putting a water garden beneath trees can result in maintenance problems—there are falling leaves and the potential for tree roots cracking the walls of hard pools. Besides, excavating around tree roots can harm the tree. If a site under a tree happens to be the best place, consider an aboveground water garden.

If you're going to create a belowground water garden, it can be made of a variety of materials:

• Natural mud-bottom ponds have clay bottoms that create a rubberlike waterproof seal.

• Flexible liners can be used to create any shape or size of pool.

• Polyethylene is the least expensive and least durable liner. Use the best grade and purchase enough so you can double it over itself to increase its thickness.

# CHAPTER TEN

• Polyvinyl chloride (PVC) liners are more flexible, durable, and longer-lasting than polyethylene. Depending on the gauge, they may last from five to twenty years.

• Rubber or synthetic rubber liners are even more durable and flexible than PVC. Two common materials are butyl rubber and ethylene propylene diene monomer rubber. They can last up to fifty years.

• Rigid preformed liners are made of fiberglass or plastic. Fiberglass liners are more durable and costly than plastic. Make sure the preformed pool is at least 24 inches deep if you want fish.

• Concrete pools are well suited for the warmer regions of Alabama and Mississippi; in colder areas, freezing temperatures can cause cracking unless the concrete is properly reinforced. Don't be timid about relying on an experienced professional.

See February p. 260 for step-by-step installation instructions.

## PLANTING

There are four groups of water garden plants:

1. Floating-leaved plants, such as lotus, water lilies, and water snowflakes, are rooted on the bottom of the pond and produce leaves and flowers on the surface.

2. Marginal or bog plants such as cannas, pickerel rush, and water irises grow in shallow water along the edges of ponds and generally have very showy flowers. Some marginals can handle either shallow or deep water levels, even dry areas, while others need a certain depth of water above their crowns. A vast majority need shallow water that is 2 to 6 inches deep over their crowns. Bog or marginal plants differ from moisture-loving plants, which will languish if their roots are waterlogged.

3. Free-floating plants float on the surface with their roots suspended in the water. They can spread rapidly, so use these plants with caution.

4. Submerged or oxygen-producing plants maintain the health of the water garden. These underwater "oxygenating" plants release oxygen into the water and absorb nutrients and carbon dioxide produced by animal wastes and decaying plants. They also provide food and shelter for fish.

Do not completely fill your water garden with plants. Only one-half to three-quarters of the pond surface should be covered with foliage. Refer to March Planting p. 262 for more information.

## CARE

Aquatic plants also need some attention during the season to keep them healthy and attractive. Prune and trim away dying or dead leaves on a regular basis. Any fallen leaves should be removed from the water.

Some plants will have to be removed when too numerous. Some can cover the entire water surface and will have to be periodically thinned out to expose the surface of the water to light.

Tropical water lilies and other tender plants will have to be lifted and overwintered indoors.

## WATERING

Maintain water levels throughout the season. To help the fish survive during hot weather it may be necessary to aerate the water in the pond.

## FERTILIZING

Use slow-release fertilizer pellets that are made for water plants. Other experts recommend making a sachet of fertilizer by wrapping a granular garden-type fertilizer in a paper towel; too much, however, can "burn" the plant. It may be best to use a fertilizer especially created for aquatic plants.

Bog plants do not feed as heavily as water lilies and lotuses. When fertilizing them, let their growth rate, flowering, and leaf color guide you.

## PROBLEMS

Most pests are controlled by scavengers and maintenance. Avoid using any insecticides or herbicides around the pond which may kill your fish and beneficial insects.

# JANUARY
## WATER GARDENING

### PLANNING

Whether you have a small container or a large pond, sit down and select the right plants for your water garden. As you swoon over the colorful catalogs, compile a list of plants that you'd like to add to your water garden. Study the ornamental features of each plant and their optimum water depth, but most important, know the plant's mature spread. Avoid focusing on the intense 6- to 7-inch-wide flower of the **hardy water lily** 'Escarboucle' without knowing that the plant will spread up to 7 feet. 'Pink Shadow', with 3 1/2-inch-wide off-white flowers, spreads half as much and would be a better choice for smaller pools and containers. If size is a limitation, consider dwarf cultivars, purchase fewer plants, or build a larger garden.

### PLANTING

Planting is for later in spring when you'll also have to divide and repot plants. If you don't have containers, aquatic plant fertilizer tablets, and pea gravel, get them now. Aquatic plants are commonly planted in pots for a number of reasons:

1. It keeps them from getting out of hand, which is very important when growing aquatic plants that can spread aggressively, such as **lotus** and **watershield** (*Brasenia schreberi*).

2. You can lift them for trimming, dividing, or storing for the winter without having to contend with a mass of roots.

3. You can easily set them at the appropriate depth and make regular adjustments.

4. It's very easy to remove them when it's time to clean the pool, which is best done in the spring before plant growth begins.

### CARE

Examine the **tropical water lilies** you overwintered indoors. Any tubers showing signs of rot should be discarded. Check to see that the sand is damp and hasn't dried out.

---

## HELPFUL HINTS

Some helpful formulas for water gardeners to determine how many plants and fish your pool can support:
- To determine the amount of water in your pool, use this simple formula: length x width x depth x 7.5 gallons/cubic foot = total gallons in the pond
- To determine the surface area for a square or rectangular pool, use this formula: length x width = surface area
- To calculate the volume of a rectangular pond, multiply the surface area by the depth: (length x width) x depth = volume
- To calculate the volume of a circular pool, use the formula: $\pi r^2$ or 3.14 x (1/2 the diameter x 1/2 the diameter) x depth = volume

- If you plan to dig a pond rather than construct an aboveground pool, find out where your underground utilities and pipes are located. Most gas, electric, water, and telephone companies will locate and mark their lines on your property. Either contact the company directly or call a toll-free "call before you dig" number to have your utility cables located and marked.

Be aware of any local building codes that may affect the placement of your water garden, its size, and depth. Anything that's deeper than a couple of feet could be classified as a pool, and pools often require fencing.

# FEBRUARY

## WATER GARDENING

## PLANNING

A number of plants are the "kudzus" of the aquatic world. When they escape into streams, lakes, and estuaries they form dense colonies which interfere with boating, fishing, and other recreational activities. They degrade water quality by reducing oxygen levels in the water and displace desirable plants. Millions of dollars are spent annually to control these thugs.

Beware of these commonly grown and ornamental plants that can escape and become invasive weeds. A few of the plants that are noxious weeds and potentially serious problems for the states' waterways include:

• **African elodea**
(*Lagarosiphon major*) – AL
• **Alligatorweed**
(*Alternanthra philoxeroides*) – AL
• **Arrowhead**
(*Sagittaria sagittifolia*) – AL
• **Brazilian elodea**
(*Egeria densa*) – AL & MS
• **Common reed**
(*Phragmites communis*) – AL
• **Eurasian watermilfoil**
(*Myriophyllum spicatum*) – AL
• **Giant salvinia**
(*Salvinia auriculata, S. biloba, S. herzogii, S. molesta*) – AL
• **Hydrilla**
(*Hydrilla verticallata*) – AL & MS

• **Melaleuca**
(*Malaleuca quinquenervia*) – AL
• **Monochoria**
(*Monochoria vaginalis*) – AL
• **Rooted water hyacinth**
(*Eichhornia azurea*) – AL
• **Water aloe**
(*Stratiotes aloides*) – AL
• **Water chestnut**
(*Trapa natans*) – AL
• **Water hyacinth**
(*Eichhornia crassipes*) – AL
• **Water spinach**
(*Ipomoea aquatica*) – AL

For more information on noxious aquatic weeds, contact your regional Extension agent who can put you in touch with the appropriate state government or university group, or both, who keep up to date on this subject. Also try these three sites: **www. invasive.org; http://plants.usda. gov/; or http://nis.gsmfc.org/**.

A good time to install a small water garden is in the spring when the ground can be worked. Here's how:

1. Outline the shape of a flexible liner with a rope or garden hose. Mark the border with spray paint, builder's chalk, lime, or sand. If you have a preformed pond, set it on the ground and mark its outline with the same marking materials.

2. Start digging from the edges to create an outline and excavate toward the center. Make the sides steeply sloped

(about a 20-degree angle from the vertical) to achieve good volume relative to surface area to limit algae problems.

3. Check the edge of the pond frequently as you dig to make sure it's level by placing a carpenter's level on top of a long straight piece of lumber laid across the hole. The edge should be even all around to prevent water from overflowing before it's completely full.

4. Create an underwater shelf along the inside wall to hold potted marginal or bog plants and rocks. The shelves are typically 10 inches long and about 18 inches wide (if raccoons are in your area, these shelves will be used as fishing platforms!). You can grow marginals in shallow water by placing them on clean bricks or upside-down flower pots.

5. Dig the hole at least 2 feet deep, allowing for a 1- to 2-inch layer of sand. With a preformed liner, dig the hole about 2 inches deeper and 3 to 5 inches wider than the liner.

6. For flexible liners, apply a 1- to 2-inch layer of damp river sand, old indoor-outdoor carpeting, or any other soft materials to protect the liner from sharp rocks.

To calculate the size of the pond liner, outline the area and decide on a depth.

1. Measure the length and width of the pool. If it's a circle or irregularly shaped, draw a square or rectangle around it and use the length and width of the square or rectangle.

2. Use this equation to calculate the length and width of your pond liner:

Length = maximum length of pond + (2 x maximum depth) + (2 x edging allowance)

Width = maximum width of pond + (2 x maximum depth) + (2 x edging allowance)

3. Center the liner over the hole and weigh down its edges with smooth stones or bricks. Slowly fill the pond with water. As the pond fills, gradually take the weights off the edges so the water will fill into the crevices. When the water comes within 1 inch of the top, shut it off and cut away any excess material, leaving about a foot beyond the rim. Line the edge of the pond with stones, pavers, bricks, or other suitable materials.

## HELPFUL HINTS FOR AVOIDING AQUATIC WEEDS

Submerged "oxygenating" plants that grow completely or mostly underwater produce oxygen as they photosynthesize. This dissolved oxygen is important for supporting aquatic life. The plants also provide food and cover. However, some of these oxygenators can become invasive and have been labeled aquatic nuisance weeds. **Anacharis** can be one of three possible species: **Canadian elodea** (*Elodea canadensis*), **Brazilian elodea** (*Egeria densa*), or **hydrilla** (*Hydrilla verticillata*). Only **Canadian elodea** can be legally sold in Alabama and Mississippi. When you purchase submerged plants, ask the scientific name of the plant. Here's where knowing its botanical name will help you make the right purchase. If you're buying "**anacharis**," make sure it's the right one.

4. For preformed pools, spread an inch or two of damp sand on the bottom. Set the form in the hole so the rim is just above ground level. Take it out and make any adjustments. When it's level, firmly pack soil around its edges. Fill the pool with water. Hide the rim with rocks or use a spreading ground cover.

## CARE

Check the tender aquatic plants you overwintered indoors. Make sure they're covered with water and don't allow them to dry out. Clean the pond of any debris.

Only Canadian elodea (also called anacharis) can legally be sold in Alabama or Mississippi. Find out the botanical name of what you're buying.

# MARCH
## WATER GARDENING

 PLANNING

If you're planning on introducing fish to your water garden, spend some time this month learning more about them. Visit your public library, visit water specialty centers, read mail-order catalogs, and talk to other water gardeners. Not only do fish add ornamental interest and movement, but they'll improve water quality as they feast on mosquitoes and their larvae, algae, and plant debris. The plants will be fertilized by the waste created by the fish, and the submerged plants will use the carbon dioxide they exhale to produce oxygen.

Many different kinds of fish are available, such as the typical goldfish-in-a-bowl variety (which can grow up to a foot in length in ponds), long-lived colorful koi, speedy golden orfes, and mosquito fish. If you lack experience and confidence with fish, start small with a few inexpensive goldfish. As you sharpen your water-gardening skills, you can add more fish later.

 PLANTING

Plant aquatics in nursery pots, plastic laundry baskets, shallow pans, and large tubs. Use a heavy clay-based garden soil that you can dig from your own yard. Bagged potting soil is too

light. Avoid amending it with peat moss, vermiculite, or perlite, which tend to float away. Submerged plants can be planted in containers filled with sand or tied to a stone so they're kept just below the water surface.

After you pot up your plant, add a 1-inch layer of pea or aquarium gravel on the surface to prevent the soil from muddying up the water. Before submersing the container, water it thoroughly and then place it in the pool.

In the warmer parts of Alabama or Mississippi, **hardy water lilies** may need to be divided every year or two. They can be divided at any time during the growing season, start-

Plastic laundry baskets can be used to hold aquatic plants.

ing six weeks before the last expected freeze. Here's how:

1. Lift the pot out of the pool and take the clump out of the pot.

2. Look along the length of the rhizome for buds or growing points called "eyes." Tiny lime-green or bronze leaves may be emerging from the growing point.

3. With a sharp knife or pruning shears, cut sections of the rhizome into 3- to 4-inch-long pieces or divisions that have eyes and accompanying roots.

4. Repot the division, making sure that the growing point is above the soil level.

Divide both **American lotus** (*Nelumbo lutea*) and **Asian lotus** (*N. nucifera*) at the same time you divide **hardy water lilies**.

About a month before the last expected freeze, check to see if the **tropical water lilies** you stored indoors over the winter have sprouted. If they haven't, put the tubers in water near a sunny windowsill to coerce them into growth. Once they've sprouted, pot them up in temporary pots:

1. Fill a 5-inch pot with soil and plant the tuber about ¼ inch deep. Add a layer of pebbles or gravel to the top and label it.

2. Move the pots to an aquarium or a large bucket. Add enough water so the tops of the pots are covered by 3 inches of water. The water should be 70 to 80 degrees F., so an aquarium heater may be necessary.

3. In two to six weeks, when new leaves have formed, move the plants into bright light.

4. Transplant the tubers into permanent containers (see May Planting p. 266). Wait until the water warms up to 70 degrees before placing them in your water garden. Very cold water can shock the plants, slowing down the growth of leaves and flowers for many weeks.

## CARE

Inspect the tender aquatic plants you kept indoors over the winter, making sure that they're healthy and haven't dried out. Keep the containers filled with water. If the area is too warm, move them to cooler temperatures of 40 to 50 degrees F.

Prune away any winterkilled leaves from the plants around your water garden before or when the new growth emerges. Compost these trimmings or bury them in the vegetable garden.

Remove any floating debris from the surface of the pool. If you have to empty and clean the pool, it's best to begin this job before plant growth begins in the spring.

Draining and cleaning the pool is a drastic measure that may be unnecessary if you regularly remove floating debris and groom the plants. You can even occasionally siphon out sludge from the bottom. When you do empty and clean your pool, don't scrub it free of algae. A small amount of algae is an essential part of a healthy pool.

# APRIL
## WATER GARDENING

### PLANNING

Know someone who's apprehensive about an in-ground pond? Consider water gardening in a container. Anything that holds water and does not have a toxic lining can be used. Containers can vary from plastic to concrete to ceramic to wooden barrels with plastic liners. Any of the plants used in water gardening in pools or ponds can be grown in a container. Keep in mind, however, the mature size of the plant. The plants can be grown in individual pots and the pots staged atop bricks or other supports so that their rims are at the appro-

priate level. You have a wide variety of plants to choose from. Here are some of my favorites:

1. The first group of plants are those that are happy with wet feet but whose crowns can stick above the surface of the water, like **striped giant reed** (*Arundo donax* 'Variegata'), **elephant ear** (*Colocasia esculenta* 'Black Magic'), and **giant taro** (*Alocasia macrorrhiza*).

2. The next group of plants are those that like their crowns to be level with the water surface. These include yellow-flowered **water canna** (*Canna* 'Ra'), **dwarf papyrus** (*Cyperus papyrus* 'Nanus'), and *Hibiscus moscheutos* 'Blue River II'.

3. Third, there are plants whose crowns should always be covered by several inches of water like cultivars of **lotus** (*Nelumbo* 'Angel Wings' and *N.* 'Baby Doll' are both suited for pot culture) and **parrot's feather** (*Myriophyllum aquaticum*).

Pot the plant in a clay-based soil topped with a layer of gravel to prevent the soil from washing into the water. Put the container on rollers before planting so you can move it around easily.

### PLANTING

**Hardy water lilies** and **lotuses** that have spent the winter in the deeper parts of your pool to protect their roots from freezing need to be returned to shallower depths when any ice has melted completely.

**Hardy water lilies** are sold dormant/bare-root or nondormant with a few leaves, roots, and perhaps buds. It's important that you prevent the rhizome from drying out. Put the rhizome in a bowl of water before planting. Here's how to plant a **hardy water lily**:

1. Select a roomy container with a drainage hole. **Hardy water lilies** grow horizontally, so select a container that is wider than tall. A pot that is 7 to 9 inches deep and 15 to 17 inches wide is fine for most; more vig-

Papyrus is one of the aquatic plants that likes conditions so that the crown is level with the water surface.

orous types need a container a few inches wider. Fill the container one-third full with slightly damp, heavy, clay-based garden soil. Insert a water lily fertilizing tablet. Depending on the manufacturer, one fertilizer tablet may be required per 5 quarts of soil.

2. Fill the container to the top with soil and then add water until it seeps out the drainage hole.

3. Dig out a depression in the medium for the rhizome. Set it near the side of the container at a 45-degree angle, with the cut end at the side and the crown pointing up and oriented across the container. The rhizome should be deep enough to be covered with an inch of soil.

4. Fill the pot to within an inch or two of the rim. Let the growing tip protrude through the surface. Press the soil in, being careful around the crown.

5. Water the pot again. Top off the pot with pea gravel, leaving the growing point visible.

6. Place the pot in the water. Lower the pot slowly at an angle to allow any air bubbles to escape and to prevent the water from becoming clouded with mud.

7. The crowns of most **hardy water lilies** can be located 6 to 18 inches below the water surface. To keep them at this depth, place them on bricks or an empty overturned pot. To speed up their growth, place them on a pot 6 inches below the surface. As more leaves grow, move the plant gradually to deeper depths.

Divide your bog plants just before or as new growth is emerging. Rhizomes such as those of **striped rush** can be divided into sections with shoots and roots. Fibrous-rooted plants such as **pickerel rush** can be teased apart into separate plants. Keep these marginal plants confined to containers like a nursery pot, which makes fertilizing and future dividing easier. Use the same heavy clay soil used for planting **water lilies** and other floating-leaved plants.

Place them on the shelf inside the pond or set them on bricks, weathered cinder blocks, or upside down pots so they're at the appropriate depth.

Any submerged plants that have become overgrown need to be thinned out.

Compost the trimmings or incorporate them into the vegetable garden. You can propagate the trimmings by anchoring them in pots filled with sand.

## CARE

If you didn't cut back the dead leaves from your marginal plants in the fall, now is a good time to remove them before or as the new growth emerges. Compost the trimmings or recycle them in the vegetable garden where they can be mixed into the soil.

Continue to remove fallen leaves and any floating organic debris from the surface of the pond.

## FERTILIZING

Fertilize bog plants with aquatic-plant-fertilizer tablets when new growth emerges. Instead of the tablets, you can use a slow-release nitrogen granular fertilizer following manufacturers' instructions for perennials. Avoid spilling any fertilizer into the pool. Feed **hardy water lilies** once a month with the aquatic fertilizer tablets pushed into the soil when the water temperature goes above 70 degrees. Keep the tablet about 2 inches away from the rhizome or tuber.

## PROBLEMS

Any diseased leaves should be removed and disposed of promptly.

# MAY
## WATER GARDENING

One of the benefits of a water garden is that you can grow bog or marginal plants in it as well, such as these iris.

## PLANNING

Consider expanding your pool to include a bog garden. Creating a bog will be easy if you have a naturally low, poorly drained area that collects water.

If you're going to install a bog garden, you can dig a shallow depression outside of the water garden that can catch any overflow. Extend the flexible liner over this basin and fill it with soil.

To create a bog:

1. Dig a hole 2 to 2¹/₂ feet and as wide as you like. Twelve to 15 square feet is the minimum size.

2. Lay a thin liner over the hole and press it in. Weigh the ends down with bricks or stones to keep it in place.

3. Fill in the hole with soil to within 3 or 4 inches of the top.

4. Trim the edges of the liner and fold them back into the hole. Add the remaining soil to hide the edges.

5. Wet the soil heavily and then let it settle for a day or two before planting it.

6. Water your bog garden whenever the surface feels dry. Stop watering when water starts to come up to the surface.

## PLANTING

Time the planting of your **tropical water lilies** with the planting of your tender vegetables and warm-season annuals a few weeks after the last freeze. They can be planted in your water garden when the water temperature stays above 70 degrees.

**Tropical water lilies** are sold dormant and bare root or nondormant with a few leaves, roots, and perhaps buds. It's important that you prevent the tuber from drying out. Put it in a bowl of water before planting. Here's how to plant a **tropical water lily**:

1. Select a roomy container with a drainage hole. **Tropical water lilies** grow from a tuber so a deep 5-gallon pot that allows for more vertical growth than horizontal growth would be fine. Fill the container one-third full with slightly damp heavy, clay-based garden soil. Insert a water lily fertilizing tablet. Depending on the manufacturer, one fertilizer tablet may be required per 5 quarts of soil.

2. Fill the container to the top with soil and then add water until it seeps out of the drainage hole.

3. Plant the tuber in the center of the pot. Look for a white line on the tuber. This is where the soil level should be once you refill the pot.

4. Fill the pot to within an inch or two of the rim. Let the growing tip protrude through the surface. Press the soil in and be careful around the crown.

5. Water the pot again. Top off the pot with pea gravel, leaving the growing point visible to prevent soil from washing away. (Though experts feel that pea gravel is unsightly and is not necessary if you lower the pot slowly into the water.)

6. Place the pot in the water. Lower it slowly and at a slight angle allowing any air bubbles to escape. This will prevent it from muddying the water.

7. The depth for **tropical water lilies** should be between 6 and 12 inches from the crown to the water surface.

## CARE

Remove faded, dying, or dead leaves from **water lilies**, **lotus**, and bog plants.

Bring your **hardy water lily** flowers to enjoy indoors. Cut

---

## HELPFUL HINTS FOR MANAGING FISH

• To adequately maintain fish and plants in aboveground pools, choose a deep container that holds between 50 to 100 gallons of water. Position this container in an area that receives morning sun and afternoon shade to benefit the aquatic plants and the fish. Be careful if you're going to place this container on a deck because water is very heavy and extra support may be needed.

Fish such as koi carp and goldfish can be grown successfully in garden ponds or pools. An unaerated pond can carry 1 to 6 inches of fish (measured from tip to tail) per 5 square feet of surface area. Aerated ponds can carry 12 inches of fish per 5 square feet of surface area.

Make sure you're using dechlorinated water before introducing any fish to the pond. To dechlorinate treated water, allow the water to stand for at least one week before introducing any fish. Aerated water will dechlorinate in 24 hours. You can also use a dechlorinating agent available from water gardening suppliers.

• Fish are a lot like houseplants that have been indoors all winter. Both need to be acclimatized to allow them to get used to their new environment. When you bring new fish home, leave them in their plastic bag in a shady spot in the pool until the water in the bag reaches the same temperature as the pond water. This may take about twenty minutes. Then open the bag and release the fish.

---

them on their first day of bloom—they'll last for three or four days in a vase or bowl as if they were still in the garden.

## FERTILIZING

When the water temperature stays above 70 degrees F., fertilize all **water lilies** at least once a month (or follow label instructions) with a tablet-form of fertilizer especially formulated for aquatics. It should contain both slow- and fast-release nitrogen. Follow the manufacturer's instructions regarding the amounts and frequency of application.

## PROBLEMS

Trim off any diseased leaves from your **water lilies** and marginal plants and discard them.

# JUNE
## WATER GARDENING

 PLANNING

For **water lilies** (*Nymphaea* spp.) in containers, choose a watertight one that's at least 18 inches in diameter and a foot deep. Fill the container with water and let it sit for about twenty-four hours to allow any chlorine to evaporate and for the water to come to air temperature. They will need at least six hours of direct sun. Some **hardy water lilies** that do well in aboveground containers that stay above freezing in winter are yellow-flowering 'Chromatella' and *N.* x 'Helvola'; white 'Hermine'; deep-red 'Froebelii'; and orange-red 'Graziella'.

 PLANTING

Grow bog plants such as **water canna**, **umbrella palm**, and **Japanese iris** in containers of ordinary garden soil placed on ledges in the pool or on inverted pots at their required depths. Marginal plants provide shelter for wildlife and shade and protection for fish. Some marginals can handle either shallow or deep water levels, even dry areas, while others need a certain depth of water above their

*Leave the spent flowers on lotus if you like the ornamental seedpods.*

crowns. If your pool doesn't have shelves, raise or lower the plant by using inverted pots, bricks, or weathered cinder blocks.

Submerged plants are essential for releasing oxygen into the water and competing with algae for nutrients to keep the water clear. Some of the most popular are **Canadian elodea** (*Elodea canadensis*), **cabomba** (*Cabomba caroliniana*), **coontail** (*Ceratophyllum demersum*), and **tape grass** (*Vallisneria americana*).

You can plant **hardy** and **tropical water lilies** now.

 CARE

Deadhead **water lilies** to encourage more flowers. The difference between **hardy** and **tropical water lilies** is most **tropical water lilies** hold their flowers above the water.

Leave the spent flowers on **lotus** because the ornamental pods that develop will look terrific in flower arrangements.

Remove any leaves that are yellow or damaged by insects or diseases. Continue to remove organic debris—grass clippings, fallen leaves, needles, etc.—from the pond.

Keep an eye on invasive plants and trim or remove them so they won't crowd out more restrained growers. Some of the plants that float free on the surface may grow with abandon. **Pond lily** (*Nuphar* spp.) and the chartreuse-green **water lettuce** (*Pistia stratiotes*) can become a pest if left unchecked. You may want to experiment with a tropical floating aquatic such as the lacy delicate **mosaic plant** (*Ludwigia sedioides*).

Keep track of water pH, ammonia, and nitrate levels, especially if you have fish. If you

# HELPFUL HINTS FOR A HEALTHY POND

A healthy pond is a thriving community of bacteria, organic matter, plants, fish scavengers, and a small amount of algae.

Brief explosions of algal growth called "blooms" commonly occur in ponds, especially during the first few weeks in newly constructed ponds or in early spring. This growth spurt occurs because there's no competition: The plants are just beginning to come out of dormancy and grow and the fish and scavengers haven't yet awakened. With plenty of sunlight and dissolved nutrients, the algae grows with abandon. Once the surface of the pool becomes shaded, the plants compete with the algae for nutrients, and the fish and scavengers start feeding on the algae, the water should clear up by itself—if the water garden is in balance.

An out-of-balance pool can look like month-old pea soup in a short time. There are a couple of solutions:

1. Feed your fish only what they'll eat in three to five minutes. Any uneaten food will decompose and encourage algae. Many water gardeners have found that when they stop feeding their fish and the fish are restricted to eating algae, plants, and insects, their water becomes clearer.

2. Add more plants. Remember that between one-half and three-quarters of the surface area of a mature pool should be covered with leaves.

If all else fails, consider installing a pump and mechanical or biological filter. In addition to having cleaner water, you can enjoy the sound of moving water.

Again, aquatic plants are active biological filters, and if you get the right balance between the number of plants, the number of fish, and the amount of nutrients the pool receives, no other filtration may be necessary.

don't stock your aboveground half-barrel or other water container with fish to consume mosquito eggs and larvae, mosqui- toes can become a problem. Buy a few briquettes of mosquito larvae killer sold as Mosquito Dunks® (it contains a bacterial insecticide called *Bacillus thuringiensis* var. *israelensis*). One bri- quette can treat 100 square feet of water regardless of its depth. Break them up into four pieces and put them out at the start of each month to float on the surface of the water.

## WATERING

Add water to your container or pool to maintain it at the appropriate level. Add the water slowly.

## FERTILIZING

Fertilize **water lilies** with aquatic fertilizer tablets, using the amount prescribed by the manufacturer. Bog plants can be fertilized based on their growth rate and appearance. To play it safe, fertilize them at half the rate of your **water lilies**.

## PROBLEMS

Black water lily aphids can disfigure leaves and flowers. Remove them with a strong spray of water or submerge plants and give them a shake. Spider mites can appear on the undersides of **water lily** leaves and **lotus**. Clip off heavily infested leaves and dislodge the mites with a strong spray of water from the hose.

Handpick brown snails from **iris** leaves.

Continue to trim away any dead, damaged, or diseased leaves.

# JULY
## WATER GARDENING

 PLANNING

This is a good month to update your gardening journal and make plans for improvements to your water garden next year. Did the **tropical water lilies** look as good as the pictures in the catalog? Have some of the aquatic plants turned out to be thugs in disguise by taking more space than you allotted to them?

Record your observations in your journal; include newspaper and magazine clippings of articles by local garden writers who touted certain aquatic plants. Perhaps you heard some recommendations from friends and other water gardening enthusiasts regarding some aspect of pond care. Compile these notes and plan to act on them next season.

 PLANTING

If less than half your pond is covered with plants, consider adding more **water lilies**. This will help control algae.

If you find choice marginal plants that will complement the planting you already have, go ahead and purchase them and plant them in your water garden.

Divide your **irises—Japanese iris** (*Iris kaempferi*), variegated **rabbit ear iris** (*I. laevigata* 'Variegata'), **yellow flag** (*I. pseudacorus*), and **Louisiana hybrid irises**—in late summer and repot them.

 CARE

Remove spent flowers to encourage the production of more blooms. You may want to allow some flowers to remain so you can harvest the fruits and sow the seed to produce some homegrown plants. Yellow leaves should be trimmed off and discarded.

Remove any debris from the surface of the pond and add it to your compost pile.

 WATERING

Check the level of your pool to see if the level has dropped. Tap water shouldn't be added directly to a water garden containing fish because the chlorine is toxic to them. If you add less than an inch of tap water to your pool, a dechlorinating agent won't be necessary. For larger amounts, a dechlorinating chemical will have to be added.

Chloramine is another water treatment agent that's used to treat tap water. Unlike chlorine, it doesn't escape naturally from the water, and a special water conditioner needs to be added to remove it. Contact your local public water department to find out which chlorinating product is used in your water supply, and use a dechlorinating agent designed for that product.

 FERTILIZING

Fertilize floating-leaved plants with slow-release aquatic plant tablets available from water garden suppliers. Bury the tablets in the soil so the fertilizer will be available to the roots and not leach out into the water (which can stimulate the growth of algae).

 PROBLEMS

**Water lilies** and some marginal plants may be attacked by aphids, which can be found clustered at the tips of new shoots.

# HELPFUL HINTS FOR POND MANAGEMENT

• The two most serious threats to pond fish are a lack of oxygen and high ammonia levels in the water. The warmer the water, the less oxygen there is. At the same time, high temperatures speed up fish metabolism, increasing their need for oxygen. Aerate the water with a pump or fountain, keep a good supply of submerged plants, and monitor water quality to keep oxygen available to the fish. Keep fish populations low. Ammonia is produced by fish waste and decaying plant debris and other gases are produced as it breaks down. High levels of ammonia are toxic to fish and lead to their quick death.

• Gardeners who cannot enjoy the blooms of their **tropical water lilies** during the day can enjoy them in the twilight hours. Tropicals may bloom either during the day or at night. **Hardy water lilies** bloom only during the day. Night-blooming **water lilies** bloom at dusk and their flowers usually remain open until late the next morning—even longer if the day is cloudy. They also permeate the air with a musky fragrance that's alluring to pollinators and gardeners alike. Tropical night-blooming **water lilies** are very vigorous and need plenty of room—at least a bathtub-sized pool. Here are a few recommended nocturnal **water lilies**:

    White: 'Missouri' and 'Woods White Knight'
    Pink: 'Texas Shell Pink' and 'Emily Grant Hutchings'
    Red: 'Red Flare' and 'Jennifer Rebecca'

A "waterfall" is a good way to keep the water aerated. Including submerged oxygenating plants is another way.

Dislodge them and knock them into the water where they can be eaten by fish. Holes in **water lily** leaves may be caused by water lily beetles or midges. Simply pick off the infested leaves to destroy the insect eggs or larvae.

Several diseases may occur while hot and humid conditions prevail. Trim off and discard any diseased leaves.

# AUGUST
## WATER GARDENING

 PLANNING

Shade is a welcome respite from the blazing sun. And there are some **water lilies** that will perform well with as little as three hours of sunlight. To decorate your shady water garden you can use traditional shade-loving plants like **hosta**, **astilbe**, and **ferns**, which will also benefit from the moist soil at the garden's edge. The following plants perform best with six hours of sun, but they will flower and grow with as little as three or four hours of sun each day:

**HARDY WATER LILIES**
'Charlene Strawn'
'James Brydon'
'Virginia'

**TROPICAL WATER LILIES**
'Albert Greenberg'
'Director George T. Moore'
'Panama Pacific'

**MARGINAL PLANTS**
**Elephant ear** (*Alocasia* spp.)
**Cord grass** (*Spartina* spp.)
**Papyrus** (*Cyperus* spp.)
**Taro** (*Xanthosoma* spp.)

 PLANTING

**American lotus** (*Nelumbo lutea*), commonly known as **water chinquapin**, is native to the eastern half of the United States. It is closely related to the **water lily** and produces a large, round arrangement of floating leaves joined by stalks to a thick, below-ground stem or rhizome.

As new growth emerges over the course of a season, aerial leaves shaped like shallow bowls are produced on stems that rise high above the pad, sometimes 5 feet or more. Magnificent flowers are borne high over the water on a thick stalk above the aerial leaves. The flowers may be white, pale yellow, pink, or deep rose, depending on the species, and range from 4 to 12 inches across. In the center of each flower is a yellow receptacle with tiny holes that looks like a shower head. This "seedpod" enlarges as it matures, changing to green and then to brown. By that point the individual seeds are held loosely in depressions on the pod's face. Because of their decorative value, these seedpods are often dried, bronzed, or silvered and used in floral arrangements.

To sow seed, scarify or abrade the impervious seed coat with sandpaper or a file prior to sowing. Sow the seed in a mix of two parts heavy garden soil and one part coarse sand, in a nondraining container. Plant the seed at a depth twice its diameter and fill the container with water so that the mix is submerged by 2 inches.

Set the container in a window with a southern exposure where the air temperature is above 75 degrees F. and the water temperature above 65 degrees. The seed should germinate in two to three weeks. When three leaves have appeared, the seedlings can be transplanted to larger pots filled with heavy garden soil. These pots can then be set in a larger container of water.

Transplant again whenever a seedling has filled its pot. Allow the delicate root tips to protrude from the soil and make sure there is enough water to support the developing leaf pad.

Young **lotus** plants can be moved outdoors into water that is at least 70 degrees F. Each plant should then be given a container at least 9 to 10 inches deep and 16 to 20 inches in diameter.

Use $1/2$ pound aquatic plant fertilizer per bushel of soil. Add a 1-inch layer of pea gravel on the surface. Before submersing the container, water it thoroughly; then place it in the pool. The gravel layer should be 3 or 4 inches below the water surface. As growth continues, the **lotus** plants can be moved to deeper water, 6 to 12 inches below the water surface.

But choose the site carefully: **Lotus** is a very invasive plant. In a few growing seasons it can spread rapidly and overtake a shallow pond. Keep the surface of the pond covered so that one-half to three-quarters of its surface is covered with leaves.

## CARE

Inspect the submerged plants in your pool and thin them out if necessary. Compost them or recycle them in the vegetable garden as mulch.

Trim off spent flowers and clip away any leaves that may be in the water. The leaves and other organic matter can break down in the water, especially in hot weather, and can harm plants and fish. Clean the surface of the pond of debris to prevent it from sinking to the bottom and fouling the water.

## WATERING

Check the level of your pool to see if it has dropped. Tap water shouldn't be added directly to a water garden containing fish because the chlorine is toxic to them. If you add less than an inch of tap water to your pool, a dechlorinating agent won't be necessary. For larger amounts, a dechlorinating chemical will have to be added.

## FERTILIZING

Fertilize floating-leaved plants with slow-release aquatic plant tablets available from water gar-den suppliers. Bury the tablets in the soil so the fertilizer will be available to the roots and not leach out into the water, which can stimulate the growth of algae. Bog plants can be fertil-ized based on their growth rate and appearance. To play it safe, fertilize them at half the rate of your **water lilies**.

## PROBLEMS

Your aquatic plants may be attacked by insects. Cut off any infested plant parts. You can also remove the offenders by sub-merging them in the water and giving them a shake. Handpick brown snails from **iris** leaves. Trim away any dead, damaged, or diseased leaves.

Inspect any iris plants, such as these Japanese iris, for brown snails or dead, damaged, or diseased foliage.

# SEPTEMBER

## WATER GARDENING

Notice how this water feature is integrated into the overall design of this garden.

they grow and fill in, they'll create a natural look on the edge of the pool. Think about picking up some of the variegated colors of the aquatic plants and repeating the colors in a nearby flower bed.

To get some design ideas, study water gardens in person and those featured in magazines and books. If you do visit, take along your gardening journal and a camera.

### CARE

Continue to trim spent flowers and foliage that has matured on your marginals. Clean up any leaves that may have sloughed off into the pond, and compost them.

### WATERING

Fall is a dry season. Maintain the water level in the pond.

### FERTILIZING

As the water temperature cools, the plants will cease growth and begin to go dormant. They do not have to be fertilized.

### PROBLEMS

Trim away any damaged, dead, diseased, or pest-ridden leaves. Compost them or bring them into the garden to be buried to enrich the soil.

### PLANNING

Although your water garden may be a focal point in your landscape, it should blend harmoniously with the rest of your terrestrial plantings of trees, shrubs, perennials, annuals, ground covers, and bulbs. Plan to grow some woody or perennial ground covers about 3 to 4 feet from the edge of the water garden. As

### HELPFUL HINTS FOR A CLEAN POND

• Fallen leaves in water will decompose, releasing minerals and gases that are toxic to fish—and the decaying organic matter will encourage algae. To prevent leaves from nearby trees and shrubs from falling into your pond, use netting to capture the leaves. Buy plastic bird netting sold for protecting fruit trees and stretch it over the pond; it won't be noticeable from distance. After the leaves have collected on the net, drag it off or roll it up and move the leaves to an area where they can be shredded with the lawn mower and composted or used as mulch.

• Terrestrial plants that need to be fertilized should be located far enough away from the edge of your water garden to prevent fertilizer from washing into and polluting the water. Consider using hardscape instead of plants at the edge, such as paving stones, gravel, or mulch.

# OCTOBER

## WATER GARDENING

### PLANNING

Make plans this month to evaluate the plants in your water garden and decide whether you're going to save questionable plants: those that have become too invasive for your garden, some that looked shabby all season long, and tender plants that will have to be overwintered indoors. Some gardeners treat tender floating-leaved and marginal plants like annuals and replace them. But if you want to save your **tropical water lilies**, plan to find some room indoors.

### CARE

Before freezing weather arrives, bring tender marginals and others that you want to save indoors, where you will store them.

Oxygenating plants should be cut back hard in the fall. Remove dead leaves from marginals. Move any cold-hardy aquatic plants to the lowest part of the pond or water garden. After the first killing frost, trim away the dead leaves of your **hardy water lilies**. In areas where ice could form on the ponds, move the pots to the deepest part of your pond (at least 2 feet or more in depth). Rest assured that **hardy water lilies** will overwinter (they are hardy to Zone 3) as long as their roots are protected from freezing. To store a **tropical water lily**, follow these steps:

1. When they stop blooming in the fall and are going dormant with the cooler fall temperatures, take them out of the pool. Gently remove the plant from the pot and wash away the soil.

2. Look for a smooth black walnut-sized tuber (many form when the parent is potbound) beneath the crown. Separate the tuber and put in water. If the tuber sinks, it's alive and can be stored over the winter. If the tuber floats, discard it.

3. Store the tubers over the winter in a plastic bag filled with cool damp sand. Put the tuber inside the bag and top it off with more sand. Seal and label the bag with the name of the variety. Store the bag in a cool 55- to 60-degree F location.

If you want to overwinter your tropical marginal plants, move them indoors and treat them like houseplants. Set them on a water-filled saucer in a bright, south-facing window. They need ten to twelve hours of light to remain healthy throughout the winter months, so consider supplementing natural sunlight with fluorescent light. Prevent the pond from freezing—any organic matter trapped at the bottom of the pond may decay, producing toxic levels of methane gases that can be toxic to fish. Install a pump or a heater designed for water garden pools. Remove any fallen debris or dead plants in the water.

After the first hard frost, trim away any dead leaves from marginals left to freeze and compost them.

### WATERING

Maintain the water level in your pond. The plants and fish that overwinter outdoors in the pond can use the depth.

### PROBLEMS

Trim away any damaged, dead, diseased, or pest-ridden leaves. Compost them or bring them into the garden to be buried to enrich the soil.

# NOVEMBER
## WATER GARDENING

### PLANNING

I hope that you have an enjoyable water gardening experience that inspires you to learn more about this exciting field.

Remember that many water gardeners are happy to share their experiences with you. To learn about a water gardening society in your area, speak to an aquatic nursery staff or water garden supplier.

Surf the Internet for water gardening infor- mation to learn about different approaches and techniques. The Water Gardeners International website offers a directory of water gardening clubs and associations. You can find these and much more at **www.watergardeners international.org**. You can also subscribe to a water gardening magazine.

### CARE

If your pond is too shallow or you have tender plants that won't survive the winter, you need to overwinter them indoors. Lift **hardy water lilies** out of the pond, cut away the leaves, and move them to a cool location (40 to 50 degrees F. is ideal). Keep the soil moist. (This also works for most hardy marginal plants.)

Tropical floating plants are inexpensive to replace, so they can be discarded after the first frost. Allowing them to remain in the pond can cause them to rot and foul the water.

Aboveground water containers such as tub gardens can freeze during extended cold periods, so move them into a greenhouse or indoors in the colder parts of the state.

To prevent ice from forming on the surface of your pond—trapping carbon dioxide and other noxious gases that can kill fish—keep the water pump running. This will create water movement, preventing at least a small area from freezing so the top of the pond won't be completely sealed.

If the water does ice up, avoid the urge to smash a hole in the ice; this could damage plants and injure the fish. Set a kettle or pan of hot water on the surface of the ice to melt an opening.

To prevent ice from cracking the walls of the pool, float several tennis balls or other air-filled or rubber balls before hard freezing weather. The balls will absorb the expanding pressure from the ice and will relieve pressure from the pool walls.

### PROBLEMS

Trim away any damaged, dead, diseased, or pest-ridden leaves. Compost them or bring them into the garden to be buried to enrich the soil.

Large or small, a water feature can be a wonderful addition to your garden. It's good to remember what it can look like when you're cleaning up for the winter.

# DECEMBER
## WATER GARDENING

### PLANNING

There's not much to be done with the water garden this month except to plan for next season. Review your journal and draw some conclusions about this past year's water garden. If there were problems with algae or if the fish weren't thriving, you need to look back at your journal to see if your observations will lead you to a solution. As with most garden maintenance, monitoring the garden on a regular basis will prevent many serious problems from occurring.

Make plans to spruce up your water garden next year with some exciting plants. The nursery industry is responding to the popularity of water gardening with new colors and forms of **water lilies** and marginal and edge-of-the-pond plants that have variegated stems and leaves. And "smaller is in," with a greater selection of smaller **water lilies** and compact marginal plants.

Just when you thought you were going to enhance your border with more perennials, you may be forced to choose between your perennials or your aquatics. Why not just splurge and give both gardens a makeover with some new plants?

### HELPFUL HINTS FOR GOOD BOOKS

Check out some books that will help you become a water gardening expert:

*Water Gardens* (from the editors of *Horticulture* magazine). Primedia Special Interest Publications, Boston, MA, 1998.

Dunn, Teri, *Can't Miss Water Gardening for the South*. Cool Springs Press, 2005.

Slocum, P. D., P. Robinson, and F. Perry, *Water Gardening*. Timber Press, 1996.

Tomocik, J., *Water Gardening*. Pantheon Books, Knopf Publishing Group, New York, 1996.

### CARE

In the warmest areas of Alabama and Mississippi, gardeners need to thin out the submerged plants if that wasn't done last month.

Remove the dead leaves from your marginal plants.

Trim dead leaves from **hardy water lilies** and cold-hardy aquatic plants and discard them. If there's a threat of ice forming on your pool, move the plants to the lowest part of the pond or pool.

Aboveground water containers such as tub gardens can freeze during extended cold periods, so it's best to locate them in a southern exposure for most of the winter. Cover them during the cold nights to trap stored heat and to offer some protection from freezing. Prevent the pond from freezing because any organic matter frozen at the bottom of the pond may eventually decay, producing levels of methane gases that can be toxic to fish. Install a pump or a heater designed for water garden pools.

Remove dead leaves and other debris that may gather around the pond or on the surface of the water.

### WATERING

Maintain the water level in your pond for the plants and fish who spend the winter outdoors.

# USDA COLD HARDINESS ZONES FOR ALABAMA

| ZONE | Average Annual Minimum Temperature (°F) |
|------|------------------------------------------|
| 7a | 5 to 0 |
| 7b | 10 to 5 |
| 8a | 15 to 10 |
| 8b | 20 to 15 |

# USDA COLD HARDINESS ZONES FOR MISSISSIPPI

| ZONE | Average Annual Minimum Temperature (°F) |
|------|------------------------------------------|
| 7a | 5 to 0 |
| 7b | 10 to 5 |
| 8a | 15 to 10 |
| 8b | 20 to 15 |

# GLOSSARY

**Alkaline soil:** soil with a pH greater than 7.0. It lacks acidity, often because it has limestone in it.

**Annual:** from a botanist's perspective, an annual lasts no longer than one year. To the gardener, an annual is a seasonal plant, growing until winter's cold or summer's heat causes it to decline or die.

**Balled and burlapped:** describes a tree or shrub grown in the field whose soilball was wrapped with protective burlap and twine when the plant was dug up to be sold or transplanted.

**Bare root:** describes plants that have been packaged without any soil around their roots. (Often young shrubs and trees purchased through the mail arrive with their exposed roots covered with moist peat or sphagnum moss, sawdust, or similar material, and wrapped in plastic.)

**Barrier plant:** a plant that has intimidating thorns or spines and is sited purposely to block foot traffic or other access to the home or yard.

**Beneficial insects:** insects or their larvae that prey on pest organisms and their eggs. They may be flying insects, such as ladybugs, parasitic wasps, praying mantids, and soldier bugs, or soil dwellers such as predatory nematodes, spiders, ants, and beetles.

**Berm:** a narrow raised ring of soil around a tree, used to hold water so it will be directed to the root zone.

**Bract:** a modified leaf structure on a plant stem near its flower that resembles a petal. Often it is more colorful and visible than the actual flower, as in dogwood or poinsettia.

**Bud union:** the place where the top of a plant was grafted to the rootstock; usually refers to roses or fruit trees.

**Canopy:** the overhead branching area of a tree, usually referring to its extent including foliage.

**Cold hardiness:** the ability of a perennial plant to survive the winter cold in a particular area.

**Complete fertilizer:** powdered, liquid, or granular fertilizer with a balanced proportion of the three key nutrients—nitrogen (N), phosphorus (P), and potassium (K). It is suitable for maintenance nutrition for most plants.

**Composite:** a flower that is actually composed of many tiny flowers. Typically, they are flat clusters of tiny, tight florets, sometimes surrounded by wider-petaled florets. Composite flowers are highly attractive to bees and beneficial insects.

**Compost:** organic matter that has undergone progressive decomposition by microbial and macrobial activity until it is reduced to a spongy, fluffy texture. Added to soil of any type, it improves the soil's ability to hold air and water and to drain.

**Corm:** the swollen energy-storing structure, analogous to a bulb, under the soil at the base of the stem of plants, such as crocus and gladiolus.

**Crown:** the base of a plant at, or just beneath, the surface of the soil where the roots meet the stems.

**Cultivar:** a CULTIvated VARiety. It is a naturally occurring form of a plant that has been identified as special or superior and is purposely selected for propagation and production.

# GLOSSARY

**Deadhead:** a pruning technique that removes faded flower heads from plants to improve their appearance, abort seed production, and stimulate further flowering.

**Deciduous plants:** unlike evergreens, these trees and shrubs lose their leaves in the fall.

**Desiccation:** drying out of foliage tissues, usually due to drought or wind.

**Division:** the practice of splitting apart perennial plants to create several smaller-rooted segments. The practice is useful for controlling the plant's size and for acquiring more plants; it is also essential to the health and continued flowering of certain ones.

**Dormancy:** the period, usually the winter, when perennial plants temporarily cease active growth and rest. Dormant is the verb form, as used in this sentence: Some plants, like spring-blooming bulbs, go dormant in the summer.

**Established:** the point at which a newly planted tree, shrub, or flower begins to produce new growth, either foliage or stems. This is an indication that the roots have recovered from transplant shock and have begun to grow and spread.

**Evergreen:** perennial plants that do not lose their foliage annually with the onset of winter. Needled or broadleaf foliage will persist and continues to function on a plant through one or more winters, aging and dropping unobtrusively in cycles of three or four years or more.

**Foliar:** of or about foliage—usually refers to the practice of spraying foliage, as in fertilizing or treating with insecticide; leaf tissues absorb liquid directly for fast results, and the soil is not affected.

**Floret:** a tiny flower, usually one of many forming a cluster, that comprises a single blossom.

**Germinate:** to sprout. Germination is a fertile seed's first stage of development.

**Graft (union):** the point on the stem of a woody plant with sturdier roots where a stem from a highly ornamental plant is inserted so that it will join with it. Roses are commonly grafted.

**Hands:** the female flowers on a banana tree; they turn into bananas.

**Hardscape:** the permanent, structural, nonplant part of a landscape, such as walls, sheds, pools, patios, arbors, and walkways.

**Herbaceous:** plants having fleshy or soft stems that die back with frost; the opposite of woody.

**Hybrid:** a plant that is the result of intentional or natural cross-pollination between two or more plants of the same species or genus.

**Low water demand:** describes plants that tolerate dry soil for varying periods of time. Typically, they have succulent, hairy, or silvery-gray foliage and tuberous roots or taproots.

**Mulch:** a layer of material over bare soil to protect it from erosion and compaction by rain, and to discourage weeds. It may be inorganic (gravel, fabric) or organic (wood chips, bark, pine needles, chopped leaves).

**Naturalize:** (a) to plant seeds, bulbs, or plants in a random, informal pattern as they would appear in their natural habitat; (b) to adapt to and spread throughout adopted habitats (a tendency of some nonnative plants).

**Nectar:** the sweet fluid produced by glands on flowers that attract pollinators such as hummingbirds and honeybees for whom it is a source of energy.

**Organic material, organic matter:** any material or debris that is derived from plants. It is carbon-based material capable of undergoing decomposition and decay.

**Peat moss:** organic matter from sphagnum mosses, often used to improve soil texture, especially sandy soils. It is also used in seed-starting mixes and in container plantings.

# GLOSSARY

**Perennial:** a flowering plant that lives over two or more seasons. Many die back with frost, but their roots survive the winter and generate new shoots in the spring.

**pH:** a measurement of the relative acidity (low pH) or alkalinity (high pH) of soil or water based on a scale of 1 to 14, 7 being neutral. Individual plants require soil to be within a certain range so that nutrients can be available to them.

**Pinch:** to remove tender stems and/or leaves by pressing them between thumb and forefinger. This pruning technique encourages branching, compactness, and flowering in plants, or it removes aphids clustered at growing tips.

**Pollen:** the yellow, powdery grains in the center of a flower. A plant's male sex cells, they are transferred to the female plant parts by means of wind or animal pollinators to fertilize them and create seeds.

**Raceme:** an arrangement of single stalked flowers along an elongated, unbranched axis.

**Rhizome:** a swollen energy-storing stem structure, similar to a bulb, that lies horizontally in the soil, with roots emerging from its lower surface and growth shoots from a growing point at or near its tip, as in bearded iris.

**Rootbound (or potbound):** the condition of a plant that has been confined in a container too long, its roots having been forced to wrap around themselves and even swell out of the container. Successful transplanting or repotting requires untangling and trimming away of some of the matted roots.

**Self-seeding:** the tendency of some plants to sow their seeds freely around the yard. It creates many seedlings the following season that may or may not be welcome.

**Semievergreen:** tending to be evergreen in a mild climate but deciduous in a rigorous one.

**Shearing:** the pruning technique whereby plant stems and branches are cut uniformly with long-bladed pruning shears (hedge shears) or powered hedge trimmers. It is used when creating and maintaining hedges and topiary.

**Slow-acting fertilizer:** fertilizer that is water insoluble and therefore releases its nutrients gradually as a function of soil temperature, moisture coating, and related microbial activity. Typically granular, it may be organic or synthetic.

**Sucker:** a new growing shoot. Underground plant roots produce suckers to form new stems and spread by means of these suckering roots to form large plantings, or colonies. Some plants produce root suckers or branch suckers as a result of pruning or wounding.

**Tuber:** a type of underground storage structure in a plant stem, analogous to a bulb. It generates roots below and stems above ground. A dahlia is a tuberous root. A potato is a tuber.

**Variegated:** having various colors or color patterns. The term usually refers to plant foliage that is streaked, edged, blotched, or mottled with a contrasting color, often green with yellow, cream, or white.

**White grubs:** the larvae of scarab beetles, including Japanese beetles, masked chafers, and May and June beetles. They have plump, cream-colored, C-shaped bodies and distinctive yellow to brown heads. Most have life cycles lasting from several months to three years.

**Wings:** (*a*) the corky tissue that forms edges along the twigs of some woody plants such as winged euonymus; (*b*) the flat, dried extension of tissue on some seeds, such as maple, that catch the wind and help them disseminate.

# MORE ABOUT PEST CONTROL

Due to space constraints, the following pests could not be addressed in the monthly chapters. Take some time to learn how to identify and manage these and other pests that afflict our plants—both indoors and out. As they say, "Never stop learning."

## ROSE PESTS

The following are important rose pests in Alabama and Mississippi.

Aphid (adult)

**Aphids:** Pink, purplish, or green, these sap suckers colonize new shoots and rose flowerbuds. Leaves and stems are stunted and deformed. The sticky substance they excrete is often colonized by a black, sooty mold fungus.

*Control: Wash off the adults with a strong spray of water. Spot treat with insecticidal soap or Neem. Dormant oils help prevent their onset in spring. Summer oils can also help during the growing season if your plants are not drought-stressed. Water your roses before- hand and spray in early morning or on cloudy days to reduce the risk of injury. Your Cooperative Extension Service can recommend other appropriate pesticides.*

**Flower thrips:** These tiny yellowish-brown to amber-colored insects damage rose flowers by rasping the tissues and sucking up the sap that oozes out. Rosebuds become streaked and discolored and often fail to open. Flowers are distorted. Thrips are especially attracted to white or light-colored flowers. To check for them, open up a suspected flower over a sheet of white paper and watch for tiny scurrying slivers.

*Control: Difficult. Fortunately, they're preyed upon by minute pirate bugs, ladybugs, lacewings, and big-eyed bugs. Remove and discard any infested flowers. Apply recommended insecticides.*

Japanese beetle

**Japanese beetles:** Metallic green with copper-brown wings, these pests feed on rosebuds, flowers, and leaves. They leave ragged edges in buds and flowers and skeletonize the leaves.

*Control: Hand-pick and drop them in a jar of soapy water. Apply Neem and other insecticides as a control. Set out traps, keeping them far away from your roses and other plants attractive to Japanese beetles. There are many plants that are resistant to Japanese beetles that are documented by David W. Held, an entomologist at Mississippi State University-Coastal Research and Extension Center, Biloxi, MS. Dr. Held compiled a comprehensive list of woody plants and rated them according to their susceptibility to Japanese beetle infestations. Plants were rated from resistant—little, if any, feeding—to highly susceptible plants that were seriously defoliated by Japanese beetles. An abbreviated list of plants is available in the Mississippi State University Publication titled "Guide to Selecting Landscape and Garden Plants Based on Susceptibility to*

*Adult Japanese Beetles," (www. msucares.com/ pubs/publications/p233.pdf).*

Spider mite

**Spider mites:** These pests suck plant sap from the undersides of rose leaves, causing the upper surfaces to turn bronze or yellow. Eventually the leaves may turn brown and fall off. Heavily infested leaves can be covered with webs. Two kinds attack roses in Alabama and Mississippi: southern red (or "cool-weather") mites, which reproduce rapidly in spring and fall, and two-spotted spider mites (pale yellow, green, brown or red), which become active during the heat of summer. Identify them by tapping an affected leaf over a piece of white paper and looking for tiny moving specks.

*Control: Spray a dormant oil in late winter or early spring before growth starts. During the growing season a strong spray of water from the hose, applied to the undersides of the leaves, will dislodge the adults. An insecticidal soap, Neem, or a miticide will also be effective, although repeated applications may be necessary.*

## ROSE DISEASES

**Blackspot:** Blackspot is probably the most infamous and most serious rose disease in the South. Look for round or irregular black splotches with fringed margins, mostly on the upper leaf surfaces. Eventually a yellow halo develops around the spots, and heavily infected leaves turn yellow and drop off. Heavily infected plants will weaken and produce few flowers. Sometimes they die. Infections can occur anytime during the growing season, but the spots are most likely to show up during periods of high humidity or persistent rainfall. Some roses are "blackspot magnets"; others exhibit resistance. The fungus overwinters on fallen leaves and diseased canes. The spores are splashed onto newly emerging leaves and stems by spring rains.

*Control: There are several ways to control this disease: (1) Plant roses in a sunny location with good air movement to speed drying after rains. (2) Prune to open up the roses for better air circulation. (3) Avoid wetting the leaves, especially late in the day. (4) Collect and remove spotted and fallen leaves during the season and prune out dead, damaged, and diseased canes. (5) Take preventive measures. Apply fungicides on highly susceptible roses before the spots appear. This protective barrier should go on right before the leaves emerge and kept on throughout the growing season.*

**Powdery mildew:** This fungus is present when you see a grayish-white powder on the young leaves, shoots, and flower buds. It typically occurs in spring and fall when days are warm and humid and nights are cool. It thrives on plants that are shaded or crowded. Its spores are spread by the wind.

*Control: To reduce the risk of infection: (1) select resistant varieties and (2) improve air movement within the plant by siting it in an open location and by pruning out interior stems to open it up.*

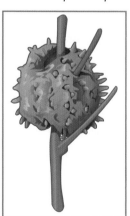

A tumorous growth of crown gall.

**Crown gall:** Suspect this soilborne bacterial disease when you see stunted, weak plants that lack normal green color. It infects stems and roots through wounds. The plant forms galls, or swellings, usually around the crown at or just below the soil surface, as well as higher on the stems. Younger galls are nearly

white. As they grow, sometimes reaching 2 inches in diameter, and age, they darken, become woody, and take on a cauliflower-like appearance. Galls constrict the plant tissues, disrupting the flow of water and nutrients to the canes, weakening and often killing them.

*Control:* Prune out the swellings when first noticed. Sterilize your pruner between cuts on the same plant with Lysol® or a 20 percent solution of household chlorine bleach to avoid spreading this disease to other canes. When using bleach, rinse your shears in water and then oil them before storing them to prevent metal corrosion. Remove and discard heavily infected plants. Remove the related soil, too, before planting healthy roses in the site, unless the soil has been replaced. Purchase healthy, disease-free plants and plant them in an area that has been free of crown gall-infected plants for at least two years. To avoid infections, avoid wounding the roots or crown.

**Gray mold or Botrytis blight:** This spring fungus infects flower buds and flowers, covering them with grayish-brown fuzz. Often they droop and fail to open. It also attacks new shoots damaged by early-fall and late-spring freezes, producing cankers that extend down the stem, sometimes killing the entire shoot. It's most active when weather is cool and wet.

*Controls:* (1) Collect and discard the infected flowers and promptly prune discolored canes back to healthy tissue. Disinfect pruning shears (see Crown Gall) between plants to avoid spreading this disease to healthy plants. (2) After pruning, treat plants with a recommended fungicide to protect the wounds.

## PESTS OF TREES, SHRUBS, VINES, AND GROUND COVERS

**Voles, meadow and field mice:** These rodents damage ornamental and fruit trees by gnawing the bark and roots. Some tunnel through lawns and gardens.

*Controls:* (1) Barriers—use hardware cloth cylinders around trunks to keep them away. Bury the bottom edge at least 6 inches below the surface. To avoid injuring roots, remove it after one or two years or reinstall it further away from the trunk. (2) Population control of voles—reduce the numbers of these efficient reproducers by trapping or by using rodenticides. Snap traps are especially effective in fall and late winter. Rodenticides or toxicants work best in warmer months. (3) Trapping—locate vole tunnels by probing with a stick. Open them at 10-foot intervals, removing enough soil to allow a mousetrap to sit crosswise on the bottom. Bait the trap with peanut butter. Light must not reach the trap sight, so cover it with an inverted flowerpot. Check traps daily until no rodents are caught for a week. In multiple planting beds, treat one bed at a time. (4) Rodenticides—use with care. They are potentially lethal to children, pets, and other nontarget mammals, including birds and fish. Place the bait in runways next to tunnels or in burrow entrances, or broadcast it evenly over the entire infested area. Usually baiting every other day for five days will take care of the problem. Anticoagulant baits are slow-acting and must be consumed over a period of five days or more to be effective. The bait must be available until the pest population is controlled.

**Whiteflies:** These are common pests of gardenias and other shrubs. They suck plant juices from the undersides of the leaves and excrete a sticky "honeydew" that is often colonized by a sooty mold. The leaves develop a sooty-looking appearance. Lightly infested leaves develop a mottled look. Higher populations cause leaves to yellow, shrivel, and die prematurely. These tiny mothlike pests are barely visible until you shake the plant and they fly away in a white cloud.

*Controls:* Spray with an insecticide or use one of the following non-chemical approaches. (1) Encourage natural enemies such as minute pirate

bugs, lacewings, lady beetles, and big-eyed bugs. Trim away only portions of heavily infested young shoots. Mature foliage provides predators a refuge from which they will attack the whiteflies remaining on the new growth. (2) Use traps. Whiteflies are attracted to bright yellow surfaces. You can trap them with commercially available yellow sticky traps. Wash off the bothersome honeydew first with a strong stream from your garden hose. You can create your own traps by coating bright-yellow cards with mineral oil. Empty yellow antifreeze or oil jugs can be recycled to make whitefly traps, too. Cover the jug with clear plastic wrap and coat lightly with mineral oil. Set traps out when you first observe whiteflies on your plants. Place them at intervals very close to the plants as the insects must see them to be attracted. (3) Spray with horticultural oils, Neem, and insecticidal soaps to suppress whitefly populations. Take care to cover the undersides of leaves thoroughly with the solution.

**Bagworms:** The larvae of this pest live in cocoon-like bags that hang from branches of the host and eat its leaves. The bag is covered with bits of leaves from the host plant and therefore looks quite different from plant to plant. Needle-type evergreens like blue spruce and hemlock, as well as arborvitae, juniper, and Leyland cypress, are favorite targets. They also attack the leaves of many broadleaf shrubs and trees including rose, sycamore, maple, elm, and black locust. Excessive defoliation may kill conifers within one or two seasons. The spindle-shaped bag is carried around as the larva feeds, enlarging the bag as it grows. Eggs hatch inside the bag in early spring. When the larva matures, it stops feeding and firmly attaches the bag to a twig. In late summer, winged males emerge and mate with the wingless females in the bags. The female moths lay 500 to 1,000 eggs and die. The eggs overwinter inside the bag and hatch the following spring.

Control: Handpick and dispose of the bags in a jar of soapy water or in deep containers that allow any parasites to escape but keep the larvae in. Bacillus thuringiensis is effective when the bagworms are small, during May or early June. Other insecticides are available.

## PESTS OF ANNUALS AND PERENNIALS

**Snails and slugs:** The most characteristic signs of their presence are the damage they do and the trails of mucus they leave wherever they crawl. They feed on both decaying and living leaves, stems, and belowground plant parts. They produce large, ragged holes in leaves of a wide variety of plants and can completely consume young seedlings. You don't see them at work. They feed at night and on cloudy days; during the day they hide in damp places such as thick mulches and groundcovers. These soft-bodied, wormlike animals are similar to each other except snails have hard shells and slugs do not. Their activity begins in the spring and continues until the first frost. They are particularly fond of wet, damp areas, since moisture is needed for their survival. They become less active during periods of drought.

Controls: (1) Sanitation—discourage slugs and snails by removing mulch and leaf litter near plants. (2) Handpicking (when you find them). (3) Trapping—set simple, effective traps. They are attracted to and will drown in a shallow pan of stale beer sunken so that the container lip is level with the soil surface. Or place a board on the ground, raised about an inch above the surface. It provides a daytime hiding place for these pests. Lift the board and dispose of the pests. (4) Barriers—protect seedlings by sprinkling diatomaceous earth around them. It is sharp enough to scratch the skin of soft-bodied critters, resulting in dehydration and death. It must be reapplied after

*a rain or watering. Slug baits are also available to poison them.*

## BULB PESTS

**Aphids and spider mites:** Inspect the leaves of your bulbs for them. For controls, see below.

## VEGETABLE PESTS

**Aphids and mites:** Aphids are soft-bodied insects that range in color from green, yellow, red, and gray to black. They suck the juices from leaves and stems, causing stunted or deformed buds and flowers and sometimes curled or puckered leaves. Expect many generations per year. For additional discussion of mites, see page 284.

*Controls: Encourage beneficial insects such as lady beetles and syrphid flies. Aphids can sometimes be washed from plants with a strong stream of water. Insecticidal soaps are effective. Many other insecticides are available.*

**Whiteflies:** Whiteflies are tiny insects that attack tomato, pepper, bean, cucumber, squash, melon, and okra. Their name is derived from the white waxy covering on the adult's wings and body. If you happen to disturb a plant infested by whiteflies, look for the adults rising upwards in a white cloud. The tiny mothlike adults (about $1/12$ inch long) usually lay eggs on the undersides of the leaves. Upon hatching, the nymphs or crawlers feed, like the adults, by sucking plant sap from the leaves. Lightly infested leaves develop a mottled appearance while higher populations cause leaves to yellow, shrivel, and die prematurely. Heavy infestations result in sticky leaves covered with a thin black film of sooty mold, a fungus that feeds on the honeydew excreted by the whiteflies. They produce many generations per year.

*Controls: Yellow cards coated with mineral oil will trap adults. Insecticidal soaps and Neem are effective. Other insecticides are available.*

**Slugs and snails:** These are soft-bodied and wormlike. Snails have coiled shells and slugs have no shells. They feed at night, producing large holes in the leaves, stems, and below-ground parts of plants. Slugs and snails leave characteristic trails of mucus wherever they crawl.

*Controls: (1) Protect plants by wrapping copper strips around the bases of stems. (2) Attract the pests with pieces of potato or cabbage underneath a board; collect and destroy them during the day. (3) Trap the pests in shallow pans of stale beer sunken deep enough so the container lip is even with the soil surface. (4) Protect young seedlings by sprinkling bands of wood ashes or diatomaceous earth. (5) Chemical baits are available.*

# ALABAMA & MISSISSIPPI PUBLIC GARDENS

## ALL-AMERICA ROSE SELECTIONS, INC.

AARS, Inc., headquartered in Chicago, Illinois, has been testing roses since 1938. Its nationwide network of Official Test Gardens, each located within a select public garden, receives new roses from growers every year to be planted and evaluated for performance. They are given average—not necessarily expert—care, and after two years scored points on each of these categories: Vigor, growth habit, disease resistance, foliage, flower production, bud and flower form, opening and "finishing" color, fragrance, stem, and overall value. The results give us an idea of which new roses will be the very best introductions. For more information on AARS, visit **www.rose.org**.

Alabama has five official AARS test gardens: Dunn Formal Rose Garden, 2612 Lane Park Rd., Birmingham 35216; Fairhope City Rose Garden, 1 Fairhope Avenue, Fairhope 36532; Mobile Public Rose Garden, Springhill Municipal Hospital Complex, Dauphin St. and I-65 Service Rd., West, Mobile 36606; Battleship Memorial Park, Battleship Parkway, Mobile 36601; and Bellingrath Gardens, 12401 Bellingrath Gardens Rd., Theodore, AL 36582. Other public gardens, including Huntsville Botanical Garden, have roses for viewing.

Mississippi has two official test sites: Mississippi Agriculture Museum, 1150 Lakeland Drive, Jackson 39216; and Hattiesburg Rose Garden, on the University of Mississippi Campus in Hattiesburg. Other rose gardens which are open to the public include the Magnolia Botanical Gardens at the Verona Research Station, Verona (just south of Tupelo), and Wister Gardens in Belzoni.

There are over half a dozen organized rose society chapters in Alabama, from Gulf Shores and Mobile to Montgomery, Birmingham and Dothan, up to Cullman and Gadsden. Organized chapters can be found in Mississippi from Bay St. Louis and Gulfport to Hattiesburg, Jackson, Cleveland, Starkville, and on up to Tupelo. Each group holds regular meetings, demonstrations, and flower shows, and all offer encouragement to visitors and new members.

To get the most up-to-date contact information for the one nearest you, as well as lots of tips on growing roses in Alabama or Mississippi, contact the American Rose Society, located just west of Shreveport, Louisiana, at their website **www.ars.org**, or call them toll-free at 1-800-637-6534.

## ALL AMERICA SELECTIONS DISPLAY GARDENS

All America Selections Display Gardens are a great place to view the new AAS winners. A network of nearly 200 dedicated AAS gardens includes 55 locations in the U.S. and Canada. Gardens in Alabama and Mississippi are listed here. You can find them all and more information about the AAS program and AAS flower and vegetable winners at **www.aas.org**.

### Alabama AAS Gardens

AUBURN UNIVERSITY BEDDING PLANT TRIAL
North Donahue Drive & Woodfield Drive
Auburn University, AL 36849

BELLINGRATH GARDENS AND HOME
12401 Bellingrath Gardens Road
Theodore, AL 36582

# ALABAMA & MISSISSIPPI PUBLIC GARDENS

BIRMINGHAM BOTANICAL GARDENS
2612 Lane Park Road
Birmingham, AL 35223

NORTH ALABAMA HORTICULTURE
  RESEARCH CENTER, AUBURN UNIVERSITY
765 Count Road 1466
Cullman, AL 35055

## Mississippi AAS Gardens

MISSISSIPPI STATE UNIVERSITY COASTAL
  Res. & Exp. Center
711 West North Street
Poplarville, MS 39470

MISSISSIPPI STATE UNIVERSITY MAGNOLIA
  BOTANICAL GARDENS
5421 Hwy. 145 South
Verona, MS 38879

MISSISSIPPI STATE UNIVERSITY TRUCK
  CROPS EXPERIMENT STATION
Highway 51 South
Crystal Springs, MS 39059

## Alabama Public Gardens

ALDRIDGE BOTANICAL GARDENS
3530 Lorna Road
Hoover, AL 35216
(205) 682-8019

The former estate of Eddie and Kay Aldridge, who owned Aldridge Garden Shop and Nurseries, this beautiful 30-acre site showcases hydrangeas and picturesque gardens. **www.aldridgegardens.com**

ANNISTON MUSEUM OF NATURAL HISTORY
800 Museum Drive
Anniston, AL 36207
(256) 237-6766

Wildflower garden, nature trail, and tropical garden. **www.annistonmuseum.org**

BELLINGRATH GARDENS AND HOME
12401 Belllingrath Garden Road
Theodore, AL 36582
(251) 973-2217

Sixty-five meticulously landscaped acres including an Oriental garden and a 906-acre woodland setting. Many tropical and "old South" plants. **www.bellingrath.org**

BIRMINGHAM BOTANICAL GARDENS
2612 Lane Park Road
Birmingham, AL 35223
(205) 414-3950

Many fine plant collections and vignette gardens, including extensive Oriental garden, rose, daylily, vegetable, herb, iris, fern, and *Southern Living* display gardens; tropical conservatory; and library. **www.bbgardens.org**

BLOUNT CULTURAL PARK
6055 Vaughn Road
Montgomery, AL 36116
(334) 274-0062

Three hundred acres with Shakespearean garden (includes all plants in Shakespeare's plays and poems), maze garden, English landscapes, thatched pavilion, and many sculptures.

CONDE-CHARLOTTE HOUSE
104 Theatre Street
Mobile, AL 36602
(251) 432-4722

1822-23 Spanish walled courtyard plantings, very well researched and authentic, with fountains and wrought iron.

# ALABAMA & MISSISSIPPI PUBLIC GARDENS

DONALD E. DAVIS ARBORETUM
Garden Drive and College Street
Auburn, AL 36849
(334) 844-5770

Located on the campus of Auburn University, the arboretum is home to 150 different tree species native to Alabama and the Southeast. A brochure identifies the species along the walking trails.

DOTHAN AREA BOTANICAL GARDEN
5130 Headland Avenue
Dothan, AL 36303
(334) 793-3224

Rose, herb, camellia, and demonstration gardens, pond and greenhouse.

HUNTSVILLE-MADISON COUNTY
  BOTANICAL GARDEN
4747 Bob Wallace Avenue
Huntsville, AL 35805
(256) 830-4447

Annuals, butterfly, daylily, herb, perennial, rose, and vegetable gardens as well as a fern glade, aquatic garden, wildflower walk, and dogwood trail. Don't miss the children's garden and butterfly house. **www.hsvbg.org**

IVY GREEN AND INTERNATIONAL GARDENS
300 W. North Common Street
Tuscumbia, AL 35674
(256) 383-4066

Lovely landscaped gardens contain plants donated as gifts from 25 nations. The grounds around Helen Keller's home are well maintained.
**www.helenkellerbirthplace.org**

JASMINE HILL GARDENS AND
  OUTDOOR MUSEUM
3001 Jasmine Hill Road
Wetumpka, AL 36093
(334) 567-6463

Twenty acres reminiscent of ancient Greece with jasmines, azaleas, flowering cherry trees, Japanese magnolias, water plants, and Greek statuary. Open only in spring; call for hours.

LOUISE KREHER FOREST ECOLOGY PRESERVE
3100 North College Street (Hwy. 147N)
Auburn, AL 36849
(334) 502-4553

Walking trails of the 110-acre preserve offer opportunities for birding, wildlife observation, and identification of trees and wildflowers. Focal areas include wetlands, a butterfly garden, GPS, fern, reptile, and wildlife trails. Open Tuesday, Saturday, and Sunday 8 a.m. – 7 p.m.

MINAMAC WILDFLOWER BOG
13199 MacCartee Lane
Silverhill, AL 36576
(251) 945-6157

Hillside meadow beside 5-acre lake with unusual wildflowers including pitcher plants, native orchids, lilies, and blazing star. Blooms April through September. Tours by reservation only.

MOBILE BOTANICAL GARDENS
Pat Ryan Drive, P.O. Box 8382
Mobile, AL 36608
(251) 342-0555

Native azaleas, camellias, ferns, magnolias, hollies, perennial displays, herb garden, and a fragrance and texture garden accessible to the physically challenged.
**www.mobilebotanicalgardens.org**

UNIVERSITY OF ALABAMA ARBORETUM
Pelham Loop Road, Box 870334
Tuscaloosa, AL 35487
(205) 553-3278

Arboretum with herb, vegetable, and annuals displays, and greenhouse.
**http://bama.ua.edu/~arboretum**

# ALABAMA & MISSISSIPPI PUBLIC GARDENS

## Mississippi Public Gardens

### CLINTON COMMUNITY NATURE CENTER
617 Dunton Road
Clinton, MS 39056
(601) 926-1104

Interpretive center and 2$^1/_2$ miles of all-weather walking trails through 32 acres of woodland area.

### CROSBY ARBORETUM OF MISSISSIPPI STATE UNIVERSITY
370 Ridge Road, P.O. Box 1639
Picayune, MS 39466
(601) 799-2311

Premier native plant conservatory in the Southeast. Seven protected natural areas covering nearly 1,000 acres are prime examples of local ecotypes, including pitch plant bog, pine and grass savanna, wetland, and woodland areas, and include many stages of native plant development. Inspirational pavilion by Fay Jones won the prestigious Gold Medal from the American Institute of Architects. Guided tours are available. **www.crosbyarboretum.msstate.edu**

### MAGNOLIA BOTANICAL GARDENS
5421 Hwy. 145 S.
Verona, MS 38879
(662) 566-2201

On the grounds of North Mississippi Research & Extension Center. All America Selections display, rose, native plant, and water gardens. Mississippi Medallion plants on display, plus a learning and demonstration garden. Monthly gardening seminars are offered.

### MYNELLE GARDENS
4736 Clinton Boulevard
Jackson, MS 39209
(601) 960-1894

Azalea and camellia trails, white garden, Oriental island, naturalized bulbs, daylilies, perennials, and annuals. **www.visitjackson.com**

### PALESTINE GARDENS
201 Palestine Gardens Road
Lucedale, MS 39452
(601) 947-8422

Walk-through miniature scale model of the Biblical Holy Land at the time of Christ. Native and hardy "Old South" trees and shrubs. Secluded; check website for directions. **www.palestinegardens.org**

### STRAWBERRY PLAINS AUDUBON CENTER
285 Plains Road
Holly Springs, MS 38635
(662) 252-1155

Strawberry Plains Audubon Center encompasses 2,500 acres of diverse wildlife habitat and has 15 miles of walking trails for exploring forests, fields, and wetlands. It has more than 200 species of birds, extensive gardens of native plants, and an antebellum house. Visitor programs, including the Hummingbird Migration Celebration, are offered throughout the year. Open 8 a.m. – 4 p.m. Tuesdays through Saturdays; closed on holidays. Call ahead for winter hours. **www.msaudubon.org**

### WISTER GARDENS
500 Henry Road
Belzoni, MS 39038
(662) 247-3025

Semiformal garden collections of flowers, trees, and shrubs on 14 acres, including roses and hardy perennials. **www.wistergardens.com**

# SELECTED BIBLIOGRAPHY

*Aquatic Plants and their Cultivation*, Helen Nash with Steve Stroupe, Sterling Publishing Co., Inc., NY, 1998.

*Bulbs for Warm Climates*, Thad M. Howard, University of Texas Press, Austin, TX, 2001.

*Bulletproof Flowers for the South*, Jim Wilson, Taylor Publishing Co., Dallas, TX, 1999.

*Can't Miss Water Gardening for the South*, Teri Dunn, Cool Springs Press, Franklin, TN, 2005.

*Commonsense Vegetable Gardening for the South*, William D. Adams and Thomas LeRoy, Taylor Publishing Co., Dallas, TX, 1995.

*Daffodils for American Gardens*, Brent and Becky Heath, Elliott & Clark Publishing, Washington, DC, 1995; 2002.

*Easy Roses for North American Gardens*, Tom Christopher, The Reader's Digest Association, Inc., Pleasantville, NY, 1999.

*The Encyclopedia of Ornamental Grasses*, John Greenlee, Michael Friedman Publishing Group, Inc., NY, 1992.

*The Encyclopedia of Roses*, Judith C. McKeon, Rodale Press, Inc., Emmaus, PA, 1995.

*Garden Bulbs for the South*, Scott Ogden, Taylor Publishing Co., Dallas, TX, 1994.

*Garden Perennials for the Coastal South*, Barbara Sullivan, The University of North Carolina Press, Chapel Hill, SC, 2003.

*Herbaceous Perennial Plants*, 2nd Edition, Allan M. Armitage, Stipes Publishing L. L. C., Champaign, IL, 1997.

*Landscape Plants for the Gulf and Atlantic Coasts: Selection, Establishment, and Maintenance*, Robert J. Black and Edward F. Gilman, University Press of Florida, Gainesville, FL, 2004.

*Manual of Woody Landscape Plants*, 5th Edition, Michael A. Dirr, Stipes Publishing L. L. C., Champaign, IL, 1998.

*Ortho®'s All About Roses*, Tommy Cairns, Meredith® Books, Des Moines, IA, 1999.

*Ortho®'s The Complete Perennials Book*, Marilyn Rogers, Meredith® Books, Des Moines, IA, 2003.

*The Palm Reader: A Manual for Growing Palms Outdoors in the Southeast*, **http://pubs.caes.uga.edu/caespubs/horticulture/Palmreader.html** compiled by members of The Southeastern Palm and Exotic Plant Society.

*Perennials: How to Select, Grow and Enjoy*, Pamela Harper and Frederick McGourty, HP Books, Tucson, AZ, 1985.

*The Practical Gardener: A Guide to Breaking New Ground*, Roger B. Swain, Little, Brown and Co., 1989.

*Rodale's Successful Organic Gardening: Trees, Shrubs, and Vines*, Bonnie Lee Appleton and A. F. Scheider, Rodale Press, Emmaus, PA, 1993.

# SELECTED BIBLIOGRAPHY

*The Rose Book*, Maggie Oster, Rodale Press, Emmaus, PA, 1994.

*Roses for Dummies*, Lance Walheim and the editors of the National Gardening Association, IDG Books Worldwide, Inc., Foster City, CA, 1997.

*Southern Living® Garden Problem Solver*, Steve Bender, ed., Oxmoor House, Inc., Birmingham, AL, 1999.

*The Southern Gardeners Book of Lists*, Lois Trigg Chaplin, Taylor Trade Publishing, Rowan and Littlefield Publishing Group, Latham, MD, 1994.

*The Southern Living® Garden Book*, Steve Bender, ed., Oxmoor House, Inc., Birmingham, AL, 2004.

*Sunset Annuals and Perennials*, Sunset Publishing Corp., Menlo Park, CA, 1993.

*Treasury of Gardening*, C. Colston Burrell et al. Publications International, Ltd. Lincolnwood, IL, 1998.

*Trees for Urban and Suburban Landscapes*, Edward F. Gilman, Delmar Publishers, Albany, NY, 1997.

*Tough-As-Nails Flowers for the South*, Norman Winter, University Press of Mississippi, MS, 2003.

*Tough Plants for Southern Gardens: Low Care, No Care, Tried and True Winners*, Felder Rushing, Cool Springs Press, Franklin, TN, 2003.

*Water Gardening*, Joseph Tomocik, Pantheon Books, Knopf Publishing Group, NY, 1996.

*Water Gardening: Water Lilies and Lotuses*, Perry D. Slocum and Peter Robinson with Frances Perry, Timber Press, Inc., Portland, OR, 1996.

*Water Gardens*, Thomas C. Cooper, Ed., Primedia, Inc., Peoria, IL, 1998.

*The Well-Tended Perennial Garden: Planting and Pruning Techniques*, Tracy DiSabato-Aust, Timber Press, Portland, OR, 1998.

*The Year in Trees: Superb Woody Plants for Four-season Gardens*, Kim E. Tripp and J. C. Raulston, Timber Press, Portland, OR, 1995.

\* \* \*

## MAGAZINES:

*Fine Gardening*, **www.tauntonpress.com/finegardening**
*Horticulture*, **www.hortmag.com**
*Louisiana Gardener*, **www.Louisianagardener.com**
*Neil Sperry's Gardens*, **www.neilsperry.com/cfbeta/**

## ASSORTED PUBLICATIONS FROM:

ALABAMA: **www.aces.edu**
MISSISSIPPI: **http://msucares.com**

# BOTANICAL NAME INDEX

# BOTANICAL NAME INDEX

# COMMON NAME INDEX

# COMMON NAME INDEX

# COMMON NAME INDEX

# COMMON NAME INDEX

# COMMON NAME INDEX

# COMMON NAME INDEX

# COMMON NAME INDEX

# MEET BOB POLOMSKI

Bob Polomski is widely known and respected for both his down-to-earth gardening expertise and knowledge of the latest technical information. He shares his gardening know-how with gardeners through numerous articles, radio broadcasts and television appearances, and even online.

Polomski's numerous publications range from scientific papers to magazine and newspaper articles. He has written over 250 Clemson Extension *Buds 'n Blooms* press releases distributed to newspapers statewide. His column *Garden Works* is published tri-weekly for the *Anderson Independent-Mail*, and he writes a monthly column for *The State* newspaper (Columbia, SC), *Living in South Carolina*, published by the Electric Cooperatives of South Carolina, and a quarterly column for *South Carolina Farmer*, published by the South Carolina Farm Bureau Federation.

*Bob Polomski*

Since 1994, he has been the "Questions & Answers" columnist for *Horticulture*, and has also published articles in *American Rose, Carolina Gardener, Fine Gardening*, and *Public Garden*. He appears on television programs devoted to gardening and hosts a half-hour question-and-answer radio program sponsored by Clemson University, *Your Day*. These radio programs are broadcast statewide on South Carolina Educational Radio with listeners in portions of North Carolina and Georgia. He has also conducted garden study tours in England and France.

He is a Certified Professional Horticulturist (a program administered by the American Society for Horticultural Science) and a member of several associations, including the American Nursery & Landscape Association, American Society of Horticultural Scientists, American Association of Botanical Gardens and Arboreta, Garden Writers Association of America, International Plant Propagators' Society—Southern Region, Royal Horticultural Society, and the Southeastern Palm and Exotic Plant Society.

In addition to *Month-by-Month Gardening in the Carolinas*, his first book for Cool Springs Press, he has also written *Month-by-Month Gardening* books for Mississippi and Alabama. These books are an extension of his daily responsibilities as Clemson Extension Horticulturist at Clemson University and State Coordinator of the South Carolina Master Gardener Program.

Currently he is pursuing a Ph.D. in Plant and Environmental Sciences at Clemson University.

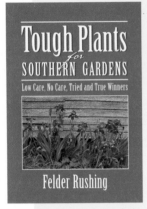
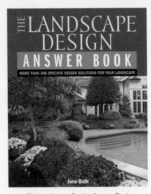
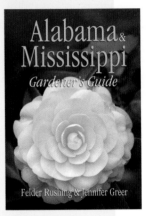

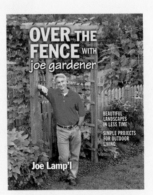
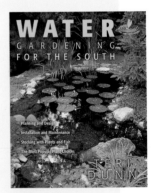